SUNDAY

DOUBLEDAY

New York   London   Toronto   Sydney   Auckland

SUNDAY

A HISTORY OF THE FIRST DAY FROM BABYLONIA TO THE SUPER BOWL

CRAIG HARLINE

PUBLISHED BY DOUBLEDAY

COPYRIGHT © 2007 BY CRAIG HARLINE

PUBLISHED IN THE UNITED STATES BY DOUBLEDAY, AN IMPRINT OF THE
DOUBLEDAY BROADWAY PUBLISHING GROUP, A DIVISION OF RANDOM HOUSE,
INC., NEW YORK.

WWW.DOUBLEDAY.COM

DOUBLEDAY AND THE PORTRAYAL OF AN ANCHOR WITH A DOLPHIN ARE REGISTERED
TRADEMARKS OF RANDOM HOUSE, INC.

LIBRARY OF CONGRESS CATALOGING-IN-PUBLICATION DATA
HARLINE, CRAIG.
    SUNDAY : A HISTORY OF THE FIRST DAY FROM BABYLONIA TO THE SUPER
BOWL / CRAIG HARLINE.—1ST ED.
        P.   CM.
    INCLUDES BIBLIOGRAPHICAL REFERENCES.
    1. SUNDAY. 2. DAYS. 3. UNITED STATES—SOCIAL LIFE AND CUSTOMS.
    I. TITLE.
  BV111.3.H37 2007
  263'. 3—DC22
                                    200602364

ISBN: 978-0-385-51039-4

PRINTED IN THE UNITED STATES OF AMERICA

10 9 8 7 6 5 4 3 2 1

FIRST EDITION

CONTENTS

A WORD BEFORE

Super Bowl Sunday, Recently

While most in the basement viewing room rush off with the rest of America to the kitchen buffet, or join the annual great flush that so worries local water departments, the colored lights, music, and smoke of the halftime show go up on the big screen. Remaining behind with my ninety-year-old grandmother, I wonder which of the Jacksons will be performing this year and what my grandmother will think of it all. Comfortable in her favorite recliner, she's no fan of football or pop music, but she recognizes a cultural spectacle when she sees one and likes to join in the fun. She also likes, I know, to have yet another look at *what the world is coming to now*, as a sort of reassurance that things were indeed better in her day. It isn't long before she raises her eyebrows and utters her trademark "Good Night!"—sure signs of disapproval. Watching all this, I'm struck by the thought that my grand-mother cannot be the only one wondering at the moment, "Just exactly how did we get here?"

In fact, I'm now wondering myself. But I don't have in mind the halftime show, or, like my grandmother, the general decline of just about everything. Instead, I'm struck by the *Sunday* part of "Super Bowl Sunday." How did that happen? For all the fanfare of the big day, the phrase itself has become a cliché, like Tuesday Night Bowling or Wednesday Night Bridge or Friday Night Fights, hardly worth a second thought. Yet that "Super Bowl" ended up as an adjective for "Sunday" was no simple matter, I suspect—nor was Sunday's partner-ing with such seemingly innocent words as "outing," "driver," "shop-ping," "movie," or "brunch." In my own neighborhood, for instance, plenty of people are at this very instant lamenting the Sunday part of the Super Bowl, as well as any other exuberant activity that upsets their sense of the day. Some neighbors watching the big game are un-easy about their choice to do so: they tune in without real enjoyment. Some, including genuine sports fans, refuse to watch at all out of prin-ciple against *Sunday* sport: they will record it and watch tomorrow in-stead. A few others are not allowed to watch: one high school football star has recently told me, with a slight tremor in his voice, that he has never seen the Super Bowl because his family, on religious grounds, keeps the TV turned off on Sunday. All this helps to explain why any local "get-togethers" today remain just that, rather than "parties." They're few and subdued, even semiclandestine, with nothing loud or extravagant or too many cars out front.

Such restrained sentiments about Sunday—Super Bowl version or otherwise—hardly lie within the mainstream of American culture nowadays, but I understand them perfectly well because I grew up with them. A subdued Sunday, in one form or another, was simply part of life. Yet like the football star, I too sometimes fretted about it. As a boy in California in the 1960s, I wondered why most of my friends seemed to enjoy Sunday more than I did. It wasn't a dreadful day, be-cause my own family was pleasant and church had its helpful and even light moments (such as when we children, after another record-setting prayer by Brother Hill, turned to each other with wide-eyed giggles and practically shouted in disbelief, "Seven minutes!"—to the mortification of our parents). Rather, Sunday was a nondescript, rather sterile day, characterized partly by long hours in church but mostly by a constant, low-grade anxiety over what should be done—or more precisely *not* done—during those precious hours outside of church. Should we see friends, buy an ice cream, turn on the TV, and play or watch our beloved sports? Even when we did engage in these activities, there was enough uncertainty about their propriety that we might feel guilty anyway.

If such anxieties about Sundays present and past are not necessarily typical, over the years I have come to realize that they are hardly unique. Especially recently, whenever it emerged that I was writing a book about Sunday, people far and wide began flooding me with their own anxious tales of the day, featuring surely exaggerated scenes of unbearable tedium, severe constraint, and heroic endurance straight from an Ingmar Bergman film. Steve, a Protestant from Belfast, dutifully read Foxe's *Book of Martyrs* on Sunday afternoons as a boy, was "once thrashed" for bicycling on Sunday, has therefore never done so since, and out of habit still refrains from posting letters on Friday lest someone need sort them on Sunday. The English Annette and her sister spent countless Sunday afternoons, as young girls, in their dreary, upstairs suburban bedroom, quietly staring out the window for hours at nothing but an unilluminated street lamp. There was also the American Martin, whose Methodist grandmother tried not to use electricity on Sunday and therefore in mashing potatoes for Sunday dinner attached only a single beater to her two-headed mixer (ironically costing twice the effort and electricity). And the American Jim still vividly recalls his frustration at missing the first half of the Joe Namath Super Bowl because of his duties as a Catholic altar boy.

These examples, all not coincidentally from the English-speaking world, interested me because they were familiar. Yet even more interesting were those unfamiliar examples I heard that contained the fondest of sentiments for Sunday—the "best day of the week!" In France it was a day for memorable family dinners and exuberant outings, and in Belgium a day for sugar bread at breakfast, fine meals, games, adventure, youth groups, music, and visiting at home or in cafés—so pleasant that the novelist Ernest Claes could define his childhood vision of heaven as "a month of Sundays."

I concluded that here was yet another inane binary grouping into which the world might be divided: those who don't love Sunday, and those who do. In fact a few psychologists had already concluded much the same thing, bestowing the grand name "Sunday Neurosis" upon those feelings of dread that, in some people, pop up every Friday or Saturday; the looming Sunday, it is explained, marks the suspension of reassuring routines, thus forcing an unpleasant psychological encounter with the ultimate "why" of those routines, even with the why of one's very existence. Surely it is this condition that lies behind the recent bumper sticker "Thank God It's Monday," or Kris Kristofferson's angst-filled "Sunday Mornin' Comin' Down." Yet could "Sunday Neurosis" not be broadened to include as well those who dread Sunday's coming less because routine is suspended than because it is replaced with a more disagreeable routine, unique to Sunday? And might not even lovers of Sunday, who delight in the day's lack of structure and who confront the big questions of existence through their revitalizing meditation or carefree play, experience a Sunday Neurosis of their own—namely, in the day's ending?

This last is expressed in the (also not coincidentally) French film *A Sunday in the Country,* whose protagonist senses so deeply the joys of Sunday that as the afternoon wears on each happy event fills him with sorrow, for each reminds him that this extraordinary day, this day removed from common time, must end after all. It is also expressed in the French play *The Sunday Walk,* in which the son, although bored, says, "I don't want tomorrow to be Monday . . . I want it to go on being Sunday." Similarly, the old song "Sunday Kind of Love" sadly concludes that Sunday makes Monday feel cold. And there's the social scientist's far less romantic explanation that Monday feels cold to the lover of Sunday because it represents leaving the attractive world of Sunday rest, playfulness, and intensive contact with loved ones for the mundane, serious, and impersonal world of work. Thus my earlier grouping into lovers and dreaders of Sunday must be slightly modified into simply two sorts of Sunday-dreaders: those who dread the coming, and those who dread the going.

But that was enough psychology for me, if I may dignify such amateurish reflections with the word: it was certainly not my forte. Here I must reveal another bias (in addition to my assorted anxieties) behind this book: my preferred approach to understanding most anything, including anxiety, is historical and cultural. Individuals experience Sunday as part of a group, not merely as islands, as I realized from the differences in Sunday observance all around me. Hence, I wanted to know not only how we got here, but more specifically how one group of people arrived at one place in their Sunday habits, and other groups at other places.

One person with only one lifetime will not answer this question completely, at least not with a single book. The topic of Sunday ranges across unmanageable centuries, places, and perspectives, while potential sources of information regarding Sunday behavior and attitudes are as limitless as the God of the Nicene Creed: everywhere and nowhere at the same time. Despite these difficulties, I still thought it worth trying to understand Sunday historically.

Certainly the hundreds of studies written just in the past century on some aspect of Sunday in Europe and the Americas gave me hope and ideas. These studies include often intricate scholarly tomes on Sunday's origins, on the evolution of Sunday laws over many centuries, on the "true" day of Christian worship, and on the theory and practice of Sunday in specific times and places. They include popular depictions of Sunday customs here or there, in the form of short books and leisurely photographic essays on Sunday in the park, by the river, at the Met, on the farm, inside the stadium, and so forth. They also include books that use Sunday as an incidental concept in titles or stories, to suggest a certain mood, such as *A Lazy Sunday, No Fun on Sunday, Sunday's Fun Day, The Pangs of Sunday,* and *Fifty-Two French Omelette Recipes for Sunday Evenings,* or such steamy romances as *Any Sunday* and *Sundays: One Day a Week She Was Good.* And they finally include numerous pastoral and inspirational works designed to promote Sunday as a day of spiritual renewal, or to offer practical advice for Sunday schools. In short, studies of Sunday have worn many faces—rules, inspirational suggestions, fond and unpleasant impressions, great debates over origins and meaning, assorted practices, and more.

This book draws upon many of these traditions, but has its own twists. I wanted to look at Sunday over a long period of time, but in more than one place, to give variety. I wanted it to be historically reliable, yet appealing to general readers. And to promote that appeal I especially wanted to focus on actual Sunday observance rather than on tidy rules and often tiresome debates. The chief virtue of studying observance is that it lends a flesh-and-blood quality to the story. The chief problem is that it's terribly messy to get at, which is only compounded when treating a variety of times and places. Sources are so overwhelming—including mountains of laws, sermons, newspapers, letters, journals, novels, and treatises, to list a very few—that one must make severe, even arbitrary choices and limits. In other words, you leave out a lot. Admittedly, "leaving out a lot" doesn't sound like much of a method, but it is one of the eternal verities in writing about Sunday, even in such a big book as this.

Eventually I settled on areas of the Sunday-observing world I happened to know best—namely, western Europe and the United States—at what seemed to me interesting moments. Chapter 1 sets the backdrop, treating the emergence of Sunday in the ancient Mediterranean; the most abstract part of the book, it sketches broadly because records are scarce and because Sunday's birth and rise were prolonged. Chapter 2 begins the more focused look at Sunday observance through examining its now mature shape in medieval and Catholic Europe. "Sunday Reformed" offers a glimpse of how longstanding Sunday practices and ideas were challenged (or not) by new forms of Christianity. Chapter 4 goes beyond these fundamental religious influences by examining the Sunday of late nineteenth-century France, arguably the most famous model ever of the day. "Sunday Obscured" treats Sunday in wartime, more precisely in Belgium during World War I, suggests what a world without Sunday might be, for war made Sunday seem to disappear. The later English Sunday of Chapter 6 reveals the notorious counterpart of the lively French Sunday, and some of the changes to Sunday after the Great War. And finally "Sunday All Mixed Up," on an American Sunday in the 1950s, shows the convergence of various European trends as well as the development of distinctly American habits, including in the realms of commerce and professional sports.

These are obviously not the only interesting places and moments in the history of Sunday: I am more aware than anyone of just how many others remain, in Europe, the Americas, and elsewhere. But I hope that the combination I have chosen might offer at least a pleasant taste, and be more satisfying and memorable than utter satiation—not to mention suggest familiar patterns for places and times not treated in detail here. By the end, I hope that you will have a much better sense of the question that has occupied me and many others for so long: Just how did Sunday get to be exactly where it is, in this place or that? But we must start at the beginning, even if this beginning is murkier than most.

1

Origins to Around AD 800

Trying to find the origins of Sunday, the biblical scholar Eugene Laverdière once observed, is like trying to find the source of a great river. The delta at the end, and the long channel flowing into the delta, are easily recognizable. Yet the farther one moves upstream toward the source of the river, the trickier the going: tributaries multiply, lead astray, or go underground. And when finally located, the humble source may bear so little resemblance to the massive amounts of water downstream that one will surely wonder what the beginning can possibly have to do with the end.

But if the orgins of Sunday are vague, and thus regularly debated, a few things seem clear enough.

THE DAY OF THE SUN

It is fairly clear, for instance, that "Sun Day" emerged in the ancient Middle East, as part of a seven-day planetary week. Many early civilizations calculated a solar year at roughly 360 days (it's actually closer to 365.2422) and a lunar month at 29 (a modern mean figure is 29.5306). But these civilizations showed infinite variety and imagination in subdividing years and months into more manageable weeks and days: around the ancient world, weeks lasted anywhere from five to sixteen days, while days were parceled into myriad arrangements of hours. That parts of the ancient Middle East and then the Roman Empire settled on a seven-day week, with each day twenty-four hours long and named for a planet, was hardly inevitable.

One early step toward such a week was taken in Babylonia, where by 600 BC observers had identified and carefully tracked seven heavenly planets, or "wanderers," moving about the Earth. This was done largely for astrological purposes: each planet was believed to be governed by a god or goddess who exerted influence upon earthly events according to that planet's position at a given moment—hence the need to track not only where the planets moved but when.

Yet the idea of organizing a seven-day week around the planets did not come from the Babylonians themselves, who preferred lunar months. Rather, it came from the later Greek or "Hellenistic" world, which included the great centers of learning at Alexandria, Egypt, during the second century BC. Wishing to measure even more precisely the influences of the seven planets upon the Earth, Hellenistic observers laid down the basic features of a new week. First, they fixed the *number of days in the earthly week* at seven, to match the number of planets, with each day under the influence of a particular planet. Second, they fixed the *order of distance from Earth* of all planets: Saturn was farthest, then Jupiter, Mars, the Sun, Venus, Mercury, and the Moon.*

*Current English names for the *planets* are Anglicized versions of Roman (Latin) names, which in turn were taken from older Greek equivalents: in the same descending order, the Greek names were Kronos, Zeus, Ares, Helios, Aphroditê, Hermes, and Selenê. Most English names for *days of the week*, however, are taken from Germanic equivalents of the Roman gods.

Third, they fixed the *order of days in the week:* Saturn Day was the first day, Sun Day the second, then Moon Day, Mars Day (Tuesday), Mercury Day (Wednesday), Jupiter Day (Thursday), and Venus Day (Friday). And fourth, they fixed the *number of hours in a day* at twenty-four, as each such hour signified the length of time that a particular planet's influence held sway.* In short, everything about this seven-day planetary week was meant to link the heavens to Earth.

So far, there was nothing that made Sun Day, the second day, or for that matter any other day, stand out; although the planets possessed different qualities and were honored with distinct rituals, all planetary days were basically equal in stature. The idea that one day in the week was superior to others came from another ancient seven-day system: that of the Jews.

SUN DAY BECOMES THE FIRST DAY

It is not entirely settled which week is older: planetary or Jewish. But it is certainly clear that the Jews had a seven-day week of their own and were largely responsible for the custom of singling out one day of the week for special attention.

For the Jews, this extraordinary day was the seventh, which ideally was to be devoted solely to their God. They showed this devotion

---

*Note that the order of days in the week did not match the order of the planets' distances from Earth. Why then all the fuss about fixing distance? The likely answer is that astrologers were more interested in determining a planet's influence on an hour than on a day—thus the "hora" (hour) in "horoscope." Hence the order of distance was indeed observed, but in linking planets to hours, not days. The hourly order went as follows: Saturn was assigned to the first hour of the first day, Jupiter to the second hour of the first day, Mars to the third hour, the Sun to the fourth hour, Venus the fifth, Mercury the sixth, the Moon the seventh, then back to Saturn again for the eighth, and so on, through the 168 hours of a week. The assigning of a planet to a *day* followed almost incidentally: whichever planet fell on the first hour of a new twenty-four-hour segment lent its name and influence to that entire day. The first hour of the first day belonged to Saturn, hence the first day was Saturn Day. The first hour of the second day (or twenty-fifth hour in the week) fell to the Sun, making the second day Sun Day. The first hour of the third day (or forty-ninth hour) fell to the Moon (Moon Day), and so on through Mars (the fourth day), Mercury (the fifth day), Jupiter (the sixth day), and Venus (the seventh day).

by coming together to worship him, by resting from ordinary labors, and by engaging in other rituals reserved for that day—helping to explain the day's name, "Sabbath," the root meaning of which is "to cease," as in ceasing from the everyday. The Jewish week and its all-important Sabbath may have emerged as early as the reigns of David and Solomon near 1000 BC, but it was certainly present around the time of the Babylonian conquest of Jerusalem in 587 BC. Some scholars suggest that Jewish enthusiasm for a seven-day week and especially its seventh day rubbed off on the Babylonians, who likewise developed a taste for the number, as in their seven planets or their special taboos every seven days. Still more scholars, however, believe that the Jewish preference for seven was the result of forced contact with the Babylonians. Thus, with their temple destroyed and their people scattered across Babylon, exiled Jews developed sacred *time* (the Sabbath) to compensate for the loss of sacred *space* (the temple), but they measured that time under Babylonian influence.

These are just some of the chicken-and-egg problems involved in searching for the origins of the Jewish and planetary weeks, which are never likely to be settled from remaining historical evidence. For many believers in the Judeo-Christian tradition, such evidence has hardly mattered anyway: in their minds, the Jewish week came directly from God at creation, when He labored six days and rested on the seventh, setting the pattern for mortals as well. But all long-standing calendar systems—and there have been many around the globe—seem divine, eternal, natural, and self-evident to those who follow them centuries later. What can be said from historical evidence is that the Jews were observing a seven-day week organized around their Sabbath from at least the sixth century BC, and that the Jewish custom of treating the Sabbath in exceptional fashion would eventually have a big impact on the planetary Sun Day too.

It can also be said that the Jewish week, unlike many weeks around the world, was not meant to be shoehorned into nature's cycles: in other words, the seven-day Jewish week did not multiply neatly into a 29-day lunar month or a 365-day solar year, but was an artifical number deliberately imposed by the Jewish God as a sign of his superiority to nature and its pagan gods.* The Jewish week therefore stood *outside* of nature, on purpose, unlike the planetary week. That the Jewish total of seven days happened to equal nature's total of seven planets mattered little to the Jews: except for the Sabbath and the day before the Sabbath, called the Day of Preparation, days of the Jewish week were numbered, not named, and had nothing to do with planets. Moreover, while days and gods of the planetary week were, as noted above, more or less equal, the Jewish week derived virtually all of its meaning from a single day devoted entirely to their single God.

Although the Jewish week wanted nothing to do with any planetary week, two seven-day systems born in the eastern Mediterranean could hardly avoid bumping into and influencing one another. Yet whatever the degree of their mutual influence, by the first century AD they were clearly both exerting influence upon timekeeping in the new Roman Empire. The Roman calendar had long featured numerous annual festivals and an eight-day market cycle, but it had no tradition of a weekly commemoration of a particular day. During the first century AD, this changed, as Rome adopted a seven-day week of its own, shaped by Jewish, planetary, and native Roman traditions. In fact, scholars believe that if the Jews and the Hellenistic Greeks should be given credit for inventing a seven-day week, then the Romans deserve credit for popularizing it—as well as for popularizing the notion that one day of the week outshone the others.

Jewish influence on the Roman week was apparent by the mid–first century, when a growing number of Roman pagans began observing a weekly rest day. Their initial choice seems to have been Saturn Day (Saturday), first day of the planetary week, which fell on the same day as the Sabbath, seventh day of the Jewish week. Jewish influence on society, trade, and traffic had been widening around the eastern Mediterranean for three centuries, so that by this time gentiles too found it convenient to adopt Jewish rhythms of work and rest. This is sug-

---

*Some modern researchers have detected seven-day biorhythms in the human body and even in simple organisms, suggesting that a seven-day cycle may be "natural" after all, even if not connected to Sun or Moon. But it is not yet clear in such instances whether social time—in other words, the habit of keeping a seven-day week—has trained biological time and thus made the latter *seem* "natural."

gested by the Jewish historian Josephus, who proudly noted that the Jewish custom of refraining from work on every seventh day had spread to *all* peoples of the eastern Roman Empire. Perhaps because of this, by at least AD 100 Romans too regarded Saturn Day no longer as the first day of their week but as the seventh. Naturally this caused every other planetary day to shift in Rome as well—including Sun Day, which became the new first day. Hence Jewish and Roman weeks were now aligned: the Jewish Sabbath and Roman Saturn Day were both the seventh day, and the Jewish first day was equal to the Roman first day, or Sun Day.

Like the Jewish week, the old planetary week also exerted influence on the Roman week, most obviously in the naming of Rome's seven days. Moreover, Romans divided their days into the twenty-four hours of the old astrologers, if with a Roman wrinkle: while planetary (and Jewish) days began and ended at sunset, the Romans continued their custom of beginning and ending days at midnight.

Hence by the end of the first century AD, the Roman week, the week that would come to dominate the Western world, was nearly complete: each day was named after a planet, Sun Day was the first day and Saturn Day the last, one day stood somewhat above others in prestige, and days ended and began at midnight. Only one element of this now-familiar week was missing, and that began to emerge early in the second century: namely, the rise of the *first* day as the most important day of the week. This came about thanks to devotees both of the newly prominent Roman Sun God, who still called the first day Sun Day, and of the new Jewish offshoot known as Christianity, who began calling the first day the Lord's Day.

THE DAY OF THE LORD

The early Christian portion of the long-flowing Sunday river is perhaps murkier than any other. Scholars can quite happily agree on Sun Day's origins in the ancient planetary week, on the changes to that week made by Romans, and on the ultimate preeminence of Sun Day among both Roman pagans and Christians. But they have never been able to agree on this: just exactly when, where, and why did the "Lord's Day"

first emerge among Roman Christians?* Was it in Jerusalem or elsewhere? Was it the work of the apostles or later church leaders? And
most of all, was it meant to replace the Jewish Sabbath, to accommodate the pagan Sun Day, or to establish something entirely new and
uniquely Christian? In other words, just exactly what kind of a day
was it?

Based on the little evidence that has survived, no one can say for
sure. Key documents are few: a handful of New Testament texts (particularly Acts 20:7, I Corinthians 16:2, and Revelation 1:10) and a
dozen other sources from the first and second centuries. They are also
vague: in Acts 20 was Paul preaching on the first day by accident or
custom? Did the Corinthian Christians distribute alms on the first day
coincidentally or deliberately? And does the term "Lord's Day" in Revelation refer to the weekly first day, to the annual Easter celebration,
or to something else altogether? These difficulties are compounded by
another: scholars have tended to read the sources according to their
own theological preferences. Such preferences are not necessarily undesirable or wrong, but they make it tricky to find consensus on the beginnings of the Christian Lord's Day.

Readers may find all the intricate details elsewhere. It will do here
to divide the vast body of competing interpretations into three manageable, perhaps oversimplified groups, in no particular order.

The New Lord's Day. Jesus' apostles established the Lord's Day
(probably in Jerusalem, perhaps elsewhere) as a weekly commemoration of Christ's resurrection on the first day. It was thus a day uniquely
Christian, with no connection to the pagan Sun Day or the Jewish Sabbath of the fourth commandment—Christ himself had abolished the
Sabbath and every other aspect of what later Christians would call
"ceremonial" law, and Paul had reminded Christians to be no respecters of days. Moreover, while the Sabbath was observed through

---

*The old arguments about the rise of the Lord's Day do *not* revolve around the question of whether Saturday or Sunday was the last day of the week and thus the original Sabbath. By the late first century the Sabbath was again clearly equivalent to
Saturday, the last day of the Roman week, and the Jewish first day was equivalent
to Sunday, first day of the Roman week. Rather, the arguments have been over what
Sunday means to Christians and its relationship to the Jewish Sabbath.

both worship and rest, the Lord's Day required only worship; rest was a useless ceremony. Besides, the first day was a regular workday for Romans: Christians met together that day as work allowed, either early or late.

The Transferred Sabbath. Jesus' apostles transferred the Sabbath in new and perfected form to the Lord's Day—on the authority of the fourth commandment. Hence, the Lord's Day *was* the true Sabbath. For although Christians were to abandon ceremonial Jewish law, the Ten Commandments were not the least bit ceremonial but instead wholly moral, not to mention universal, a perfect summary of God's will for all people in all times. The fourth commandment therefore remained as binding as the other nine. Christ never intended to abolish the Sabbath, but to give it new meaning in a new day: the old version commemorated the Creation, the new Christ's resurrection.

One Day in Seven. Whether established by Jesus' apostles or later leaders, the first day was chosen as the day for worship on the authority of the new Christian church, not the fourth commandment. The "spiritual" element of the fourth commandment (keep it holy) did still obligate believers to worship together weekly, but the "ceremonial" element (which day?) made no difference. The church eventually settled upon the first day as the Lord's Day because of its connection to Christ's resurrection, but also because it was convenient: it immediately followed the Jewish Sabbath, which many early Christians still observed, and it was the same day that many pagan neighbors worshiped.

It's possible that one of these three basic views of how the new Lord's Day came about is wholly correct. Yet because there is some historical evidence for each, and so many ways to read the evidence, it is unlikely that the superiority of one will ever be proved to the satisfaction of all. Protestants who emphasize New Testament above Old prefer the first view. Protestants and more radical groups who regard the Old and New Testaments as basically equal prefer the second. Catholics, Seventh-Day Adventists, and Protestants who stress Christian freedom from Mosaic Law prefer the third. Some others, such as those who follow the Calvinist tradition, prefer parts of the second and third views. And there is a final obstacle to achieving consensus: early Christian worship was hardly uniform around the ancient Mediterranean, so that even if one of the views above might have been true in one time and place, it may not have been true in another.

These difficulties are formidable, but they need not bog us down. For there is at least one basic point of agreement among almost all scholars that will move the story along: by at least AD 150, and perhaps sooner, most Christians were observing the first day as the Lord's Day by coming together to worship. This alone suggests the day's new importance for Christians.

PAGAN AND JEWISH INFLUENCES ON THE LORD'S DAY

Early Christians were not alone in worshiping on the first day or in shaping it. To begin with, Sun Day mattered more than ever among Roman pagans, who still far outnumbered Christians and who may well have influenced how Christians worshiped on their special day.

The second-century pagan empire was not irreligious at all but rather was conspicuously religious, its marketplaces, buildings, streets, and hilltops filled with countless temples, altars, and statues devoted to a wide array of pagan gods and goddesses—the planetary deities, Diana, Minerva, Bacchus, and more. On Sun Day, Roman pagans began with early services in honor of the rising Sun and the Sun God. But these sunrise rituals were not restricted to Sun Day and thus did little to elevate its status: pagan gods could be worshiped any and every day, particularly the Sun, which of course reappeared every morning in the east.

The cult of the Invincible Sun, which took hold in Rome during the second century and became the official cult of the emperors by the early third, might have turned more attention specifically to Sun Day— but not necessarily. Here too the Sun Day rituals were also performed on any day of the week and thus gave no special significance to the day itself. Besides, this was not a widely popular cult.

More important in raising the status of Sun Day among pagans was Mithraism. This movement was related to the emperor's Invincible Sun cult but carried much broader appeal, especially among the empire's multitude of soldiers. Followers of Mithra *did* emphasize Sun Day, and with greater impact than early Christians. In fact, they may have influ-

enced the Christian choice of the first day for worship and some Christian forms of worship. Purification by baptism, the virtues of abstinence and self-control, belief in resurrection, setting aside heaven for
the pure and hell for the sinful, and celebrating the birth of their God
on December 25 are all obvious parallels. Another was Mithraism's
treatment of Sun Day: it was honored with rituals unique to that day,
whether during communal worship in subterranean caves or in banqueting, taking rest, and refraining from the customary daily bath at
home.

These activities were familiar to Christians, who likewise worshiped
on the first day, began their services at sunrise, faced east to pray, and
more. Of course, Christians assigned their own meanings to such practices: the first day was the day of Christ's resurrection, Christ was the
true Sun, and east was the direction in which Christ ascended to
heaven and where the first earthly paradise was found. But the similarities in worship, the new status of the first day among both groups at
about the same time, the pagan assumption that Christians were fellow Sun-worshipers, and the emergence of the Christian metaphor
"Christ the Sun" all suggest a connection of some sort.

Willy Rordorf, a leading scholar of the early Lord's Day, believes,
however, that these Roman pagans singled out the first day only after
Roman Christians already had. In other words, Christians influenced
the pagan Sun Day more than pagans influenced the Christian Lord's
Day. Even if pagans chose Sun Day first and Christians followed, this
did not make the day ultimately pagan, argues Rordorf. Christians developed their own theology of the first day, so that any similarities of
form became trivial. Finally, despite adopting the metaphor of Christ
the Sun or making other minor accommodations to pagan Rome,
Christians were still reluctant to use the pagan word "Sun Day" for the
first day: in Latin-speaking Christianity, and then in most Romance
languages that followed, the first day became forever "the Lord's
Day"—*dominica, dimanche, domingo, domenica.*

In sum, the question of pagan influence upon the new Lord's Day,
and vice versa, is another tough problem. But the adoption of Sun Day
as the high point of the week by many Roman pagans undoubtedly
boosted the day's importance.

A more certain influence upon Christian observance of the Lord's Day was the Jewish seventh day, or Sabbath—as both a negative and a positive model.

Given Christianity's Jewish roots, it was no surprise that for centuries many Christians worshiped on both Sabbath and Lord's Day and that many elements of Lord's Day worship drew upon Sabbath worship. But in the later first and early second centuries, some Christians began downplaying the Sabbath as something *not* to be observed or imitated. Here was its negative influence. This new antipathy to the Sabbath emerged partly because the Jews fell out of favor with the empire between AD 70 and 130, thanks to rebellions in Palestine; given the empire's habit of lumping Jews and Christians together, some Christians wanted clearly to separate themselves. This was true most of all in Rome and Alexandria, where as early as AD 130 Christians quit the Sabbath and began to worship exclusively on the Lord's Day. Many even fasted on the Sabbath to denigrate it, for fasting implied sorrow or gloom, in contrast to the Lord's Day, which was to be a day of joy and therefore never of fasting.

But the decision of some Christians to quit Sabbath observance was not merely a political strategy to curry favor with Roman authorities. Rather, these Christians began going out of their way to deride the Sabbath and to glorify the Lord's Day. These voices said that the Lord's Day was not merely the first day of the week but could be counted as a timeless and superior "eighth day": for if the seven of the Sabbath was a symbol of completion and the end of time, then the next day, the "eighth," represented eternity. The famous Christian author Justin Martyr was more blunt: the Sabbath was a mark of divine reprobation upon Jews, who because of wickedness required a special day to remind them of their duties to God. Christians needed no such day, because all days were holy to them. But because one day was necessary for regular communal worship, then the first day, the day when Christ resurrected, was the best choice. Justin also criticized what he regarded as the overly exact rules of the Jewish Sabbath: these were unnecessary for law-transcending Christians. Still other Christians ridiculed the supposed idleness and lewdness of a Jewish Sabbath, which they blamed on excessive rest. This paradoxical caricature by Christians of the Jewish Sabbath as both too rigorous and too idle would persist for centuries.

Yet even while Christians denounced (and often distorted) the Jewish Sabbath, they regularly borrowed from it anyway for their Lord's Day. The notion of the superior "eighth day," for instance, came straight from Jewish writings about the end of the world. Here was the more positive influence of Judaism. During the second and third centuries, certain elements of the older religion remained attractive not only among many Jewish converts to Christianity but also among growing numbers of pagan or "gentile" converts. Thus, though now Christian, these converts and their descendants admired Judaism's antiquity, its decorum, its ritual purifications, as well as other visible signs of faith, including carefully observed holy days. Such signs were similar to the paganism or Judaism in which they had been raised, or that they saw around them, and more tangible than the invisible qualities of heart, and the lack of distinction among days, urged upon Christians by Paul. How could one identify a religion and its believers without such clear signs as holy days?

If some gentile adult male Christians willingly submitted themselves to that most permanent Jewish sign of circumcision, then why not to another obvious but less intrusive sign such as the Sabbath? Indeed, outside of Rome and Alexandria, Christians continued to observe both Jewish Sabbath and Christian Lord's Day into the fourth century—and this despite Jewish efforts to exclude Christians from synagogues, and Christian efforts to root out remnants of Judaism within the church. The long appeal of the Sabbath helps to explain why most early Christians replaced "Saturn Day" with "Sabbatum" in their native Latin: in later Romance languages this would become *samedi, sabato,* and *sábado*. It also helps to explain how so many elements of Jewish Sabbath worship found their way into Christian Lord's Day worship, both before and after that magical date of 150, when sources become more clear.

THE LORD'S DAY AROUND AD 150

Like Jews on the Sabbath, second-century Christians preferred to gather together on the Lord's Day both in the early morning and in the evening—thus before and after work. It is not always clear whether an "evening service" meant Roman time (midnight to midnight) or Jewish time (sunset to sunset) and thus whether a "Saturday" or "Sunday" evening is in question. But by the early second century, Christians held both morning and evening services on the Lord's Day, Roman time. Especially those in the evening could invite trouble, given the ban in the empire on all evening study groups, regarded as subversive, and on Christian worship in particular. Yet evening services were frequent anyway.

The setting of Lord's Day gatherings was not the synagogue, as on the Sabbath, nor even some Christian church, as the first genuine churches appeared only in the third century. Until then the Roman skyline was fully pagan, and Christians met in spacious private homes or modest apartments. Justin Martyr, who around 150 wrote a detailed account of Christian worship, said that all believers "came together" on that day. Whether he meant in a single group or in several places at once is not clear, but meetings were rather small.

Before 150, Lord's Day services were apparently as varied and casual as the surroundings. Paul had written of one early assembly singing a hymn, another hearing a reading, and still others receiving a revelation or speaking in tongues. But by 150, services were more fixed, with usually an opening prayer, lessons from the gospels or prophets, an address by the presiding officer, more prayers, and the commemoration of the Lord's Supper, called the Eucharist, or "giving of thanks," which was celebrated as a full meal in the evening service. In conclusion came the collection of alms for the needy and the distribution of the remaining Eucharist to believers unable to attend that day.

Not only was much of this structure drawn from Jewish Sabbath worship, but much of the content was as well. Some prayers were taken word for word from Jewish prayers, and the practice of a sacred meal was common not only with Judaism but also with pagan religions. Christians adopted as well from the Sabbath the chief mood that was to prevail on the Lord's Day: joy, or celebration. Specifically, a Christian did not fast on the Lord's Day, for this, as noted earlier, suggested soberness. Neither did a Christian kneel in prayer on the Lord's Day, but prayed standing with arms outstretched: kneeling, another sign of soberness, was for ordinary days. And the evening fellowship or "agape" meal (the Eucharist) likewise emphasized the joyfulness of the Lord's Day.

Although the mood and many rituals of the Lord's Day were borrowed from Judaism or elsewhere, they were meant to have specific Christian purpose: namely, reinforcing faith in Jesus' resurrection through fellowship with him (believed to be present) and with other believers. Indeed if joy was the prevailing mood of the Lord's Day, then fellowship was the chief way to express that joy. Certainly fellowship was promoted simply through meeting together, but it was more explicit in the Eucharistic meal. While Jews held a large family meal right *after* the Sabbath, Christians made the Eucharist the high point of their special day. For many of the gathered, this meal was the finest of the week, not only in its contents but because for that one meal all present—rich, poor, bond, free, male, female—were ideally equal and unified. It likely seemed obvious to believers, for instance, that after Christ resurrected, he should have shared a meal with his apostles, for what better way to promote fellowship? In imitation, believers brought gifts of food to the gathering, signifying gratitude to God and generosity with others. Before the Eucharist began, believers also uttered a prayer reminding them not to approach the table until they were reconciled with all others present, else how could they be reconciled with God?

The final seal of fellowship during Lord's Day worship services also occurred just before the Eucharist: the holy kiss, on the lips, between believers. Newly baptized Christians were thus kissed by their bishop, Christians greeted one another with a "holy kiss" of fellowship, and John wrote that Christ "breathed" upon his disciples, implying a kiss. Precisely because breath was believed to come from the soul did the kiss have to be on the lips and not the less intimate cheek; the union of breath meant a union of souls. Pagan Romans found the practice odd, and it likely contributed to rumors of Christian orgies. There were abuses, suggested by warnings from church leaders against a second kiss with the same person, or against "unholy kisses," which "inject the poison of licentiousness." And eventually there was strict division of holy-kissing by gender. But the holy kiss was important enough to the sense of fellowship that despite complaints and abuses it was retained during Lord's Day services for many centuries to come.

Whether such rituals helped Christians on their favored day to be any more successful than Jews or pagans at achieving fellowship is an open question. Paul, for instance, grew angry at wealthy Corinthian Christians for refusing to share their abundant food during the Eucharistic meal. Partly because such scenes became commonplace, the Eucharist changed during the second century from a full meal to a symbolic meal of simple bread and wine, making it easier to include everyone equally. And partly because of that change, the Eucharist shifted as well to the morning service.*

Also prominent in Lord's Day services after 150 were sermons, just as in synagogues on the Jewish Sabbath. Delivered now by ordained preachers and leaders, these sermons ranged across all themes of life. Christians in Alexandria might hear Clement (b. 150) deliver his famous "Rich Man's Salvation," in which he assured wealthy Alexandrian believers that their overflowing possessions need not be renounced in a literal sense, merely a spiritual sense: their riches could go far toward helping the poor, after all, and the poor in turn helped the souls of the rich by praying for them. Believers in Caesarea would have heard quite an opposite message from Origen (d. 254), who often forced Christians to make drastic choices between God and the world, requiring them to sever ties with riches, possessions, and sex. He dramatically set the example, castrating himself in order to attain his image of sexual purity. Such demanding sermons were not well received, he admitted. In fact, his listeners displayed the same symp-

---

*It is also possible that the Eucharist moved to the morning service partly because of the Roman ban on study groups, which a lengthy evening gathering resembled, or because as the number of Christians increased it became difficult to seat everyone— the fellowship meal was eaten in Roman style, which meant reclining on couches around tables. Still, the ritual evening meal didn't disappear at once or everywhere: Tertullian around 200 explained to Roman authorities that it was still being conducted with all modesty, not drunkenness, and not as a "belly-feast" but as an act of fellowship among believers, and a time to collect gifts for the poor, widowed, orphaned, and so on.

toms that future generations of Christian preachers also would lament: inattention, chattering, even pickpocketing.

Finally, Lord's Day services around AD 150 included the singing of psalms (just as in the synagogue), confessing the Lordship of Christ and his imminent return, and the benediction "Grace be with you and peace from God our Father and our Lord and Savior." An occasional part of the day's services was the baptism of new Christians, either converts or the children of believers. The first Christians were obviously adults, but the more baptism was seen as necessary for salvation, the more urgently parents and clergy wished children to receive it early—whether by immersion, simple anointing, washing of feet, or otherwise—and the Lord's Day was the usual moment.

After morning service and before evening service, the most time-consuming activity of a Christian's Lord's Day was ordinary work—which obviously did nothing to make the day unique. Almost all Roman women were engaged in cloth production of some kind, usually spinning, weaving, or sewing at home. Most men and women in the empire worked as farmers or agricultural laborers. Men and women in towns might work in or run a family business, as there were plenty of bakers, carpenters, fullers, dyers, tanners, and more. Men might engage in law or trade. Some urban women were employed independently as nurses, saleswomen, and in exceptional cases physicians and painters. If a Lord's Day coincided with a Roman religious feast day, there were celebratory games for those who wished to attend, although in the fifth and last Roman century Christians were instrumental in putting a halt to gladiatorial games on any day.

If work did nothing to make the Lord's Day different, a few other rituals did. Christians not only refrained from fasting on the Lord's Day but unlike Jews on the Sabbath were warned more and more to refrain from sex. A negative attitude toward sex specifically on the Lord's Day was also evident when Christian women who wore provocative dress and makeup were discouraged from participating in the Eucharist. One bishop told fathers who were worried about the sexual stirrings of adolescent sons that the Lord's Day was an ideal time to take them to a favorite holy man. Sexual restraint in general became more and more the Christian sign of purity—different from

Jewish bodily purifications or dietary laws but a visible "ritual marker" nonetheless, and most obviously desirable on the Lord's Day.

The holy man raises a final possible activity on the Lord's Day during the second and third centuries, one already mentioned: the gathering of some Christians in independent study groups. These might meet on other days of the week too, but after the decline of communal evening services in the later second century the evening of the Lord's Day was a desirable time. The historian Peter Brown has reminded the modern reader how difficult it is to appreciate the importance of these groups, or to "enter into the intensity" of the small study circle of male and female believers who gathered for years around a single spiritual guide, seeking deeper spiritual growth than they received from increasingly formalized services. These believers reasoned that although Jesus willingly taught multitudes, he taught most deeply and intimately within his small group of disciples. Soon Christian leaders were as unhappy as civic leaders about such groups, and for the same reason: they were believed to breed disunity and dissent. No wonder that in the later second century, church authorities sought to define heresy and orthodoxy more clearly, driven in part by private gatherings of believers on the evening of the Lord's Day.

FROM LORD'S DAY TO CHRISTIAN SUNDAY

While the first day became the high point of the week among both pagans and Christians during the second and third centuries, the final steps in its ascendency as unquestionably supreme occurred between the fourth and sixth centuries—especially among Christians, whose numbers around the Mediterranean were now immense.

So prominent had Christians and their day become that when the Emperor Constantine in 321 officially proclaimed Sun Day as *the* weekly holy day for all Romans, some Christians believed that it was for their sake. More likely Constantine, like many Roman aristocrats of the time, was simply trying to find common ground for his mixed pagan and Christian subjects, especially his soldiers. Unity was good for the state and the emperor's power. Observing the "Venerable Day of the Sun," as he called the first day, allowed soldiers and citizens of all persuasions to honor together their one, indivisible God—even if they meant quite different things by that term.

More important than Constantine's decree in the spread of the Christian Lord's Day was the establishment of Christianity as the empire's official religion in 392. This changed the atmosphere of Lord's Day worship from one of persecution and caution to one of triumph. Gone were the days when Christians gathered in fear, at marginal hours and in marginal places. More than 350 Christian churches for public Lord's Day worship were constructed during the fourth and fifth centuries in Palestine and Arabia alone, either as visible rivals of remaining Jewish synagogues or as replacements for newly destroyed pagan temples.

Even when the western Roman Empire fell in 476, Christianity and its Lord's Day survived. And even when the southern Mediterranean was lost to Islam around 640, Christianity persisted in the eastern Mediterranean and moved upward into western and central Europe— so successfully that by 800 almost all of Europe was Christian and thus observant of the Lord's Day. Here was where the story of Sunday would continue most prominently: because of Christianity's nearly universal presence in Europe, its special day was also nearly universal, even more than during the Roman Empire.

Yet it wasn't merely the increased number of Christians that gave the Lord's Day its new stature between 300 and 800. Just as important was the continued shaping of the day. This included adding "rest" to the old tradition of "worship" on the Lord's Day, continuing to formalize the day's worship, and the common use now by Christians of the very term "Sun Day."

As in earlier centuries, paganism and Judaism again left their marks on the Christian Sunday. Certainly Christians now condemned both religions, including their holy days, more frequently and bitterly than ever. And during the fourth century, almost all Christians at last stopped observing both Sabbath and Lord's Day, instead worshiping solely on the latter. In fact by 330 the famous bishop Eusebius of Caesarea was already claiming that whatever Sabbath duties the Christian owed had been transferred to the Lord's Day. But for all this rhetoric against the Sabbath, its influence upon the Lord's Day remained strong. The very choice by Christians to give up the Sabbath altogether and to observe the Lord's Day only was based on the Jewish idea of treating one day in the week as more significant than the other six. The emerging Christian desire to make the Lord's Day a more complete and obvious holy day—beyond merely worship services before or after work—was also taken from Judaism. The Jewish Sabbath promoted holy time, or separation from ordinary time, through not only ritual worship but an entire day of rest free from work and routine.

During the later fourth and fifth centuries, Christians began moving toward such a day as well. Before this date, any Lord's Day rest among Christians had been interpreted figuratively, as in "resting" from sin. This was partly because Sun Day was long an ordinary workday, partly because of old Christian prejudices against Sabbath rest, and partly because Christians insisted that they did not need an entirely separate day to remind them to ponder God and timeless things: every day was holy. But after 300, sentiment for more literal rest on the Lord's Day grew among Christians, with advocates declaring all the while that this of course had nothing to do with Jewish rest or the Sabbath commandment. More time free from work, they explained, was only a means to an end: namely, more time to worship.

A church council at Laodicea in 364 reflected this idea, stating that when possible Christians should physically rest from work on the Lord's Day in order to worship more, but by no means were they obligated to "Judaize" the entire day with literal Sabbath-like rest. After worship those who wished to return to work were free to do so. The council's message was repeated by other councils and such influential figures as Augustine through about 500: more worship, but no Sabbath-like customs. Saint Benedict, the great monastic reformer, confirmed the widespread Christian attitude that work was preferable to idle rest on the Lord's Day: if *required* to rest all that day, then his monks, he feared, would fritter the day away, in which case they would be better off working.

The fourth century's tentative steps toward literal Lord's Day rest soon became decisive steps, especially after Rome fell in 476. Within decades, bishops and councils were urging more genuine rest on the Lord's Day. Caesarius of Arles (d. 542), in Gaul (roughly modern France), repeated the old horror of Sabbath "superstitions" and rigors, then proceeded more than anyone before him to require literal rest throughout the entire Lord's Day and to suggest that such was based upon the fourth commandment; the Lord's Day was simply the better moment to fulfill that commandment.

How did this change happen? One immediate cause in Gaul itself was that new converts from paganism needed extra convincing to switch their favorite day of rest from Thursday, day of the pagan God Jove, to the Christian Lord's Day. "Church custom" wasn't enough, but a divine reason, in the form of the fourth commandment written directly by the finger of their new God, would do. In the later sixth century, Archbishop Martin of Braga (in Spain) addressed the same sort of converts from paganism and used explicit Sabbath phrasing: servile work on the Lord's Day was sin, because the fourth commandment said so. For the first time in Christian history, a church leader had outlawed all such work on the Lord's Day on the basis of the Sabbath commandment.

A more general cause of Christian support for literal Lord's Day rest was ever greater acceptance of visible religiosity, which after all had dominated religious thinking and practice in the ancient Western world. For instance, although Augustine spiritualized Lord's Day rest as "rest from sin" and ridiculed literal Jewish rest, he promoted literal rest indirectly through his rehabilitation of the Ten Commandments—including the fourth. Many early Christians had regarded all ten as part of Old Testament ritual law and thus no longer valid, but Augustine insisted on their continuing force, for all people, not merely the Jews. Just as important was his insistence on more visible displays of Christianity: not only should believers cease even witnessing Jewish and pagan religious rites, they must avoid as well even the broadly *civic* songs, dances, and banquets of Rome. Here was a distressing choice for many upper-class Roman Christians, who had previously regarded such activities as unifying points with other Romans, pagan or Christian, much like the national anthems or other civic rituals of countries today. But Augustine was adamant: separation in one's heart from any sort of pagan rite was no longer enough; rather, it required literal, physical separation as well, especially on the Lord's Day, when Christians should behave better than ever.

John Chrysostom echoed this notion: if Jews, who obtained "no benefit at all" from their "mistaken" Sabbath observances, could bother to observe them strictly anyway, then why shouldn't Christians, whose benefits were certain, be at least as strict about their Lord's Day? Christians should also cease using pagan names for days of the week, including Sun Day. It was the "Lord's Day." In other words, Christians must separate themselves more literally from pagans and Jews around them rather than entrusting that separation to Paul's invisible qualities within. If Christians wanted literally to stand out in a religious world that considered such standing out necessary, then they would not reject visible signs altogether but rather would hold up superior Christian signs to their rivals—such as a more visibly devout Lord's Day. As a later Christian council in Paris stated, pagans had their commemorative days in honor of false gods, and Jews had their "carnal Sabbath," but Christians should exceed both in celebrating their blessed Lord's Day. One had to *demonstrate* true religion.

A few later councils and leaders continued to resist this trend, repeating worn formulas against "Jewish superstitions." The Council of Orleans in 538 insisted that rest was solely for worship on the Lord's Day and that work before and after worship was fine, while Pope Gregory the Great (d. 604) emphasized the figurative meaning of the Sabbath commandment and warned that "Jewishness" was creeping into the church. But even Gregory's hugely influential voice was silenced by winds blowing the other way.

The renowned French bishop Gregory of Tours (d. 595) promoted literal Lord's Day rest by telling stories of the miserable punishments inflicted upon those who dared to labor that day. From Ireland came more such stories, along with expanded lists of prohibited activities and of holy events said to have occurred on the Lord's Day, thus heightening its sanctity. Believers learned that Noah's ark came to rest on the Lord's Day and that the adoration of the Magi occurred on that day, as did the baptism of Jesus, the feeding of the multitude, the Transfiguration, and the changing of water into wine at Cana. With such a list, how could one then think of laboring profanely on the Lord's Day? Much talk of literal rest also came from Spain, which some scholars attribute to the many Jewish converts to Christianity there: they either wished to retain certain habits of religious obser-

vance learned in Judaism or wanted visibly to outdo their more sophisticated former coreligionists.

In short, Lord's Day rest became openly codified in church law and
an assumed part of lived Christian culture. The Council of Rouen
(Gaul) in 650 was the first church council explicitly to require a
twenty-four-hour Sabbath-like Lord's Day, to make rest and worship
obligatory, and to fix a list of penalties for violating rest—as usual after first condemning all "superstitious" rules and penalties of the Jewish Sabbath. Indeed, Rouen's rules were in some respects stricter than
the Sabbath, including cutting off hands for assorted crimes committed on the Lord's Day and prohibiting sex that day. Moreover, now any
Christian who had engaged in intercourse even on the night *before*
Lord's Day services should not approach the communion table. Christian regulations did allow some things on the Lord's Day that Jewish
regulations did not allow on the Sabbath, and Christians were quick
to point these out, but they neglected to point out the reverse.

The stricter Lord's Day of Rouen was copied not only by ecclesiastical but by secular rulers all over Europe. In 755 the Frankish king
Pepin III gathered the bishops of France, condemned Judaizing within
the Church, then promptly proclaimed a long list of prohibited Lord's
Day activities. And in 789 Charlemagne specifically denounced labor
on that day as contrary to the Sabbath commandment.

The trend toward a more visible Christianity, evident in the spread of
literal rest on the Lord's Day, was also evident in changes in worship.

In the first place, thanks to Christianity's official status after 392
and more free time than ever on the Lord's Day, worship became more
public. Services began at midmorning now, rather than at inconvenient
hours, and took place in clearly defined churches rather than in semi-
secretive houses.

In the second place, worship on the Lord's Day became more formal. The elements and order of services were elaborated even further.
Numerous brief statements of belief, or "creeds," were added to services to promote orthodoxy. For the same reason more and more collections of the sayings of safe, recognized authorities were assembled

as well, and read aloud during services. Formalizing worship also included dividing congregations by gender, age, and marital status.

Another sure sign of formalized worship was the increase in complaints from clergymen about casualness during services among the flock. John Chrysostom, lamenting—even then—that churches were filled on Easter and Christmas but empty on the Lord's Day, urged his audience to compel friends and enemies and wives and children alike to come to services weekly, even forcibly drag them along, as part of their Christian obligation to love their neighbor. And it wasn't enough that people merely show up to church: he complained about young men who giggled or laughed aloud during prayer or sermons, declaring it a wonder that thunderbolts were not cast down upon them. If such indifference was suffered by Chrysostom, whose name means "the golden mouth," then one may safely assume that other preachers suffered it as well.

One way to counter irreverence at Lord's Day services was to grab people's attention with yet another sign and method of formalization: increasingly dramatic liturgy, in the form of special music, vestments, processions, objects, and actions, all set in ever more impressive churches. Since the time of Paul, many Christians had argued that holiness was interior and that God could not be circumscribed in a particular building or place or object: the true dwelling place of God was the heart of the baptized Christian. But now more and more Christians began to see God in specific earthly places, especially churches, and even in the holy objects used within them. Pagans and Jews had likewise established holy places, but Christians gave their own explanation: if God had become incarnate in the physical world in the form of Jesus, and God had created the physical world, then surely other visible signs of him could be found on earth.

The single most important physical channeling of God's presence by this time occurred within the church, during the Eucharist, still the highlight of Lord's Day services. When the Eucharist shifted from a genuine evening meal to a morning meal of merely bread and wine, then that bread and wine took on even greater importance, as did the vessels used to hold them. More and more Christians believed that these earthly elements, once consecrated during the Eucharist, were transformed literally into Christ's flesh and blood. In addition, the old fellowship-meal table became an altar, and the vessels used for the Eucharist were no longer used for everyday meals.

The new setting of the Eucharist—the church building itself—became more visibly important than ever by the sixth century. Anyone visiting a Christian service on the Lord's Day then would have noticed the magnificent candelabra, censers, and colored marbles, all meant to increase the sense of holiness in the place. Perhaps most striking of all would have been the abundant images in mosaic, images once considered too earthbound or pagan for Christians. These portrayed not only recognizably Christian figures but also pagan deities and such elements of this world as birds, beasts, trees, baskets, fruits, vases, and even seasons. Summer might appear in a church mosaic as a bare-breasted woman wearing earrings and wielding a sickle, the ocean as a half-nude man; the church building might take a blatantly Roman form, most notably a basilica. All this did not mean acceptance of paganism, but reflected Christianity's new confidence: fear of paganism's allure was past, because paganism had been subjected. Things of this world were now holy, creations of the Christian God.

Most telling here is that even the Sun, greatest symbol of Roman paganism, no longer had exclusively pagan meaning. Some early Christians had already used, with mixed results, the Sun's imagery to speak of Christ. But such imagery became more acceptable during the fourth century, when far more Christians began calling the first day "Sunday" rather than exclusively the Lord's Day—despite even the condemnations of an Augustine or a Chrysostom. Saint Jerome himself defended the practice, saying, why shouldn't we call it Sunday, since Christ is the Sun of justice and has filled the world with his light? Jerome even claimed that Sunday took its name from Christ the Sun rather than from the physical Sun. This was a classic example of reading present desires into the past, but Jerome demonstrated perfectly the ability to take something previously seen as Roman and make it Christian.

Indeed if the "Lord's Day" dominated Latin ecclesiastical usage by the fourth and fifth centuries, "Sunday" was at the same time more and more common in popular Christian usage. And when Christianity moved into northern Europe, "Sunday" was so common among Christians that the new northern converts simply used that name exclusively. Just as pagan *forms* had been conquered and appropriated, now the greatest *pagan day* was absorbed as well. Emerging vernacular languages around the Mediterranean, where the early church was born and raised, certainly retained "Lord's Day" in common usage, but a good Christian in either north or south could now find as much Christian imagery in "Sunday" as they pleased, and thus uttered the word without a second thought. Only the later vernacular languages of eastern Christianity, and Portuguese in the west, would reject all planetary names for the days of the week as offensively pagan.

In sum, by 600 one may speak of a Christian Sunday in the old Roman provinces touching the Mediterranean. By 800 this had expanded into the large portions of northern Europe already Christianized. Like the Jewish Sabbath, Sunday had become the most important day of the week, indeed gave the week most of its meaning. Once thoroughly pagan, Sunday now had a decidedly Christian connotation. It would remain this way for so long that countless generations in the Western world would consider the day's very existence, name, and status as obvious, unquestioned facts of life, as if things had always been this way.

2

A Village in the South of England,
Around 1300, in June, When the Sun Was Soft*

All days began early in June, with the first rays of sunlight landing on the highest stones of the church's squattish tower, then gradually spreading to rooftops clustered nearby. Most of these several dozen

---

*This chapter builds upon H. S. Bennett's classic essay of a week in a medieval village, entitled "A Fair Field Full of Folk," and included in his *Life on the English Manor* (1937). About ten of that essay's twenty-four pages are devoted to Sunday; thanks to countless studies that have appeared in the seven decades since he wrote, Bennett's brief, roughed-out Sunday may be embellished with far more detail and color—which is what I seek to do here, while following his basic structure of sunrise to sunset and his emphasis on work, church, food, and play. Also, just as Bennett took his essay's title from William Langland's famous medieval poem *Piers Plowman,* so my allusion to a "soft" or fair sun is from Langland.

houses resembled a very bent "A" and featured tried and true walls of wattle and daub, fresh or old whitewash, roofs of thatch, a single door, and a small window or two covered by wooden shutters. Some were no more than hovels. The front side of all bordered the single dirt road that wound lazily through the village, while behind each dwelling lay a plot of ground, nearly an acre, where stood a shed, various patches of vegetables, a few fruit trees, and, far in the back near the stream, a pigsty. A cow grazed in the ragged grass of more prosperous back-yards.

Men upon arising swallowed some heavy dark bread and ale, then alone or with teenaged sons went to their sheds to collect needed tools before heading down the road toward the fields. Like fields surrounding many villages in Europe, these occupied hundreds of acres and were divided into three sections: one for spring planting, one for fall planting, and one fallow. So that the varying quality of soil in the fields was divided as fairly as possible among villagers, and to ease plowing, each section was subdivided into dozens of long, distinct strips, ideally about twenty yards wide by 220 yards long (one acre), and now bursting with assorted shades of green, turning the landscape into a pleasant mosaic. But the peasants did not stop today to work in their fields, where precious crops still had far to go and where the weeding of thistles would begin only after St. John's Day, on June 24; any sooner, said tradition, and the thistles would come back threefold. Rather, they turned off the main road and headed toward a meadow, where the grass stood tall, ready for cutting.

The meadow too was divided into smaller parcels, marked by large stones or sticks. Men and boys scattered to their particular allotments and with sharpened scythes turned to the business at hand, which was to make hay. Some turned the slightly damp hay that had been cut the day before, while others swung into the fresh, dewy grass. Like all their agricultural work, this could be dangerous, especially the scythes. And when the cutting and turning were finished, the loading and driving of overburdened, groaning carts would bring even more dangers. Still, accidents were more likely to occur toward the noon meal, when bodies and minds were tired, and today the work would not last that long, for it was Sunday.

They did not fret about working this Sunday, for during hay and harvest season the village priest was especially understanding. He knew, as a farmer himself, that now was the critical moment for hay—the only food for animals during winter and thus carefully protected in the meadow since Christmas. He knew that most peasants not only cared for their own hay and crops but had to care first for those of the village lord, the nobleman from whom they rented their strips in the fields and to whom they owed regular labor; every hour on their own strips, in field or meadow, was therefore precious. And he knew last that peasants were required to observe, even during harvest, still other work-free holy days besides Sunday. Hence, although a village priest might not condone Sunday work, as long as the workers returned in time for Mass, kept their labors to the morning hours, and acted from necessity rather than greed, then he would not begrudge them their mowing. Besides, even the village lord violated the Sunday prohibitions by holding court, sending messengers, and ordering necessary work in fields and meadows as he saw fit. How could priests then completely forbid it to peasants? The crowd therefore sweated away for some time, until the sun was well above the horizon, but well before eight, when Mass would begin.

WORK

The stricter, more elaborate, work-free Sunday that emerged in Christianity between the fourth and sixth centuries was only reinforced during Europe's remaining medieval centuries. By about 1200 almost everyone knew the basic requirements of the day: worship and rest. And an ever-growing number of rules was designed to enforce them. Yet as the labors of these English peasants suggest, plenty of work took place anyway on Sunday, at least in the countryside.

Throughout the Middle Ages church councils, theologians, and secular rulers all over Europe declared as a commonplace what until around 400 had still been a novel idea in Christianity: the obligation literally to rest on Sunday. The stated purpose of rest remained that people might attend a growing number of services at church. William Langland's poetic plowman Piers put it thus: "And upon Sundays to cease, God's service to hear, both matins and mass, and after meat, in churches to hear evensong, every man ought."

More prosaic observers, such as Alexander of Hales (d. 1245) and Archbishop Peckham of Canterbury, in 1281, said the same: the general principles of rest and worship contained in the fourth commandment remained in force for Christians on Sunday. Thomas Aquinas (1225–1274) explained it most famously, by distinguishing, as ancient Jews never would have done, between the commandment's ceremonial and moral aspects. If the commandment were merely ceremonial, as some Christian thinkers had said, then it would have to be thrown out with the rest of Mosaic law. But if it were thrown out, then the other nine commandments could be threatened too. Aquinas saved the fourth commandment by concluding that it was only partly ceremonial, namely in its requirement to worship on the seventh day. This ceremonial aspect the Christian could safely ignore; it was no more binding than any other ceremony in Jewish law. But the moral aspect of the commandment, namely worship and literal rest, still applied, and on the day designated by the Church: Sunday. From this time on, almost every Christian commentator on Sunday began with Aquinas's distinction: it provided the separation that Christians sought from Jewish law, yet it preserved the fourth commandment, and all others.

A more securely Christian Europe now devoted less energy to denouncing the Jewish Sabbath and more to delineating (and arguing over) just exactly what a Christian should and should not do on Sunday. So many Sunday rules and decrees emerged even before Aquinas, some at odds with one another, that Pope Gregory IX in 1234 felt it necessary to impose order upon them within the first great compilation of church law, known as the *Decretals*. Most people still got the word in simpler form through their local priest, who was sure to warn them about the three great pollutants of Sunday—money, carnal pleasure, and spilt blood—or who told frightening stories in the manner of Gregory of Tours about those who performed unnecessary work on Sunday. They got it as well from traveling preachers, including of all people a Frenchman, the Abbot Eustace of Flay, who arrived in England in 1200 to recruit Crusaders but who ended up being the first vigorous campaigner there for a stricter Sunday. John Mirk's famous instruction to parish priests, composed in the fourteenth century, merely stated what was by then obvious: "Therefore they shall their holyday, Spend only God to pay."

But such lovely-sounding rules of Sunday rest and worship were rarely so simple for peasants, who made up the overwhelming majority of the population everywhere in Europe. Of the four to six million people who lived in England by 1300, 90 percent or more were peasants, organized in villages of 150 to 600 souls and dependent for survival largely on their own agricultural labors. Life (and Sunday) in towns looked much different from rural versions, but towns were still few: for almost everyone, Sunday meant a rural Sunday. Peasants knew firsthand that wind and rain and sun were no respecters of days, including Sundays. And now there were other holy days as well, forty to fifty of them added to the Christian calendar since the sixth century, all to be observed as if they too were Sunday, or in a very few cases even more strictly than Sunday.

The long list of new holy days not only diluted Sunday's prestige but severely reduced the number of days available for work. During the wintry part of the ecclesiastical year, agricultural demands were few and abstaining from field work on Sunday was easier than in summer. But once the plowing season began in April, the pressures mounted: May was for draining fields, clearing ditches, and mending hedges and enclosures; June for harvesting of hay; July for weeding fields, and harvesting, drying, and spinning hemp and flax; August and September for harvesting barley, rye, oats, peas, beans, and wheat; and finally October for more plowing. At these busy agricultural times, weekly Sunday rest, plus an occasional weekday holy day, could be a genuine nuisance. Complicating matters, about half of the peasants in villages typically held lands that obligated them to work a certain number of days per year on the lands of their village lord, especially at harvest-time.

The church understood these burdens upon peasants and therefore allowed "necessary works" on holy days. They might disagree with peasants over what "necessary" meant, but when bad weather threatened a harvest, the local priest would likely grant permission to bring it in on Sunday. The church also made concessions by ignoring backyard gardening on Sunday and by designating different levels of holy days: no work was allowed on the chief holy days (Sunday, Easter, Pentecost, Ascension, Christmas, and Epiphany), but on lesser holy days one might work in the afternoon. Still, with so many holy days through the year, numerous exceptions were bound to be granted, especially during the high agricultural season, so that on any summer Sunday in medieval England, in any village, people were likely to be engaged in some sort of physical work for at least part of the day, with the tacit or explicit permission of their priest. Hence, were one to ask a medieval peasant what Sunday meant, then part of that answer, certainly in summer, would have included work—despite all the formal prohibitions against it.

The peasant's habit of laboring on Sunday must be qualified, however: although peasants did indeed wish to work their own lands on Sunday when necessary, they did not wish to work their lord's. In that case, the rules about Sunday rest served as a protection for peasants rather than a hindrance. Work was always hard, but even harder when performed for someone else, as suggested in this contemporary dialogue:

> *Master:* What sayest thou plowman? How do you do your work?
> *Plowman:* O my lord, I work very hard: I go out at dawn, driving the cattle to the field, and I yoke them to the plow. Nor is the weather so bad in winter that I dare to stay at home, for fear of my lord. . . .
> *Master:* Have you any assistant?
> *Plowman:* I have a boy to drive the oxen with a goad, and he too is hoarse with cold and shouting.
> *Master:* What more do you do in a day?
> *Plowman:* Certainly I do more. I must fill the manger of the oxen with hay, and water them and carry out the dung.
> *Master:* Indeed, that is a great labor.

Or as Piers Plowman succinctly put it: "Some labored at ploughing and sowing, with no time for pleasure."

"No time for pleasure" might very well apply to Sunday, for despite the legal right by now to enjoy literal rest on that day, some lords—even ecclesiastical lords such as bishops or abbots—wanted their fields worked during crucial times of the seasons. A steward of the Bishop of Winchester, for instance, did not hesitate to blow his great horn one Sunday, summoning all the bishop's tenants to come cart the bishop's hay. The peasants complained, as did the local priest, who threatened the steward with excommunication. But the steward only laughed: his lord was after all the bishop, the priest's superior, and thus he continued his summoning.

There was at least one other circumstance in which peasants might oppose Sunday labor in the fields: when other peasants engaged in it alone, or nearly alone. Those working with few neighbors nearby, a scene more likely on Sunday than otherwise, could slyly extend sickle or scythe across the narrow boundaries that divided strips, reaping from someone's else's parcel. They might even subtly move the boundary in their own favor.

MASS

While meadows or fields might buzz with activity on Sunday morning, the interiors of huts and hovels certainly did. Especially women, girls, and young boys set about collecting eggs from their hens and, if they were lucky, milk from their cows. Large pots of hot water and vegetables cooked over open fires in the main room, turning the air sooty, for most homes had no chimney and smoke escaped as it could, through doors, crude windows, and crevices in walls and roofs. Blankets were pulled up on beds. Earthen floors were swept up with large brushes of twigs, then strewn with straw. When finished with chores inside or out, women might wash themselves with water from large bowls, or spend some time arranging their hair, before removing from a sole wooden chest their best dress, reserved for Sundays and feast days. All this was in preparation for another central meaning of Sunday in the Middle Ages, just as in the ancient Christian world: attending church. On most days women usually wore long, loose woolen gowns belted at the waist, their heads and necks covered by wimples. (If they wore undergarments, they were usually of linen.) But Sunday's gown for church would be cleaner and finer, and most likely brighter as well.

Before eight, those in the meadow returned from haymaking, likewise to prepare for church. After a drink, men and boys might set aside their sleeveless working smock for a better Sunday version, or merely straighten what they were already wearing: a short tunic belted at the waist, either short stockings or long hose also fastened at the waist, a cloth cap, and leather shoes with heavy wooden soles. The poorest had simply a coarse coat, likely with holes in the hood, not to mention holes in hose, shoes, and muddy mittens as well. In colder weather the feet of the poorest easily bled from icy furrows in the fields.

Bells announcing Mass were ringing. Sometimes they rang three times: the first two to warn that the hour was drawing near, and the third time more earnestly, proclaiming that the hour had come. Everyone knew that attendance at Sunday Mass was expected, by church law and by neighbors, and if purer motives did not suffice then these were enough to cause the peasants to set out with others toward the church. Along the way, not only were surrounding fields and houses visible, but likely the tower of the next village's church, some five to seven miles away. Near their own church the stone walls of the churchyard were in chronic need of repair and thus vulnerable to pigs and sheep in search of pasture. The animals' presence always displeased the village priest, who considered it profane, or who perhaps wanted the space for his own animals.

The churchyard was meant to be primarily a cemetery for the sacred dead, with the sunny south side holding those who had died in the faith, and the shady north for suicides and others out of favor. But to villagers this holy ground was also a playground, especially on Sunday and other holy days. It was the best green in the village, a gathering place for gossip before and after Mass, for striking deals, meeting friends, singing, dancing, sporting, and marketing. Behind the churchyard, in the background, stood the priest's residence, and next to it his tithe barn, a sturdy reminder that part of every peasant's crop would end up here this year, as every year.

The church itself was over a century old by now, but thanks to its stone still looked newer than more recent structures in the village. It was also grander than the village's last church, which had been one of the first rough wooden Christian churches built in England during the Saxon period (ca. 600–1066). This stone church was in the style that later centuries would call Norman (for England) or Romanesque (for all of Europe) and was erected with six to seven thousand other new parish churches in England between 1100 and 1150. Although sturdier and larger than the thatched huts they replaced, Norman churches were still fairly simple. They were as short as thirty-three feet in length, always longer than wide, and consisted of but two or three sections within: a larger nave for the laity on the west, a narrower chancel for the clergy on the east, and sometimes a choir on the east as well. That plenty of new churches were put up more sloppily than they might have been only added to the burden of maintenance: laypeople were responsible for the nave, and the clergy for the chancel and choir, but both parts were in chronic disrepair. In some parishes, rain and wind came through the thatched or leaded roof.

Having quit their conversations in the churchyard, these houselings, as villagers were known, entered through the main door of the church, in the southwest corner, where each couple in the village had likely been married. Finding the niche for holy water just inside the door, they dipped their fingers into it, crossed themselves, then continued into the nave: women on one side, men on the other. Except for some stone benches along the walls for the aged and infirm, there were, as in most churches still, no chairs in the nave, and only straw or rushes on the hard-packed dirt floor, to ease frequent kneeling.

Meanwhile the village priest had been busy as well. Early that morning he had performed various "chantry" Masses, for the souls of departed relatives of current villagers, who had made pious gifts to the church for this purpose. Before the parish Mass, he washed his hands and face in a sink, a ritual that was supposed to remind him to be pure, just as when he removed his everyday surplice and put on his Sunday vestments he was to pray that he might be able to lay aside his old person and clothe himself in a new. Indeed each of the various pieces he put on before Mass had some symbolic meaning, such as the cincture or belt around his waist to remind him of the column to which Jesus had been tied when beaten by Roman guards. But whether each priest pondered all of these, or was numb from the routine, is of course unknown. In many parishes, a deacon and subdeacon, or at least a holy water clerk, helped the priest with his preparations, served him at the altar during Mass, sang with him, and read the day's epistle from the Bible.

When finished vesting, priest and clerk came to the front of the chancel and blessed the holy water for the week. This would soon be poured into fonts and sprinkled on the church's altars. Next the priest led a procession through the church, or on fine days he began outside, and upon reentering the building and walking toward the chancel, he sprinkled the gathered faithful with holy water, stopping when he reached the great rood, or cross, hanging from the ceiling.

The villagers were most likely silently kneeling during these early proceedings, and also when the priest and clerk began singing the *Confiteor,* or general confession, which began the service. Unlike ancient Christians, who believed that kneeling detracted from the joy of Sunday, medieval Christians knelt often during the day's services. After the *Confiteor,* the priest walked through the rood screen (the partial wall dividing chancel from nave) into the chancel and toward the high altar, where he commenced saying more prayers, often with his back to the flock. This was the signal for some in the nave to begin whispered conversations or to lean irreverently against pillars. Much of the service was after all in Latin, the language of ancient Rome and still the official language of the Church, and none of the peasants understood it, save for the occasional familiar *Oremus* (Let us pray) and *Amen.* Some in the crowd claimed that they would be more attentive if they could understood Mass "word by word" in their own language, as they did the sermon, but plenty of experienced clergymen were unconvinced. Moreover, Latin was the church's link to its Roman Christian forebears and seemed inseparable from the faith. The problem, as churchmen saw it, was not with Latin but with an inattentive flock, who if they pleased could in fact choose to be closely involved in the service.

They could, for instance, keep their hearts meek. They could keep their ears attentive when the priest made announcements or preached. They could make the sign of the cross and kneel at appropriate times. And above all they could quietly say prayers of their own while the priest was praying at the altar, such as the Our Father (with spelling here largely modernized).

> *Fader Our, that is in heaven,*
> *Blessed be Thy name to neven,* *
> *Come to us Thy kingdom.*
> *In heaven and earth Thy will be done.*
> *Our ilk-day bread grant us to-day,*

* "give utterance to"

And our misdeeds forgive us aye,
As we do them that trespass us,
Right so have mercy upon us,
And lead us in no founding,
But shield us from all wicked thing.
Amen.

Some probably immersed themselves in such prayers, keeping their hearts with the priest even when he stood away from them. For these, he was not a detached figure, removed from an ignorant, passive flock, but their living intermediary with God: his actions were performed in behalf of all, and they followed intently. But for others he was distant and hard to hear, and thus hearts and minds and eyes—especially eyes—could wander.

There was much to see inside a medieval church, after all, even in a humble village version. Compared to the houses of the villagers, the church was a fine and spacious place, even otherworldly. They might well worry about the cost of the latest repairs, but more likely they proudly laid their eyes, for the thousandth time, on what they had contributed. Here in the church's decoration was where their sweat and blood and gifts and faith took tangible form and where they expressed themselves even more articulately than during Sunday Mass. In fact if, as some scholars have alleged, monks and friars dominated Europe's spiritual life during the twelfth and thirteenth centuries, then the laity set the tone around 1300 by adorning their new parish churches.

Many women standing in the nave had washed the cloths that were draped over the church's altars, mended the vestments worn by the priest, cleaned the vast floor and spread upon it the rushes where everyone alternately stood and knelt, and set out the flowers they all admired and breathed in. Others had paid for the lamps and candles scattered about the otherwise dark interior, for the crude wooden statues of saints all around, for the stained-glass stories of saints in the windows, and for the vivid murals on the walls. This saturation of images was, as Pope Gregory the Great stated in the sixth century, the Bible of the people: What is seen lasts longer than what is heard, he insisted. Yet these images carried more than an educational meaning to the villagers: there was also something immediately real and holy about them. Knowing this, clergymen worried about idolatry, instructing believers to adore what an image represented rather than the thing itself. But who could stop the houselings from seeing things as they pleased, especially when they had commissioned it all? Who could dissuade them from believing, as they long had, that whoever looked upon the image of Saint Christopher would suffer no harm that day?

Most striking in the church, perhaps, were the bright colors—on walls and stone or wooden objects—typically painted by experts but again paid for by local believers. The most prominent mural in almost every church, because almost always situated above the unmissable arch between nave and chancel, was a mural of the Doom, or Last Judgment. A stark Christ in his glory stood with hands apart, dividing the damned and the saved as he saw fit, the saved on the right accompanied by angels, while the damned on the left cast their eyes downward and gnashed their teeth, or simply were pulled headlong to hell, the devil's flesh-hooks in their shoulders. Other favorite murals included the Annunciation, the Adoration of the Magi, the Nativity, the Coronation of the Virgin, and simple allegorical depictions of abstract concepts: lust as a man and woman embracing, avarice as a man clutching his purse, and gluttony as a man with an oversize belly.

Of greatest relevance here, however, was the genre of mural known as the "Sunday Christ."

From the fourteenth century on, dozens of small village churches in England, and many more on the continent of Europe, contained portrayals of Christ surrounded by a number of tools familiar to villagers: tailoring scissors, a weaving shuttle, a fishing hook and reel, pincers, staples, nails, a knife, shears, auger bits, yarn, an ax, spade, mattock, mallet, harrow, sickle, scythe, rake, fork, cart, flail, and more. Each tool was then connected, sharp end first, by a red line to a fresh wound somewhere on Christ's body—beyond the well-known five wounds of the crucifixion. If the message was long elusive to modern scholars, it was readily apparent to villagers: namely, using these tools on Sunday only added to Christ's suffering. Agricultural tools were less prominent in these murals because, again, the church understood that agricultural work sometimes had to occur on Sunday. But there was less justification for peasants to use other tools, as many in a village might, for they often engaged in occupations besides farming. So important was this message that the Sunday Christ was sometimes as big as the great Doom. Many were placed near or all the way around the main door, so that upon exiting the services one was reminded what to avoid during the rest of the day. Moreover, in all works of church art the Sabbath commandment was one of only two commandments (with blasphemy) treated separately from the other ten.

The visual feast inside wasn't yet finished. Perhaps the most elaborately decorated object in every church by this era was the rood screen, standing directly beneath the great rood. Made of stone or wood, the lower part of the screen was covered with painted scenes on the wainscot paneling—often saints, prophets, and patriarchs in gold background. The upper part of the rood was riddled with assorted openings so that people could see through and follow Mass. The lower half even contained peepholes for children, called elevation squints, through which they might especially look during the Eucharist. Hence the rood screen did not necessarily hide the action at the altar but rather partly revealed it, or "framed" it, to focus attention and heighten its importance. Dramatizing the altar further was a reredos, or painted altarpiece, hanging behind it. Here was where the villagers would soon gaze most intently, if they weren't doing so already.

While some in the crowd swiveled their heads high during Mass, others looked for the umpteenth time at those around them.

Although familiar, the faces all around were neither uniform nor constant. The most obvious distinction was that between the village lord and lady on the one hand and everyone else on the other. The lord was noble by birth and controlled the village's land, movable property, and court—and very likely those of other villages as well. The lord and his household were long the only laypeople to have seats in church, but even more impressively, their seats, sometimes finely carved, were located in the chancel among the clergy. Moreover, Sunday services did not start until they were present, assuming they were in residence that week.

Another distinction lay between the houselings and their priest, now celebrating Mass. England had some 30,000 clergymen in 1300, serving some 8,500 churches and chapels. An elite group of clergy clustered in a few well-to-do urban parishes, while almost all of the rest were attached to rural villages. Many of these village pastors, however, did not actually reside in the village itself but paid a less glamorous, less educated substitute, or vicar, to replace them. These vicars were usually closer in status to the peasants than to the lord, often sharing their social origins and sometimes born and raised in the parish itself. To the peasants, the vicar was their neighbor, usually even their fellow farmer working the land. His share in the fields, called the glebe, lay right among their own strips, and though by 1300 more and more vicars were renting out the glebe rather than working it themselves, many still muddied their boots. The vicar might be found before Mass taking care of sheep in the meadow. He might be shoeing a horse when someone wanted to confess. He might like to hunt or to deal on the marketplace in land and goods. And also like the peasants, he might frequent the tavern on Sunday, occasionally game or drink too much, and exhibit the most common human failings. In short, he was more like the peasants than his successors in later centuries would be.

Surely this was why the famous manual for English priests, authored by John Mirk, established quite minimal standards for them. Among other things, Mirk felt it necessary to remind priests to be sober when ascending the pulpit to preach, and to be sober as well when administering the sacraments. And they needed not worry about having a broad understanding of the sacraments but had simply to be able to administer them. He also assured priests that as long as they could pronounce the first syllable of each word in the ritual and say the words in proper order, and were full of good intent, then the sacrament was valid.

Yet even this minimal knowledge was enough to make the vicar different from peasants, so that he was not entirely one of them either. Even though they knew their vicar's foibles, they likely marveled that he could say the mysterious Latin words at all, taught to him by a previous vicar. They marveled that he was their link to heaven, administering the soul-saving sacraments they wanted—baptizing and marrying them, hearing their confessions, attending them with holy oil and the consecrated host when they lay dying, driving evil spirits from their homes and fields, and performing the miracle of transubstantiation before their eyes every Sunday. That he was also to help the poor and to mediate disputes in the village reinforced his authority and apartness, as did his ever more distinctive dress (a tonsured head, a long cassock, and special vestments during Mass). His behavior was supposed to be increasingly distinct as well: pure in thought, chief in action, discreet in silence, profitable in speech, sympathetic to all, unbending against evil, fervent and gentle at once, and especially, since about 1100, celibate. On this last, here in 1300 an unknown number of English priests still kept women; one wonders where such women sat during Sunday Mass or how they were regarded.

Aside from obvious distinctions between houselings and lord, or between houselings and vicar, assorted distinctions existed among houselings themselves. Many were married and lived in "nuclear" households, for instance, but many were not and lived in mixed households: as many as 20 percent of people, especially women, never married at all, a good number under twenty-five were not yet married as this typically occurred later, and many were widows or widowers not remarried.

Another way to divide the houselings was by social status: some here in the nave were legally free, while others were unfree, the property of their lord. But the full meaning of either status was not self-evident. Unfree peasants were certainly tied to the lord through rents and other obligations, but they typically held larger shares of land than free peasants and held village offices: the steward (in charge of the lord's fields), the bailiff (responsible for supervising work on the lord's fields), the reeve (his assistant), jurors, ale-tasters, woodwards, and so on. Free peasants were simply more mobile, and indeed were the greatest reason why the mix of people in the village church on Sunday changed from year to year, even season to season. Then within the "free" and "unfree," prosperity and poverty varied. All of them, free and unfree, large and small and middling, stood together in the nave now, while the lord and his lady sat beyond the rood screen, and the vicar prepared to come back through it for the next part of the service.

After reemerging, the vicar made his way to the new stone pulpit on the side of the nave.

First came the announcements. Recent deaths, disputed wills, and the reading of banns for couples planning to marry, villagers likely knew already from friends. Other announcements might be exciting (upcoming feast days) or burdensome (new laws, a summons to a church court, or restrictions on work during upcoming feast days). Next the vicar might recommend prayers for the pope, their bishop, the king, queen, local lord and lady, those who had honored the church with gifts, the workers and tillers of the earth, good weather, villagers in debt or sin, the sick, pilgrims, pregnant women, and deceased villagers. Occasionally at this moment the vicar performed an excommunication with all its drama—praying that the Father, Son, Holy Ghost and all the saints would curse the person in question, then throwing down a candle, spitting on the ground, and ringing a bell to finalize the deed. Any public penances would also be carried out at this time, with the penitent clad only in underclothing and even scourging himself or herself.

When these preliminaries were accomplished, there followed from the pulpit the reading of the day's gospel. And finally from the pulpit there might very occasionally come a sermon—which like the announcements would be delivered in the people's own language.

Vicars were preaching at Sunday Mass more often by 1300 than in earlier centuries, yet still only occasionally. Archbishop Peckham's decree of 1281 stated that the parish priest was to instruct his flock formally at least four times a year, regarding the Creed, the Fourteen Articles of Faith, the Ten Commandments, the Seven Works of Mercy, the Seven Virtues, the Seven Vices, and the Seven Sacraments. Yet even four sermons proved too many for some. When vicars did preach, they were invariably inferior to traveling Franciscan and Dominican friars, who made preaching their vocation and who passed through casting thunderbolts and telling marvelous tales. But most of the time friars worked in towns, and villagers had to be content with their own vicar, whose learning and eloquence were as plain as his dress.

Fortunately for the vicar, there were now more aids than ever to help him preach, in fact entire sermons that he could simply read aloud. One English collection from the eleventh century contained some forty tried and proven homilies from Augustine, Jerome, Bede, Gregory the Great, and other immortals. Such collections even told him on which Sundays a particular sermon might be delivered, for the church year was divided up into distinct periods based upon biblical events. Still, topics were flexible, so that vicars who felt an urge to preach might select a theme that suited them.

Whatever the theme, most preachers, even the most respectable, preferred the fantastic and dramatic. They knew that anecdotes and examples moved listeners more than did abstract precepts or elaborately divided and subdivided expositions. Augustine had urged preachers to be pleasant, even entertaining, to hold the easily distracted flock, but John Chrysostom, despite his own gifts, warned against such methods, believing they would make people happy but not healthy. In general, more preachers seem to have followed Augustine than Chrysostom and gave people what they wanted, even mixing in such popular folk and mythical figures as King Arthur or Charlemagne. Arthur was said, for instance, to have had an image of the Virgin Mary on the inner part of his shield, which he would behold when weary in battle and then wax fresh because of it. But such tales had limits: another preacher awoke a drowsy congregation by suddenly interrupting his sermon to shout out, "There once was a king called Arthur!" at which everyone immediately stirred. He then chastised them for preferring profane tales to holy.

Despite their taste for the fantastic, preachers relied upon the familiar too. One vicar delivered, over two months of Sundays, a series of sermons on Jacob's well, with references to soil deposits, spades and ladders, ropes and buckets, and other processes and objects known to his listeners. Another elaborated upon the symbolism of plowshares and pruning hooks in Scripture, and the methods of manuring contained in Jesus' parable of the vineyard. A vicar might linger on the symbolic armory of God, in Ephesians, and add to the usual breastplate or sword a knight's special arrows, spurs, and bits. And he might use examples from familiar nature to simplify the most complex dogmas, such as the Trinity.

> *Of water and ice and also snow,*
> *Here be three things, as ye may see,*

And yet the three all water be.
Thus the Father, Son, and Holy Ghost
Be one God of mighty most.
For though they be persons three,
In one godhead knit they be.

Such familiarity extended to biblical and saintly characters, making them almost neighbors with the villagers: Noah and his Ark, Joseph in Egypt, Adam and Eve were all spoken of as if they were old friends, or at least no more distant than the king of England. They were also dressed up to look like the king and his noble cousins. Abraham was a bold earl, Satan commanded a court of evil knights, Judas and Pilate were dubbed "Sir," Jesus was a worthy duke, Jezebel a tyrannical queen, Paul a great gentleman, the Twelve Apostles the twelve heavenly gentlemen of the jury at the Last Judgment, and the wedding feast at Cana simply a medieval wedding party.

To the fantastic and familiar in his sermons the medieval priest added as well an inclination to dwell on sin and punishment. After all, if he heard people's confessions with any regularity, he knew sin up close. Preaching manuals urged him not to overemphasize God's mercy, nor to ignore the terrors of hell; although people loved to hear talk of "the pity and sweetness of God," the priest should hold up more often death and judgment. Threats were always more effective than sweetness in getting people to mend their ways, promised experts. Be harsh as lions against sinners, not lapdogs of even lords and ladies. Use darts, arrows, thorns, nails, swords, knives to penetrate the soul and pierce it. Hold up a skull, point to the mouth once so delectable to kiss and so delicate in eating and drinking, and to the eyes so fair where worms now crawl in and out. Do mention the grace of our Lord, and Our Lady, to soothe them, but do not linger there.

The range of sins spanned as far as the horizon. The supposed wiles of women were certainly a regular favorite, as some called woman "the confusion of Man, an insatiable beast, a continuous anxiety, an incessant warfare, a daily ruin, a house of tempest, and a hindrance to devotion." Others wondered why women tampered with the handiwork of God by adorning themselves with unnatural color and hair, or

why they habitually revealed so much of that handiwork. Or during
the harvest season the vicar might unfold the awful fate of those who
failed to pay tithing, or tell stories of the miraculous benefits that ac-
crued to those who paid in full. Abundant crops, bodily health, remis-
sion of sins, and reward in the kingdom of heaven were the promised
rewards of tithe-paying. Certainly the vicar would remind them as well
that there was no income or item so small that it could not be tithed,
as proven by Jesus' story of the widow's mite.

And of course during farming and festival season the vicar would
have reason to preach on Sunday observance, to remind his listeners
that though Sunday work was sometimes necessary, they need not
overdo it. Our Lord, explained the vicar, would never expect them to
let a crop rot in the fields on Sunday, just as he had not expected the
Israelites to leave an oxen stuck in the mud, but the busy peasants
ought to consider just how necessary their Sunday work sometimes
was. Did they dread God and keep his commandments? Did they realize that of all the Ten Commandments, God charged none so straitly
as this: "Remember the Sabbath to keep it holy"?

By 1300 the Sabbath commandment had not only survived the disputes of early Christian centuries to remain fixed among the eternal
Ten, but as this last phrase and the Sunday Christs on the murals suggested, it was very possibly the most emphasized of all. Stories of Sunday violators, begun in earlier centuries, now multiplied: did they
know of the fellow who missed Mass to go hunting and ended up having his arrows fly back at him? Or of the peasant who picked peas on
Sunday and had them stick to his hand so tightly that only by going to
church and praying did they come unstuck? Or of the terrified peasant
who felled a tree and watched blood flow from its stump? Or of the
baker who drew his batch of bread from the oven on a Sunday and
saw blood flow from a broken loaf?

But no story carried a stronger warning than the "Sunday Letter."
This was said to have been written by Christ himself around the sixth
century, then dropped by angels onto altars in the Holy Land, from
where over the next many centuries it made its way to Europe. If there
was an original and single version of the letter, it did not survive, but
plenty of other versions did. The central purpose of all was the same:

to tell people in dramatic fashion exactly what they should and should not do on Sunday. Despite this quite orthodox purpose, the letter's spurious origins caused religious and secular leaders to condemn every version of it as early as 745. Still, these prohibitions did little to weaken the letter's popularity among preachers and believers: in fact, it spread all over Europe and emerged in Latin, Syriac, Greek, Arabic, Ethiopic, Old Norse, Anglo-Saxon, Gaelic, French, Spanish, German, and Slavic variations, not to mention English. By 1300 condemnations of the letter were conspicuously absent, as many churchmen at least agreed that it effectively delivered to believers the good message: do not work on Sunday but worship only.

An English village vicar by 1300 probably knew nothing of any past condemnations of the letter at all, but treated it with the same ease and familiarity that he did the equally miraculous biblical stories of Balaam's Ass or Jacob's Well. And thus he did not shy away from citing it in his Sunday sermon.

For the sermon the people stood, or sat, on the rush-covered floor. "Friends, ye shall well understand that it is written, Dread thy God and keep his commandments, for unto that intent was every creature born into this world . . . and whosoever keeps my commandments, it is he that loves me." To prove that God emphasized the keeping of Sunday above even the other nine commandments, the vicar told how "Christ Jesus himself, God's son of heaven, had written an epistle with his own hand and had an angel deliver it to the altar of the church of St. Peter, Bishop of Antioch, intended for every creature on earth." Yes, Christ had written other letters on other subjects, such as against the tyranny of wicked King John of England decades before. Even the devil had sent letters, including one expressing his delight at the sins of the English clergy. But that Christ singled out Sunday for such a heavenly letter showed how important it was to him.

The letter, explained the vicar, told all the world to observe holy days, "and in special their Sunday," so that the great and horrible cursing of almighty God lay not upon them. For if the people did not rightly observe Sunday, then they would be cursed in their villages, and in their fields, in the woods, in the earth, in the water, in their land, in their crops, and in their children—then where would all their Sunday labor and pleasure have gotten them? Stones would blizzard down from heaven, there would be scalding water, famine, thirst, darkness, monstrous creatures with the heads of lions, and worst of all pagan peoples sent "to slay you and beasts to devour the breasts of your womenfolk."

To avoid these awful fates, they must abstain especially on Sunday from uncleanness, fornication, lechery, gluttony, contending, backbiting, uncleanness of body and soul, and the seven deadly sins, more so than on other days. But especially they must cease their labors. This meant there was to be no washing of clothes or heads, no wringing, shaping, sewing, baking, brewing, shaving, hair-clipping, or gathering of herbs and grain.

To impress upon the houselings just how important Sunday was, the letter reminded them of all the marvelous things God had wrought upon Sunday—the number of which had greatly expanded during the centuries since such a list first appeared. Everyone knew that Christ rose to life from the dead on a Sunday, changed water to wine, and fed the multitude, but did they know that he also created all the angels of heaven? Or that God appeared to Abraham on a Sunday? Or divided the Red Sea? Gave the law to Moses on Sinai? Ordained Aaron as the first bishop? Fed the children of Israel with manna? Caused a fountain to flow from the rock in the wilderness? Allowed Joshua to walk through the River Jordan with dry feet? Did they know that Christ was born and circumcised on Sunday, as well as baptized? That he began his forty-day fast, sent the Apostles preaching, caused the Holy Ghost to descend, and gave the vision of the apocalypse to John on Patmos? All on Sunday? Were they aware that Christ reopened paradise on a Sunday, or would render his Last Judgment on a Sunday? And did they know that on a Sunday Christ had destroyed the Jewish synagogue and ordained our mother Holy Church to take its place? All this should tell them that Sunday was no ordinary day, but a day to keep themselves from all sin, not to mention all unnecessary labor. "You have six days in the week to work all your earthly works, but keep to me the holy Sunday."

Those paying attention surely would have thought to themselves that it was a rare summer's week indeed when they could work six days, given all the other holy days they were also to observe. But others in the crowd continued to be distracted, or mumbled with friends, just as they had earlier in the service. The sermon itself was never long, perhaps ten or fifteen minutes, because preachers believed that listeners were easily fatigued. They weren't entirely wrong. Parishioners then seem to have wanted in sermons what they have always wanted: brevity, instruction, conformity to what they already believe, a pleasing voice, no condescension, no conceit, condemnation of others' sins rather than their own, and especially impressive delivery, diversion, novelty, and entertainment. The preacher hoped from his side for attentiveness and a positive response. He did not want laughter, heckling, sleeping, or blank looks, but rather tears—especially tears, which he took as a sign that he had touched them. But he had to be careful here. One preacher who proudly observed a woman weeping was later told the reason why: his voice reminded her of a dear but recently deceased donkey she had owned. Indeed, as often as a village vicar saw tears of devotion, he saw less desirable responses.

During the sixth century the famous bishop Caesarius of Arles went so far as to lock the church doors before he preached on Sunday, lest people wander out. "What are you doing, my sons?" he called at a group of men. "Where are you going, led by some evil idea? Stay here! Listen to the sermon for the good of your souls and listen carefully!" Other distinguished medieval preachers complained that people wanted to hear only "fancy tricks of style" and "whimsical bits of information and novelties." And if they did not get them, then they chattered, or slept, like the merchant's wife in London who brought her stole to church because she had slept poorly the night before and planned to catch up during the sermon. Naturally, preachers blamed the devil for such behavior, intent as he was upon preventing people from hearing what might save them: he was said to spread ointment to make people sleep, or to send little fiends into the crowd to put their fingers over the ears and eyes of people. These same drowsy people, grumbled preachers, had no problem staying awake for an hour in the tavern or at Sunday dinners, eating and drinking into the night. "I know well that you want a short sermon and long table," said one. Specific complaints were lodged against houselings who brought needlework to church, played chess, threw dice, engaged in love trysts, or discussed business. Women were supposedly especially given to whispering. No wonder priests still shied away from preaching every week, long before Anthony Trollope noticed in the nineteenth century "that anxious longing for escape, which is the common consequence of common sermons." But some vicars persisted anyway, if not weekly; surely they took solace in the thought that Saint Paul himself had put to sleep one young man, who grew so weary that he fell from the window where he was sitting and had to be miraculously healed.

Even if some villagers found the sermon and prayers tedious, most, even the indifferent, kept coming back, Sunday after Sunday. It could have been the fine building, or the legal and social obligation, or the hope of news and the sight of new faces. Certainly most came at least in part because they believed in death, and God, and the devil—especially the devil, whose evil cohorts tormented fields and homes and barns and animals and would do so even more freely if villagers did not attend Sunday Mass. And just as certainly they came on Sunday because of what would occur next in the service: the miraculous transformation of the wafer and wine into the flesh and blood of Christ.

Certainly the social element in the Eucharist mattered to them. Just as in the ancient world, a primary purpose of Sunday meeting in general, and the Eucharist in particular, was to reconcile differences and promote fellowship. Here in medieval Christianity, this was even more imperative: all were now born and baptized into the church, all worked side by side in the fields, and all knew one another. Failure to participate could be taken as a hostile act, a rejection of common rituals and ideals.

By 1300 most believers participated in the Eucharist not by partaking of the consecrated elements but simply by watching together. People took communion rarely, perhaps annually on Easter Sunday, because they regarded the Eucharist with such awe. Still, even watching offered the chance to reflect upon their relationships. Did they harbor ill feelings toward their village lord, who could be seen as an object of terror as well as affection? Who might show benevolence at harvest time or Christmas, yet who tirelessly tried to control their lands, obligations, and labors?

And what of their vicar? Anticlerical sentiment was growing in England by 1300, fueled by stories of negligence or abuse and certainly not helped by a vicar's chronic struggle to survive materially—just like the peasants. After all, the vicar's lands lay right among the peasants', and farming disputes were inevitable. Then there were the fees the vicar collected for performing baptisms, marriages, and funerals, plus their regular tithes. This was not to mention the vicar's claim to a peasant's second-best beast upon the peasant's death (based on the assumption that the deceased had surely underpaid his tithes), or conflicting views over proper uses of the parish church, or of course proper activities on Sunday.

The houselings ought also to reflect during Sunday Mass upon their even more frequent disputes with one another. Often these were about fields and meadows, boundaries, or trespasses committed by animals. But there were also the two women cooking at the village oven who argued over a missing loaf, to the point that they took up their fists and grabbed each other's hair. And there were always those who were only too willing to watch and accuse others in this small world of close neighbors, and the more rules that emerged from the church and the state, the more easily houselings could find fault in others. Such disagreements, however, could not be allowed to fester long, largely because of the need for cooperation in the fields. Thus the importance of Sunday Mass, and especially the Eucharist, to soothe.

As important as the social function of the Eucharist surely was, it was not all that attracted believers to this climactic moment. Rather, there was especially the Eucharist's magical pull: people wanted to witness the miracle, to feel the presence of God, and at the same time reap some decidedly tangible benefits. Priests in village churches complained that people often headed for the doors after witnessing the miracle, missing the rest of the service. Priests in large churches reported that when multiple Masses were being said at once, believers tended to noisily shuffle from one to the next just to see the miracle again. And why not? It was said that merely watching the ritual could remove fetters from an imprisoned knight, prevent blindness, improve eyesight, ensure an increase in crops and worldly goods, win love, and more.

Then, among the few who partook, or among the many who partook at Easter, were inevitably some who kept the consecrated wafer in their mouths until after Mass. These wafers were then planted in fields to promote a good harvest, or placed among beehives to prevent the bees' death, or crushed and scattered over cabbages to ward off caterpillars.

Hence all eyes looked intently ahead toward the altar where the vicar stood, as he prepared to consecrate wafers and wine. In a niche on the north wall stood a statue of the church's patron saint. Along the south wall was the *piscina,* where the vicar and assistants had already washed themselves, and the *sedilia,* or a series of recessed seats where they sat when necessary. Suspended above the vicar and covered with a silken veil was the *pyx,* which contained the leftover hosts from the previous Mass and which he now lowered by a pulley. Many repeated quietly their usual prayers, hoping to "pierce heaven with their Paternosters." They also brought forward their gifts for the altar, with some furtively stashing close by the altar certain objects they wanted the vicar (unwittingly) to bless. Unhurried, the vicar prepared the holy vessels, filling one vessel with wafers (or hosts) and one with wine. Then he uttered a prayer, concluding with Christ's own words from the New Testament, "This is My Body," at which he lifted one vessel high, and then said another prayer ending with "This is My Blood." At the conclusion of each prayer, a bell rang, signifying the moment of the miracle.

Those who had learned special prayers for this moment now repeated them in a whisper: "Every day thou mayest see, the same body that died for thee, Heed if thou wilt take, in figure and in form of bread, that Jesus dealt ere He were dead, For His disciples' sake." Or: "Hail salvation of the world, Word of the Father, true sacrifice, living flesh, fully God, truly man." Or: "Glory to you Lord who is born." Or: "Ihesu, Lord, welcome thou be, In form of bread as I thee see, Ihesu! for thy holy name, Shield me today from sin and shame."

Before partaking himself of the consecrated wafer and wine, the vicar kissed the lip of the chalice, then in turn the *paxbred*—a disk or tablet, carved with the Lamb of God or a crucifix—which was then borne around to be kissed by one and all. This was a continuation in new form of the ancient kiss of peace and thus of fellowship, as well as an extension of communion, thanks to contact with the holy vessels, however indirect.

During this ceremony the vicar knew to avoid the "perils of Mass," related to the miracle of transubstantiation. For once the wafers and wine elements were transformed and became divine, they could hardly be treated like ordinary objects. Thus the consecrated wine was consumed only by priests, to reduce the chances of spillage. If he happened to spill even a drop of wine on wood or stone, he was to lick it up and wipe off the place with a mixture of water and wine, also to be drunk or poured into a consecrated font reserved for that purpose. If after consecrating the chalice he should raise it to his mouth and discover a fly or spider inside, he was either to drink it down or remove the insect to another vessel, which would be washed repeatedly with water and wine after Mass, while the insect was burned and its ashes mixed with wine—this too was to be drunk, if it could occur "without horror." The consecrated wafer, if less likely to be spilled, presented dangers too. What if crumbs should fall onto the altar cloth? In that case the cloth had to be washed twice with wine and water, and the liquid drunk by the priest or a faithful layperson. Something similar applied to his vestments: if crumbs fell upon them, then the affected piece of material had to be cut out and burned, and the ashes kept in a special vessel for that purpose. Or if a communicant should suddenly vomit the host, the priest was to carefully gather it up from the mess, rinse it with wine, then drink that wine. No drop or crumb could be left unaccounted for. If a mouse somehow managed to eat even the tiniest bit, then the priest was punished with forty days of penance, while the mouse was to be hunted down, captured, and burned, its ashes reserved in a consecrated vessel.

All this the vicar had to know while swallowing the host and wine, and while sharing the host with a few others. But for many villagers the consecration itself was, as already noted, quite enough. Some left immediately "as if they had seen not God but the Devil" in the Eucharist. Some were eager, after this service of an hour and a half or two, and despite the sermon against working, to get back to their field, or to get to the alehouse right near the church for refreshment and socializing. The vicar had repeatedly insisted that the alehouse not open until after Mass, but this was a never-ending point of conflict. Not all vicars regarded alehouses as "the devil's chapel," because they drank in them too, but they did not want them interfering with church.

For those who stayed to the end, the church offered two final attractions. First was an indulgence, or reduction of time in purgatory, to all who heard the conclusion of Mass, taken from the first fourteen verses of John. All they had to do, when the priest said, "the Word became flesh," was to kiss a designated image or their own thumbnail. Second, the vicar stood before the rood screen with pieces from the "holy loaf," which he had blessed and cut and now distributed as another sign of fraternal love. Villagers kissed his hands upon receiving their share. Now all left the church, walking through the door framed by the painting of the Sunday Christ, reminding them to watch themselves during the rest of the day.

MEAT

While some lingered in the churchyard after the service to gossip more about marriages, crimes, or accidents, others walked home with neighbors, past the clutter and through the smells, disrepair, and dust in every village. Although as usual babies were crying, geese were hissing, dogs were barking, roosters were crowing, and any peddlers and tinkers were to the vicar's displeasure shouting, cart wheels were not squealing, hogs were neither butchered nor bawling, mills were (usually) not turning, smiths were (usually) not hammering, and flails were not thwacking, because indeed it was Sunday.

It was possible that a market might be held in the churchyard—a rather formal name for a few peddlers displaying their wares, although on some Sundays the number was bigger than others. Such markets, and the irreverent sideshows that always seemed to accompany them, offended the vicar, especially when they occurred right after a sermon about Sunday work. Laws against Sunday markets were repeated often from the time of King Ethelred (978–1016), but that very repetition suggests how hard they were to stop: right after church was simply a convenient time for congregated people to buy congregated goods. Concerted efforts by church and state caused Sunday markets to decline only by the later fourteenth century.

In addition to troublesome markets, Sunday after church could mean occasional violence. Gathering together for Mass made easier not only reconciliation but arguing and defaming and fighting too, right afterward. Emma, wife of John Lylle of York, yelled one Sunday after church at Agnes, wife of Robert the cook Popilton, that she was an old whore of monks and friars. Emma then tried to hit Agnes with a club, but Agnes ducked inside her home. The sixty people who witnessed this repeated the rumor about Agnes to others, and to her detriment, for various neighbors soon refused to deal with her.

If there was no diversion or excitement in their churchyard, most villagers simply returned home, sometimes along the way arranging to help each other in the fields during the coming week. Upon reaching home, they began preparations for the midday meal, typically the largest on Sunday. While women and girls of the households assembled food, men and boys headed to the end of their gardens and poured into the pig trough the scraps of the last meal, plus some weeds or sour milk. They might putter for a while among the vegetables, weeding and thinning, until it was time to eat. At some point they would see the holy-water clerk walking along the street, who sprinkled each house and would be given something in return.

Peas, beans, an old piece of fat, and an onion were the likely ingredients cooking in the large pot over the fire all morning, keeping the air inside the cabin as thick as ever. But there wasn't much furniture to soil: perhaps a bench or two, a couple of beds, a cradle, a trestle table or barrel, and a cupboard in which to store bedding, dishes, and bowls. The pottage was poured into wooden bowls, and all sat down to dinner. In addition to pottage, the meal included such everyday fare as new cheese, nuts and roots from the woods, and big, round four-pound loaves of dark rye or bean bread. (Wheat was usually sold at market rather than consumed, for it brought the best price: thus the peasants' own bread tended to be made from oats, barley, beans, and rye.)

On Sunday the midday meal also included better ale than usual and possibly some meat. Although meat was allowed on Sunday, as in the ancient world, medieval peasants were more likely to eat it in winter, when animals were slaughtered, than in summer, unless of course someone had dared to poach a fish from the lord's pond or some wild animal from his forest. In any case, among the special occasions when peasants did eat something different, then Sunday was usually on the list. One peasant woman who fell into a river on a Sunday did so on the way to help a friend with a special meal that day. Piers Plowman spoke of curds, cream, oaten cakes, loaves of bean bread, parsley, leeks, and cabbage during ordinary meals, but pork, geese, salt bacon, and eggs for special occasions, and fine grain, cherries, and baked apples and pears only at harvest—that short period each year when food seemed plentiful.

After the meal the men often returned to their gardens, a favorite Sunday pastime now and in the future. This was better than working the lord's land that day, and part of the freedom of Sunday. The vicar looked upon gardening more kindly than he did working in the fields, or sitting all afternoon in the alehouse. Besides, the garden was another important source of food, as its fruits and vegetables added quantity and variety to the basic diet of bread and ale. Peasants did not grow all of their own food; they regularly bought ale from various women who brewed it in the village, and they might even buy bread from those who realized they had baked too much at once in the village oven. But peasants did provide much of their own, so that every bit of food-producing ground mattered. Because houses stood near streams, and because the various household animals deposited their waste around the yard, these arable patches might actually contain more fruitful soil than the strips in the fields. Hence it was important to care for them, and Sunday was one of the best days to do so.

Inside each home people stayed busy as well. From the scant records remaining, it appears that households of the time, whether nuclear or mixed, averaged between three and five people. All bore a limited number of Christian rather than Anglo-Saxon names: William, Thomas, Robert, and John, Matilda, Margaret, Emma, Alice, and Agnes were some of the favorites. Nuclear households were small because of high mortality among children, due mostly to stillbirths and especially to disease: a mother might bear eight children, but some died at birth, others died in the first few years, and only two or three survived to adulthood. Never-married young people, stepparents, and single parents were plentiful in households, but grandparents and never-married elderly people were not: only about 10 percent of the population seems to have been over fifty.

Also present inside the house were likely a pig, chickens, hens, dogs, and cats, all scattering the dung and filth that had been swept up that morning. Where the human members of the house lived, after all, was not easily distinguished from where the animal members lived; sometimes there was no dividing wall, for the warmth that came from the animals helped to warm the entire house, even if their smell filled it too.

Except at harvest-time, a woman was often around the house rather than in the fields, and she slowed down somewhat on Sunday. If she were a brewer, for instance, as so many women in England were, she would refrain from that on Sunday, as she would from carding, spinning, and beating flax. But animals still had to be cared for, water still had to be fetched from wells (a more dangerous job than it seemed, given the slippery ground around wells, ponds, and ditches), meals still had to be made, wood still had to be collected and hauled home on their backs, and fires still had to be lit. Young children followed her around, or wandered as well, adding to her responsibilities more than helping her. She often tied any baby into a cradle, so that she wouldn't have to keep a constant eye out when the pig or dog came through. One problem with this increased security, however, was that it helped to make cradle fires the leading cause of accidental death among infants, as the pig or dog might accidentally bump the cradle into the household fire. And when babies grew old enough to crawl and walk, the hearth became even more dangerous. Older boys followed their father to learn his tasks in fields, roads, forest, and, on Sunday, the back garden. They and their sisters might help in getting water, or with herding and gathering nuts, herbs, and wood, or, if along the coast, even collect shellfish.

Toward two o'clock a small crowd of villagers gathered at the church for evensong, which was usually shorter than Mass and sparsely attended. In theory, any tavern that had opened its door after Mass was now supposed to shut briefly. But taverns were free to open again at the end of evensong, around three, when the recreational part of Sunday truly began.

FUN

Just as peasants set out together on Sunday mornings in summer to work in the fields and to attend Mass, so on Sunday afternoons they came together for fun. Here was the third and last great meaning of Sunday for medieval people (or fourth, if a slightly better Sunday dinner is counted too).

Adam le Schirreve and his wife, Cecilia, of the parish of Marden in southeast England, were two such fun-seeking peasants. They would never forget one particular Sunday afternoon near 1300. Shortly after the end of evensong, they decided to do what they often did on fair Sundays: walk to a tavern in the hamlet of Wisteston, about a mile away, to drink ale and socialize.

The couple, in their twenties, left their several children at home, under the care of the eldest, or a grandparent, or a friend. But after going some distance, Adam and Cecilia realized that their five-year-old daughter, Joanna, was following stealthily behind them. Rather than take time to see Joanna back home, the couple decided to bring her along, for at the tavern there would be other children from the parish with whom she could play. Indeed upon arriving they found some one hundred other people already engaged in recreation and talk. Joanna stayed for a short while with her parents, but was quickly drawn outside by the fine weather and three young friends, including her godmother's four-year-old son, and thus her "spiritual cousin," John Schonk.

Some time afterward the younger adults of the parish, led by John's father, Thomas, began their usual dance line, which proceeded through the tavern's garden and up around a nearby pond. Reaching the pond, Thomas and three others in the front of the line saw what looked like a child's body floating on the surface; they immediately supposed that it was the daughter of a local beggar woman, thrown in by her mother to drown. Believing the girl already dead, they decided not to tell the others in line, nor to raise the troublesome "hue and cry." This old tradition required the discoverer of a crime immediately to yell it out, and persons standing nearby to continue yelling, until the cry went from village to village and finally reached the regional officers of the law, who were then to ride and investigate. Whoever raised the cry was also required to wait until the officers arrived, which was inconvenient to say the least: those who raised the hue were often suspected of the crime itself and were required to appear in court if a trial followed. Yet those who failed to raise the cry or who moved a dead body were severely punished: a village's well or pond might be filled in, at village expense, or an entire village might be fined. Thomas Schonk and the lead dancers therefore took a huge risk when they ignored the body and an even bigger risk in deciding to return that night to move it from the pond and into a nearby river, where they hoped it would more easily be discovered by someone else or carried downstream. In the meantime they danced on for another hour or so, back through the tavern and up to the public road. The body in the pond continued floating.

The dancers were wrong in their identification: in fact the drowned body was that of Joanna le Schirreve, who had been out playing with her friends while her parents were inside the tavern. Joanna and young John Schonk had begun their play away from the pond. Like other medieval children, they might have climbed trees or dangerous woodpiles, hunted for birds' nests, spun tops, and sung rhymes along the way, such as "Clim, clam, the cat leapt over the dam" or "The hare went to the market, scarlet for to sell, the greyhound stood him before, money for to tell." But eventually Joanna and friends found their way, as children often do, to water. The pond, about twenty-four feet wide, sixty feet long, and over six feet deep in places, was surrounded by sparse vegetation, but the bank was mostly mud, sand, and dirt. It appears that Joanna and John were throwing rocks into the pond when John either bumped into Joanna and knocked her in, or playfully pushed her, not realizing the awful consequence. There was a drop of four feet from the bank to the water; on her way down Joanna, unable to swim, grabbed at weeds on the bank and screamed for help before going under, but no one saw or heard her except her frightened friends, who dared not follow her.

The boy John ran into the tavern to tell his mother, Joan (Joanna's godmother) what had happened. But Joan was busy talking to Joanna's mother, Cecilia: either the women did not understand the message or were preoccupied with their conversation. Events here are not exactly clear or consistent from later testimony, but it seems that someone did hear the boy correctly and ran outside to tell his father, Thomas

Schonk, still in the dance line. Thomas, realizing what had happened, went inside the tavern, grabbed his boy John by the ear, and led him home, about a hundred yards away. One of two things then occurred: either Thomas went back to the tavern and told Cecilia and Joan what he knew, or the boy John broke out of the house several hours later, went back to the tavern, and told his mother himself—this time successfully.

However Cecilia and Joan finally came to understand the devastating news, they at last dashed to the pond and saw Joanna's now submerged body. It had been at least a couple of hours since her accident. Cecilia was eight months pregnant, and therefore perhaps hesitated to jump in, but Joan, Joanna's godmother, did not: though not knowing how to swim, she was moved "by a kind of passion," having lifted Joanna as an infant from the baptismal font after all. She also understood that her task as godparent was not only to teach Joanna her three prayers, not only to care for her should her parents die, but specifically to protect her from the perils of fire and water until age seven. Hence Joan plunged desperately in and managed to get hold of the girl, drag her to the bank, and throw the body up onto it. Joanna's face and clothes were so disfigured and covered with mud that her family and friends did not recognize her. Her tongue was also sticking out between her clamped teeth. But her shoes with red tie-strings, which Cecilia had bought for her just the day before, confirmed the terrible truth.

Joanna's father, Adam, was still in the pub while this was going on, until someone finally came to tell him. He too ran outside and saw Joanna, with everyone mourning and crying around her. All were well acquainted with death, for likely up to half or more of their children had died before adulthood, but this did not make death any easier. Adam was "stirred to my paternal depths," as he later put it, and wept. Someone wanted to raise the hue and cry, but Adam preferred to go down on bended knees with the weeping women and seek divine intervention. He had heard recently of purported miracles performed by Thomas of Cantilupe, former bishop of Hereford, who had died in 1282 and whose tomb lay just six miles away in the cathedral of Hereford.

And so Adam prayed that Thomas of Cantilupe might intervene for his daughter, then urged others present to call upon Thomas as well. To demonstrate his good faith, Adam followed the custom of measuring Joanna's length with his belt, promising to purchase a candle of that size for the cathedral if Joanna survived. Then he used his knife to cut Joanna's belt, because her stomach was so swollen, and then carefully used his knife again to open her rigid mouth. This action successful, a great noise came from within Joanna; some said it was God breathing life into her, through Thomas's merits.

Adam stayed next to the pond from sunset until it was dark, in prayer, and both men and women removed their hose so that they might utter on bare knees all the prayers they knew. About two more gallons of water came from Joanna's mouth and cavities during all this time, and one man turned her upside down to get out more. Cecilia held her daughter in her arms and mourned. Against the wishes of her husband, who feared trouble from the law, and with some collusion from others, who agreed to say that Joanna wasn't yet dead, Cecilia then carried her into the tavern. But not wishing to get the tavern-owners involved in the matter, Cecilia finally took her girl home. Joanna's body was now so cold that Cecilia decided to get into bed with her, near the fire, and hold her.

It was only the next day, Monday, that the miraculous occurred: at dawn Cecilia felt movement from Joanna. Then the girl began vomiting and speaking, eventually coming to full consciousness: she was alive after all, and with no apparent ill effects. At sunrise her thankful parents carried her to their own parish church and laid her on an altar while the church bells rang, signifying a miracle. People from the village heard and came to see, including the lady of the village, Margery Wafre, who brought her entire household. Adam decided to take his daughter immediately all the way to Hereford, to visit Thomas of Cantilupe's tomb. About thirty people came along, all wanting to touch and kiss Joanna; many from nearby villages joined as well. At the church a canon performed an initial inquiry into the miracle, the bells rang here too, and a huge procession of thanks began while the miracle was publicized.

One wonders whether Adam and Cecilia continued to socialize with their once close friends, the godmother and namesake of their child, Joan, and her husband Thomas. Obviously Joan's rescue of Joanna was heroic, but Thomas Schonk's behavior much less so. Still, some years later Thomas Schonk did come forward to testify at the official inquiry into this alleged miracle, as did a dozen or so other witnesses from that dramatic Sunday. Partly on the strength of Joanna's miracle, Thomas of Cantilupe was indeed made a saint in 1320. All the witnesses noted that since the miracle they had become more devout. But none of them could remember exactly what year or date the events had occurred—only that it had been a Sunday. This was not because of the miracle, which might have happened on any day, but because of the visit to the tavern, which was for Sundays only, and which despite their newfound devotion they continued to visit, for they saw no contradiction at all between fun and church on Sunday.

Although thankful for this miracle, which was perhaps the most widely reported of the time in England, churchmen would have been less than pleased with its setting at a Sunday tavern.

The medieval church did not necessarily oppose play and recreation, including on Sunday. Just as it recognized the need for time free from work, so did it recognize the need for people to "refresh" themselves as part of that rest and thus to engage in honest recreation outside of Sunday services. The question was, what did "honest recreation" mean? Now that rest was an integral part of Sunday, did it simply mean "no work" or did rest also include "play"? And what kinds of play? Indeed, as much as the church condemned Sunday work, it condemned certain kinds of Sunday play even more, pitting, as one source put it, the *taberna contra tabernaculum*, or the tavern against the tabernacle.

The church itself designated in the middle of Lent a "refreshment Sunday," alluded to famously by the wife of Bath as a blessed time to refresh her carnal needs but intended more generally as a time of relief in the middle of that strenuous season of denial. The pious devotional work *Dives and Paupers* admitted that people should make mirth on Sundays and holy days, to refresh body and soul. But many clergymen would have defined "mirth" differently from Adam or Cecilia and their friends. True, some clergymen were still recreating right alongside their flock, but more than ever they were expected to stand apart and to set an example, as well as to prescribe for their flocks an increasingly narrow definition of recreation on Sundays. Some clergy therefore lamented that the greater the holy day, the greater the depravities.

To the clergy, Sunday was meant to be a busy day, just like a workday, but concerned with work of the soul rather than of the body. John Mirk's famous book instructed vicars to ask their flock, "Hast thou kept the holy days?" or in other words gone to church and avoided work, riotous company, shooting and other sports, and especially church ales and bride ales (often riotous festivities held in churchyards, meant to raise money for one cause or the other through selling ale). "The holy day only ordained was, to hear God's service and the Mass." Church-approved activities on Sundays included giving alms, visiting the sick, reconciling with neighbors, saying prayers, singing psalms and hymns, and eating modest meals. Together with services at church in morning and afternoon, these were enough to fill an entire Sunday and to set the proper mood. This prescribed mood was no longer one of outward joy, as in the ancient Sunday, but of inward joy. The outward mood, however, was one of somberness. Preachers held up to their flocks the example of the king whose family asked him why he was always of such heavy cheer and did not make merry as they did. He responded that the seven deadly sins were always ready to stab him in the heart, causing him constantly to be fearful for his soul. And "whosoever should take this example to heart, he shall have more delight to be sad than to laugh, to sigh than to sing, to cry out than to rhyme, to grieve than to dance; so that he shall find awareness of death the chief help against all manner of sin." In other words, ultimate joy came through inner stillness and deep sobriety.

Most villagers did not agree or feel satisfied with merely the prescribed list of activities. The things they preferred on Sunday afternoons are known less through such rare records as those about Adam and Cecilia than through the many denunciations of such Sunday activities as drinking and carnality, in all its forms.

"Drinking" per se was not objectionable: people drank ale every day, as their main drink and an important source of calories. The problem on Sunday came when they drank together in a crowd, and drank more than usual, which led, believed the church, to a rise in bodily temperatures. This came out in the form of dancing, rude songs, low tricks, lewd conversation, carnal pleasures, and violence, all unbecoming in the eyes of the church but particularly on Sunday. Priests complained that people loosened their tongues more at the tavern than they ever did to their confessor, and even told jokes of vague factuality about priests, such as the priest in Worcestershire who was kept awake all night by people dancing in the churchyard and singing a song with the refrain "Sweetheart have pity," so that the next morning at Mass, instead of uttering "Dominus vobiscum," he too blurted out "Sweetheart have pity." Or another who supposedly did not know the difference between Saint Jude and Judas Iscariot and thus on the feast of Saint Jude and Saint Simon advised his congregation to honor only Simon. Or a priest named Richard Helmyslay who concluded that a royal decree of 1215 requiring all people of both sexes to confess annually applied only to hermaphrodites. Priests of later centuries could tell jokes about priests too, but when told by laypeople they were clearly not meant to flatter. Priests therefore complained that even parishioners in church on Sunday often had their souls in the tavern, the devil's school, where the lessons taught included gluttony, lechery, swearing, forswearing, lying, slandering, and telling evil tales.

But again the arousal of carnal desires at taverns was the biggest fear among those who criticized common sorts of Sunday fun. To them, lust simply seemed to be more present on Sunday than on other days, not only in taverns but in such "lovely places" as the village green or flowery meadows. Since the ancient world, Christian authors (virtually all of them sworn to celibacy) had defined piety more and more in terms of sexual restraint specifically and bodily restraint generally. Lack of such restraint on Sunday, the ultimate holy day, seemed to them the ultimate impious act. Officially by now, sex was prohibited on Sundays, Wednesdays (regarded as the day Jewish leaders conspired to kill Christ), Fridays (the day of crucifixion), Saturdays (the day of darkness before the resurrection), all of Advent, the forty days of Lent, forty days before or after Pentecost, and on days before receiving communion. This left fewer than one hundred days in the year for licit sexual relations—as long as the woman was not lactating or menstruating, of course, which were also proscribed days. How many Christian villagers kept to such a schedule is unknown.

Dancing, also popular on Sundays and holy days, was another favorite target of the clergy because of its carnal connotations. Augustine's saying, that it was better to spend the whole day digging than dancing, was a well-worn platitude by now. Stories recounted the awful fates of dancers, such as several men and women who danced inside a church on Sunday, including during Mass. When the priest asked them to leave, they scorned him instead. But soon the dancers realized that they were powerless to stop: they danced through the day and night, until one fell dead from exhaustion. Here was a lesson to all. A Dominican preacher complained that women, the "devil's amazons," were to blame for most dancing, enticing men away from church, armed with horns and elegant headgear of flowers and fine material, plus a bare neck, a colorful brooch on their breast, and other vanities. Who could resist their deadly shafts, the fatal attraction of their looks? Still, people continued dancing despite the warnings, especially on Sundays and holy days.

Much the same can be said for all sorts of games. Many were condemned as slothful or lighthearted, reflecting lack of concern for one's soul, while others were condemned because they were violent. Handball, or Fives, was seen as inherently irreverent because it was played on the church wall, the only relatively flat and solid stretch of large wall anywhere around. Tumbling was condemned with reminders that King Herod's daughter was a tumbler. And many sports allowed on other days were banned on Sunday—partly because they interfered with church, partly because they occurred in that favorite play area the churchyard, and partly because they often led to noise, jangling, crying, striving, and fighting, "unbecoming" of the day. There were plenty of stories, for instance, of boys who went swimming on Sunday and drowned. Thomas Aquinas seemed hesitant about sports generally, but certainly discouraged them on Sunday. This was all quite in contrast to ancient cultures, which included sports among their holy day rites as something pleasing to the gods, and thus regarded them as deadly serious, even as conveyors of ultimate meaning.

Still, all the repeated condemnations and complaints about Sunday games suggests that they were regularly played anyway and thus implicitly seen by participants as not necessarily incompatible with faith.

These included games of chance, such as cards, dicing, backgammon, and even chess, but also physical sorts of games, such as wrestling matches, shooting, stone-casting, and ball-playing. Some churchmen, for instance, realizing how popular wrestling was, simply accepted it, and used wrestling metaphors in sermons against the devil: "In wrestling, when a champion may lift another's foot, then he throweth him down—right so the fiend!" The church's general opposition to Sunday sport was also diluted when various English kings urged people to practice on Sunday those sports connected to military prowess, such as shooting and wrestling. Edward III in 1365 even ordered men to practice only archery on Sunday rather than engage in "useless" sorts of games. The Italian churchman Bartolomeo Pisano allowed running, wrestling, and throwing the javelin on Sunday because they were all good for the body. Other churchmen concluded that hunting, fowling, and fishing were acceptable on Sunday if they were engaged in for recreation and food, but not for business—and certainly not when the village lord was at Mass, which made poaching in his woods and lakes too easy. Still, it was due to overwhelming amounts of participation, and not to theorists, that games of chance and exercise were as regular a part of Sunday as taverns through the Middle Ages.

All such games were often connected to fairs (from the Latin word *feria,* referring to "holy day"), which usually included such recreations as dancing, dramas, and markets. Sunday fairs were discouraged by the church, partly because some people had to work at those fairs in order for others to have fun. Smaller and less regular versions of fairs were bride ales, church ales, bede ales, and more, often held on Sundays. One should not conclude that a medieval Sunday or holy day was one ribald round of feasting and overconsumption; there was simply not enough time or food and drink for there to be regular plenty. But perhaps this helps to explain why on abundant Sundays the celebrating was so intense.

Even the miracle plays of a Sunday fair might be condemned, sometimes because of dubious content, sometimes because exotic traveling actors kept people out of church. For although clergymen occasionally acted in these plays too, plenty were full of heresy or bawdiness, just like ordinary sorts of plays. One apparent favorite portrayed a literal fight between a friar and a pardoner (who sold indulgences). Each struggles to be heard over the other, the friar promising the audience "I come not hither for meat nor for meal, but I come hither for your souls to heal, I come not hither to gloss nor to flatter, I come not hither to babble nor to clatter, I come not hither to fable nor to lie, but I come hither your souls to edify." The pardoner meanwhile promises just as loudly that the indulgences he holds, bearing the papal seal, would be more effective than any sermon in saving them. Eventually, neither man can make himself heard over the other, and so they begin to fight. More insults follow amid the blows, until the local vicar separates the two rivals, but only briefly. For after urging them to penance, they fight again, and the vicar must call in a strong parishioner to help.

In sum, the medieval church, like the ancient church, still feared sloth and depravity on Sunday even more than it feared labor. Indeed, clergymen familiar with the case of Joanna le Schirreve could have pointed out that it was thanks to their visit to the tavern that her parents so sorely neglected their child, necessitating the miracle that brought her back to life that Sunday. But these churchmen might not have pointed out that children were just as likely to be neglected on weekdays, if for a different reason: their parents were so often overwhelmed with work. This was precisely why so many looked forward to Sunday: there might be some work on that day, as other days, but there would certainly be some rest and socializing and fun.

As a Sunday night in summer wore on, the laughter and conversation grew louder, the stumbling increased, and the chances for liaisons and violence escalated. But those who carried their drink well needed no reminding, at least not in June, that tomorrow was yet another important workday. Thus there was also strong incentive to go home and sleep at the end of a long Sunday. They likely dreaded running into the lord's beadle, who often appeared at the end of any day this time of year to say that the village lord had requested, in addition to the usual required work in his fields, some extraordinary work, or "love boon," on the morrow. This would mean that work in the villagers' own fields would again come second. The love boon might include a meal with it, but it was still an annoyance.

When the day was done, usually the woman of the family tucked in any children and blew out any candle, which is known from the number of times candles were *not* blown out and thus fell into the straw and started fires. But most often the houses simply went dark, and weary people slept deeply until the next day, a workday. And thus the weekly cycle of work began once more, and the grace and leisure of Sunday, the finest day of the week, came to another end.

3

A Town in the Dutch Republic, in Winter 1624,
When the Sun Was Low

Like medieval peasants before him, the Dutch schoolteacher David Beck rose early on Sunday mornings. But while rural peasants hoped to get in some work before Mass, this urban creature simply had too much on his heart and mind to sleep well, even in the black of a winter's night.

Sometimes he awoke early because of frightening dreams, such as when he imagined himself and his brother Hendrik being clamped into chains by Turks—the bogeymen of early modern Europeans—and then left to die in prison. But most of the time he awoke because of dreams about his wife, Roeltge, who had just died in December while giving birth to their third child. Once he dreamed that he cried tears of grief until he was blind, but then Roeltge appeared behind him, drying his tears and restoring his sight.

Other things upset his sleep as well. The new baby, named after her mother, was not among them: only a month old, she would stay with the wet nurse for another six months. But David's other two young children, Adrian and Sara, sometimes stirred in the night, and night or day he was now solely responsible for them. He had recently become also responsible for his teenage sister, Diliana, and his ten-year-old brother, Abraham, who had moved from Cologne to live with him here in The Hague. Diliana was at least a great help, especially in watching the children while David worked or went out. But Abraham was a worry: he kept running away from home and from apprenticeships David arranged for him, and had been found more than once begging in the streets, full of lice and scabs. What would David tell his parents in Cologne? Yet they may very well have been dead by now, which would explain why the two young siblings were in David's charge. He had still other family in The Hague, and they were a big reason why David had come here himself seven years before, but they could not bear away his many troubles. In the depth of sorrow, on his thirtieth birthday in January 1624, he wrote in his unusually personal and detailed journal that truly his youth was behind him.

Still, David had not lost all energy and hope. Long hours teaching children, in the schoolroom attached to his home, helped him to cope, as did his Sundays. Thanks to the watchful eye of Diliana over the children, David had on that day more time than usual to take long, reflective walks and to visit with sympathetic friends. Yet Sunday's extra time for pondering, walking, and conversing could be a mixed blessing: it relieved his sorrow, but just as often intensified it. After all, freed from his weekday routine of teaching from eight in the morning to as late as eleven at night (among irregularly scheduled students), much of his Sunday was spent with people who had also known and loved his wife, and thus who mourned her as well.

It was still dark when David set out at four-thirty for the first of his Sunday walks, from his home in High Street *(Hoogstraat)*. He proceeded back and forth and across and around this prosperous capital city of eighteen thousand souls, with its swarms of diplomats, its gabled brick houses, governmental buildings, tidy streets, and frozen waterways. Unlike rural people, who walked in order to get somewhere, David Beck walked for recreation—to think, to renew his body and spirit, and to see things. When the weather and light were better, he walked on Sunday in the large woods that bordered the city, or he walked across the dunes to the sea, just an hour west, to see a storm. To the south and west were also frozen meadowlands, seemingly extending, in the winter bleak and cold, to the edge of the horizon.

In winter he usually kept to the city's well-ordered streets and bridges, passing again and again the attractive buildings and ponds of the Binnenhof, where the States General gathered, or strolling behind the palace of the country's greatest nobleman, the Prince of Orange, where come spring David would hear nightingales. Sometimes he circled around the city's surrounding walls, which lay behind moats lined with trees. Sometimes he walked so long on Sunday mornings that he had to stop for a drink of *jenever* water (gin), which he bought from a vendor at a bridge. And sometimes he walked until it was time for the midmorning service at one of The Hague's Reformed churches, where he entered and took his place, for he was a communing, faithful member and rarely missed on Sunday.

THE WORD

Unlike his medieval predecessors, or even most of his contemporaries in the rest of Europe, David Beck had to choose which version of Christianity he would follow. And this choice would naturally have consequences for his Sundays.

The medieval church had hardly been uniform, but the splitting asunder of Roman Catholicism begun by Martin Luther during the 1520s gave dramatically new variety to the religious order. Within decades Catholics were still the majority in Europe, but there were also such numerous organized protesters, or "Protestants," as Lutherans, Calvinists (Reformed), Zwinglians, Anabaptists, Spiritualists, and other eternally subdividing Christian confessions, as well as Jews, and still more. Unlike most countries of Europe, which promoted a single, official religion, the young Dutch Republic was home to almost all of these groups. And although most followed ancient and medieval

Christians in retaining Sunday as their biggest day, the "Reformation" made a difference in how each group observed it.

Because David Beck's Reformed Church enjoyed the status of public or "prevailing" *(heersende)* church, it felt entitled to shape Sunday for all the Dutch, of whatever faith. And it was this Reformed version of Sunday that David largely followed.

That version included long hours in church. Whether up early to walk, to receive a guest, to drop off the wet nurse's wages, or to sing a psalm near the fire with Diliana, by nine o'clock on Sunday he was to be found at a Reformed service in either the Great Church, the Convent Church, or the Old Church of The Hague. Sometimes he attended as well the early service, at six.

The Reformed service, like most Protestant services, differed purposely from the old Catholic Mass. The Reformed focused on hearing the Word, while Mass highlighted the Eucharist and engaged all of the senses. Reformed preachers called themselves "servants of the Word of God" rather than "priests." And the Heidelberg catechism, the most basic statement of the Reformed religion in all of Europe, stated that Sunday was instituted especially for preaching.

When David Beck walked into a Reformed church, he understood all of this implicitly, for the interior reflected the emphasis on the Word. Like other Gothic, once Catholic churches in the Dutch Republic, those in The Hague had been converted to Reformed settings. Especially during the 1580s, altars, crucifixes, surplus candles, relics, statues, and paintings of Catholic worship were stripped away, seen as vestiges of superstition and idolatry. In addition, murals were painted over with whitewash, so that the cumulative effect was one of an oddly stark, cavernous interior. There was still decoration, but generally of a different sort: now there were wooden boards containing the Ten Commandments and other biblical verses. Shields bearing the insignia and motto of prominent local families were attached to every pillar. And walls and ceilings were painted in a single popular color of the day, usually Berlin blue, olive green, or mahogany red. Yet the most telling change inside the church for Sunday was that the centerpiece was no longer the choir, where the Eucharist had been performed, but the pulpit. Although still propped up against one of the pillars in the nave, it was now ringed with a small fence to set it apart from the rest of the church. The choir was reserved for weddings and monthly communion, and thus was used sparingly.

These conversions of Gothic spaces into Reformed spaces were not ideal. Some were downright inconvenient. Obstructed views and limited voice range restricted the usable space of a refurbished Reformed church to the area right around the pulpit. Women typically sat directly before it in movable chairs, while men stood to the side of and behind the chairs or sometimes sat on benches; fixed pews would become more common only toward 1700. A few new urban churches were built specifically for Reformed services, usually in octagonal shape, with the pulpit set along one side and therefore visible to all. Smaller village churches simply rearranged old rectangular interiors by changing the focal point to a pulpit centered against one of the two long walls. But in towns, the large, old, remodeled, inconvenient church known to David Beck was the norm.

The focus on the Word was also evident in the structure of Reformed services: this included a few prayers in biblical language, some sung psalms straight from the Bible, and especially a lengthy sermon on a biblical verse or two. Even the preliminaries emphasized the Bible. If David Beck arrived a bit early to a Sunday service, he would hear a fellow schoolmaster reading aloud from it, to set the mood, and in the faint hope of keeping people quiet as they came in. But then precisely at the designated hour the preacher (or *dominee,* as he was called in Dutch) climbed into the pulpit, took off his hat, and began with prayers or announcements.

Unlike a Catholic priest, a *dominee* wore no special clothing, merely the usual clothing of the learned: a plain black robe with buttons and loops, and either a white ruffle under his chin or two cloth bands hanging from his collar. The local church council, seated within the fenced area of the pulpit, also wore hanging bands, as did all male members of the church on monthly communion days. Only during prayers did members of the congregation remove their own hats ("free men take off their hats only to God"), to the astonishment of foreigners, who kept them off during the entire service.

After the introductory prayers, which sometimes lasted an hour, came psalm singing. Some new hymns found their way into Dutch Reformed services, but in theory psalms were preferred, for who could

improve upon God's Word? The 23rd and 103rd were general favorites, but each congregation had its preferences and sang them
heartily without the accompaniment of an organ. While some Protestant faiths destroyed old organs, regarding them as a popish invention,
and others played them loudly each Sunday, the Dutch Reformed followed a middle way: they kept organs intact but until 1680 would not
allow them to play during services, for various reasons. Organs were
not specifically mentioned in the Bible. They might detract from the
Word. And they potentially made music too seductive. Hence, to hear
the assorted famous organs and organists of Reformed churches, one
had to arrive an hour early or stay after the service, as David Beck occasionally did.

The effect of silent organs on psalm-singing was all too obvious: it
suffered miserably. Any worries about the seductive powers of *this* music were wasted. The Amsterdam *dominee* Geldorpius had choice
words for his congregation's singing, calling it crippled, dragging, and
heavy, like a ship being towed upstream. Another *dominee* said that it
was like birds pecking at different moments: one rose, another descended, and all cried out *in extremis.* The famous thinker and aesthete
Constantine Huygens blamed it on the habit Reformed members had of
stubbornly sticking to a favorite version of a psalm—in regard to both
its translation and its musical setting—on all occasions, regardless of
what the conductor or others were singing. David Beck, who often sang
psalms at home, never complained about the music at church, perhaps
because there was nothing to be done, or perhaps because he was
among those who took the lack of refinement as a sign of sincerity.

Emphasis on the Word was most evident, of course, in the sermon,
to which everything else in the service led. It lasted at least as long as
the sand in the hourglass placed conspicuously near every pulpit, as a
not-so-subtle reminder to preachers, but often a sermon went much
longer. If expectant members of the congregation eagerly watched the
last grains of sand fall from the top to the bottom chamber, they were
disappointed when the *dominee* simply turned it over and kept right
on talking. David Beck occasionally noted that because of an especially
long sermon, the morning meeting, begun at nine, did not end until
twelve-thirty, so that he had to rush home and grab something to eat
before the afternoon service began at one.

Reformed sermons were not only much longer than Catholic sermons, but since Huldrych Zwingli of Zurich initiated the practice in 1519, they were more closely focused on a biblical text. A Catholic sermon also began with a biblical text, but one usually connected to the current moment of the liturgical year—Lent, Easter, Pentecost, and so on. Reformed preaching, on the other hand, paid little attention to any liturgical calendar and instead worked steadily through one book of the Bible at a time, a few verses at a time. The New Testament gospels were treated during the morning service, and New Testament epistles or the Heidelberg catechism in the afternoon. Old Testament books received attention during a weekly Thursday sermon. In this manner it might take fifteen years of Sundays for a *dominee* to complete just the gospels.

This sort of focused, intense preaching demanded much energy from both preacher and listener, even more than in the ancient and medieval Sunday. Unlike medieval predecessors, *dominees* avoided colorful allegory or anything else that made the sermon sensually attractive, and instead favored explaining one biblical text by citing dozens of others. They occasionally cited from the classics, but sparingly, to avoid the allures of pagan ways. The preacher's job was simply to elucidate Scripture, explain why the Reformed view of a verse was correct, and inspire his listeners to penance. In this last he was very much like medieval preachers, who also focused on vices and sin and fiery punishments. But a Reformed *dominee* did this all at much greater length than his medieval counterparts. "How their zeal burned, how often the pulpit shuddered and smoked!" said one lover of long, impassioned Reformed sermons.

Reformed preachers had one other thing in common with ancient and medieval predecessors: they often complained about the behavior of their audience. *Dominees* growled that people ate too large a breakfast on Sunday and grew sleepy, for a "full stomach has no ears." They fretted that people still chatted and looked about during the sermon, but now they also read books or fussed too much about the preacher's style. Preachers ridiculed "name Christians" who could hardly get out of bed because they'd been "gazing too deeply into a beer can" the night before. Preaching to such a congregation, said one *dominee*, was like hitting an anvil: the more you hit it, the harder it got. And despite close attention to the Bible, and the expectation that it would make Christians far more theologically literate than before, *dominees* still complained of ignorance, with some sadly concluding that they had labored all their lives for nothing. Perhaps inattention was due to Dutch cold in wintertime: despite whole teams of stove-lighters in churches by now—plus small individual stoves, cushions, and footstools—the vast buildings were rarely comfortable. One British visitor did note that the Dutch coughed less during church than did the English, but this was hardly proof of real comfort or reverence.

Beyond prayers, psalms, and sermons, other elements of the Sunday service were occasional only, such as monthly communion—one of two sacraments recognized by the Reformed religion, in contrast to the Catholic seven. David Beck noted in his journal when he communed, or when others had, suggesting that the ritual still carried great significance, if not the overarching significance of the Catholic Eucharist. The ritual's importance was also reflected in the finer dress of communion Sunday (the men wearing black cloaks and broad bands), in the restricted access to communion through monthly checks on worthiness, and in the shorter length of the sermon that day, to allow sufficient time for the ritual.

Those deemed worthy to commune proceeded to the remodeled choir, where a large table had been set up. Divided by gender, they then alternated in sitting or standing at the communion table to receive bread and wine, which had been blessed with a brief prayer. Those not allowed to commune were members who had violated the grounds of fellowship, or who were among the far more numerous *liefhebbers,* or friends of the church. These showed support by attending services, but they were not bound by the church's strict requirements for full membership.

Before people headed out the door, there was a last ritual of Sunday worship: collection. This was not for the pastor, who was paid by the Dutch state, but for the poor and for maintenance of the building. Even during the psalm-singing, various deacons walked down the aisles holding long sticks with bags connected to them; a little bell on the bottom of the bag rang to announce the deacons' coming, then rang again when a contribution was dropped, hinting at its size.

After the nine-o'clock service, if the weather wasn't severe, David Beck and other churchgoers engaged in the usual chatter outside. But often he went directly home to warm himself by the fire or stopped at the home of his best friend, the painter Herman Breckerfelt, to discuss Scripture or to read in the Heidelberg catechism in preparation for the afternoon sermon. The two friends also regularly sang a psalm together, surely with less dissonance than during services. Visitors to the republic often remarked on hearing this ritual as they walked past open windows of Dutch homes.

Herman Breckerfelt regularly visited David as well after morning church, bringing such items as letters from German friends that contained highly elaborate writing and embellishment; these were useful models for the parchment certificates David created as prizes for his young students. And there were plenty of other visitors, or other places to visit, right after morning church: a grandmother, an uncle, or dozens of friends, with whom he discussed current events, a favorite translation of the Psalms, and recent poetry. While engaging in these midday visits, David typically ate a modest lunch, such as cabbage, bacon, and sausage, or buttermilk and blood sausage, but it was the company he cared about most, often "cheerier and happier than if they'd been to a wedding feast." During one midday meal, David's brother Hendrik, also a schoolteacher, quoted Solomon's saying that a plate of mash served with love was better than a fatted calf served with hate and envy; when David asked how one would say that in French, the company started laughing so hard at the various attempts that no one could even raise their spoon. Such a meal helped to ease his worries, wrote David in his journal that Sunday.

Most of his Sunday cheer, however, he would save for social calls later in the afternoon; unlike medieval Sundays, the Reformed noon meal was usually short, so that people might return for the afternoon service at one. Obviously the Reformed Church's answer to the question, "What should people do on Sunday afternoon?" was the same as the medieval church's: attend more church. But the Reformed services during both morning and afternoon were twice as long as medieval services. Still, David Beck rarely missed the afternoon sermon. His older brother Hendrik, who often visited from nearby Delft, was no great fan of it, however. And so sometimes when Hendrik was in town, David stayed at home from the service to chat with him, or Hendrik waited alone, looking through David's books, until church let out. When baby Roeltge came back home in September, then David alternated services with Diliana: he went to either morning or afternoon service, and she to the other.

The afternoon service required little attention, for it ran much like the morning service. The main difference was that the sermon was taken from the Heidelberg catechism, one topic at a time. Over several months, for instance, the preacher might treat one phrase a week from the Lord's Prayer, dissecting it for an hour or two: "Thy kingdom come" one week, "Thy will be done" another week, and so on. The afternoon service also differed in that it was the moment for weddings and baptisms. Because of the Reformed Church's public status, all inhabitants of a town, regardless of religion, were entitled to be baptized, married, and buried inside it. In urban churches, Sunday weddings were clustered together, especially in the favorite month of May, with as many as seventeen couples marrying at once. Often there were so many in attendance at weddings or baptisms that *dominees* complained, mainly because the regular congregation left before the extra ceremonies, while those arriving for those ceremonies came in only at the end, and pushed forward with much noise.

DUTCH TREATS

When the afternoon service finished, usually no later than four, David Beck had what remained of Sunday to himself, for "rest." Much as in the Middle Ages, this was the favorite part of the day among laypeople, if among *dominees* the most aggravating.

David Beck did not always rest as the *dominees* preferred, yet outside of *dominees* and their families, or visiting Puritans from England, his Sunday afternoons were about as restrained as any in the Republic. The preachers would have praised David's psalm-singing, Bible-reading, and quiet contemplation by the fire. But they would have lamented that David, like many of the Dutch, was also a tireless visitor, dining companion, host, and excursion-taker after church. Even his long, solitary Sunday walks would have offended, at least if unaccompanied by "constant pondering of God's marvelous works in nature." And this was not to mention that David, again like many other Dutch, attended more than one apparently simple Sunday meal that soon grew into a scene of excessive merriment.

The recreational activities began almost immediately after the last service, as David sometimes joined the crowds who now jammed inside the church to hear the organ, especially when it was played by the "blind but artful" Pieter Alewijns. When crowds were thinner, David listened while walking around the church. And when it was particularly cold outside, or unbearably warm, he walked even longer inside, once for an hour and a half with a friend.

But usually David left immediately after church to go warm himself again by his fire. Back at home, he enjoyed reading in his French Bible; his school, after all, was a "French School," intended for the sons of merchants and anyone else desiring a curriculum useful in trade. Sometimes he read a volume of poems or history. When he had company on Sunday afternoon, he chatted, with a mug of Breda beer for himself and his guest, discussing not only general news but also his own difficult situation as a grieving widower.

After an hour or so of conversation, David often took another walk, as many as five on Sunday. There were plenty of Sunday walkers in Dutch towns, on the streets or in churches, for here was another way to warm oneself. David's Sunday walks might include a practical purpose, such as ordering more turf or wood at the turf market, or visiting a leather-worker to have his belt fixed, or fetching something at the apothecary's on the main market. Sometimes he was merely in search of curiosities, even celebrities, both of which were plentiful in The Hague. Sunday wedding parties, for instance, ubiquitous in the republic, were especially lavish here, as evidenced by the "glorious" Spanish trumpets David heard announcing an exceptionally well-born bride. More appealing still was the endless flow of famous personalities, who frequented public places on Sunday; David sometimes bumped into them on the street or shamelessly sought them out. He proudly noted one Sunday that he sat during the entire sermon directly opposite the exiled King Frederick of Bohemia, right in the king's "line of vision."

Another Sunday, Prince Frederik Hendrik of Orange rode out with seven or eight carriages, and David followed on foot as long as he could. And David made sure to note the Sunday he passed by Jacob Cats, famous poet and future grand pensionary of Holland, who was walking with Constantine Huygens, the great thinker. At least twice on Sundays David engaged in that other favorite urban spectator sport of the time: watching a great nobleman and his entourage eat dinner. Once, he watched inside the Binnenhof, where Frederick of Bohemia was dining, and once he watched for an hour at the tavern called the Golden Lion, where the Count of Mansfeld, commander of Protestant troops during the current German war, was busy filling himself. That Sunday night David wrote that he went home afterward and ate in good Mansfeld fashion himself: one good rabbit with applesauce, doves, and omelettes, plus a good pot of wine, with great conversation near the fire.

Yet for all of his warmth-seeking and contemplating and errand-running and celebrity-watching, David's long Sunday afternoon walks always carried a social purpose. One wonders, were he still married, whether his Sunday regime would have meant fewer walks and longer hours at home. He certainly spent some free time at home on Sundays, but he spent even more with his Uncle Adrian and Aunt Liesbeth, his brother Steven, his friend Herman Breckerfelt, his mother-in-law, his tailor, and many others, to whose homes he walked to chat, drink, and eat. With his closest friends and family, David felt free to drop in unannounced, and vice versa: sometimes David came home and found three or more people waiting for him by the fire. The inevitable drinking during such casual visits usually included beer and two or three *roemers* (tall, narrow glasses) of wine—three being the typically polite amount, and the point from which excess was measured. For full-fledged meals he usually extended or received an invitation in advance, often through third parties, a necessity in a day when an invitation had to be delivered physically.

Such meals were often the focal point of a Sunday evening. In fact, among the Reformed, this was the largest and most elaborate meal of the day, with plenty of food and laughter over many hours. One of David's own Sunday dinner parties at home, which he helped prepare, included a modest veal in the pot and other delicacies. By the end, he noted, everyone was "sweet and merry," but there had been nothing to excess. Still, when he walked several of his guests home afterward, they invariably insisted that he come in for another "three or four" *roemers* of wine. Over the course of one such Sunday evening, David too freely mixed wine, beer, and gin received at various places, and suffered for it all through the night. Although a doctor reassured him the next day that overloading on drink was occasionally good for the system, because it purged one "below and above," David took little comfort.

More comforting by far, and most common of all for David on Sunday evenings, were his visits to his mother-in-law, Anna van Overschie, often to dine but just as often for the company. Here was one of the most interesting people in David's highly interesting social circle, and someone with whom he felt much in common. Nearly fifty now, she had been widowed herself only three years before, by Lambrecht van Belle, long a messenger for the States General. And of course Anna had been deeply saddened, like David, by the death of Roeltge. David visited whenever he pleased and was invited regularly to dinner on Sunday evening. Anna's large heart was evident not only in her kind treatment of David but in the presence of two other people in her household: her elderly aunt Judith, and nineteen-year-old Jacomijn van Belle. Aunt Judith required extra help, while Jacomijn had been fathered by Anna's deceased husband, with another woman, while Anna was still married to him. Her status wasn't quite that of other members of the family; David purposely never taught her to read, for instance, as he did Diliana, yet Jacomijn was easily included in the family circle and was Diliana's dear friend.

On a Sunday night or otherwise at Anna's, David was freer than elsewhere to mourn and restore himself. He went there especially when he felt low, such as the night he walked all around The Hague while crying. Anna tried to lift both of their spirits by inviting other interesting characters to dine, including a burgomaster of Amsterdam and a shareholder in the East Indies Company, with whom they talked long about war, art, learned men, and the East Indies.

Occasionally, David's Sunday dinner parties took place outside The Hague, especially at the home of his brother Hendrik, in Delft, just an hour away by canalboat. Sometimes David simply arrived here unannounced on Sunday, but often Hendrik sent a messenger that day to ask him to dine, or, when Hendrik was ill, to ask whether David could take his school too the next day. In every circumstance, Hendrik was a gracious host; when his health returned he invited David and others who had substituted for him to a banquet of thanks on a Sunday evening. There he served much "good, expensive food and wine," and festivities went so long that David stayed the night, returning early the next morning to The Hague in time for school at eight. On special occasions, such as during Kermis, David even missed the Sunday afternoon sermon in The Hague to visit his brother. One of the most memorable Sunday banquets at Hendrik's occurred on a night of such foul weather that "not even the dogs would go out." David and the four other invitees hesitated whether to make the trip, but finally, because "love conquers all," they boarded the seven o'clock canalboat and arrived at eight. Hendrik put on a fresh fire for his determined but thoroughly soaked friends; half a side of beef was already roasting, and the guests were soon served *hutsepot* (thick stew), blood sausage, other sorts of sausage, and fine drink, which they consumed over conversation and warm fire until midnight.

Thus went the busy Sundays of David Beck.

Of course David did not experience or record *every* aspect of the Dutch Sunday, not even of the Reformed Sunday he knew best. In fact plenty of his coreligionists seem to have passed their Sunday afternoons and evenings "resting" with even more enthusiasm than he.

David Beck, for instance, never mentioned visiting a single tavern on Sunday, yet here was a favorite Sunday pastime, in town or country, among the Reformed and otherwise. In fact, just as in the Middle Ages, Sunday still seemed the ideal moment for such a visit. The Reformed Church was hardly against all use of drink; this would have been a disaster for the many brewers who sat on the church council of Delft, for instance. Instead, the church held up the evils of taverns and excessive drinking. Still the seventeenth-century town dweller had far more possibilities in the way of Sunday taverns than had medieval predecessors. Legion in number, these taverns were no longer half-disguised homes, but were full-blown drinking and eating establishments. Bearing such memorable names as The Swan, The Red Lion, The Chapel, The Heavenly Kingdom, The Golden Wagon, St. George, The Thirsty Hart, or The Blue Hand, a few were immortalized by such painters as Frans Hals.

Especially taverns outside town walls offered inviting spaces to rest, drink beer or wine, eat, and play games. Of the republic's 1.5 million inhabitants spread across seven provinces, about half lived in the largest province of Holland. Half of these lived in towns of ten thousand or more. And one of the chief recreations of town dwellers was to go into the countryside on Sunday afternoons. The destination was usually a tavern, where the setting was more relaxed than in town and where prices for food and drink were often cheaper. Tavern games included ninepins, cards, and more violent goose-pulling. This involved tying a rope between two trees, across water, hanging a live goose upside down from that rope, spreading fat or soap on the goose, then leaping out, grabbing onto the goose's head, and trying to slide across. In winter, Dutch people of many faiths ice-skated to the countryside, again visiting taverns and now playing games on the bounteous ice, such as fishing or a kind of golf. One Sunday in 1621, thirteen hundred sleds bypassed taverns altogether, riding out onto the frozen Harlinger Sea to pitch tents, drink beer and wine, and otherwise recreate. The wealthy might engage in other Sunday games and avoid popular taverns, but they too went outside towns, to pursue the new elite fad of owning a country house. People of lesser means began to regard Sunday as a fine time to tend a garden plot outside town.

Another favorite Sunday activity in the Dutch Republic, also never mentioned by the still-mourning David Beck, was courting. For this, as with taverns, Sunday was not just another day but *the* most popular day of the week. Boys often went out on Sunday afternoons in search of girls, and the time they promised to call on them at home was nine o'clock that same Sunday night. If the suitor arrived early, the door supposedly was not opened; if he arrived late, it was considered an insult to her honor. If the suitor came on time three Sundays in a row, then contemporaries thought it possible that a bond had developed between the two, and the suitor might then arrive even earlier on Sunday night (plus call on Wednesdays as well). David occasionally talked with Diliana about courting in The Hague, but she never seemed to cause him any worries in this way.

This was not true of the fifty-six-year-old tailor Gerard Udinck, who lived in the north of the republic and who was temporarily responsible for the well-being of his teenage niece, Maria Jasons. Like David Beck, Gerard spent much of his Sunday at Reformed services, but during the first three months of 1664 he also spent a good chunk of his Sundays engaged in a timeless ritual among parents and guardians: worrying about the social life of a teenager. Fortunately, Gerard Udinck too kept a journal, in which he recorded his anxieties.

Sometimes, he noted in irritation, Maria did not return home from the afternoon sermon until seven-thirty that evening, and then after eating she liked to go out again. One Sunday night in January, Gerard and his wife Janneke waited until ten o'clock for Maria to return home; when she did not, the couple went to bed. At midnight they awoke to discover that she still wasn't home. A worried Janneke went looking for her, only to discover that Maria hadn't been at all where she had told them she would be. Instead she had gone sleigh-riding with a boy of whom her aunt and uncle did not approve: he had no money and was said to be in taverns all the time. Every Sunday it was the same: Maria would say that she was headed to a nearby cousin's but would end up with this boy somewhere else, until ten or later. Eventually the weary Gerard and Janneke sent Maria back to her parents.

Sunday was also arguably the favorite time for the final step of courting, mentioned only in passing by David Beck: weddings. If the Dutch had already developed a reputation for thriftiness, this had not extended to their weddings. The great celebrated them three days long, beginning on Sunday, while people such as David Beck stood gawking. The middling and poor celebrated on Sunday only. So important was a grand wedding and feast that neighbors often helped pay for the celebrations of the most poor, or more than one couple celebrated together to spread expenses. One reason the wedding ceremony was always conducted during the Sunday afternoon service in Reformed churches, rather than the morning services, was that the inevitable feasting that followed would otherwise have begun even sooner. Still, it began too early anyway for *dominees,* often at the moment the couple entered the church for the ceremony: especially in rural areas this was greeted with shooting in the churchyard and other racket, while guests continued their drinking all the way up to the church doors. Sometimes the bride's ladies might preen and groom her while she stood before the pulpit, then immediately after the service she was crowned with flowers by her friends and led noisily away.

Soon after the ceremony the marathon wedding feast commenced, often featuring enormous slabs of beef, plus countless morsels of lamb, pork, chicken, and duck. Sometimes entire pigs were set on the table, thirty rabbits and hares were laid out on separate plates, and fish might be stacked in pyramid form. All the while wine and beer flowed continuously. Neighbors and friends also brought edible presents, including giant pancakes, and wine or brandy laced with a cinnamon stick. Running into the feast were the ever popular dances and flirtatious games of a Dutch wedding, which might last for days on end.

Of course such Sunday feasting did not occur only at weddings, as David Beck's own Sundays have already shown. This was true of other Reformed members as well. The devout Gerard Udinck faithfully recorded the texts of the three Reformed sermons he usually attended on Sundays, and also the gargantuan meals to which he was invited, how much was drunk, and how much it probably cost—without a hint of criticism or a sense that such meals were opposed to the spirit of a proper Reformed Sunday. He also noted that his niece Maria invited nine friends over for waffles another Sunday evening, all of whom stayed until eleven.

One great lover of banquets showed even more enthusiasm than David Beck or Gerard Udinck. He described a banquet as if it were a military assault, reflecting the violence and eagerness that might be present at a groaning Dutch table on Sunday night. He titled his account *The Relation of the Marvelous Battle and Siege of the Table, a Very Important Place, Taken by Assault, by the Lovers of Good Cheer and Their Allies.* The Commander was Taste, the Field Marshal was Good Appetite, the Colonel was the Nose. The Lords of Wet-Throat and Jaw-Bone led the terrible regiment of the Teeth, ready to cut the enemy into small pieces. Arms and Hands were the Support Troops, who saw to it that the regiments of fingers, spoons, forks, and knives fought gallantly. After taking reconnaissance of the table and offering prayers and sacrifices to assure happy results, the attack began. First captured were bisques in Swiss fashion, including Queen White bisque, Asparagus bisque, and more. Then followed charges against calf breasts, stuffed doves, partridges, and roasted pork. Putting up stronger resistance were roast beef, various cutlets, sheep's tongue, meat pastries, pistachios, artichoke leaves, mushrooms, and young hens. All were soon subjected, as were various wines from the famous arsenals of Beaune, Aix, Arbois, and Chablis.

Reinforcements replaced the fallen defenders, and the battle was courageously joined once more, against more doves, rabbits, pheasants, and especially the greatest resister, wild pig, who was nevertheless cut to pieces, bit by bit. Lemons and oranges were wounded in the neck, shoulders, legs, and buttocks, and fortresses named salads, strengthened by capers, olives, and other delicacies, fell at last. Still the battle wasn't over, as beef tongue, Austrian ham, and various venisons now entered the fray, along with regiments of eggs in a hundred different styles. When these too were dispatched, a round head of cheese appeared, but ladders were made ready and the cheese was soon scaled and defeated, along with Bologna sausage, pickled herring, and still more wines in reserve. At last hunger was conquered, and a weary General Taste sang a hymn of triumph to Bacchus.

More ordinary Sunday banquets were accompanied by singing too—and not merely the pious psalms preferred by David Beck. One tract, dedicated to the young women of the republic, listed dozens of popular songs and lyrics for banquets, such as "Cupid's Hunt," "Pure Through Love," "Small Cupid, Who Gives You Such Power?" "Only One in My Heart," "Whom Cupid Has Touched," "A Pure Maiden Quite Delicate," "A Praised Maiden," "Sweet Goddess Whom I Love," "You Young Men Who Court," "O Venus Highly Praised," "O Heavy Sorrow and Pain," "O Painful Love," and "Old Woman I Don't Want You."

Another aspect of Sunday play neglected by David Beck also bears mention. Namely, that for the elite whom David liked to watch, Sunday was just another day of revelry. Willem Frederik of Nassau, for instance, renowned as the most Reformed member of the princely

Orange family, engaged in strikingly full Sundays, yet these looked much like his other days. Certainly Willem Frederik always heard a sermon or two on Sunday, even when he was on military campaign, but the rest of the day, like the Sundays and weekdays of other nobles, contained both large amounts of work and recreation as it suited him. Like David Beck, Willem Frederik often "walked" on Sunday—but on horseback or by carriage. He also made social and official visits, but these he made every day. One Sunday he ate with a friend and stayed until three in the morning, again something he did regularly on other days. Like the teenager Marie Jasons, Willem Frederik had friends over for pancakes or waffles on Sunday night, then also other nights. Sunday evenings also meant the sort of banqueting and high-stakes gambling that occurred every night, and Sunday evening discussions included topics that might occur any day, from major affairs of state to the current gossip at court.

Some of Willem Frederik's Sunday activities raise a final aspect of Sunday hardly touched upon by David Beck: work. David Beck mentioned walking to the open-turf market and pharmacy on Sunday night to buy goods. But he did not mention those merchants who were working at home or in their stores that day, hoping to get a head start on the week's business. He also paid no special attention to the hirelings in shops who, like medieval peasants, were less keen about Sunday work than were their bosses. Yet, some workers wanted shops open on Sundays because they were paid on Saturday evening and wished to buy things the next day. Industries such as textiles and brewing found it difficult to skip any day of work at all, given the long process involved in the manufacture of their wares and the possibility of spoilage—and the economic importance of these crafts to cities made town rulers reluctant to tell them otherwise. In the countryside, especially the farmers of Friesland were, like medieval agricultural workers, notorious for laboring on Sunday. Reformed synods complained that even preachers there were out working in the fields that day, and that markets were regularly held as well.

All these elements, too, beyond the rather restrained experiences of a David Beck, might be part of a Reformed Sunday.

SABBATH IDEALS AND OBSTACLES

This was not how Reformed preachers had envisioned it.

The Reformation of Christianity by Protestants was supposed to include the Reformation of Christianity's special day as well. *Dominees* did not wish to muddle along in what they considered to be the old, lax, Catholic Sunday. And they could make their wishes known not only from the pulpit, as in the Middle Ages, but through the printed word, thanks to the republic's notoriously free press and highly literate populace.

Like medieval predecessors, *dominees* condemned the restrictions of the Jewish Sabbath before proclaiming their own restrictions upon a proper Reformed "Sabbath," as they called it. One Reformed catechism is striking for both its typically urban concerns and the finality of its answers.

Q: May one travel on Sunday?

A: No.

Q: May a hunter hunt on that day?

A: No.

Q: May a student that day study worldly arts and sciences?

A: No.

Q: May a dance master that day hold dance school?

A: No.

Q: May a lawyer compose and write briefs that day?

A: No.

Q: May one go around with a pen that day?

A: No.

Q: Should a merchant postpone all his correspondence until that day?

A: No.

Q: Should one go around collecting debts on that day?

A: No.

Q: Should men transfer notes from a draft book to a final book?

A: No.

Q: Should one count money on Sunday?

A: No.

Q: Should one clean house on Sunday, and other such work?

A: No.

Q: Should one hold meat and fish markets on Sunday, and other markets?

A: No.

Q: But the fish will spoil if one waits until Monday.

A: Doesn't matter.

The rest of the catechism likewise stressed what should *not* be done that day, identifying thirty-four current Sunday activities, involving both work and play, that the author hoped would soon disappear: laboring during and after the sermon, transporting goods, brewing beer, preparing beer barrels, riding on wagons and carriages, unloading and loading ships and boats, baking bread, milling, cutting hair, cleaning porch or house, bleaching linens, hawking sweet-milks, fruit, birds, brandy, tobacco, fish, and meat, frying and boiling as on no other day, settling accounts, paying wages, goose-pulling, shooting at stuffed parrots on tall poles or roofs, shooting slingshots, gambling, bowling, relaxing too long with friends, crowding about in markets and streets, tapping in taverns, and committing various abominations in taverns and hostels outside of towns.

Sermon after sermon, tract after tract, and meeting after meeting of preachers repeated these complaints—and not only in the Dutch Republic but in Switzerland, Germany, France, and anywhere else the Reformed influence was present. One *dominee* labeled three undesirable sorts of Sabbaths he saw around him: a Donkey's Sabbath (lying about and doing nothing, like a lazy animal), a Golden Calf's Sabbath (filled with pleasure, banqueting, and riding), and a Devil's Sabbath (silliness, whorehouses, drunkenness, bawdy songs, and dancing). Another preacher came up with seven unsavory Sabbaths: a Lazy Sabbath, a Joshua Sabbath (longing for the day to end, as the sun seemed to stand still), a Pleasure Sabbath (playing and sailing), a Sensual Sabbath (when the Egyptian fleshpots smelled better than the heavenly manna), the Devilish Sabbath (drinking and clinking), the Trimmed Sabbath (being in church as little as possible and when there counting grains of sand in the hourglass during the sermon), and the Outward Sabbath (observing the day without enthusiasm).

Other preachers hammered on the same broad themes, sometimes inventing new metaphors or merely repeating old ones. Sunday was Sinday, the rest day was a workday, the Lord's Day was the Devil's Day, with drinking and clinking, gambling and playing, dancing and jumping—all "serving the Devil better than God himself." Too many would rather be in the tap-house than the church, hear the fiddle in the tavern rather than the harp of David, sing the foul songs of whores instead of the glorious hymns of Israel, heed the noise of table-brothers more than the voices of shepherds and teachers. If there was one day of the week when the devil worked upon the children of disobedience and blinded senses, a day on which the Dutch Children of Israel were like an unbound calf and determined to do evil by following the pagan gods of play and sin, then truly it was Sunday. When, cried *dominees*, were taverns fuller, propped up by crowds of young people and old? People inside shrieked like stuffed birds, in towns and villages, and fought more than ever, as if they wished to slap God himself in the face. More than merely a Devil's Day, Sunday was also a Salon-Day, Leisure-Day, Permissive-Day, Romp-Day, Whore-Day, and Tavern-Day. Even for some who observed it strictly, Sunday was too often a Sorrowful-Day, which people impatiently wanted to end.

The preachers never failed to single out dancing—abominable on any day but especially on Sunday, when it happened to be most popular. According to them, dancing was always accompanied by kissing, romping, and caressing, and "each leap was another step toward hell." It was "dirty, unvirtuous, unsuitable, unashamed, and unbridled," something to be avoided at all times. The dance hall was an antichurch, or better yet "a synagogue of Satan." People were dancing and leaping in one home, reported the church council of Zevenhoven, "as if no Christians lived there." Although "respectable dancing," with only "chaste steps" and movement, was possible in theory, even this should be avoided, especially on the Sabbath, for all dancing offered too much opportunity for "fleshy lasciviousness, vanity, highmindedness, and smoldering unchastity." Merely watching it was wrong, and anyone who taught dancing should be barred from communion. Some physicians chimed in too, arguing that "all vehement movements and great shakings of the body" were detrimental to one's health.

According to Dutch preachers, Sundays of the good old days were devoid of all such ills. When the Reformation first came to the Netherlands, they said, people regarded the Word of God as sweeter than honey and costlier than gold. On Sundays congregations veritably ran after preachers like sheep to the meadow, just to hear the "sons of thunder." Yet now there was "utter neglect" of God's word. In fact, by the end of the seventeenth century the ministers of Holland would lament at one meeting that "there was no day on which sin was more thorough and common, more public and unanimous, and Satan more diligently served, than the day of the Lord." Another preacher by 1678 was just as pessimistic: Sabbath violations had been complained about since the birth of the republic, yet little had been done to halt them. In fact, Sabbath-breaking could truly be called *the* sin of the Netherlands. It not only threatened her with ruin but had already done so: weren't recent disastrous wars with France evidence enough of God's wrath at the desecration of his holy day?

Yet despite the message of peril they sent out, despite their zeal and energy, and even despite the public position of their church, the Reformed preachers never could implement the sort of Sunday they envisioned for the republic.

One obstacle was the preachers' own elimination of practically all holy days except Sunday from the Reformed calendar. This put more emphasis on Sunday worship, as intended, but it also reduced the number of days available for fun. Except for the elite, almost all free time and recreational activities were now concentrated into a single, desirable day each week, making that day busier than ever. Preachers could rail against undesirable activities and urge Dutch rulers to halt them, but they could not stop such activities themselves.

This raises a second obstacle to the preachers' sort of Sunday: their "public" church was not an "official" church. It was not even a majority church—no church in the republic was. By 1600 perhaps only 10 percent of the 1.5 million Dutch were Reformed, 20 percent in some towns. This was an extraordinary thing in Europe, where nations and towns had assumed since the Middle Ages that an official, universal religion was a requirement for good order and God's favor. The

Dutch thought otherwise. During their war of independence against Spain, begun in 1568, many Dutch grew wary of a powerful state religion. They also grew generally unwilling to force the many Catholics, Lutherans, Mennonites, Spiritualists, Libertines, Neutralists, Jews, and others who lived among them either to convert or leave. Instead the Dutch created, in rather willy-nilly fashion, their odd compromise of the "public church." Only the Reformed Church would receive public funds and be allowed openly to worship on Sunday. But other faiths would be allowed, if in semisecret, and the Reformed Church would be *subordinate* to the state, not part of it. This meant that the shape of Sunday was ultimately in the hands of the Dutch "regents" who governed provinces and towns. And most of them, like most laypeople, preferred a wider range of Sunday recreations than did *dominees*. The most regents would typically do was to prohibit certain activities during the hours of Reformed services. And even these prohibitions were loosely enforced.

A final obstacle to implementing the sort of Sunday desired by Reformed preachers was this: the preachers could not even agree among themselves on what that Sunday should be. As long as there was no single vision of Sunday in the Reformed Church, much less the entire republic, there could be no hope of trying to make such a vision real. Thus the Dutch Sunday would remain as wildly varied as it always had been.

The Dutch were hardly unique in arguing over Sunday. In fact, it was an old habit by now among Christians everywhere, present almost from the start of the ancient church. But such arguing was aggravated by the trauma of the Reformation.

In the first place, after 1521 Sunday became a way for Catholics and Protestants to further distinguish themselves from each other. Protestants, for instance, typically insisted that Sunday was the only day of worship sanctioned by Scripture; the many other "holy days" cluttering the calendar had simply been declared so by the Catholic Church and should therefore be thrown out. Catholics responded that holy days were indeed declared by the Church, including Sunday: if Protestants were going to throw out holy days, then they would have to throw out Sunday too. Until they did, their Sunday worship implicitly acknowledged the authority of the Catholic Church.

In the second place, often hair-splitting arguments over Sunday did not stop with Catholics versus Protestants. For especially in the process of refuting Catholics, Protestants began to reveal angry disagreements among themselves. Martin Luther (d. 1546), for instance, accepted that Sunday worship had been established by the Catholic Church, not divine decree. It didn't matter on which day Christians worshiped, and Sunday was as good as any. Where Catholics—and now some Protestants—had gone wrong, continued Luther, was in making Sunday a sort of Jewish Sabbath. To Luther, the Sabbath had been invented solely for the Jews; Christians were free from Moses' Law and required no rules of extraordinary behavior on Sunday, as every day was holy to them. They were therefore free to rest and recreate after church, but according to daily standards of Christian decorum and not because the defunct Sabbath commandment said so.

Many other Protestants, however, saw the Sabbath as still binding. To John Calvin (d. 1564) the Sabbath was a "perpetual" institution, established at Creation for all peoples and times. This did not mean that the specific rules and regulations of the Old Testament Sabbath still applied to Christians. Instead it meant that the lasting spiritual truths behind the Sabbath commandment simply required new form. That form did not include a "true" day of the week; Calvin agreed with Luther that Sunday was as suitable a day as any for worship. But that new form of Sabbath did include specific Christian standards of worship and rest on the day chosen. Calvin tried to exclude from those standards both the strict legalism and the excessive levity said to mark the Jewish Sabbath, and thus held up a "moderate" Sabbath. He himself was said to have bowled on Sunday; he certainly sailed one Sunday on Lake Geneva to wish his brother a happy birthday, and he walked in the nearby mountains. But his Sunday was a Sabbath nonetheless.

There were still other distinctions among Protestants, but Calvin's moderate Sabbath was the version adopted by most Dutch Reformed preachers. Their complaints reviewed above, about taverns and levity and irreverence on Sunday, were based upon Calvin's ideals. But some Reformed preachers were still not satisfied—and this was how the biggest argument of all over Sunday began.

In the early seventeenth century a few *dominees* concluded that

Calvin's moderate Sunday, already poorly observed, was neither strict enough nor properly grounded in Scripture. To get a better Sunday, the republic needed a new and improved *ideal*. They found it in England. This ideal said that Sunday was more than merely a suitable moment to celebrate the Christian Sabbath, as Calvin alleged: instead it was the true, original, and actual Sabbath as God intended it and ought therefore to be observed with the strictest of care.

The fighting that ensued when some *dominees* tried to impose this English-inspired Sunday on the Dutch church embroiled the republic off and on for over a century. But even more important, the fighting showed that when it came to Sunday, the essential dividing line in the Christian world lay not between Catholics and Protestants, or even between this Protestant and that, but between the English and just about everyone else. For centuries to come, a more moderate Sunday would prevail on the European continent, including the Dutch Republic, while a stricter Sunday would dominate England and its colonies, including the Americas. The Dutch did as much as anyone to help draw that long-standing dividing line, and it is therefore worth examining more closely.

THE SHADOW OF THE ENGLISH SABBATH

What exactly was this English Sabbath, and how did it come to be such an issue far beyond England?

Although not the only part of Europe to produce Sunday Letters and Sunday Christs, England supposedly had a reputation for strict Sundays even before the Reformation. *After* the Reformation its reputation was secure—for if King Charles II, champion patron of actresses and the racetrack on any day, was busy proclaiming and enforcing Sunday laws during the 1670s, then the notion of a good, strict Sunday surely lay deep in English bones.

The famous English Sunday crystallized somewhere between the Middle Ages and Charles, most famously during the late sixteenth and early seventeenth centuries. This was partly the work of a small but vocal group within the English church known as Puritans. It is wrong to think that all Puritans agreed on the topic of Sunday observance, much less anything else, or that they were the first in England to promote a strict Sunday. Indeed their views of Sunday probably had more in common with their English rivals than with most Christians elsewhere. But certainly Puritans became the most prominent face attached to the strict English Sunday.

The single most famous Puritan statement on Sunday, influential across centuries and oceans, was Nicholas Bownd's *The Doctrine of the Sabbath,* which appeared in England in 1595 and ran to more than five hundred dense pages.

Bownd declared, like Calvin, that the Sabbath was not merely for the Jews. But he went beyond Calvin's "perpetual" Sabbath by insisting that the Sabbath was "natural." In other words, it was not *established* at Creation but instead was *rooted* in Creation and the very order of things. Bownd also insisted that the old distinction between "moral" and "ceremonial" aspects of the Sabbath was meaningless: there was nothing ceremonial about the Sabbath at all. Indeed if it were regarded as the least bit ceremonial, then people were likely to consider it as something temporary and for the Jews alone. The Sabbath had to be eternal to be obeyed.

It also had to have been transferred to Sunday by divine mandate, not by merely the authority of the church or "tradition." Here too Bownd exceeded Calvin. He asserted that the shift of the Sabbath to Sunday was made by Christ and his apostles themselves, not by some later arbitrary decision of the church, because in fact Sunday was *the* true and proper day to celebrate it. Of course the original Sabbath had been observed on the seventh day, to commemorate Creation, but Christ himself chose Sunday to replace it, for Sunday marked the beginning of his new creation—and humanity's new creation—in the resurrection. In short, argued Bownd, the Sunday Sabbath was no convenience but a necessity. It was even the key to all Ten Commandments, for in practicing it one was likely to practice all the others.

What did this high-flying theology mean in practice? Bownd devoted the balance of his book, about half, to showing how a proper Sabbath should look. Sunday rest was indeed to be literal, as the commandment stated, and not merely spiritual, as many Protestants argued. It was so literal that no ordinary work of the week should be done that day, even in an "emergency" such as hailstorms threatening a harvest. Yet literal rest did not mean lying about: it required vigor-

ous activity of a spiritual sort, through worship, all day long. Like
Calvin, and even the Dutch *dominees,* Bownd wanted plenty of church
on Sunday, with morning and afternoon services, plus Scripture-
reading, praying, psalm-singing, and acts of charity the rest of the day.
But if Bownd's desire for lengthy public and private worship on Sunday was not so terribly different from the ideals of other Protestants or
Catholics, he exceeded them all in forbidding even emergency work,
and especially in allowing so little scope for play. Here was another famous characteristic of the famous Puritan Sabbath. The "cease from"
element of the "Sabbath" included ceasing not merely from work but
from anything "worldly," which Bownd took to include play. Contrary
to stereotypes, Puritans were not against all sport: rather, they opposed
certain kinds of violent sport, such as bear-baiting and cockfighting,
and all *Sunday* sport. Even lawful sport should cease on the Sabbath,
argued Bownd. Sport's inherently playful character was not in keeping
with the eternal matters that should prevail that day. Moreover, although sport and recreation were necessary for life, they were less necessary than work—and if work should cease on Sunday, then how
much more should play? Bownd's answer to the old question, "Did
Sunday rest mean merely no work or did it also mean no play?" was
clear.

This Sabbath of Nicholas Bownd was what some Dutch *dominees*
sought to implement in their own land. Not coincidentally, many of
them came from Zeeland, the southwesternmost province and thus
closest to England. One of the most prominent, Willem Teellinck,
spent a good part of his young adulthood in England and became acquainted firsthand with this new vision of Sunday. He fondly recounted a Sunday he spent with a family in Banbury, a town already
known for its Puritan flavor. In the morning the family came together
before church to read a chapter in the Bible and pray. At church, all
paid close attention to the sermon, even copying it down, for the children and servants knew that later they would have to give an account-
ing of what was said. Back at home, each pondered the sermon alone
and prayed to God for a blessing from it. At table they spoke about the
sermon, then sang a psalm, after which each person sought further
seclusion for prayer and pondering, in preparation for the upcoming
afternoon sermon. That evening the entire household came together

again to review both sermons and to point out those things that had special application to the household. When this was all done, they prayed together a final time. And whenever they walked together during the day (not for fun but to go to church or to return home or to visit the needy), then they sought a companion who might better explain the sermon or psalm or Bible chapter to them. It went without saying that the town's stores were closed and that the whole day passed with very little visible activity.

Not all the English observed Sunday this way, of course, but this was the sort of living example that caused Teellinck and other Zeeland *dominees* to believe that Bownd's Sunday was more than a dream on paper, and might actually be achieved. These *dominees* therefore decided to make Sunday a national issue for the Dutch, specifically at the Reformed Synod of Dordt in 1619. Yet the Synod, famously strict in Dutch history for other reasons, rejected their strict Sunday. The Synod went along with a condemnation of "abominable and multitudinous profanations" of the Sabbath in the republic, but it even more forcefully condemned certain "foreign opinions creeping into the land, to the unsettling of pious consciences," that favored an *excessively* strict Sunday, one that would prohibit all "honest recreations," the bringing in of grain during wet weather, and merely uttering a single word about business! The fun-loving, merchant-dominated Dutch would not hear of this new English version, and most *dominees* agreed.

Despite this defeat, Dutch advocates of a stricter Sunday persisted. The arguing raged most furiously during David Beck's lifetime and then again after 1655, with the loudest voices and most imaginative arguments coming usually from the strict-Sabbath side. The theologian Johannes Hoornbeeck, for instance, sought to bolster the divine origin of the Sunday Sabbath through performing some biblical calculus: he reckoned that because the sundial of Achaz went back ten degrees (Isaiah 38:8), and Joshua made the sun stand still for hours (Joshua 10:12), and there were three hours of time-stopping darkness at Jesus' crucifixion, then a full day was lost in the week. Added all together, it meant that the Sabbath had literally been moved to Sunday! The leading anti-Sabbatarian theologian, Johannes Coccejus, who regarded Sunday as a day unique to Christians and therefore not the Sabbath, disputed this calculation: these stoppages of time would have moved the week not forward but backward. Any recalculated Sabbath would therefore fall on Friday, the Muslim Sabbath. But even this would not have bothered Coccejus tremendously: like Luther and even Calvin, the specific day of worship didn't matter to him, and Sunday or Friday would have been just fine.

By the late seventeenth century it seemed that the entire Dutch Reformed Church was in uproar over Sunday, demonstrating as ever the restful day's unusual ability to provoke unrest. But at each phase of the debate, those in favor of a stricter Sunday were in the minority. Important exceptions existed in Zeeland and a few pockets elsewhere, but in general David Beck and his Dutch coreligionists preferred Sunday in its old, often immoderate style.

The best evidence that this was the case came not so much from never-satisfied *dominees,* whose gloomy assessments have already been noted, but from English visitors to the republic, who knew better than anyone the difference between a Dutch Sunday and their own. Puritan and non-Puritan visitor alike found it a "great scandal" that Dutch goods were so casually sold, and Dutch stores so blatantly open, on Sundays. "A good bargain relishes better with them than a long prayer," concluded one Englishman. Others noted that more of the Dutch were at the market than at church on Sunday, people traveled freely, windmills operated normally, and farmers labored visibly. Only in Zeeland did people seem somewhat devout on the Sabbath, decided English tourists.

But the harshest criticism of the Dutch Sunday certainly came from Puritans. Many of them were not merely passing through but had quit England and the English Church and were living in exile among the Dutch. These "Separatists" had been attracted to the republic because it seemed to offer them the chance to practice their religion as they pleased, among people—the Reformed—whom they supposed would be religious allies. Yet in the end it was this very freedom of religion in the republic, and the perceived laxity of Reformed "allies," that drove Separatists to pack up again and head to the New World, turning them into "Pilgrims." What the Separatists wanted was not religious freedom for all but freedom to set up their particular religious community without outside influence. And in the Dutch Republic there were too many such influences, too many competing churches, and too much indifference for Puritan tastes. In other words, if Pilgrims left England to seek religious freedom, they left the Dutch Republic because there was too much of it, especially on Sunday.

Puritan exiles often expressed disappointment with how their new Dutch neighbors observed the Sabbath. Everywhere on Sunday were strolling players, jugglers, and worldly attire. Young men put on hats with ostrich plumes, sported frivolous locks of curled hair, and wore ostentatious velvet breeches. The dresses even of Reformed girls and women featured slashed sleeves, rich silken undergarments, and dainty bonnets trimmed with lace—precisely what had offended Puritans in England. The Reformed clergy too wore what Puritans considered offensively elegant clothing. Even in Middelburg, heart of Zeeland, complained one Puritan, one might see a Reformed family on Sunday in colorful attire rather than the dull gray and black of English Separatists. The mistress of the household wore a hood of light blue satin, folded back to reveal her blond curls and to highlight her dark blue velvet dress, while the master, who was a Reformed elder, wore fluffy white lace ruffles around his throat, a yellow satin coat, puffed brown velvet breeches, and white silk stockings. When the English visitor expressed surprise, the Dutch hosts assured him that their religious convictions were essentially the same as his, but they simply liked a bit of color in their clothing on Sunday.

Exiled English Puritans grew weary of such attitudes after a couple of decades and began sailing in steady numbers to the New World from 1619 on. They worried that staying would cause not only their language but their distinctive ways to be swallowed up, in Dutch society and Dutch Sundays. Indeed, one reason stated repeatedly by the departing English was how little they had been able to reform the Dutch Sabbath around them. Surely their children would adopt these Dutch ways as well, and this the Separatists did not want. And so each year after the sailing of the *Mayflower*, the number of Puritans in the Dutch Republic diminished. Some assimilated into Dutch society, most sailed onward. There was just too much labor, too much dancing, too much beer and wine and brandy on the Dutch Sunday. The stricter Sunday would be transported to North America, or stay in England in slightly different form.

BABOONS AND PAPISTS ON SUNDAY

Just as David Beck was silent about assorted aspects of the Reformed Sunday, so was he silent about the Sundays of a boatful of other faiths in the republic.

The remarkable variety of religions here, and the lack of a single Dutch policy for Sunday, did not mean that all the Dutch enjoyed the day in the same sort of comfort and ease as David Beck. In contrast to him, many non-Reformed Dutch could find Sunday a day of stress precisely because of their status outside the public church. In theory this should not have mattered: to be Dutch, one did not have to be Reformed. But despite marveling foreigners who saw only religious license, the view from within non-Reformed religions was more severe.

If the republic was known for its religious freedom, it was not because Reformed preachers or even many laypeople wanted it that way. Certainly some of them were beginning to articulate ideas in favor of tolerance, but the existence of so many religions in the republic had at least as much to do with economic needs and political arrangements as with any abstract philosophy. Neighbors might interact regularly with the Lutheran baker or Mennonite farmer or Catholic butcher, attend each other's weddings, and generally avoid the physical violence that marked religious conflict in most European states. But these interactions were from necessity and then habit, rather than principle or preference, and were certainly not universal. The regents themselves, reluctant as they were to be ordered about by Reformed preachers, still felt an obligation to promote the "public church" for the sake of good order. In practice, regents allowed those of other faiths to worship on Sunday, as long as they did so in private and did not upset public order. But this could be interpreted arbitrarily, and the local sheriff might suddenly decide to conduct a raid, especially when he was in a mood to collect fines. Hence if a Mennonite or Catholic service was a regular Sunday occurrence in the republic, it always involved some stress.

Probably most tolerated among the divergent groups were the Mennonites, who by the mid-seventeenth century were even allowed to build visible churches (called the *vermaning*, or "exhortation house") where they worshiped on Sunday. At first their Sunday meetings featured silent prayer, but over time they came to be structured much like a Reformed service, with a focus on the sermon. One thing they always retained was a rejection of the Sabbath commandment: when services were complete, Mennonite believers returned to work.

Far more stressful than the Mennonite Sunday in the republic was that of the Remonstrants, so called because of "remonstrations" made to the government. This small group within the Reformed Church was actually expelled from the church, and from the entire republic, in 1619, for upholding a softer view of predestination than most Reformed. Before the expulsion, enemies gave Remonstrants the usual range of derogatory labels, including *baviaanen,* or baboons, and violently broke up their Sunday meetings—kicking down doors, destroying windows, chests, chairs, and linens, and grabbing jewelry and money from the assembled. Although already confident enough to return and build a visible church in Amsterdam in 1629, the Remonstrants felt so much pressure for years that they moved their meetings to a day other than Sunday, when rivals would have less free time to spy them out. Moreover, their preachers were forced to travel in disguise, as they had a reward on their head of five hundred guilders—more than the annual wages of most workers and even some preachers.

There were many other non-Reformed Sundays in the Republic, but most common of all was the Catholic Sunday, the largest rival faith to the public church. Catholicism had been gradually outlawed in the republic from 1573, including in provinces where Catholics held a majority, but in practice this simply meant that priests were outlawed. There were far too many lay Catholics to expel, and so they were free to stay, on the usual condition that they worship only in private.

This was not as simple as it sounded. Mass required a priest, and priests were illegal. And so Sunday for a Dutch Catholic typically meant searching out clandestine meetings served by smuggled-in priests. Most of the three hundred or so priests who moved about the republic *stayed* on the move, disguised in lay clothes, baptizing, performing marriages, preaching, and saying Mass, sometimes all in one night.

Until the 1620s most such secret meetings occurred on Sundays in homes, or a nobleman's private chapel, or even a barn. Some drew such a crowd that they could hardly be considered "private"—four or

five hundred at one, even three thousand at another. Steep fines by local authorities and confiscation of precious liturgical objects convinced
believers that smaller and more secretive gatherings were wiser. After
1620 Sunday meetings then might be found in urban churches disguised to look like large homes or warehouses. Many people (Catholic
and otherwise) knew the locations of these buildings, but believers
were generally left alone in exchange for subdued behavior and regular payment of protection money in the form of a tax or bribe.

We can therefore imagine a Catholic Sunday after 1620, set inside
an ordinary-looking home or storefront, say in Amsterdam, with its
dozens of hidden churches *(schuilkerken)*, where people entered a few
at a time for safety's sake. Believers had been notified of the meeting
time by so-called *klopjes,* single women who devoted themselves to
caring for the secret meeting places and the priests who frequented
them, and who went around town knocking at various hours upon
doors they knew well, then whispering the information. Clothed in
their black dresses, black veils, and flat black hats coming to a point
on their foreheads, these women also stood on street corners when
meetings were under way, to anticipate and signal any trouble to those
inside. After entering what seemed like a storefront, then climbing a
spiral staircase, believers reached a door at the top. Behind it stood a
lookout, who peered through small holes drilled into the door to see
who knocked. When satisfied, he opened the door and welcomed the
person in. Holding a candle in one hand, he might motion with his
other toward a holy water font just around the corner. Bells were ringing—but not from this building, rather from the Reformed church
nearby. Catholics preferred to hold their services at about the same
time, so that they, like ancient Christians surrounded by pagan Romans on Sunday, would be less conspicuous. But sometimes Catholics
waited until evening too, when civil authorities were busy with their
own Sunday activities at home.

Inside, behind the building's ordinary facade, ceilings and beams
had been stripped away, for two or three stories upward, to form an
astonishingly open meeting space. The windows of the "church" were
covered with heavy curtains to muffle the sounds of singing within, but
most churches didn't dare sing, lest it be heard on the street and taken
as a public affront. Mass was read at a portable altar at the front of

the room. An image of Christ hung behind the altar. Also behind the altar was often a secret door or window, through which a priest might escape in the event the meeting was invaded by the sheriff or his men. Priests who avoided detection could lodge in a secret room also built into the church. If a priest was caught, then the entire congregation would typically have to contribute toward his ransom; hence there was also economic incentive to keep priests safe, not to mention economic motive for authorities occasionally to interrupt these meetings and levy fines.

Such Sundays too, simmering with tension, occurred weekly in the Dutch Republic, throughout the life of David Beck and beyond.

NIGHT

At the end of a long Sunday, especially in the dark days of winter, Catholic Masses in The Hague were likely the last church services to end, while everywhere in the city banquets were drawing to a close. If David Beck was not returning home from one of these, then certainly at around midnight he was returning home from his mother-in-law's or from visiting another relative or friend.

Sometimes the musicians in the streets were still playing at that hour, sometimes "very divinely," compelling David to stand and listen. One Sunday night he watched the last of a huge fireworks show on the frozen pond of the Binnenhof, in celebration of a recent victory over the Spanish. At home, even when late, he read a bit in his Bible, or sang a psalm or the Lord's Prayer. If Diliana, who had already put the children to bed, was still awake, then he chatted with her by the fire, "about the young people of The Hague, and weddings." He sometimes wrote a bit too, usually in a small journal, four inches by six, in his tiny, cramped hand: by the end it would reach 110 pages for 1624 alone, and survive the ravages of time. But on Sunday evenings he usually did not prepare for school, nor work on his long series of poems mourning the loss of Roeltge, including his "Shout Angels but Grieve Ye Nymphs of The Hague."

David Beck composed these poems out of sorrow. He seems to have kept his extraordinary journal mostly out of sorrow as well. Whatever his motives, what he wrote in his journal was unusual for its highly

personal quality: rather than big, newsworthy events, or such impersonal minutiae as daily expenses, he recorded frank revelations of his
feelings, his comings and goings and everyday life, and of course his
Sundays, his best days—when he didn't have to teach, when he went
to church, and when he had more time than usual for walking and
visiting.

Only when he finished writing did he blow out the last burning candle and retire to bed, where he so often dreamed of Roeltge.*

---

*David Beck recovered enough from his sorrow to remarry in 1630 and to father
three more children. He died in 1634, at a mere forty, leaving behind a young wife
with young children—just as his first wife had left him behind. It is not clear what
became of David's troubled brother Abraham, but his sister Diliana was married by
1639, then died in 1641. Shortly after David's death, his brother Hendrik and his
best friend Herman both named their newborn sons David.

4

Paris, in the 1890s, a Sunday in Mid-Spring

The sounds of early Sunday morning were fewer than those of other mornings, but still wholly disorienting to the protagonist, a man accustomed to sleeping late today, as every day. If the clatter of a milkman's horse and wagon on cobblestone didn't disturb him enough, then a host of other terrifying sensations would: an open window, cool air pushing through it, a cage with singing birds, bright pine furniture and colorful flowers all around, and indeed this entire modest apartment five ghastly stories above the street. What time was it? Where was he? How did he get here? And where was his dear Pompon?

This last question brought to his side the elusive woman herself, laughing at the protagonist's groggy confusion while embracing him fondly. But instead of reassuring him, her appearance only confused him more: this was not the Pompon of his usual morning. *That* Pompon slept punctually until eleven, her "pink snout" burrowed deeply into a tangle of lacy sheets. Nor was this the Pompon of his evenings: just last night, in the most elegant salon of Paris, she had as usual "played the decadent queen" with assorted famous socialites in fancy ties, who held her hand and recited verse to her. Yet now she stood before him all Sunday-fied—*endimanchée*—in bourgeois fashion, hair wetted and pulled back, clothed thus far in a calico chemise embroidered with scallops and a corset of gray linen. She had all the makings of a shop assistant. What in the world had happened?

The protagonist had already forgotten, or perhaps never knew. And so Pompon explained: the night before, increasingly bored with their usual routine of witty conversation in a salon followed by late dinner at a cabaret, he had succumbed to the influence of too much drink, talking "the inverse of good sense" until at last he was "stupified." That was when Pompon decided they needed new diversions, new sensations and joys, to occupy them. Within minutes she had conjured up a plan, something they had never tried before: the popular *dimanche,* or Sunday, of Paris. Each Sunday through the spring and summer, the two of them would venture out and experience this great weekly event among the people—starting immediately. Hence the answers to his original, hazy questions were these: (1) it was 6:30 A.M., (2) rather than their own well-appointed apartment, surely on the prestigious *première étage* right above the street, they were in a simple room she had arranged just for Saturday nights, to set the mood for their Sunday excursions, (3) he had been carried upstairs in a semiconscious state by the footman and another servant, and (4) right now, she, the "architect of his pastimes," was busy with preparations for their big day, as a bourgeois housewife should be, and she had no more time to waste.

Handing him some bourgeois literature about Sunday, as a sort of crash course—he assumed this included some witty dialogues, a Maupassant story, a few pages of Zola—Pompon left to finish dressing. Alone again, the stunned protagonist slowly warmed to the idea: why not share "the special joys of Sunday," so unfamiliar to him, with each social class. Yes, they would stay in Paris this year for their taste of the strange and new! Why should they run off with so many others to

London, Madrid, or Amsterdam, the same old thing, among legions of Cook's tourists, just so that back home they might join unbearable conversations about the "splendor" of the Boboli gardens, or the "character" of Brittany? Reduced-price voyages, and insatiable thirst for things foreign, had made travel so tiresome. Why, even Pompon's concierge had spent three weeks at the Swiss resort of St. Moritz! Hence they would do the truly exotic: remain in Paris and follow the people of Sunday.

The protagonist got another idea: not only would he and Pompon venture out each Sunday for their own enlightenment, but he would write down their adventures in a book, for the enlightenment of others. After all, Parisians of his sort knew Tunisia or Constantinople a hundred times better than they knew their local Sunday pleasure parks. It was a brilliant plan! Still, he knew that his friends would criticize him for so vigorously pursuing the vulgar, the common, and the clichéd (and thus the distasteful, the tedious, and the uniform) pleasures of "the rabble." He also knew his response: did their snobbery not impose a certain tedium and uniformity of its own? "Why should we sing like imbeciles in that delicious monotone of snobbery?" he would say. In fact, "sheeplike snobbery" was the plague of their time, in art, literature, theatre, and all else. There was now snob cuisine, snob drinking, snob everything! But with this Sunday idea Pompon was teaching him to "thumb his nose at prejudice," to quit snobbery, to take steps alone on unknown paths, even to carve out new paths. He would go see the local Sunday for himself, rather than assume it to be insufferable. Oh, how expansive he felt! Just yesterday he was accused, like other artistic types, of narcissism, of being an "androgynous aesthete who spouted vague obscurities." But here he was, about to join the people and gorge on common sense and fresh air.

At the moment, however, the fresh air was giving him a chill. His initiation into Sunday rituals would clearly have to be gradual. But his enthusiasm was genuine, and he happily recited aloud the stereotypical pleasures of the popular Parisian Sunday that surely awaited them: breakfast at Duval's, a promenade on a donkey, a visit to the Grévin Wax Museum, a boat outing, and . . . Pompon, within earshot, stopped him. They would do all of these things, she said, but not at once, for as part of their experiment they would restrict themselves to a modest, bourgeois-like ten francs each Sunday. If they spent more, they would revert to their usual excesses and grow bored again.

With that, she handed over the Sunday outfit she had put together for him: a pink shirt with white collar, a vest, pants, and waistcoat, a white regatta tie, some yellow and white leather shoes, a ring on his little finger, a watch chain of nickel covered with "sportive attributes," a little pomade for his hair, and a specially shaped bowler from the boulevard Rochechouart—worn not too far back lest he look like a panderer. With his bowler on correctly, for whom would he be taken? he wondered aloud. They settled on either a hairdresser's assistant or a bath attendant. If it was all the same to Pompon, he said, he preferred the first.

Pompon's *toilette,* or "outfit," consisted of a simple dress costing three francs and a hat of fifteen sous (a sou was one-twentieth of a franc, or five centimes). But she looked as charming, refined, and distinguished as ever, and spoke knowingly of "trousers" and *"liquettes"* (his special shirt) and other bourgeois mysteries. Where did she learn these things? he marveled.

While dressing, he could see out his window into a courtyard and into many other windows. Behind these, the sorts of people with whom he would spend his Sundays were dressing as well. All prepared themselves with extra care: old balding men passed combs over the bare ground of their heads, young beardless men applied great piles of unnecessary lather to shave, skinny women adjusted the false fronts of their dresses, other women pulled "like longshoremen" on the strings of their corsets. A fat man plunged his head into a washbowl and blew water through his nose "like a sperm whale." Others polished boots, admired themselves in the mirror of their armoire, adjusted ties, and unrolled curlers. Outside, a young man and woman were about to miss their train, because they were intent on kissing every exposed bit of skin and caressing every ringlet; exhausted by work six other days, and intent on savoring the joy of the seventh in a way the protagonist had never known, they wished not to waste a moment.

Suddenly Pompon stood before him and readjusted his bowler, and they were off—descending the stairs, going out the front door, and walking down the street past all the other Sundayed-up people already gliding along the sidewalk at that early hour.

At least two things are clear from this opening scene of *Parisian Sundays: Notes of a Decadent* (1898) by the then-acclaimed French illustrator, painter, caricaturist, and humorist Louis Morin.

First, like the medieval lord of the manor, or Prince Willem Frederik of the old Dutch Republic, the wealthy, leisured classes of the nineteenth century—including the couple here—did not really understand the importance of Sunday to ordinary people. To the great, who possessed money and stature enough to work and play as they pleased on any day, Sunday remained quite like any other. As one contemporary put it, "Life among the leisured knows no Sunday, for their days flow into each other monotonously. Only the people and the bourgeoisie know Sunday." And for this overwhelming majority, the exceptional quality of Sunday was arguably even stronger during the industrializing, urbanizing, bourgeois-dominated world of the nineteenth century than in the past.

Before the Industrial Revolution reordered the Western world, peasant and urban artisan alike certainly knew what it meant to work long hours and to find relief through Sundays or rural holy days. Yet whether one was engaged in agricultural or urban work, and whether one was Protestant or Catholic, the line between working and recreation was often vague in the preindustrial world. Rural workers drank, smoke, chatted, sang, and stopped to play during workdays, while on Sundays they might decide to work. Artisans in towns likewise mixed work and play, as they were paid by the piece rather than by the hour and usually worked from home. But after 1800 or so, when industrialization introduced its long and rigid hours, its fixed workplace, and its discipline of the clock, the line between work time and free time became more distinct, and it was basically drawn around Sunday. After some uncertainty in the beginning, Sunday by around 1860 was the one free day, and even free night, for working people.

Industrialization also meant urbanization, which besides much else changed the familiar rural setting that had dominated Sunday for more than fifteen hundred years. David Beck and other Dutch knew an early sort of urban Sunday, but theirs paled next to that of nineteenth-

century Paris. Already enormous in the sixteenth and seventeenth centuries, the city's population reached 600,000 by 1800, and then 3 million by 1900.

Urbanization in turn brought new social arrangements that would
also affect Sunday. Most new city dwellers belonged to the expanding
urban working classes and the swelling bourgeois (or middle) classes.
Especially the bourgeoisie, who defined themselves as those not engaged in physical labor, grew in number during the nineteenth century,
from about 15 percent of the total population of Europe in 1800 to
around 30 or 40 percent by 1900. Although still fewer in number than
the urban working classes, the bourgeoisie grew in influence as well,
to the point that many historians consider the nineteenth century to be
the bourgeois century, and France the quintessential bourgeois nation.
True, France was slower to industrialize and urbanize than were some
of its European neighbors: Britain, Germany, and Belgium were ahead
in both areas, while France, Austria, Italy, and Spain lagged behind.
Yet despite this, the bourgeoisie after 1870 dominated French politics,
culture, and style to such an extent that the public face of the nation,
and of its Sundays, was a bourgeois officeholder.

Industrialization and urbanization therefore helped to reshape Sunday everywhere, by heightening its importance and giving it a new
physical and social setting. But there was one more development of the
time that helped to reshape the French Sunday in particular: after 1830
France had no established church, traditionally the main architect of
Sunday rules. Abolished during the French Revolution, then briefly
reestablished by King Louis XVIII in 1814, the church was detached
from the French state for good by 1830. This is not to say that some
vague process of "secularization" necessarily explains why the French
seemed to find more pleasure than others in Sunday, or why the possibilities of Sunday seemed so happily infinite there. After all, Europeans
with official churches were quite capable of finding illicit Sunday fun,
as we saw in Chapter 1, while religious devotion in France hardly died
after the Church was disestablished: most of the French remained
Catholic, and in such areas as Brittany attendance at Sunday Mass remained almost universal. Rather, pointing out the lack of any sort of
official religion in France is simply to say that church on Sunday was
no longer obligatory, and that no particular religion could even *pre-*

sume to prescribe legally binding rules for all the French: even the less-than-official Reformed Church had at least been in a position to try that in the Dutch Republic.

It was in these new settings, both broad and particular, that late-nineteenth-century France, the European capital of style and culture, produced the quintessential pleasure-seeking Sunday of the modern, urban Western world—for those who loathed or loved it. Novelists elaborated it (all of Zola's Parisian novels but one include scenes of Sunday outings), such artists as Georges Seurat immortalized it (in scenes of crowded parks, lively cafés, and raucous dance halls), poets and songwriters versified it (from the sublime to the bawdy), but most of all the bourgeois and working classes of France celebrated Sunday so memorably that it became one of the defining characteristics of this so-called Belle Epoque. In fact, although Sundays around mainland Europe had much in common by now, when contemporaries spoke of the "Continental Sunday," the model they had in mind was inevitably French or, more specifically, Parisian: everything else of the genre was a variation on a theme.

A second striking thing evident in Morin's opener is that the leisured classes not only failed to appreciate how meaningful such a Sunday had become, they didn't much like it. Despite the couple's good intentions in going to see for themselves what the commotion over Sunday was all about, their unease with wild enthusiasm for the day is already apparent. A well-deserved day of rest they might appreciate in the abstract, but what the great could not endure was the frenzied determination, the insistent pouring into the boulevards, parks, train stations, and suburbs, and the so predictably "Sunday-fied" dress. Indeed the term *endimanchée* was a derogatory one, meant to poke fun at the special care the masses took for their clothing that day as one of the rituals meant to heighten its importance. "Respectable" people cared for their toilette every day.

Such a dismissive attitude toward the popular Sunday suggests that those who knew only flexible leisure time simply could not grasp the urgency felt by those who had but one indisputably free day from which to squeeze every drop of pleasure, one day on which they felt free to control their lives. Nor did the leisured appreciate that theaters, music halls, and ballrooms all catered to this urgency by lowering prices on Sundays to attract those who lacked time and means during the week, thus jamming Sunday streets. Indeed, the elite of Paris increasingly took care to avoid going out on Sunday during the busiest hours. In provincial Rouen the upper bourgeoisie made Sunday an indoor day, for family, games, reading, the piano, or letters—partly because of new bourgeois emphasis on home life, partly because they had time on other days for outside activities, and partly out of a desire to miss the crowds. There was a final thing the leisured classes could not understand about the popular Sunday, and which they abhorred perhaps most of all: the sudden craving of so many Parisians for the countryside. Why then did people choose to live in Paris?

Ungenerous sentiments toward popular events such as Sunday were typical of all leisured classes but perhaps especially of that small portion known as *décadents,* as Louis Morin at least playfully and perhaps truthfully labeled himself in the subtitle of his book. These were typically well-to-do artists, such as Morin, professional critics, or wealthy self-appointed guardians of style and culture. The term *décadent* was rooted in numerous theories of decay, beginning with Greeks, who believed it was constant, or even ancient Christians who saw decay culminating in the end of the world. But in late-nineteenth-century Europe *décadent* had a more specific meaning, akin to the English "dandyism" embodied, for instance, by Oscar Wilde.

Philosophically, this most recent version of decadence admitted that civilization was unnatural and corrupting. But unlike Romantics of the earlier nineteenth century, who sought an antidote to civilization by fleeing to nature, or later Realists who condemned civilization by focusing on its miserable aspects, the *décadents* reveled in corruption: for even when corrupt, civilization remained superior to nature, grounded as it was in human invention. They reveled as well in the abnormal and deviant—in *décadent* eyes, further "proof of man's superiority to natural law."

Stylistically, *décadents* therefore delighted in the unusual and artificial and excessive. They regarded refined conversation as a sign of advanced civilization, preferred unusual words, and favored wild colors and styles in clothing and decor—"Overdressed and Overeducated Since 1890" proclaims one modern Web site for dandies. They could bear to live only in cities, which accentuated one's distance from unbearable nature. And they delighted in anything that promoted independence: for although they loved the conveniences of industrial civilization and the myriad possibilities of urban living, even blessed city life could promote the horrors of conformity, in appearances, manners, and style. Thus their contempt for stable bourgeois living, their deliberate ignorance of the working classes, and their utter disdain for popular culture—including its enthusiasm for Sunday. In the eyes of *décadents*, "class" and "popular" by definition reflected and nourished widespread conformity, and nowhere was either more evident than on Sunday.

If elite ignorance and mistrust of Sunday are apparent in Morin's opening scene, less so is how accurate this colorful account of Sunday adventures might have been, or how reflective of Morin's own views. Is he even the protagonist?

The opener certainly suggests the *décadents'* typical discomfort with the masses and love of detailed description for its own sake, yet later in the book Morin will sympathize with the popular Sundays he sees. He will even state that art "is not solely for the fortunate of this world," a view completely foreign to true, elitist *décadents*. Perhaps Morin's social origins linked him too strongly to the popular world to leave it completely: one great-grandfather was a clog maker, one grandfather was a cooper and rural policeman, and his father was a tutor. And more than one of Morin's relatives "could dream of nothing grander" for him when he was young than that he might one day be elevated to the dreary post of rural notary. In other words, his distant family was working class, his immediate family new bourgeoisie, and he himself had already ascended to the leisure class. His familiarity with all social groups may explain why he both praises and criticizes all of them as well: he knew something of each, up close.

But the real key to making sense of Morin's *Parisian Sundays* may be that above all else he was a humorist, or, as he styled himself in discussing his art, a "fantasist"—someone able to "find the joke" in practically everything. This orientation was in direct response to the "joyless, colorless" childhood he claimed to have endured, including dull academic lessons from his elderly father and terrifying days with his mother in Paris during the Franco-Prussian War of 1870–71. Weary of joyless things and displaying talent in drawing, he decided as a young man to become, against his family's wishes, an artist. Thanks to the "supple fancifulness" of his pencil and his "exquisite talent," as later critics called it, his life was thenceforth deliberately light and full of humor, as reflected in most of his nineteen thousand illustrations and paintings. Many of these stood alone, and many served as illustrations in dozens of books authored by himself or others, ranging from a prize-winning children's book, to occasional pornography, to such literary works as *Parisian Sundays*. No more "joyous draughtsman have we seen," exclaimed one reviewer of Morin's drawings. "Fun" was certainly his mantra.

However *Parisian Sundays* should be read, one thing is certain: despite its sometimes condescending views toward the popular classes, despite its likely comic exaggerations, despite the uncertain factual quality of his and Pompon's great Sunday experiment or the very identity and position of Pompon herself (Morin was married, but Pompon is a frivolous, *décadent* sort of name and her status in the book rather vague), this work treats in highly memorable fashion the favorite activities on a Sunday in Paris during the later nineteenth century. It is therefore an excellent starting point for a journey into that world.

ON THE BOULEVARD

It was only fitting that Pompon and the protagonist (who might here be called Louis, just in case) should begin their Sunday excursions on the boulevards of Paris, promenading for two hours from the Place de l'Opéra toward the Drouot crossroads.

By now the Sunday promenade was popular all around urban Europe, but the model and name rightly came from France. Some guidebooks described Paris as one big "Sunday walk," "365 days a year," the "only city" where one could find amusement merely by walking. Still, the Sunday crowd was different from that of other days: during the week, tourists, the leisured, and the high bourgeoisie dominated streets, but Sunday was the day for workers and shopkeepers. This was especially so after 1870, when Sunday as a regular day of urban rest became more common, and when the many wide boulevards laid down a decade earlier by Baron Haussmann, the famous rebuilder of Paris, had been thoroughly "democratized."

Yet even before Haussmann, Honoré de Balzac (d. 1850) felt that Parisian streets were livelier and more varied than promenades elsewhere: The Hague had its woods, Venice its canals, Milan its Corsia dei Servi, Rome its Corso, St. Petersburg its Perspective, Vienna its Graben, and London its Regent Street, but most were dominated by the bourgeoisie and thus lacked the "vivifying sun of the soul" in more diverse Paris. Still, there was little doubt that Haussmann's new boulevards popularized Sunday promenading more widely than before and bestowed a "common right of possession and enjoyment" among all classes. Walking was so popular that even on the new widened boulevards the going was rough, thanks to dense crowds of people, countless horse-drawn carriages, omnipresent manure, and soon, dangerous cars and trams. One guide book listed as its "second commandment" of walking in Paris: "never leave the sidewalk."

Part of the purpose of a Sunday promenade was the same as in the time of David Beck: to see things. That was indeed the main desire of Louis and Pompon today. But equally important was another purpose: to *be* seen. Contemporaries made the distinction between the promenader, motivated largely by the second purpose, and the *flâneur,* the stroller, who was motivated by the first. The *flâneur* was a distant, often solitary observer of the "spectacle of the world," who stopped to gaze contemplatively at the Seine along the way, or shamelessly walked up and down busy streets to see accidents. Pompon and Louis were somewhere in between the *flâneur* and the promenader: not quite solitary enough to be *flâneurs,* but too much the socially superior observers to care much about being seen themselves.

Today on the street a carnivalesque atmosphere reigned. Vendors sold fatty beef from sidewalk stalls, and everywhere people were behaving in rather silly fashion. Louis liked it, at least at first. Streamers suspended from trees gave all vegetation a "bizarre appearance." Two contrary flows of people moved over the sidewalks and spilled into streets. Colored confetti covered shoes and ankles, as promenaders greeted each other with handfuls of the stuff, making conversation and introductions unnecessary. Louis and Pompon were enormously amused. Perhaps he could like popular Sundays after all, he told her:

he was growing accustomed to his clothing, and his "popular heart" was beating enthusiastically in his breast.

But he grew less amused as they went on. There was the awful brass music, which "peeled the skin from our ears," and a "disgusting odor" of fried food. But an enthusiastic Pompon ignored his complaints and marched onward, beneath a densely flowered hat that almost swallowed her head. When a "hooligan" made fun of Louis's shiny spats, Pompon said not to worry: in three minutes they would be gray with dust and no one would notice. A sudden blow to the head made Louis forget his spats: he turned in time to see his bowler rolling along the ground, then be dragged under three or four dresses, losing its luster. The culprit approached and announced happily: "That was me!" Holding up the enormous cardboard hammer that had struck the blow, the man added, "Buy this, and you can do the same to others!" Pompon laughed and paid the man two sous for his hammer, light as a feather. Louis walked on, hitting other people and yelling, "Hit your mother-in-law in the trap, only two sous!" When someone threw confetti in Louis's mouth, he swung his new hammer too late. Pompon was delighted. And she wanted to try everything she saw, from the Ferris wheel to the mechanical racing horses.

Pompon urged a now-subdued Louis onward, saying that it was wiser to investigate why certain customs had been popular for so long than simply to declare them imbecilic. "What philosophizing!" responded Louis, "and right in front of the crêpe vendor!" And so they went on to the Ferris wheel, but instead of a frightened Pompon burying her head into Louis's shoulder, it was the other way around. He could not describe adequately the "horrible sensation" he felt at each descent. Nor could he understand the laughter from the crowd when he emerged, pale and defeated, his suspenders ripped from every button, so that he had to hold up his pants with one hand.

Things grew only slightly better when the crush of people forced them into the narrow avenue leading to another amusement: the enormously popular Grévin Wax Museum. Here they filed past replicas of famous figures, equally divided among "people of merit, criminals, and buffoons." Right before their eyes was the famous assassination of the Revolutionary hero Marat, scenes from Zola's *Germinal,* the coronation of the Russian czar, a street in Cairo, the papal cortège, the volcano of Pompeii, and more. Popular every day, such museums overflowed on Sunday, so that Pompon and Louis were pressed against countless backs and chests. Louis's joints suddenly stiffened, and in a small black staircase he was overcome by a "terrible oppression." It could have been worse: they might have been pushed by the crowds into that other popular favorite of the time, the Paris morgue, through which a million visitors a year passed, especially on Sunday, to see the laid-out corpses. The ostensible purpose was to identify bodies: only in such a huge city was it possible to die anonymously. But clearly, simple morbid curiosity was at work as well; not until 1907 was the morgue finally closed to the public.

It was a very mixed Sunday by the end.

OF CAFÉS AND DANCE HALLS

Louis and Pompon ventured out nineteen more times on Sundays, both in and around Paris, and more often than not especially Louis would come to quite the same mixed conclusion. But neither felt any mixed sentiment during their visits to Paris's famous cafés, which they both roundly disliked.

Cafés originated in the seventeenth century, specializing as their name suggested in the latest trendy drink, and designed to be a more sophisticated urban form of the old medieval tavern. By 1900 the cafés of Paris numbered almost 27,000 and served much more than their original coffee. Moreover, along with their cousin wineshops, cabarets, and taverns, they served as focal points of public life every day, including Sunday. At least one observer thought them even more vital on that day: if the cafés of Paris closed on Sunday nights as they did in London, he contended, then 30,000 people would surely hang themselves.

Cafés were typically associated with the bourgeoisie, and taverns and wine merchants with the working classes, but the destination of Louis and Pompon attracted a more varied audience, especially on Sunday, when even students visited. This was the café-concert, which featured singing and dancing performers and which was introduced to them by Louis's ne'er-do-well young cousin, Gontran. Cooped up all week with books and forced to dress "in an awful uniform that made him look like an artillery officer," Gontran took his revenge on Sundays in the café-concerts.

Arriving at the appointed establishment on the Champs-Élysées, Louis was surprised to learn that admission was free. Like most of the 260 or so other café-concerts of Paris, this one made its money on food and drink. The small stage for singers likely grew out of the *goguettes,* where people used to gather to sing on Sundays, while the café-concerts were in turn already growing into such larger music halls as the famed Folies-Bergères. But in whatever incarnation of popular music Louis and Pompon might have found themselves, they would not have felt at ease. And they would have found no relief in the guidebook that promised that absolution from the pope was not necessary after attending such a place—for the objections of the couple to the café-concert were not religious but aesthetic.

Amid the racket and the crowd of merchants, employees, "lovers of lowlife," and girls in special Sunday toilettes, an unsettled Louis looked around for his cousin. Though only seventeen, he was the "herald of the coming century, possessing every vice necessary" to succeed in his chosen path, and "particularly gifted in the art of causing money to leave other people's pockets." Suddenly Gontran appeared, hardly recognizable in his garish outfit: a gray felt hat with a large brim, a high 1830-style collar up to his ears, a wide, flowered, dark red tie in a special knot held in place by a cameo tie-clip, a pleated, ruffled shirt, a flecked silk waistcoat *à la papa,* a jacket of gray pearl wool with tails, matching pants, yellow spats, white leather gloves, a monocle, and an enormous hooked cane—in short, a walking caricature of all current fashion.

Gontran announced his entrance by striking his cane on a whole row of chairs, then seated himself and demanded that the singing begin. Not yet seeing Louis and Pompon, he sat next to a thin girl "swallowed up in a large, exaggerated cape" and an immense flowered hat "representing all the flora of Paris." Suddenly the curtain went up, and various singers took their turn entertaining the crowd—and discomforting Louis. A woman with a raspy voice led off, followed by a man wearing equestrian breeches who juggled his hat while singing. Whenever he tried to place it on his head, the audience yelled *"Chapeau! Chapeau!"*

until he took it off again. Gontran of course led the yelling and the bursts of laughter that followed, but Louis and Pompon did not get the joke. The coup de grâce was a lovely woman wearing a big hat, who sang of her trysts with English, Chinese, Japanese, Russians, and Americans but who had saved her real attractions for the "little Frenchmen."

At this, the "amorous hearts in the audience commenced howling," noted Louis, so that the singer could no longer be heard. Gontran himself stood on the table jumping with enthusiasm "among the cherries of the liqueurs." A waiter rushed over to make him climb down, but Gontran fell into the arms of the girl next to him, who uttered a loud cry. When a supervisor ran over, serviette on arm, and asked Gontran to leave, the boy simply dashed from one place to another, hiding, until at last several customers delivered him to the guard at the door, who threw him out. It was not a proud moment for Louis. "What an abyss in the brain" of his cousin, he thought. Snobs may indeed be "carried away excessively by art and literature," but at least they were interested in things of the spirit, Louis thought. They never spoke to Gontran that day after all.

A visit on another Sunday to the dance halls of Paris was little better for the intrepid couple: more than merely annoying, these establishments could be distressing.

They decided to visit such a place only because it was raining. Like two-thirds of Paris on a Sunday morning, Louis and Pompon had their noses to the window and their eyes on the barometer, hoping for sun, and then went out anyway in the rain. They would have their Sunday out, even if it was indoors.

Louis and Pompon settled on the Moulin Rouge and Moulin Galette, on the (in)famous Montmartre. The atmosphere there was calmer during Sunday afternoon dances than during wild nights, when tourists and the bourgeoisie dominated. The Sunday afternoon dances attracted young people of the working classes and lesser bourgeoisie, plus "their mamas and papas, especially their mamas." The atmosphere was rather "like a provincial, tree-lined walkway where young, slicked-down boys paraded in front of bedazzled girls, and vice versa," much as depicted in Renoir's famous painting of the Galette.

Mothers sat with their daughters on benches, in a large circle, smiling at passersby and preparing "to make a hearty welcome to any respectable-looking gallant fellow" who came to ask for a waltz or polka. The young lady would be handed over immediately, without extensive introduction, for each dance gave the couple ten minutes to strike up conversation. The mothers did not worry as much as Louis thought they might, perhaps because being there watching was better than pondering that "her shop-attendant daughter walked home every other night of the week with a strange young fellow" whom the mother had never seen. These mothers had no wide social contacts and no tempting dowries; they were there to seek a son-in-law, and fast, before some stranger won their daughter's heart. Promising young men circulated at this dance, but also ridiculous older men "looking for the elusive composite of all their past loves," plus noncommissioned army officers hoping to impress with their blue coats and fitted red pants. If the dancer offered a drink to the young lady, he offered one to the mother as well, and if the conversation revealed that he was sufficiently placed and had some future, and the girl "knew how to enchant," then the couple "might end up at the town hall." Louis praised these mothers who "braved the benches of such a diabolical place on Sunday afternoon," for they were acting out of necessity.

Pompon found it all too anonymous; she preferred the fair of a small town, where people knew each other already. She coaxed Louis into the garden, where the sun had begun to shine. Eventually they went back inside, this time into the Galette, where the atmosphere was much more "lugubrious," according to Louis. This place could have been "queen of the *guingettes*" (Sunday's suburban pleasure gardens), mused Louis, perfectly situated at the edge of Paris and overlooking the magnificent skyline. Instead it was now seedy, even on Sunday afternoon, filled with "rascals old and young" searching for unsuspecting, unaccompanied girls, and pimps in search of new hirelings.

Indeed there were 35,000 prostitutes in Paris by 1859, not counting the unregistered. And this was a prime recruiting ground. There was a feeling here of the police, "of the pawnshop, of dirty bars where the public was forced to rest its rough hands." It was a sad and mean atmosphere, where the waiters seemed intent "primarily on insulting the public" and where the girls fell into the arms of the first man who approached, because "even before their need for love was their need for food." A man or two walked by, "assessing this line of lanky dress-makers' errand-girls as if they were bolts of fabric," to determine their quality. These men were villainous monsters, decided Louis, but would they exist if there weren't so many girls desperate for survival, and so much demand for their services? It was hard to know who to blame, he concluded sadly.

This Sunday ended up being dismal. Moreover, it ran quite contrary to Louis's original plan to seek out only places where there was at least hope of finding color, diversion, and gaiety. But darker places were also part of a Parisian Sunday.

MASS?

More than a few people might be surprised, admitted Louis, by his decision another Sunday to attend Mass.

After all, many had seen him shake hands with "old anarchists and fossilized republicans," both decidedly against the Church. Moreover, many nowadays regarded churchgoers as "idiots and morons." How could any cultured person at the end of this nineteenth century "possibly confine oneself to such a narrow manner of seeing, fit only for inferior classes whose misery drives them to believe anything"? Indeed many other books on Paris didn't bother to mention church among the possible activities of Sunday. But Mass continued on here too, as it had since the medieval world, and Louis was perfectly willing to try it: since the age of thirty he had considered himself an "eclectic" anyway.

A number of *décadents* likewise displayed a soft spot for Catholicism: aesthetes like Louis, perhaps they enjoyed the ceremony of it all. Indeed, declared Louis, the Mass of internment was the "most beautiful tragic poem ever written by man." Because he enjoyed services especially on Palm Sunday, "the day when nature awakes," he and Pompon made their way to St. Severin—in his opinion, the "most suggestive" of all the old churches in Paris. Right and left of it were cabarets, "ignoble houses" that Haussmann's demolitions had inexplicably missed, and other "low places," but this setting was as aesthetically pleasing as the Mass to come: it framed the church in beautiful, profound contrast. On the cobblestoned square before the church, older ladies huddled together to sell "palms" (actually boxwood branches here in palmless northern Europe), chattering interminably and yelling occasionally at the "thieving brats" who peddled their own branches sneakily in side streets.

Inside, the church was almost dark, despite the pale lights of the altar. Like many a devout churchgoer (or aesthete) before him, Louis was overcome with awe and reverence, confessing that he'd never been able to laugh in a church. Although he did not perpetually meditate upon the "mysteries of the altar," although he did not know precisely the steps of Ignatius Loyola's famous spiritual exercises, he knew well that a sojourn in a church such as this predisposed one "to a particular state of soul, favorable to the evolution of thought."

While in his reverie, he noticed that only a few of the regulars responded in similarly awestruck fashion. Most people, he concluded, came out of habit, "dumb and blind," or social convenience, and had no clue to the profound mystery around them, a complaint heard since the ancient world, of course. Young people yawned, the old snored, and no one seemed to mind. Was there an impish altar boy here like the one in Zola's *The Sin of Father Mouret,* who swung the censer loudly and high, with great clatter and smoke, hoping to make people cough? And once, recalled Louis, he had seen, and heard, the entire bench of churchwardens at Sainte-Marie-des-Batignolles "sawing logs," filling the vault with their snoring, until the verger discreetly "struck a hard blow on the flagstones to the right of the improvised dormitory."

Louis did not approve of such irreverence. Nor did he approve of those who came here as "an act of elegant society" and entered— preferably late—in "the same mood with which they went to afternoon tea at the baron's," to show off their toilette. Upon being seated, such people began looking for acquaintances in the crowd and exchanging discreet salutes. The *messieurs* crossed their arms impatiently: at the elevation of the Host they inclined their heads dutifully, but as soon as the concluding *"Ite missa est"* was uttered, they grabbed their canes, hats, and gloves and were off. A number of ladies were collapsed in prayer upon the *prie-dieux,* in a posture "suited to show off their figure and neckline"; with rapid circular glances they inspected those around them, guessing the price of someone's toilette as they ran through their prayers, and "in two seconds" of looking they had enough material to gossip all afternoon.

Louis and Pompon, in contrast, found "delicate charm" in the Mass. They listened, breathed, and looked; there was music, incense, and exquisite stained glass. As in a medieval Catholic service, the senses were still appealed to—at first only smell, sight, and hearing, but eventually, during the Eucharist, even taste and touch. Louis was distracted for a moment by the thought of how wonderful it would be to experience a church where all the senses were satisfied at once, perhaps even drinking exquisite liqueurs in the middle of it all, but Pompon, intuiting that he was about to do something stupid, interrupted and advocated against employing the sense of touch too enthusiastically in this setting.

After the entrance, the exit was the most important act for many, especially the young, who crowded together outside, forming a hedge of sorts, using their hats to exchange blows, shaking hands, winking at waltz partners of the night before or even early this morning, then huddling together closely. But this morning their consciences were clean, they believed, because they had done their duty and attended Mass. Still, he could hardly condemn them, because they weren't much different from many churchgoing adults over the centuries—including an old diplomat Louis had seen at a ball on Good Friday. "Surprised to see me here?" said the man. "You shouldn't be, I did my duty earlier today, and the good God doesn't ask more."

AU RESTAURANT

Was it on that Sunday after Mass, or on another Sunday, when Louis and Pompon decided to venture into the eating places of Paris?

Here was a favorite Sunday activity in provincial cities as well. One could dine variously at a café, cabaret, brasserie (where beer was brewed and simple meals served), tavern, *table d'hôte* (pension), or wine merchant's (who served meals as well as drink). But for a finer experience, particularly the bourgeoisie sought something else on Sunday afternoon: the restaurant, where one found special relief from the monotony of everyday meals.

French cuisine began to distinguish itself in the time of the Sun King,

Louis XIV (1638–1715), but its most renowned setting—the restaurant—was established only in the late eighteenth century. Originally
the word "restaurant" had a narrow meaning: bouillon of meat undi-
luted by water, a dense concoction meant to "restore" one. Some
places serving this specialty simply called themselves a "bouillon." A
certain Boulanger, often credited with opening the first restaurant
around 1765, wrote confidently if irreverently above his door, in Latin,
"Come unto me, all ye who labor in stomach, and I will restore you."
Antonin Carême's (1783–1833) tireless codification of procedures and
his zealous pursuit of ideal blends of flavors beyond bouillon spread
the fame of French cooking and expanded the meaning of the restaurant. By 1825, when restaurants in Paris numbered nine hundred, the
word had also come to mean a place open at any hour (rather than a
few hours) to all comers (rather than only men), where the atmosphere
was decent and clean (rather than the usual), where diners ate on small
individual tables (rather than all together), where everyone was served
the same-size portion from a menu (rather than whatever was at
hand), and where announced prices for a variety of items allowed one
to choose as one pleased (rather than be presented with a single plate
at a mysterious price). Naturally Sunday became the favorite day for
most to visit such an attractive place.

By the time of Louis and Pompon, with fifteen hundred restaurants
in Paris and eleven thousand people employed in them, there was further nuance unrelated to the food: at a restaurant one took time to eat,
discussed anything except politics, and was conscious of engaging in
"an act of refined elegance." Georges Auguste Escoffier (1846–1935),
the leading spirit behind much of this, understood that "refined elegance" was as important as the food, and made sure that hotel restaurants in particular were "eminently adapted to the favorable exhibiting
of magnificent dresses." Still, it was the taste that one most remembered. Not even Mark Twain could find something to satirize about his
first meal in Paris, but instead blubbered like a typical, overwhelmed
tourist: everything was "so tidy, the food so well cooked, the waiters
so polite, the company so affable, so moustached, so Frenchy!"

Louis was less enamored of these places. For one thing, he understood better than tourists how greatly restaurants varied in quality. At
the best establishments, one could expect to pay at least eight francs

per person for a single meal, and at the very best more than forty. Middling restaurants ranged typically from three to seven francs. This last was the sort of place chosen, with self-conscious courage, by Louis and Pompon, who generically called it a "Duval," or a large dining establishment catering to the lesser bourgeoisie. Such were especially popular on Sunday, when the well-to-do could give their servants a break, or when middling bourgeois families simply wanted a meal out. Indeed, dining out mattered more by now to the French middle classes than it did to, say, their English counterparts.

It was Pompon especially who wished to dine here, insisting that there was just as much snobbery in the culinary arts as in letters or painting, and that one could therefore dine as well at such a popular restaurant as anywhere in Paris. In fact, she expected that she was more likely to find in this place the fondly remembered but perpetually elusive aromas and flavors of her youth: mutton with young hen, minced meat with egg, and more, served up to her by an old baroness-aunt, and which their own cook, Joseph, could never seem to imitate. Louis was better disposed than Pompon to Joseph. Although a steady diet of Realist art and literature, with its main course of misery, might have damaged Louis's psyche, his father had fed him at least a single grain of saving good sense: an "invincible prejudice" toward restaurants. Even if their man Joseph failed to satisfy Pompon's childhood memories, he at least scoured the world for good ingredients and gathered sacred recipes whispered by distinguished chefs on their deathbeds.

The couple arrived in an immense hall, clinking with the "joyous sounds" of plates, glasses, and silver. It was absolutely packed, and to reach an empty table they had to walk through the "narrow avenues" separating many other tables and along the way inhale a "wild variety" of aromas. Finally they found a place near the door. Pompon ordered her mutton with young hen, followed by minced meat with egg, and topped off by strawberries and sugar. The waiter placed napkins and two portions of bread on the marble table, while Louis looked around. He decided quickly that what he disliked about such a place was "the promiscuity" of eating before so many people he did not know. Coatracks stood everywhere, piled with overcoats and capes, and there were mirrors behind them on all sides, so that the hall went

on infinitely. All this only added to the sense that one was eating under "the breath and eye of a thousand strangers." If one looked upward, there were galleries as well, with hundreds of diners, and the
incessant walking of waiters, back and forth, over one's head. The
mass of employees and merchants seated at the tables didn't seem to
care, but instead seemed delighted. Families eagerly took possession of
tables, children running ahead and hauling themselves up, impatient
for this extraordinary meal discussed for days. Their legs were "constantly in motion, full of happy fever." Mother followed, "dolled up in
her lovely toilette, scrubbed and soaped." Father was freshly shaven,
"full of a childish but proud air that he could sponsor such a party for
his wife and little ones," a day of happiness. And all this despite the
certainty that by ten o'clock that evening this man would be exhausted
from the exertions of the day, the woman ill-humored, and the children
almost certainly crying.

The meal was less memorable to Louis and Pompon than to those
around them. At first she optimistically insisted that this was the taste
she remembered! But her "small grimaces," and her failure to finish
her portions, betrayed her. Yet even if the food did not live up to Pompon's memories, Louis admitted that it was well prepared and fresh:
good bourgeois cuisine, without the annoying, predictable odors of a
more pretentious restaurant—namely, Madeira, truffles, and meat
broth. He would reserve judgment on the house wine, mindful of the
maxim that one knew only the next day whether wine was good. The
service was prompt, the only sin the rapidity of the army of rushed
waiters and their refusal to hear any complaints, such as "over-
cooked," "undercooked," or "too salty." And a few of his fellow diners perturbed him, some small outbursts of anger here and there "from
famished and forgotten clients," or the "sanguine airs of elderly drapers' assistants acting before their young misses as if they were gentlemen accustomed to being obeyed." All things considered, this Sunday
experience, like many others, wasn't quite for him, or even Pompon.

Neither was the walk she insisted upon taking later that day
through the garden behind the Louvre, nor the very bourgeois picnic
in the park she planned for their dinner. Luckily Louis escaped the picnic, for Pompon became preoccupied with confessing her disappointment at the afternoon's meal. While she spoke, he thought how

grateful he was to have escaped the horror of eating on the grass, sitting cross-legged in the midst of soiled napkins and newspapers. They finally returned to their own apartment, where Pompon reconciled with their cook, Joseph, having decided that all was indeed for the best in the best of all possible kitchens: their own.

THE INFIELD OF LONGCHAMPS

Despite their Sunday forays into the crowded boulevards, cafés, churches, and restaurants of Paris proper, on most Sundays Louis and Pompon followed the example of another great mass of Parisians and went in search of green.

The closest pastoral destinations were the parks just beyond the old city walls. And the most prominent of these was the massive Bois de Boulogne, on the western edge of Paris, erected as one of the two crowning jewels of the city's eighteen hundred new parks after 1850. Zola considered the Bois, despite its eighty-five kilometers of footpaths and extensive woods, to be part of the city still: he wanted working people to venture out even further for their Sunday promenades, away from unhealthy Paris. But for tens of thousands of working people seeking to avoid Paris's crowded streets, such parks were countryside enough; thus they flocked to the Bois on Sunday, and in even greater number to its counterpart on Paris's eastern border, the Bois de Vincennes. Both were inspired by the same model, Hyde Park in London, yet each possessed a distinctly different character. Boulogne was thronged daily, for it was a playground and fashion runway of the great. Vincennes came alive only on Sunday, when working people engaged in games and promenades. But on Sunday working people made their way to Boulogne as well, especially after late spring when the horse-racing season began, so that the Bois too felt different on that day. Races occurred daily at the track called Longchamps, a park within the Bois, where the biggest purses were offered on Friday but the biggest crowds arrived on Sunday. Indeed about forty thousand people frequented all of Paris's tracks on any given Sunday by now, a large chunk of them going to Longchamps.

Louis and Pompon had attended races here before, but for their special Sunday excursion they wanted a perspective different from their customary place in the grandstand. This time they would watch from the infield, where there were more bookmakers and smaller bets. And they would travel there by public omnibus rather than their usual landau, that favorite carriage of the great.

On the appointed Sunday, at the Place Clichy, toward the western edge of Paris, their omnibus did not arrive as expected. Louis and Pompon therefore walked on toward the Bois while bicycles, cabs, and many other forms of transport noisily bounced past on the cobblestones. Finally they spotted a monstrous *char à bancs* (or "wagon with benches") pulled by six horses—and with two places free! Ordinary omnibuses, pulled by a mere two or three horses and seating forty to fifty people, had by 1888 already carried 150 million passengers around Paris, contributing significantly to the city's racket and causing such sensitive souls as Marcel Proust to shut his windows and soundproof his walls with cork. But far more than fifty filled this gigantic heap approaching Louis and Pompon, who were motioned aboard by a woman in front. Did they hesitate? Guidebooks warned them that they should, "lest you deform your hat, your odor, and maybe your principles." Moreover, the drivers were supposedly untrustworthy, because they read "free-thinking papers," cast "gallant looks at skirts," saluted churches "with an air of irony" and wine merchants "with reverence," and talked woefully about their eleven children in hopes of a large tip. But there was no time to hesitate, for the wagon stopped only momentarily to pick them up, then rumbled on again with Louis and Pompon standing precariously on board, searching for the final two seats.

Where were those seats exactly? In front, came the answer. There they saw a tiny space on either side of a very large woman. The ride did not go smoothly in any sense. Some of the men ended up fighting over the merits of two racehorses, and in the ensuing fracas Pompon was nearly thrown from the wagon. The couple decided to walk the rest of the way. This gave them even more opportunity to observe the masses of humanity around them. All along the road, people played and sat on the tiniest bits of green. Chic mothers and fathers lined up their *chaises* and watched the finely dressed parade by. The well-to-do, making their "health promenades," were followed closely by their coaches, which stopped every six meters in order to stay behind their plodding owners. Among these, Louis and Pompon spied many acquaintances, but the acquaintances did not spy them, thanks to the couple's temporary bourgeois clothing.

At the track they paid one franc apiece to enter the infield, then crowded along the rope to watch the next race. All talk around them was of betting, and it was deadly serious: should I bet to win or to place? Hesitation abounded: am I right or wrong? The sport in the infield wasn't for fun; they weren't here primarily for the excitement of huge stakes or the chance to show off one's toilette, like Zola's Nana, who at Longchamps on Sunday held her blue silk sunshade while clothed in a dramatically "voluminous" dress, her pampered dog on the ground beside her. Instead, Louis and Pompon saw quickly that a bet of one hundred sous (or five francs) was of genuine importance to entire families for the coming week. Prognosticators circulated in the crowd, making people doubt themselves even more and predicting to each person a different winner; for when the race ended, of course, one of his "picks" would have won, and the prognosticator would have a new client for future races.

Louis's description of the race failed to match the brilliance of the scene in *Nana,* in which "the whole crowd had thrown themselves impetuously against the barriers, and a deep clamor issued from innumerable chests before the advance of the horses and drew nearer and nearer like the sound of a foaming tide. . . . A hundred thousand spectators were possessed by a single passion, burning with the same gambler's lust, as they gazed after the beasts, whose galloping feet were sweeping millions with them." Rather, Louis simply noted that when the race ended, the infield was full of excessive enthusiasm and dancing among some and only partly hidden despair among others. Cashiers walked around to make immediate payment, cocoa and *limonade* vendors sold their wares. Some ordinary people were certainly here to relax and enjoy the air and sun. But most were there for business. It was not fun here, Louis decided, nor on the wagons one rode to get here.

TO THE COUNTRY!

Even more foreign to Louis and Pompon than the infield of Longchamps were the mysterious great stretches of fields and woods beyond, where at least half of Paris seemed determined to go on Sundays—on foot, by train, or by bicycle.

Just as the industrial clock heightened the desire for Sunday, so did the enormous expansion of Paris heighten the desire for the country-side around it. David Beck could walk through the seventeenth-century Hague and into the surrounding woods in little time, with little effort, and in solitude. But for most Parisians the countryside lay much farther away, and the effort required to reach it was much greater, even after the establishment of trains in 1849 or the development of the bi-cycle from the 1880s.

Precisely for this reason, the idyllic quality of the countryside was magnified. A poem by Coubard d'Aulnay had a worker say that he se-questered himself for six days, "in our Babylon, with black soil and filth," and it was only natural that he sought the countryside on his day off. What was more idyllic than seeing the wagon of the produce man basking in the sun, his children pulling up weeds, and women gathering vegetables? Jean Gabin sang into the twentieth century that on Sunday, when all filed off to the suburb of Nogent, life was sud-denly charming. "How lovely everything becomes, when one prome-nades beside the water! What renewal! Paris in the distance is a prison to us now, the heart is full of songs. A single Sunday beside the water, the singing of small birds, make all other days lovely."

Some saw the countryside as an antidote to the city and its debauch-ery. Some saw it as simply a place where food and drink were cheaper than Paris, or the dance halls larger. Whatever their motive, to many Parisians, Sunday was a day to escape to the forests and water all around, or to the suburban villages whose names now rang out fondly in the most citified sections of Paris: Nogent, Argenteuil, Croissy, La Grande Jatte, and more. The downtown station of St. Lazare saw 203 trains departing and arriving each Sunday, carrying some 142,000 peo-ple, most headed to the fields and villages. Ironically, the countryside too might become crowded on Sunday.

Émile Zola was glad for it, and indeed thought it happened too rarely. Too many workers on Sunday stayed in their cramped, muddy section of Paris, such as the Mouffetard, because they did not know where to go for fresh air, or had too little money. Thus they settled for cabarets, or whatever low pleasure was at hand. Yet even in their absence the countryside was still full, as Zola himself knew: the heroine of his *Thérèse Raquin* and her small party walked "along roads and paths crowded with parties in their Sunday best. Girls in gay-colored frocks ran along between hedges, a crew of oarsmen sang as they passed, processions of worthy couples, elderly folk, office workers and their wives sauntered along beside the ditches. Every path seemed to be a noisy and populous street." Even "tarts from the Latin Quarter" were out in the suburbs, enjoying the sun and singing "a nursery round."

Pompon decided that they too should pursue this pastoral idyll, beyond Longchamps—and not on the train but on that latest symbol of industrial progress and mobility, the bicycle. Mass-production of bicycles began in the 1880s, and 375,000 had been sold by 1898 and 3.5 million by 1914. Pompon gave Louis a week to learn how to ride, though of course she required much less time herself to become proficient. She also made an appointment for them to acquire the proper clothing, from tailors who specialized in cycling gear. Louis wore an outfit of mouse-gray velvet muslin, an officer's "peaked cap with bouffant pediment" adorned by a medal saying TCF, plaid socks, spikes, and gloves of badger skin. Pompon wore a silk daffodil blouse and prune bouffant breeches, black socks with gold corners, black shoes with heels, a black boating cap with a cut feather, and a veil bound tightly to hold her hair. Anything they wished to carry was in a knapsack on their backs, including the inevitable new "kodak" to take pictures of their adventures, which was "sure to be broken into a thousand pieces" on their first fall.

Where were they going? They had no idea. The goal, gathered Louis, was simply to ride along the lovely routes leading away from Paris, and not to see the sights but simply to be able to say, "I covered so many kilometers today!" Anxious to avoid blowing out their tires, they chose routes with as few stones and as little mud as possible. Whichever paths they chose, there were swarms of cyclists all around. In fact, the farther they went, the more crowded it became, as if they were "in a river with a thousand tributaries." Pedestrians were so few that they received odd stares from the riders passing by, but they did not look for long. Glancing to left or right was a dangerous action, because of bumps in the road and the crowds. As for resting—that was why they had a kodak! Clack, Clack! There was no planning for such pictures, noted the painter Louis, no thought of angle or lighting, no solitary artist trudging along roads, burdened down by pallet and brushes and paint, seeking to find emotion, atmosphere, or fantasy. Instead there was simply running to some arbitrary point and clicking.

Still too preoccupied to talk to each other or fellow riders, Louis and Pompon soon lost track of the kilometers and whizzed past places most Parisians never saw, including the scores of cafés now popping up in the countryside and special stops for the repair of "sick tires." The road was completely covered, in two directions, with cyclists, so that all of humanity seemed to be on bicycles. Suddenly they scattered at the "terrible sound" of a horn—belonging to a car. This new invention, even more recent than bicycles, was still the exclusive toy of marquises, counts, barons, and other rich sportsmen, all of whom had left Paris later than Louis and Pompon but now arrived in the country before them. Some passengers in the car stood, some sat; all covered their heads with enormous goggles, the "queens" in the party behind windshields. If Louis lamented the bicycle, he lamented the automobile even more, especially on crowded Sunday afternoons.

After four or five hours Louis and Pompon finally arrived with the rest of the peloton at their "destination," in the woods near the famous royal château of Fontainebleau. Today this spot was serving as the finish line for a big race that had begun in Carcassonne, far in the south of France. The couple descended from their bicycles and watched fellow riders wipe off sweat and brag of their exploits. Within an hour the professional racers arrived, causing Louis and Pompon and the rest of the crowd to rush to the grandstand to see. Soon the exhilarated crowd was hoisting the winner's bicycle and cheering: he had broken some record by three whole seconds! But the winner himself lay in a tent, now with other riders, who all needed medical care. Louis and Pompon caught a brief glimpse of the champion, lying on his back, still in cycling posture, blood flowing from his nostrils, his face ashen gray. The cheering crowd seemed not to notice.

It wasn't long before there appeared overhead the great foe of all Sunday afternoon outings: a cloudburst. Everyone darted to the village seeking shelter. Louis and Pompon waited for a break in the weather, then rode to the nearest station, where, weary of Sunday cycling, they took a train back to Paris.

AND AGAIN!

From now on Louis and Pompon went only by train to the suburbs, and they went again and again. By the end of the summer they had visited on assorted Sundays all the great pleasure parks surrounding the city including Sceaux-Robinson, Versailles, Le Marne, Bougival, St. Cloud, and more.

Perhaps their favorite was Sceaux park, popularly called Robinson because of its well-known treehouse restaurants, inspired by the famous adventures of the Swiss family. On Sunday, Robinson was a favorite of students: unlike Louis's cousin Gontran, who stuck to his urban roots on Sunday and stayed in Paris, students who flocked to Robinson typically came from the provinces of France, finding in this park something of the rural flavor they knew at home.

But there was more than that: Robinson also had fantasy, including its "silly promenades on donkeys." Certainly much of the silliness stemmed from the students' immobility during the week and their "grateful release" from it on Sunday: how their spirits and muscles would atrophy "without a Sunday romp"! The study of law was punishing and boring, a knowledge of math required years of austere labor, medicine was not only difficult but full of sadness and disgust. No wonder, thought Louis while observing such fellows on the train, that today they wanted to climb onto a horse and laugh convulsively with friends. All had a little money from their parents to pass Sunday happily with each other and with plenty of young women "decked out a little like the devil."

The famous donkeys and horses of Robinson were the first thing Louis noticed upon arriving. All saddled and bridled, the poor beasts would need a whole week to recover from Sunday labors. The boys tried predictably to get their horses galloping, with little luck. The girls on donkeys were more picturesque, for the "badly coiffed appearance" of the animals contrasted humorously with the "delicacies of the young ladies." When the donkeys began trotting, hair came undone and toilettes unraveled, so that the scene was even more "rustic and burlesque." The boys did not mind, nor did Louis: it was a "grace to see their hair floating in the wind," and a "lovely occasion" for the girls "to show off legs and the roundness of their calves, to coquettishly reveal skirts and bloomers." And "if a small bit of pink flesh" appeared beneath her garters, then attention was rapt. A similar scene occurred when the girls ascended the swings hanging just outside Robinson's famous treehouses. The young men "can't keep their eyes off the dresses blowing in the wind, like butterflies. They're tantalized by it, and take the most poignant pleasure in the rapid seconds when the lower leg is revealed to them." Louis Morin, illustrator extraordinaire and frequent composer of frolicking nudes and "slightly undressed" figures, did not condemn the boys for their attentions. Instead he considered them preferable to the much fleshier exposures of the Moulin Galette or Moulin Rouge, and was pleased that there was "romance in the souls of these youth!" Louis did not mention Pompon's opinions on all this.

Also prominent in Robinson on Sunday was the singing. "Little groups form who hardly know each other, but they know the song and that's enough!" The appearance of a brass band, or fanfare, increasingly popular around Europe at the time, signaled that there was still more music to come, but this was a sight and sound Louis could have done without. Just as he feared, the "cacophonic orchestra, fifty instruments all in discord," suddenly broke out on the grand avenue of Robinson Park, with a predictable result: the mounts of the young ladies jumped, the young men grew furious, and the beasts fled. Accidents were also part of Sunday in Robinson.

Louis and Pompon could of course not leave this park without eating in one of the treehouses. As with his other experiences in public dining, Louis was not at ease here—this time less because of the food, which was pulled up on ropes, than the heights at which they dined. But the day was not wholly lost: watching the young men and women return late that evening from their promenades around the park, then climb onto trains, he guessed that most would get only a few hours of sleep that night, before taking up the puzzles of law and mathematics again in the morning. Yet this very vitality was what caused him to conclude, "Youth is beautiful!" Here was one of his truly enjoyable Sunday experiments.

He was less enthusiastic about other excursions to the countryside. The waters of Versailles were too crowded. A boat trip one Sunday toward the suburb of Nogent depressed him because of the endless, shapeless storefronts along the waterway. A journey toward Bougival was ruined by a well-meaning companion who, as "a disciple of Louis Pasteur," pointed out the infinite microbes around them in the food, the parks, the river, even on the people—making them afraid to eat anything so that they returned home that evening quite hungry. A Sunday spent in the fields, picking bouquets of wildflowers, of all things, had its charm, but Louis's gardener, unaccustomed to his employer's sudden interest in flowers and wandering in fields, told the maid that Louis was not well. An adventure to watch a line-fishing contest on one of the many crowded canals surrounding Paris was frustrating, as those fishing grew irritated at any observer who dared giggle or speak aloud. More fun was a visit to a suburban café-concert, where Louis and Pompon became mixed up with a wedding party, all of whom were soon at the mercy of Pompon's charms and graces. But this affair too ended badly for Louis when he suffered cramps and headaches after consuming, in order, *pommes frites,* fresh cow's milk, a *raspail* meant to counter the cramps, and finally an absinthe that caused him to pass out. A contented Pompon administered smelling salts to him and suggested he learn better the trick of emptying his glass under the table.

Clearly their results in the country were, as in the city, mixed. What tilted the balance once and for all against further excursions was the inevitably crowded train station each Sunday night. As the sun descended and bodies converged, people cried out names and laughed and sang, but then grew angry as the realization hit them that not only this train was full but the next one too, and the next after that. Thus commenced the pounding on windows, the rude gesturing at the train's employees, and the quarreling and uttering of oaths. Those lucky enough to be on board, including Louis and Pompon, were struck momentarily by the sight of the skyline of Paris coming into view: the 32,000 gas lamps showed the city to good effect. But it was not a quiet of awe or joy they felt: for most people it was the sobering thought of returning to "another asphyxiating week."

On disembarking from the Sunday night train, there was a final race among passengers, for the last Sunday night omnibus to their neighborhood. Here, thought Louis, was the real symbol of Sunday melancholy, for the omnibus quickly filled with sleepy people and crying children, but again not all could get on. These "sad beings" set out slowly on foot for distant homes. Bouquets they had picked, already limp, were tossed aside. Children were warned that they would not be carried, and "all the mamas were insisting that this was the last time, yes the last time," that they would follow the crowd to the countryside on Sunday.

PLEASURE TRAIN

Having gamely tried almost everything around Paris and its suburbs, there remained but one final popular adventure for Louis and Pompon: the Sunday pleasure train to the distant beach.

Long a place to avoid, the beach was by this time in fashion, especially on Sundays and in summer. For Parisians, this was often Le Touquet, or Paris-plage (Paris Beach), on the coast of Normandy. At the inevitably crowded station, with Louis plastered into the wall, the spirit of anticipation soared, and the "flame of enthusiasm" among those gathered helped ease Louis's momentary suffering. Pompon was her usual calm self, and she delighted in the scene, even when the waiting began to try everyone's patience and voices grew louder.

Louis noticed that people were in groups of five to ten, never in couples; the man of the people, he concluded, required an audience greater than his wife alone. The bigger the crowd, the bigger the laughter, and laughter was their measure of fun. In every group was an "Alfred," whose real name might be Jules, Edouard, or Gustave. He was the funny man of the group, and his hilarity would only expand with today's lighthearted mood. If there were two Alfreds in a group, so much the better, for each man would compete to be the funniest. Also striking was the extraordinary number of packages everyone carried—provisions, parasols, and suitcases—which must have been accumulated over at least ten days. Louis and Pompon, with no provisions except a purse, feared that they would be found wanting and be exploited in the cabarets and taverns at the seaside.

The gates to the platforms opened, and packages and people all squeezed through, racing to get to that most desirable of all places in each car: the corner seats. Pompon and Louis, unaware of this, sat naively in the middle, across from each other, amid "a shop of singing florists." "Parrotlike chatter" penetrated the din, and in no time at all the couple was quickly up to speed on their neighbors—the *monsieur* of the shop, his friend, and so on. Monsieur looked ready, under the severe stare of Madame, to fall asleep. Monsieur's friend was the Alfred of the group; Louis suspected that Madame had brought him along to direct all female attention his way, rather than toward Monsieur. The train pulled out, and the party grew more animated still.

The biggest preoccupation along the way proved to be eating and drinking. Food flew from packages and was passed endlessly back and forth and over and behind Pompon and Louis, who had "never smelled so much garlic sausage." The Alfred added to the hilarity by bringing out his potent little sack of Roquefort cheese, whose odor filled the air immediately, to his delight. Behind them they heard a man reproach his wife for having received a friend just when they were about to leave, causing them to arrive too late for a corner seat: "How comfortable is that, with all these packages you had to bring!" Louis could not see the couple, because there were indeed a lot of packages in the way, but he heard them well enough.

After a couple of hours of this, at last the sea approached and faces went to the windows. Some claimed to taste salt in their mouths already. All the florists inclined that way, their "small pink tongues agitating on their pale lips" to try to taste it themselves. Some were disappointed at seeing only water, having expected more. Others were in ecstasy, determined to find paradise here, whatever reality might bring. When the train stopped, everyone hurried out, Pompon right behind eager to follow. All the Alfreds made jokes, astonished that they could not see England across the way! Violating their usual rules, Louis and Pompon decided to leave the crowd and dine in a showy hotel, for they had no provisions and did not trust the ordinary cafés.

Soon, however, they returned to be among their new acquaintances
on the beach, who had just finished their picnics and were ready to begin exploring the ocean. The florists, as well as the (still) quarreling
couple, all wanted to taste the sea water, just briefly, and make the customary grimace. Some eagerly filled bottles, to show friends back in
Paris. Young ladies dipped their feet, shoes and socks off, skirts hiked
up to their calves, but not high enough, for even small swells soaked
them to their knees.

Toward four the tide rolled in and the moment for more serious
swimming approached. The economical pulled out their own swim-
suits, "constructed during wakeful nights" by mothers in anticipation
of this happy hour and decorated with the inevitable marine anchors.
Behind makeshift tents fashioned from open umbrellas, most noisily
changed their clothing, then ran into the sea. The woman of the quarreling couple had chosen a camisole and a linen petticoat, assured by
Monsieur that this would do at the beach, for this was what she wore
on warm days in Paris. She passed modestly before Louis and Pompon,
but the sea was "saving its treacheries for her." The first wave
drenched her wholly unsuitable costume, rendering it "a thousand
times more transparent" than anything ever worn at an ancient Roman orgy, Louis was sure. Mortified, the poor woman faced resolutely
out to sea, desperately calling for her husband, who finally came running, red and huffing, his feet cut by the rocks, and carrying a skirt and
bodice for her. But these too were soaked by the next wave, so that
Madame was forced to "duck under the water to preserve her modesty" until he could run and find something else. Louis and Pompon,
"overcome by discretion," looked away, but most observers, "a bit
cruelly," twisted with convulsive laughter. Louis was certain that in
this single incident there were grounds for a lifetime of quarrels.

Those who had not brought their own swimming outfits went to
rent one on the boardwalk, where they formed a "most marvelous collection of comic figures" sure to tempt the pen of any caricaturist such
as Louis Morin. Those who provided the costumes randomly handed
out suits left by past swimmers, regardless of the age, size, or gender
of the person now before them. As chance would have it, the skinniest
always got the largest suits, "disappearing in outfits of abundant
folds," while the large strained every button of some smallish suit. And

this was not to speak of color: black, blue, and red "had all acquired through the chemical reaction of sun and sea the most bizarre nuances," unknown even to the colorful palettes "of the English Pre-Raphaelites." One bathing cap reached above the ears, another past the neck, and all disappeared in the first wave anyway.

By the end of the day all were "wearied beyond measure," so that they scarcely had enough energy to get back to the train. And the disembarkment was pitiful, the ill, gray faces of the passengers telling everything. Here was the reward for their relaxing Sunday outing: sunburn, exhaustion, nausea. Louis and Pompon decided to wait, dine in a restaurant, and take a later train, again breaking their new Sunday rules. But they justified it by saying that they stayed behind in order to allow their traveling comrades extra space on the train back to Paris.

In the end, the greatest strength of *Parisian Sundays* is not merely the range of possible Sunday activities it describes, for other works did that too, but rather Morin's ability—despite his comic exaggerations and prejudices—to capture the hopes, disappointments, and meanings of the day for so many Parisians. It was never entirely clear where his own sympathies lay: he criticized the snobbery of *décadents* often enough in the book and found some virtues in the popular Sunday (Pompon almost always thoroughly enjoyed herself), but he also condescended and suffered real discomfort.

The final Sunday scene gives a last clue to his thoughts. Fittingly, he and Pompon chose the suburban park of St. Cloud, the most melancholy park of Paris according to Louis and thus ideal for contemplation. It was now autumn, and the trees shimmered with gold, brighter than ever in the sharp light of late afternoon. Despite gusting wind, there were the usual crowds of Parisians on every lane, determined to visit their parks, and heroically setting up picnics with their children.

Pompon was quieter than usual: was she contemplating a conversion to suburban or even country life? wondered Louis. No, she responded, she merely wondered whether Louis regretted all their Sunday promenades, for it wasn't as if all had ended happily. He did not regret them, he assured her: their excursions into Paris and environs had had an unexpected effect. Specifically, in contrasting his daily life of pleasure to the Sunday pleasures of the people, he had been forced to reflect, not always to his advantage, upon the snobbism he had practiced for so long. "Our kind lead a life far too refined: under the pretext that boredom is the sure fruit of uniformity, we despise uniformity and sweep out of our lives anything ordinary, common, vulgar, facile." Yet snobs grew bored nonetheless, running to foreign places and seeking exotic adventures, like Zola's Nana, whose "monotony of existence" included repeated "drives in the Bois, first nights at the theater, dinners and suppers at the Maison-d'Or or the Café Anglais, not to mention all the places of public resort, all the spectacles to which crowds rushed," just so that she might avoid solitude, "which brought her face to face with the emptiness and boredom within her." The Sundays of the "little people" were "no more ridiculous" than the pastimes of "our people," decided Louis. "We are full of chic," yet the people's Sundays were not necessarily any more vulgar, common, tedious, and clichéd than "our own."

With their Sunday experiment complete, would the couple then return to their old monotonous life? wondered Pompon. Perhaps. But Louis admitted that their Sundays had also caused to grow within him a wholly unexpected desire for the country! He didn't think it would last, but at that moment he, unbelievably, thought that he would like to try a life outside of town. In fact, soon after the publication of *Parisian Sundays,* the real Louis Morin did indeed move to the rural Loire valley. Eventually he felt "uprooted" there and so returned to the city. But such a daring experiment was surely the influence of the adventurous Pompon, who if not an actual person represented at least this protagonist's popular conscience—and such a conscience longed for the country on Sunday.

WORKING SUNDAY

For all of its insight and heroically broad sweep, Morin's *Parisian Sundays* largely avoids less pleasant aspects of the day of rest.

Even when he or his subjects were disappointed in the outcome of a Sunday, Morin took for granted one crucial thing: that great crowds of people in France were at least in a position to *try* finding that elusive, perfect day. What he neglected was another sizable crowd not able to do even this. Despite the filled pleasure palaces, museums, and parks of Paris and its environs each Sunday, many people were too busy working, or were too miserable, to join in the fun. Morin was aware of this. He knew that many in Paris would have gladly traded their Sunday of work or poverty for a Sunday of sunburn and inconvenience at the beach, or a few caterpillars and cloudbursts at the park. But he chose mostly to ignore that fact, determined as he was to show the lighter side of things, always. Extended exposure during his childhood to the Realism of late-nineteenth-century letters and art had failed to convince him, he explained, that a relentless focus on the ugliness of life had done much to improve life or "to halt the tripling of suicides in France." His remedy was to find what fun and joy he could in his society and its Sundays, even though he knew perfectly well the less pleasant aspects. Not even the death of Morin's only son, Jean, at the slaughter of Verdun during World War I would alter Morin's determination to show the lightness of life in his art.

Yet Morin's approach to art and life obviously did not remove France's woes. Indeed if Paris, and its Sundays, was a place of style and fun in the late nineteenth century, it was just as much a place of struggle and misery. For masses of people it was no Belle Epoque at all, but a time of bitter conflicts over class, labor, and religion, of the infamous Dreyfus affair that revealed widespread anti-Semitism, and of 300,000 deaths from smallpox between 1875 and 1905. One guidebook went against its usually cheery genre in freely admitting Paris's many problems, but even that was ultimately to exploit them: promising a change of pace from the usual tourist attractions, it was titled, *Paris horrible et Paris original* (1882) and included a chapter on "Thirty-Six Ways to Steal." Zola urged working people to avoid the Bois de Boulogne on Sunday not only because it was too close to Paris but because upon seeing all the wealthy "rascals" around them at the park, they would angrily wonder why such rascals earned so much while workers earned so little.

But again, anyone in any park on Sunday at least had the day free. For an unmeasurable but visible enough minority of workers in the nineteenth century, Sunday was like any other day. This, ironically, was something they had in common with the leisured classes, but in much different fashion: the leisured Sunday included discretionary work and play, while the working Sunday was filled with compulsory work alone.

How could this want of Sunday have come about, when the idea of a Sunday free from labor had been almost universal in Europe since the Middle Ages? The French Sunday had long been such a free day as well. It underwent small changes regularly, such as the stunning music, wigs, and pomp of church services during the eighteenth century, and the even greater stress on play after 1730, to the chagrin of certain church and civic leaders. But the essential element of a free Sunday was long intact. So popular was Sunday in old France that it withstood attempts to abolish it during the Revolution; in 1792 the most radical imposed a new ten-day week and renamed months and days. Yet even before this revamped calendar was officially dropped in 1805, the vast majority of French were already ignoring it and continuing to observe their old Sunday.

What threatened Sunday most came after the Revolution in France: again, industrialization and urbanization. If the greatest threat to the old religious Sunday had long been excessive play, the greatest threat to Sunday after industrialization was excessive work. The new industrial clock culture heightened the importance of Sunday's free time for those who *had* free time, but for some the industrial clock never stopped. With efficiency-driven shop and factory owners determining most of France's laws after 1830, there was little to prevent them from requiring hungry, poorly paid workers to labor seven days a week. An 1814 Sunday law that restricted both labor and play was largely ignored for decades.

By the mid-nineteenth century, France had the least regulated labor force and longest working day and week of any industrial nation. Workers who refused to labor on Sunday could easily enough be replaced. Many bosses held, like Saint Benedict, the ancient idea that workers would dissipate free time if they had it; hence both individual and society were better off if people worked instead. Indeed the French bourgeoisie championed, if less famously than in England or the United States, the spread of a "work ethic," suggesting that work was not just a necessity but a noble form of devotion. Bosses also largely suppressed the old, inefficient tradition of frequent holy days, still present in largely Catholic France.

The seven-day work week in French cities began to crumble only after 1850, when voices for a weekly day of salaried rest grew louder. The old religious arguments for Sundays free of work were still championed by the Catholic Church (and by smaller Protestant churches); but the churches' arguments were, alone, no longer broadly appealing enough to arouse popular support. Other tactics were developed instead. Even religious-minded people began stressing the importance of a free Sunday on the basis of hygiene, relaxation, and self-improvement, not to mention the need to counter a declining birthrate: lack of free time on Sunday deprived workers of the "joys of the hearth." A typical title was J. Lefort's *On Weekly Rest, from the Point of View of Morality, Culture, Intellectual Life, and Industrial Progress.*

The campaign for a free Sunday succeeded first among industrial workers. Such novelists as Charles Dickens in England and Émile Zola in France had in decades past championed the cause of a shorter workweek, with at its heart a free Sunday. Now well-organized unions and moralists picked up the theme and emphasized its tangible benefits for both workers and bosses: a weekly day of rest, even paid rest, made workers more efficient, productive, and reliable than did a seven-day week, and thus a factory could earn more.

Reliability was the cornerstone of this argument, as industrial bosses were still fighting the old irregular weekly rhythms of the former craft system. Craft workers had typically taken two days off each week, and not Sunday but rather Monday and usually Tuesday. "St. Monday" was their day for reverie with fellow workers, but it often spilled over. When the craft workers entered the new factories, they brought St. Monday, and its frequent drinking companion, Tuesday, and even part of Wednesday, with them. But such irregularity simply did not fit the industrial timetable, certainly not when factories ran seven days. By 1880 the sides had developed a compromise: bosses would guarantee one day off each week, Sunday, if workers would give up St. Monday once and for all. Most workers agreed.

The free Sunday of factory workers inspired employees in other occupations, more numerous by far in still-industrializing France, to seek the same, starting with the new, large department stores. After 1880 these also regularly closed on Sunday, although Denise of Zola's *Ladies' Paradise* suggested that it wasn't always much of a day off: her weekday hours were so long that Sunday remained her only day to clean at home and bosses might whimsically decide to rearrange the store on Sunday. Long less successful in securing at least an official free Sunday were the employees of France's countless small shops. Shopkeepers argued that Sunday was the only day many of their working customers could shop. And precisely because large stores were closed, Sunday was a day for small shops to pick up business and stay afloat. In fact, Sunday was their biggest day of the week, and they needed their one or two employees to work that day. There were also culinary reasons to stay open on Sunday: bakers knew that their fellow French would not tolerate stale bread on any day, while all sorts of other fresh products were needed for the inevitable special Sunday dinner. Finally there were intangible arguments for Sunday shops: "commercial animation" was what made the atmosphere of a French Sunday "so agreeable" in comparison to the gray English Sunday, where everything was shut tightly up. But it was also true that the employees who made that animation possible enjoyed no lively Sunday at all themselves.

These are of course generalizations. They take on greater meaning and nuance when a few flesh-and-blood examples are added.

Some of the best emerge from a remarkable collection of interviews gathered over forty years by the pioneering sociologist Frédéric Le Play. Carried out among the working classes of France, the interviews make clear that to understand workers' Sundays, one must understand as well their weekdays and general living conditions.

One memorable couple, named Jean and Marie, lived on a quay in the ninth arrondissement of Paris. Like millions of others in the city, both had been born in the provinces but later moved to Paris to find work. In their early forties at the time of the interview, they had two children still living—Marie had given birth to four others, but all had died of "intestinal afflictions" before eighteen months. Their apartment was on the top, or sixth, floor and consisted of two modest, simply furnished rooms: the windowless entry room, where the children slept, and the main room with a dormer window, where the couple slept. The ceiling in each was about six and a half feet high.

Jean, of medium size with thinning hair and traces of smallpox from when he was three years old, had left home at fourteen to learn carpentry. His *compagnonnage,* or trade union, gave him his craft, his morals, and instant social connections with three thousand other carpenters of Paris. Work had been fairly regular over the years, save for one period when he had been humiliated by having to sell newspapers in the street, then fruits and vegetables at Les Halles (the famous open market) with Marie. Otherwise, from March to December his workdays were ten hours long; from December to February, if there was work, only eight. Save for two weeks of vacation each July, he worked every day, including most Sundays. Only the first Sunday after payday, when there was a bit more money to celebrate with the family, did he have Sunday free. He did not attend church that day, but he did not dissipate his free time either. Rather, he conducted himself "in all decency" and applauded the progress of his fellow workers in improving "their habits of drunkenness and debauchery once all too evident on Sunday."

Marie, of medium size with chestnut hair, "good humor," and "intelligence," came to Paris when she was twenty-two, weary of the "brutalities of her drunken father," and found employment in domestic work. There she learned the habits and skills of economy that she still used in her family, so that she could even send a little money to her impoverished mother. She had once learned the trade of a polisher but was forced to quit because of a "paralysis" in her right arm. Now she devoted all of her energy to household tasks—making and remaking shirts, pants, and work clothes, and doing some outside sewing for pay as well. Sunday was only a little better for her. She usually attended Mass that day with the children, although she admitted having "no religious zeal," except for fasting on Good Friday.

Like Jean, Marie looked forward to that Sunday of the month right after payday. Then the family went out together and usually walked down the Champs-Élysées in their Sunday clothes, or made a promenade near some old fortifications around the city. Some workers stayed away from crowded boulevards on Sunday, mostly to avoid stark and humiliating confrontations with the superior Sunday-fied toilette of the bourgeoisie walking past. Jean wore a topcoat, his fourteen-year-old dress suit from his wedding, and its accompanying cashmere vest, black silk hat, and black satin tie. Marie wore her dark secondhand Sunday dress, a black wool overcoat, a shawl, hood, black tulle bonnet, and high-button shoes. She rarely wore her black silk wedding dress, even on Sunday.

On their Sunday outings they usually bought a few small things for the children, aged twelve and seven. Four Sundays per year they alternated visits with a cousin who also lived in Paris, and dined together—usually in a bit more style than on weekdays. This meal was the same each time, so that expenses were equal on both sides: *pot-au-feu* (stew), ragout of lamb or veal, salad, fruit, a small cup of coffee with water, and a small glass of spirits. A few other exceptions occurred too. Twice in their thirteen years in Paris the couple had saved enough money to attend the annual ball of the *compagnonnage*. And very occasionally Jean's boss distributed "drink money" at the completion of a job, which they used for the great treat of a meal in a restaurant. Almost certainly this occurred on Sunday, as in Zola's *L'Assommoir,* where working families on Sunday crowded together to eat fried fish in the garden of a restaurant, which did almost all its business that day. If Jean and Marie ever went out with others on Sunday, they divided up the cost between them, "never arguing over the odd penny." When simply at home on Sundays, Jean and Marie and their two children often entertained themselves by playing with their caged canary.

Another worker in Paris, from the Auvergne, was one of the few remaining water-carriers in the city by around 1880. He lived near the fountain on the Place St. Michel, where one could still take water freely. Burdened on his back by a pole with a full bucket of twenty liters on each end, he made thirty to forty trips a day up and down stairs. On Sunday he rarely attended Mass, because he had little time for it, much less for recreation that day—no balls, no shows, no cabaret, no tobacco. Two or three times a year he dined on Sunday evenings with friends in the suburb of Grenelle, and in the winter he sometimes received those same friends with crêpes, wine, spirits, and cards—the loser paying the expenses of the meal.

Restricted on Sunday more by her poverty than by her job was a certain "sewing maid" *(lingère)* named Sophie-Victoire, of Lille, in northern France, a woman "at the bottom of society." One of nine children, both her mother and father had died when she was young.

Charitable institutions helped some but "embarrassed" Sophie-Victoire as well; seeking to avoid them, she sought help elsewhere and was easily "seduced" by a young man and became pregnant. Abandoned by the young man, and now her angry family as well, Sophie-Victoire and her new baby fell into even deeper destitution.

Since then she had learned to make a living sewing from her miserable room, ten hours a day, earning about one-third the income of Jean the carpenter in Paris. Her nourishment, and that of her child, now seven and pale and skinny, was "almost perpetual abstinence." For breakfast they had a little bread in milk or chicory, then bread and potatoes for lunch, and bread in milk for supper. Coffee was rare, wine nonexistent. As a result, she and the child were regularly sick, usually with violent migraines accompanied by vomiting; and when sick, of course, she earned no money at all, for she was paid by the piece. The apartment only aggravated their poor health. It was a single room on the predictable top floor, with a single window in the ceiling, bare walls, sad furniture, and a cholera bed, so-called because it was the usual bare model used by cholera patients. There was a straw mattress, a sign that Sophie-Victoire had not quite reached the absolute bottom of poverty, for the last thing to be pawned was one's mattress. There was also a small stove, but she could not afford fire anyway and in winter simply wrapped her child in more layers of her own clothing to keep him warm.

Sunday did nothing to relieve this misery, for though she went to Mass she understood little of it, and she was ashamed to wear her everyday clothes—her Sunday best she had long ago taken to the pawnshop. After church she at least did not work at her job, but she had no time or money for Sunday recreations and usually spent the day washing her floor, cleaning the room, laundering, making food, and mending their clothes. Her biggest recreation was the very occasional Sunday dinner with the extended family who had not rejected her; this dinner featured seasoned rabbit with onions and prunes.

And so it went among Le Play's multitude of workers, from the better-off to the poorest, varying from a fairly regular free Sunday to a very occasional. A fifty-nine-year-old laborer in Paris, whose forty-three-year-old wife had endured nineteen pregnancies, worked hard but had no money or time for the cabaret, tobacco, and other recreation on Sunday; he rarely even took his children on free walks in the nearby public garden, but for relaxation very occasionally attended the evening service at church. A more fortunate woman, married to a cabinetmaker of Paris, attended Sunday Mass as a girl, to show off her toilette, but today she and her husband preferred socialism and regarded Sunday as a time for family parties, including excursions to the Bois de Vincennes to ice skate in winter or picnic in summer. She still liked to dress in her best on Sunday. On some Sundays her husband played billiards with friends in a café, the loser buying lunch, or they visited a café-concert or theater when someone happened to give them tickets. A surveyor for a factory in Guise took his family each Sunday to a garden in the suburbs and cultivated vegetables, eating the same food on Sunday as other days but always improving the Sunday meal with good wine. And a tailor in the provincial town of Meusnes took his only child to Mass each Sunday, partly because the man was paid after Mass at the office next door to the church. Upon receiving his pay, he went to a café, followed by a visit to the home of a friend to play cards; in the afternoon he worked in his garden, just like medieval peasants.

Even more burdened by Sunday labor than Le Play's workers was that great symbol of overwork in France, the postmistress. The first female directors of French post offices were appointed in the eighteenth century, and by 1863 there were more women than men as directors and distributors, some 3,900 of them. Especially the women were "doomed to slavery," as one commentator put it, expected to work fourteen-hour days seven days a week. This resulted from an old belief, evident beyond France too, that if the mail stopped, the country would stop. Hence there was no free Sunday, no distinction at all among days, for the postmistress; and because of her gender she could rise only to the second-highest of four levels of pay. That an overwhelming surplus of women kept applying to such positions says something about the opportunity it seemed to represent, but that very surplus was what kept the postmistress's existence so miserable: if one person would not carry out the impossible task, someone else would.

A postmistress of 1870 put her day, including Sunday, into verse form. She arose at four, in order to meet the courier bringing the mail to her office. Get up, she urged her body, even though she had just finished her work of the previous day only hours before. How she envied the austere Trappist, Carmelite, and even Chartreuse monks, for they had at least six hours of sleep and did not have to work when sick! She entered her cold office, with no time to light a fire, despite her cruel rheumatism or inflammations: the courier could not wait, and the letter carriers would arrive soon after.

When she opened the window to the public, they made demand after demand and handed her a stream of poorly packaged items that they expected her to repack—"surely it's not much trouble"—because they were in a hurry. Or a young lady would ask her to double-check for a letter from a lover but "please don't tell my mother." She was followed invariably by the mother herself, demanding to see any letter sent to her minor daughter, barely sixteen, and ranting when informed that a letter could be delivered to the addressee only. "Do you mean to tell me that a mother has no right to intervene in the life of a crazed child?!"

Another postmistress listed the basic requirements of the job, Sunday or other days: always show patience and friendliness to the public, learn the entire postal code, work thirty years in the same place, and pay heed to "an immense concert of lamentations in this human purgatory," not to mention the same inane comments and questions over and over again, or the umpteenth lawsuit caused by an error in the books because she had worked too fast. Yet another developed the twenty-seven commandments of the job, including: Always a slave you will be, feast day and Sunday alike; you may have no heart or spirit; you must never ask for justice; you must renounce promotion; you will eat rarely with your family (if you have one); you will hide your talents from the world; you will never have rest; you will never make mistakes without a lawsuit; you will never attend a party or visit your parents without an inquest; you will endure the ill treatment of the public; never respond proudly; you will renounce the joys of the world for thirty years; you will not marry without the consent of your boss; you will never be sick unless you pay your replacement yourself; and you will say all the while Blessed be God and the government. Such was the Sunday, and every day, of the postmistress.

———

By the end of the century, momentum to secure Sunday rest for all workers was strong in France. Various unions took the lead: in 1890 there were two popular demonstrations for Sunday rest, by 1905 there were twenty-three. Small-shop employees complained publicly now of the strenuous physical effort masked by their nice bourgeois clothes (43 percent of employees in coiffeur shops died before age thirty-nine, for instance), the poor pay (and women usually earned less than half of what men did), the difficulty of quitting an unpleasant job (your boss would speak poorly of you to other bosses), a long working day (often fifteen hours), and among women the unwanted advances of male superiors on any day. Around the rest of Europe and the U.S., the pattern was the same.

Such arguments began to overwhelm the resistance of shop owners in France. Finally in 1906, despite the opposition of small shop owners, and under pressure from unions, religious groups, and violence against stores that refused to close, France became one of the last European nations to pass a law that guaranteed workers the right to have twenty-four hours off every seven days. It did not guarantee that Sunday would be the day, but most workers assumed it. The French law came nearly thirty years after the first nation to pass such a law (Switzerland in 1877) and one year before the last (Italy).

Certainly loopholes remained. The 1906 law exempted domestic, rail, and agricultural workers, whose hours were still potentially unlimited; indeed agricultural workers were said to be working more often on Sunday than in the past. Plenty of problems remained with the law as well, such as there being far from enough inspectors to enforce it. Moreover, the 56 percent of married French women employed in 1906 were also expected to do the household work, including shopping, and Sunday was their best day to do so. Finally, almost all workers wanted Sunday off, not another day, because Sunday was the most common day off for family and friends. This would be solved only in 1919, with the adoption in France of the "English week," which meant that workers had Saturday afternoons off for shopping.

Hence if Louis Morin's Sunday scenes included a huge portion of working people, they were not the same people out each week, and some never got out at all. Before and even after 1906 Sunday was a working day for a significant minority of the French.

While Morin deliberately left unsketched such darker contours of a French Sunday, other observers did not.

Zealous condemnations by Sabbatarian-minded English and American critics, of the overwork and overplay that they saw in an active French Sunday, were regular and predictable. More striking was the large number of unfavorable accounts left by native French artists, novelists, and journalists. These stood in sharp contrast to already popular images of the French Sunday as one long, licentious carefree day of pleasure. That such native accounts were more numerous than favorable accounts was likely because the overwhelming majority of the French simply pursued their cherished Sunday rather than write about it. As in most societies, only a few bothered to reflect critically, in writing or in other enduring forms, on the regular, accepted doings of their world. Yet it is these reflections that typically survive.

Most critical accounts by the French themselves focused upon the bourgeois Sunday, which the largely bourgeois authors knew painfully well. In fact, if the limited and even nonexistent working-class Sunday was one part of the day's darker contours, then the banality and emptiness of the bourgeois Sunday expressed in these accounts was another.

A few critical accounts share Morin's generally light touch. Charles Foley's satirical monologue, "Sundays of a Bureaucrat," has the man recall, in a tone of resignation, the misadventures that seemed to follow him on Sundays. He loved his "charming wife" and his four "chubby children as plump as brioches" but he dreaded the long excursions she insisted upon, every sunny Sunday, to the Bois de Boulogne. The children cried out they were hungry, then became sick from eating too much spice bread, and to top it all off the clear skies turned black with rain and soaked them through—including his wife's flimsy pink sun umbrella, now bleeding red. The bureaucrat ended up walking home, as there wasn't enough room for him in the cab that they were fortunate enough to hail.

But many such accounts carried a more tragic tone. Zola's *Thérèse Raquin* portrays miserable Sunday walks on the Champs-Élysées by the bored bourgeois heroine, who felt compelled to "stop in front of shop windows with silly wonderment, silly comments and silly silences" simply because her husband loved to show her off that day. Sunday also gave him greater opportunity, during long picnics in the fields beyond the suburbs, to tell "feeble stories" about his job, which moved her to pretend to sleep. Guy de Maupassant's dour "Sundays of a Bourgeoisie" featured a pathetic, middle-aged, fourth-class government clerk who stumbled through a succession of dreadful Sundays in the countryside, which had very little that was humorous or redeemable. More ominous was his Sunday story "Two Friends." It began with two old drapers, during the Franco-Prussian War, happily deciding to go fishing together, as they used to on Sundays before the war, and ended with them being shot as spies.

Even the most famous visual reflection on French Sundays, Seurat's *Sunday on the Island of La Grande Jatte,* was meant more likely as a criticism of Sunday than a celebration. One may certainly see Seurat's depiction of this favorite suburban destination as an idyll, with the cane-holding figure possibly representing how lovely it was to do nothing, to abandon one's dignity for a day! Others have read the painting as an illustration of the happy mixing of working classes and bourgeois enjoying Sunday afternoon along the Seine. But still more have read it as a show of the banality of the bourgeois Sunday promenade, without real pleasure and instead a series of clichés, engaged in because everyone else was engaging in them. As for social mixing, there is little of it at all; rather, the figures happen to be near one another yet remain lonely, remote, inhuman, and joyless—suggesting the alienation and divisions of modern life.

Arguably the darkest Sunday of all came from the "Bohemian" Jules Vallès, in his *The Sundays of a Poor Young Man: The Seventh Day of a Condemned Soul.**

The term "Bohemian" has many definitions, from the scholarly "appropriation of marginal lifestyles by young and not so young bourgeois, for the dramatization of ambivalence toward their own social

---

*The subtitle reveals that the notion of Sunday as the seventh day was present even in non-Puritan France.

identities and destinies" to the simpler "pursuers of art," the "under-world," and followers of a "gypsy lifestyle." In late-nineteenth-century France, all those with any artistic pretensions seemed to be calling themselves Bohemian. Some were posing or passing through a stage, but some were deadly serious, especially about their art, their inde-pendence, and their rejection of bourgeois society, from which most of them had come. In all these respects they resembled *décadents,* but there was at least one unmistakable difference: Bohemians were des-perately poor. While the purses of "dandies" were, according to the poet Baudelaire, "long enough to indulge without hesitation their slightest whims," Bohemians slaved away at their writing or painting with little return.

Many Bohemians were proud of that fact and wore poverty as a sign of commitment to true art and its necessary rejection of the world. They stubbornly refused to take, at least for long, the ordinary office jobs and steady incomes that their family connections might have se-cured for them, fearing that such would mean the acceptance of a pre-dictable bourgeois fate. They would stick it out in their art and condemn society—especially bourgeois society—for not understanding and supporting them better. And naturally this extended to Sunday, one of the great bourgeois institutions.

Vallès himself came to Paris as a student in 1848 but was soon es-tranged from his bourgeois father. Desperate for money, he worked among other things as a journalist and eventually ran for political of-fice as the "the deputy of misery." In 1861 the agitating newspaper *Le Figaro* published serially Vallès's bitter account of Sunday, as seen through Bohemian eyes. Other Bohemians would leave similarly bleak portrayals of Sunday—the poet Jules Laforgue comes to mind, for in-stance. But this Sunday by Vallès displayed most convincingly the sort of Realism blamed by Louis Morin for France's increase in suicides. To heighten the sense of misery, Vallès used the second person and the present tense, putting the reader right in the young man's shoes.

Your Sunday begins at eight, no later, because for "men of letters" the day to sleep in is Saturday. On Sunday there is too much anticipa-tion and noise in the stairwell, as it is full of "running, colliding, cry-ing, singing, embracing, and big laughing." The heavy monotone of the church bell makes it hard to sleep anyway. It's pale and melancholy outside, and your heart tightens—why? A lacuna in one's novel, an improbability in one's article, a hole in one's pants? Certainly all of these, but even more deflating is this: IT IS SUNDAY. And as usual, it will be long and sad.

You hear footsteps and fear a creditor. But it's Sunday, so it's a different sort of creditor: a friend from whom you have borrowed a suit and he needs it back. The suit has been soaked in beer in numerous brasseries, and you brush it while the lender speaks worriedly of his small children. He leaves only because someone else is knocking: the laundress, who's brought your weekly wash and has stuck a white butterfly to the top shirt. It says, "3 francs." You have only one. How to escape? Give her more laundry, or a book by a friend marked "3 francs" inside. You wash, dress, and head downstairs, twenty sous in your pocket. The street is different today, everyone going fast, lots of gloves and canes. "Sunday is the Mardi Gras of gloves and canes." Tailors carry packages, for Sunday is the day of bargain prices on frock coats and breeches, if you dig deeply enough in the pile. Two "consumptive horses" pull a muddy cab, while a "dog-tired simpleton" sleeps on the shoulder of a prostitute. Where are your friends, who might ease your boredom? On Sunday they're at father's, a mistress's, or like you looking for something to eat.

You take your usual morning fare at the creamery, some rice and chocolate, but the clientele is different today. Some smile at you like a comrade in misery; others won't share the free newspapers. The waitress is sad, the milk sour, and you don't have enough money for something more. Where to borrow money today . . . the pawnshop! Your trousers and coat are still worth something. But what a fool: on Sunday pawnshops only redeem, they do not lend. The government has decided that no one is hungry on Sunday, no one needs money on Sunday to pay a doctor. At least today you do not have to suffer the humiliation of placing your shirt or blanket on the pawnshop's counter, having the man sniff it for a terrible minute while you go cold with agony, and hearing him declare: "We cannot take this, items must be worth at least three francs."

You head to the morgue with everyone else, out of curiosity. Then a café, where today it's more agitated than in the week: people play interminable card games, or "filthy dominoes," or bump you in the head

with their billiard cues. But there are always cheery fellows, with pink
expressions and long waistcoats and yellow gaiters, happy to buy you
a proper drink. Worst is when you leave, for you trip over an assortment of dogs, children, and skirt hems, while people mutter "Lout!"
"Clumsy!" and someone else calls your name—a creditor! "Did you
forget about me?" he asks with feigned discretion, so that every head
turns.

You try Mass but find this depressing as well: people are indifferent,
there is much flirting, and when you drop a paltry sou into the collection bag upon exiting, the woman holding it gives you a dirty look.

You try the street, mostly empty and silent by afternoon. Stores are
closed, doors are shut, for all of Paris is outside on the boulevards, in
the parks, or in the suburbs. You join the promenade but regret it, for
there is the shame of moving among the sparkling new toilettes while
wearing a threadbare overcoat and reddish cap. And you don't dare
look any lovely women in the face, draped in their silk and velour ar-
mor. Worst of all, you hear the jangle of coins in the pocket of even the
humblest employee or craftsman; in your pocket there's an incomplete
manuscript crumpled on the edges. All pleasures are forbidden you
without money, even the café-concert, for they expect you to buy
something. What about love? Ah, a poor young man has for a mistress
only the mistress of everyone else, or someone's wife. That of everyone
else goes today where pockets are full, while someone's wife is at home
on Sunday.

By six the gardens and parks are empty, the streets repeopled, and
restaurants begin to fill. The restaurant bosses stretch out linens, fill
carafes, and prod the chef. Families sit down, "kidneys leap in delight,
the bourgeoisie tremble with anticipation, and the orgy commences before your eyes." The view of the fine food puts your stomach in a bad
humor, the "molars gnashing together, the stomach quivering. Your
tape worm struggles, for all men of letters carry one inside them."
Your dream is to do as all the world does today—to dine!

The bookstores are all closed. You pass by even finer restaurants,
the aromas "taking you by the throat" so that you stop and stare with
haggard eye. The cooks are dressed in white, like attendants at ancient
altars, teasing the fire, passing a plump partridge along the spit, or
tending the legs of mutton "crying warm tears in the dripping pan."

The "onions simmer, the butter sings," and outside you are cold and hungry. There's a family in the street of Perpetual Fasters, where you can take your Sunday meal at eight, but the father goes into contortions if anyone speaks of painting, theater, or novels.

And so you return home. On the way you might enter a brasserie where two hundred people are jammed inside, but you don't know a soul: it's all families and couples. In your own quartier the streets were sad at midday—what about now? They are death. Just yesterday people collided in them, goods were displayed, but tonight the gas is off and the doors are shut. Drunkards and embracing couples stand against the dark walls. The grocer is open, but he's reluctant to come from the back room, where he's playing cards with his family; when taking your last sou, he says not a word of thanks, then quickly ducks back inside. The "Herbalist and Leeches" is open, it's always open, displaying its mysterious bottles, powders, handcuffs, forceps, sponges, and ointments, but you've never seen anyone go inside. You don't go there either.

You finally reach your room, number 19 at the Hotel Etoile, somber and sad. Yesterday you were troubled by noise; today you are troubled by the silence. There's only the sound of church bells now, telling you that you are aging, sadly and unknown to others, so that the days are long and the years short. You think about the Sundays of your youth in the provinces, which passed so quickly and happily. You go to bed but don't sleep. You sit at the table to write, but you write poorly. "It's a beastly day, full of chagrin, Sunday."

If such devastating observations as all these were even close to the truth, one wonders what kept pulling and pushing crowds of people to the boulevards and suburbs on Sunday. There was no single answer, of course, for anyone. Most obviously, as even Maupassant admitted, plenty of people truly enjoyed their Sunday, and that kept them looking forward to the next; indeed even one good Sunday could be enough, despite frequent disappointments, to keep hope alive. Only a very few people saw Sunday through Bohemian eyes.

But the answer most critics gave as the deepest motive for Sunday-going, especially among the bourgeoisie, was the force of bourgeois habit, including the constant pressure to keep up with neighbors. People at Morin's beach outing filled their jars with water mainly to show their friends. The chief desire of Maupassant's clerk was to be able to tell neighbors of his tremendous success at fishing. And even a guidebook poked fun at people whose chief purpose on Sunday, miserable or not, seemed to be that they wished to tell others they had spent their Sunday in the country! The packed railway stations, the joining of the insatiable quest for green, the impossibility of getting a good meal in a crowded country restaurant or a good piece of beef in a depleted country store, the possibly poisonous mushrooms everyone loved to pick, the enthusiastic gardeners on their tiny plots of land outside Paris who after great labor at last picked a melon the size of a small nut, the cloudbursts that soaked chiffon dresses and created form-fitting trousers (usually to great disadvantage)—for what were they all endured? Or more precisely, why were they so easily forgotten, and the day glorified anyway, and the pursuit begun again the very next Sunday? Because no matter how frightful the day in reality, said critics, people were determined to make their Sunday live up to the expectations that they, and their neighbors, imposed upon it.

Such native depictions of predictable, conformity-inspiring, even disastrous Sundays stood in sharp contrast to the popular image of the French Sunday as one long, carefree day of pleasure.

HOLY SUNDAY

There is one final native view to consider of the French Sunday, and that came from religious quarters.

Whereas Jules Vallès and other bourgeois critics disliked Sunday for its emptiness, some others disliked the French Sunday, even in supposedly irreligious France, for the most old-fashioned of reasons: because it offended religion. Some of these quite traditional voices even claimed, like their medieval predecessors, to be supported by Mary, the Queen of Heaven herself.

On a June Sunday in 1873, in the southern French village of St. Bauzille, Auguste Arnaud, thirty-two years of age, went to work in his vineyard. Like medieval peasants, he worked briefly on Sunday mornings, ordinarily from five until seven, when he stopped to eat a modest breakfast at the edge of the vines. After eating, he leaned back and smoked, contemplating his neatly cultivated rows and anticipating what was sure to be an abundant harvest this year. Suddenly there appeared not two meters from him an "extraordinary personage" in the form of a woman, standing above him in the air, about one and a half meters off the ground. Her costume was of a "dizzying whiteness," her head was covered by a crown and white veil, and a "resplendence" extended from the summit of her crown to below her feet.

Auguste's first reaction was stupefaction, even fear. But he was calmed by a light "more radiant than what he saw with his own eyes," which revealed to him the miserable state of his soul and the evil of working on Sunday. He fell prostrate, stricken by the knowledge of his faults, yet he also felt a sweet confidence descend upon him, which gave him hope. When he finally gathered courage to ask who she was, she replied in Auguste's own dialect, "I am the Holy Virgin, have no fear." She then gave him specific information and instructions, most notably that his vines, as healthy as they looked, were actually quite sick, because of his Sunday labors. He was also to tell his father and his pastor about the vision and return in a month for further instruction. Then she rose into the heavens, disappearing in the clouds.

A shocked Auguste finally recovered enough to go home and tell his father and priest, as directed. His father believed him, but the pastor was reluctant: he couldn't decide whether he had to do with "an imposter or a fool." The church believed in visions and holy manifestations, as always, but it was also, as always, skeptical of the overzealous, who may have "simply been suffering indigestion." The pastor therefore frankly told Auguste that he did not believe him, but that if the Virgin had in fact appeared to him on this Sunday when he was working, then he was fortunate to be standing there at all, for by working today he was in revolt against her Divine Son and she might have struck him down.

Auguste paled at this thought. People in the village considered him an honorable, pliable, tranquil man, even "incapable of lying." But like many men in the village, he was poor with a large family and needed all the income he could get. Like them, he therefore worked all week at another job for wages, then worked in his vineyard on Sunday, hoping to earn extra money by selling his crop at harvest time. His conscience was never completely easy about it, but so many in the village did the same that those few who would not work on Sunday were even called "lazy" by the others. Now the priest's words, and the messenger's in the vision, made Auguste determined to cease. He was just as determined to carry out the rest of the messenger's instructions, even though the priest had explicitly told him not to. "I don't want to disobey you," Auguste told the priest before leaving, but with the confidence of Paul speaking about his experience on the road to Damascus, he added that "the Holy Virgin really appeared to me, and I know I saw her, just as I see you before me now, and I heard her speak just as I hear you now."

A month later Auguste did indeed receive another vision, containing further instructions. This time it happened in the presence of two thousand curious people who, though they themselves saw nothing in the heavens, saw how Auguste reacted to what he was seeing. When the vision finished, at least nine people saw a meteor sweep over Auguste's field, a sight they testified to still twenty-four years later. Then he escaped the crowds and went to his room, where he revealed the content of the vision, as follows: one must not work on Sunday.

When one thinks of France and its famous Sundays, this is not usually what comes to mind. It sounds like an event straight out of Gregory of Tours in the sixth century.

Yet in Catholic countries more appearances of the Virgin Mary were alleged and recorded in the nineteenth century than perhaps in any other. Was this because of the threat posed by rational industrialization to what Max Weber called the "enchantment of the world?" The number of alleged visions always increased in a time of crisis, which the age of industrialization certainly was. And there was even more disenchantment than industrialization at work in nineteenth-century France: military defeat by Germany in 1870–71, and the replacement of the Catholic-friendly Second Empire by the anticlerical Third Republic.

Whatever the cause of the spate of visions, most interesting here was their regular attention to Sunday. Their message might be, especially in the countryside, about abstaining from work, as in Auguste's vision. Or it might, especially in towns, condemn the sorts of Sunday fun portrayed by Louis Morin. In either case, the message was much the same as in earlier centuries: no work, much worship, and a little honest play.

The first Sunday vision in France probably came in 1814, to Marie-Jeanne Grave, aged fourteen, a shepherd girl, who was told that her parents were blasphemers for working on Sundays, and that if they did not change, they would die within a year. Everyone laughed upon hearing Marie-Jeanne's report, but both of her parents indeed died as predicted. In 1821 a nun in Alsace was ordered in a vision to write to the king of France and say how much the violation of Sunday irritated God, and that if the king did not restore Sunday, then he would be chased from France—as occurred in 1830. In that same year, a nun named Catherine Labouré brought the often rural Sunday visions to urban Paris.

Then came more visions at Tours in 1843, La Salette in 1846, and most famously of all in France at Lourdes in 1858, where half a million visited every year by 1900. Nine more visions, including Auguste's, were recorded in France alone during the 1870s, five in the 1880s, and two in the 1890s. The message of all was similar: nowhere else was Sunday transgressed "more audaciously and impudently" than in France.

As Auguste's pastor suggested, visions were a tricky matter for Catholic leaders: they believed such were possible but were irked by the claims of excessively enthusiastic people, especially laypeople and nuns, typically the recipients of such visions, and perhaps not coincidentally those without official authority in the church. But even if the church was nervous about its visionary members, it was quite in agreement with them—and with the small number of Protestant allies in France—about the need to restore what they perceived to be the old Sunday. In the old days, claimed one pious book, work on Sunday was the exception, and anyone who did work always asked the permission of the pastor. Now such permission was never asked, and France had been cursed for it. As for Sunday Mass, most church leaders seemed to see it only in decline: an observer in 1845 said that one-tenth of Catholics didn't believe at all, half came to Mass a few Sundays a year, and the other half came even more irregularly.

Despite near-universal attendance in some regions, in others—especially working-class districts of large cities—people lived "almost completely apart" from the Catholic Church by 1900. Fifty percent of Marseille attended church in 1840, for instance, only 16 percent in 1901. Hence a multitude still went to Mass, but it was a smaller and less consistent multitude. Women were most likely to attend, the young and men less so. The Bishop of Verdun, in typical older-generation fashion, declared that never had the youth of the nation shown itself more frivolous, more independent, and more forgetful of their duty than now, and it was all because they did not observe Sunday. Other churchmen were more general: all of France's problems might be blamed on Sunday profanation: strikes, social unrest, socialism itself, epidemics, earthquakes, floods, and even the blight that struck French vineyards so hard in the 1870s, as predicted to the vintner Auguste. In order to revive France, then revive Sunday.

Some church leaders laid blame for the neglect of Sunday at the shop doors of greedy bosses: in how many stores did "pitiless masters traffic less in merchandise" and more in forcing employees to work that day? Children, women, young men by the hundreds, "obligated to earn their bread at the price of forced labor," consumed rapidly their "flowering youth in corrupt air and excessive fatigue, the unfortunate victims of avarice," declared one. Such a statement reflects that after 1870 the church followed other agitators for Sunday rest by pointing out as well its nonreligious benefits, including economic efficiency, personal hygiene, family relations, and good morals. It also held up the wealth of such strictly observant Sunday nations as England and the U.S.: Was this not proof enough that prosperity resulted from resting each week? Certainly England sometimes went too far in Sunday strictness, noted many, but the basic idea of Sunday rest leading to greater prosperity was worth imitating.

Of course, to churchmen, keeping Sunday free of work was only part of the battle. Another was to promote piety and condemn irreverent recreations on the day. Specifically, they put the burden of a pious Sunday on the shoulders of women. Not only did women attend Mass in greater numbers than men, but the Church looked to women to make Sunday right even beyond Mass. A woman's job that day, wrote the lay Catholic Emile Cheysson in 1898, was to turn her husband away from unsuitable friends and debauchery and to chase gloom from the home, filling it with tranquillity, reading, games, and edification. The clergy agreed: having a clean house, a better meal than usual, and sweetness in the home were the keys to a proper Sunday, as well as getting everyone to Mass, and all were the domain of women. Indeed, women should take a nap on Saturday afternoon so that they might be ready for the responsibilities of Sunday!

Important as scattered sermons and publications may have been, some sought a more organized reform of Sunday on a national scale. The largest movement was headed by the Catholic layman Louis-Joseph-Gustave Courtôt de Cissey. His noble name reveals that he was no ordinary layman. Schooled in law, active in local politics and pious works like the old local nobleman (he lived in the family château in Chalon), and overseeing the vineyards of his estate, Cissey had always been a busy man. But his true vocation came to him only at age fifty-seven, in 1871, the year of the humiliating defeat to Germany, when he heard about a Society for the Sanctification of Sunday, which met in nearby Lyon. He attended a meeting and was so overcome by the story told there of the Virgin appearing at La Salette that he joined immediately. He participated in the first national pilgrimage to La Salette in 1872, designed to draw attention to the need to improve Sundays, and from that he was inspired to make the revival of Sunday in all of France his life's mission.

Perhaps because of Cissey's noble stature, or the force of his personality, or because they simply thought it right, the local clergy and bishop supported Cissey's plans to journey to Rome, gain an audience with the pope, and receive his blessing as a missionary of Sunday. The Society for Sanctification had begun in Lyon, but Cissey wanted to spread it to all of France. He did make his trip to Rome, but did not get his papal audience: instead he received a private letter from the pope encouraging his efforts, and the support of a Cardinal Pitra as well, who confirmed that "no nation has such a scandalous dishonor of Sunday as France," and that France's example in all things was highly contagious, for good and ill.

Cissey put the pope's letter to good effect in the coming years, reading it aloud in gathering after gathering of the Society, especially in the north and center of France, where he became known as the "Apostle of Sunday." He regularly recorded the large size of his audience, the flow of tears that he brought to the eyes of his listeners, the loud applause, the kissing of his hands by grateful people, and the electricity in the air—especially when he repeated the words of the Virgin of La Salette: "If my people do not submit themselves, then I am forced to let go the arm of my Son. It is so heavy and weighty that I cannot hold it back any longer." He urged people to cease working on Sunday and bosses to cease requiring people to work, then criticized all sorts of maladies and industries in France. Attendees pledged not to work on Sunday, not to make their children or servants work, not to open their stores or factories without genuine necessity, not to shop at stores that were open on Sunday, and to urge others similarly.

In private, Cissey sometimes complained that more than a few Catholics, including clergy, sought to check his zeal, accusing him of excess. Also in private, his wife complained that Sunday was her enemy, because it took him from her every week. But he continued anyway, riding through all sorts of weather in uncovered carriages, all year long, determined to set up more branches of the society and to get the state to pass a Sunday law. Success was less than he had hoped, he later admitted; despite his glowing accounts of his many emotional gatherings, terrestrial joy reigned, he lamented.

He died in 1889, before the Sunday law of 1906 was passed, but in the end that law was the result of union and secular forces more than religious. In fact, even among fellow French Catholics, and despite his enthusiastic reports of emotional meetings and impressive figures, Cissey's message in the long run achieved only limited success. As one French churchman concluded in 1908, thirty thousand sermons a week by thirty thousand pastors in France "have not stopped French Catholics from arriving at a state of anemia" on Sunday or other subjects. Another prominent Catholic complained that Protestants, especially the English, had preserved Christianity, "despite their heresy," better than the French, because of superior Sunday observance. Despite the emergence or even renaissance of Catholic spirituality in France in the late nineteenth century, especially in the countryside where most Sunday visions occurred, Sunday was far from where these reformers wanted it to be.

This wasn't because French believers were indifferent to religion; it was because many enjoyed their lively Sundays and saw them, in contrast to such coreligionists as Monsieur Cissey or the local priest, as quite compatible with their beliefs. These churchgoers disliked the harshness of certain clerics, who were "always saying no"—no drinking on Sunday or during processions, no Sunday morning markets, no fishing on Sunday—or who refused absolution to all girls who danced or to all boys who went to taverns. Some clergy were so opposed to dancing, still a favorite Sunday activity, that they flung down crosses at dances and then dared the dancers to walk over them on their way across the floor; or they broke violins, or made girls leave their benches at church and kneel before the altar for having danced at a ball the night before. Some priests were even rigorously against promenades. But to many laypeople, such clergymen were simply too lazy to adapt themselves to popular customs, or wished to avoid dealing with unfamiliar things in the confessional. Many laypeople felt their Sunday activities were perfectly reasonable and respectable, and priests who too vigorously opposed them would be repaid with their parishioners staying away from Sunday Mass, or losing faith altogether.

The poet Arthur Rimbaud wrote in just this way of his disheartening childhood Sundays. At age seven he feared the "pallid Sundays of December," when, "all pomaded," he was to read from a Bible with gilded edges, lying on a mahogany table. Yet he loved not God "but men," who on Sunday in the "fawn-colored or black evening" entered the suburbs for entertainment and diversion. He dreamed of the romantic meadow, where "luminous swells, healthy scents, and downy gold" moved calmly and sprang to life. Priests knew these attractions: some combated and forbade them, others openly admitted that they felt obligated to tolerate certain "lesser evils" on Sunday in order to avoid greater. But to parishioners these were not evils at all, any more than they were to their medieval forebears: Sunday fun fit as much into their religious lives as the rituals of the agricultural year.

In the end, for all of the criticisms of Sunday from religious and areligious quarters, throngs of people continued their pursuit of that perfect Sunday which seemed especially possible in France. The leisured classes found the popular Sunday tacky, Bohemians and bourgeois critics found it conventional and empty, the poor could hardly participate in it, and the very devout found it impious. But most of the Sunday-fied crowd simply said with their actions that the sort of active Sunday portrayed by Louis Morin was their desire and ideal, unfulfilled though it might be at times—and criticized though it might be by Morin himself, or Zola, Maupassant, Foley, Vallès, the Church, and others.

Pursuers of the French Sunday were openly proud of the "native expansibility" of their day, compared to what they saw as the "consternation of the London Sunday," where museums, expositions, theaters, and cafés were all dead. In contrast, Parisians could find any of these at their pleasure, plus the elegance (or anxiety) of the race track, or ice skating on the lake in winter, or the countryside and boulevards in the summer. Even when trees were bare and the air was cold, they promenaded anyway. Some Sundays in France were certainly for crying, at least among those who could afford the expenses of the day or among such poor as the seamstress from Lille. And for those who ventured out there was certainly inconvenience at the crowded train station or tram. But for so many in France, Sunday remained, even after all the disappointments, filled with the spirit embodied by Morin's female character and alter ego, Pompon—namely, the hope of physical and spiritual relief, diversion, and renewal through especially a wide range of recreations concentrated on that day.

5

Belgium, August 2, 1914

On the last Sunday before the Great War, most Belgians followed their usual Sunday pleasures. In Brussels the afternoon crowds quite resembled their counterparts in Paris—walking along busy boulevards, heading for suburban fields to seek the sun, taking cover in the shade of lush woods, or, if they were poor, spending the day miserably. In Belgium's ubiquitous villages (all 2,633 of them), young couples strolled along country roads through glistening fields, old people sat before their doors, neighbor ladies chatted over garden hedges, boys swam in the river and looked for birds' nests, while men young and old cared for their doves or gathered in taverns.

But even as people went about their resting, there was tension in the Sunday air. Rumors of war between Europe's great powers, and neutral Belgium's likely familiar place in the middle of it all, had spread for two years. In fact, the German army had mobilized only days before, alarming the Belgians into mobilizing their much smaller army in response, just in case. And this very afternoon, while people strolled, the Belgian ministers of justice and finance hastily organized a meeting with leaders of the national bank to discuss emergency financial measures. Finally at seven that evening, while people prepared dinner, the minister of foreign affairs received the dreaded ultimatum that true believers in international treaties and good neighborliness thought would never come: Germany wanted unfettered and immediate passage through Belgium in order to wage war on France. Any resistance would be regarded as an act of war, thus causing Germany to attack Belgium as well.

Early on Monday the Belgian government answered that there would be no free passage for German troops. On Tuesday morning, Germany, as promised, moved into Belgium. The Great War, which would suck in most of Europe and then others far beyond until some called it World War I, had commenced, right here in Belgium. In the cities of the great powers, people danced and paraded in the streets, happy for the release of pent-up tensions and certain of quick victory for their side. No such happiness or optimism prevailed in little Belgium. The Flemish writer Ernest Claes put it most tragically: a small land was overrun by a big land; the small land was peaceful and hard-working and its name enjoyed a lovely sound in the world, but the big land wanted to be bigger still, and the small land was foolish enough to believe in accords, signatures, and negotiations. War was the result, and it changed everything.

If Claes was a bit idealistic about his native land and simplistic about the causes of war, he can be forgiven, for he was exactly right in saying that war changed everything—including Sunday. Certainly other changes were even more devastating, as all together some ten million people were killed, twenty million more were wounded, and cities and landscapes were obliterated. But in Sunday-loving countries such as Belgium, the loss of their favorite day was no small thing. It forced them to confront the gloomy prospect of life without Sunday. For make no mistake, during war, Sunday seemed to disappear.

War minimized all lovely glimpses of transcendent things. It made genuine rest impossible at any time. It made Sunday's usual diversions feel unseemly and irreverent. And most of all, it erased any distinction whatsoever among days, so that Sunday was in effect no more: all days blended into one dreary shade. Of course other forces might also homogenize time and thus diminish Sunday—such as constant work, or constant play, or even the ancient Christian idea of eternity as a constant holy day. But constant war diminished Sunday most painfully and thoroughly of all.

OLD SUNDAY

Before the Great War, Sunday in Belgium was the best day of the week.

Belgium was hardly alone in this. A similar sentiment, even similar Sunday habits, were evident in Ireland, Spain, Italy, Germany, Austria, and elsewhere, and of course in Belgium's trendsetting neighbor, France. Yet for all of the similarities among continental Sundays generally, each had its own shades and hues. In particular, for all the likenesses between France and Belgium* and for all the talk of Brussels being a smaller and quainter Paris, Belgium was not France, nor its beloved Sundays quite French.

In the first place, the old Belgian Sunday was, like old Belgian culture as a whole, a rural idyll. Here lay a great irony. Before the Great War, France was largely rural, yet was dominated culturally by Paris. In contrast, Belgium was the most densely populated country in the world, the first country on the European mainland to industrialize, the fifth-greatest economic power in the world, and the fourth-greatest trading nation, boasting a capital city of 750,000—yet it was grounded culturally in village and small-town life.

A key reason was this: unlike Paris, Brussels did not spread its physical and cultural tentacles to pull in everything else. There simply wasn't enough space or inclination to do so. Moreover, the new train network was the densest in the world, distances were short, and travel

---

*Most obviously, about 40 percent of Belgians spoke French as their first language, and French still prevailed in public life throughout Belgium, including in the military; the majority of the population spoke various Flemish dialects, related to Dutch, but even in Flemish areas children were expected to learn French. There were also similarities between the countries in style and cuisine.

was fast, easy, and cheap. All this meant that even after industrialization, most of Belgium's 10 million people could continue to live in
small towns or villages of 10,000 or fewer while commuting to new
jobs elsewhere. Yet many of these continued to farm as well, still some
800,000 in 1914, one-quarter of the working population. Moreover,
the rural landscape, though hardly flawless, was not made unrecogniz-
able by industrialization: even mining areas looked more like agricultural areas, with the usual church towers, cows, and fields, and still far
preferable to the blackness of London or the overcrowding of Paris. In
short, if Parisians flocked to the countryside on Sunday, six in ten Belgians were already there, and mostly stayed there.

A second important difference with France was the decidedly
Catholic context of the Belgian Sunday. Many here would have echoed
the Irishman who said, "What a source of manifold graces and comforts and blessings is the Sunday! Anywhere, but especially Sunday in
a Catholic country-parish—in an unsophisticated, rural place." Unlike
France, Belgium was still officially Catholic. It was not universally so,
certainly not in cities. Yet 80 percent of Belgian children aged six to
fourteen received a Catholic education in 1910. And although the Liberal Party and Socialist Party boasted significant minorities, the
Catholic Party dominated politics from 1884 until the outbreak of the
Great War. In fact, an important reason Belgium remained culturally
and demographically rural was the pressure from the church to make
rail lines plenteous and rail prices next to nothing—for an urbanized
populace would be a Socialist populace, feared the church.

This very cultural and political dominance of Catholicism has led
historians to point out that Belgium had no excuse for not passing a
law against Sunday work until 1905, only a year earlier than "godless"
France. The Catholic Party could have passed such a law twenty years
before had it pleased, but not enough were pleased to do so, and then
when the law finally came, it was in part under pressure from Socialist unions. In Belgium as in France, business interests were the stumbling block: just as anticlerical laissez-faire industrialists in France
were not initially persuaded by the need for Sunday rest, neither were
Catholic laissez-faire industrialists in Belgium. Still, even before 1905
and certainly after, Belgians found many ways, especially in the countryside, to celebrate their Sundays.

"The Sunday, well that is just the finest day of the week—no work, clean shirt and socks, spending money, going out, ninepins, cards, sleeping in." Thus wrote Ernest Claes, perhaps the greatest expositor of the old rural Sunday in Belgium. When a boy, Claes's ideal image of time was "a month of Sundays." And he regarded anyone who was able to smile at the ordinary cares of life that occupied most people as a "Sunday person."

Claes was as capable as anyone of distorting the old Sunday, especially since he wrote about it mostly after the Great War, when the *memory* of that Sunday became a dream, even better than the thing itself. As the exiled Abraham Hans wrote during the war, "I know, there were abuses too, but in our memories these vanished, and we saw only the lovely and dear." Yet Claes also gave his memories more flesh and blood and dimension than most Sunday observers, and he never forgot the perpetual hardships of the typical rural week that helped to make Sunday's relief so important. All these combine to make his portrayals worth an especially close look.

Claes's Sunday began, like that of so many other rural working people, with the anticipation of it in the days before. Like a young cowherd described by another Flemish writer, Stijn Streuvels, Claes's characters found all their "comfort and anticipation in Sunday." And when one Sunday ended, they began almost immediately to think about the next. One form of anticipation for men and boys in Belgian villages was the Saturday night shave and haircut, just for Sunday. In France the busiest day for barbers was Sunday morning, but not in Belgium, where many people attended early Sunday Mass. Belgian women more likely went to a coiffeur in the nearest town on Saturday afternoon, not trusting themselves to the village barber, who did this job on the side.

The barber in the village of young Ernest Claes, named Fiel Ekster, was by trade a shoemaker and by avocation a reader. During the Saturday night barbering sessions in the main room of his modest home, where a single lamp burned next to his shaving chair, he told all that he had read to the wide-eyed crowd, which sat on benches or chairs, waiting their turn. While he talked of his favorite subjects—Napoleon and wild animals—he also worked. First he wetted the customer's face with warm water, then took a piece of soap over it and rubbed it into a lather. Next he sharpened his razor and began shaving. When he came to the cheek, Fiel stuck two of his fingers inside the customer's mouth, to round it out; for those who had "a little more standing in the community" or were willing to pay a penny or two more, he used a spoon. With one customer, Jan Kieper, neither was necessary: Jan chewed a fat wad of tobacco at all times, and so when Fiel began shaving, Jan simply asked, "Which side first, Fiel?" And that's where Jan moved his tobacco. Young Ernest Claes needed only a haircut, and when it was his turn, Fiel would pretend to be dangerous with scissors, saying that just last week he had cut off the tip of someone's ear. But the boy shouldn't worry: Fiel had sewed it back on with a needle and thread, then "smeared a little cat fat on it, and it looked fine." At that very moment he would touch the cold steel of the scissors to Ernest's ear, making him jump.

Shaved and trimmed, the boys and men were ready for Sunday. In Claes's village the day began early—and not with work like their medieval ancestors, nor with early Mass like some neighbors, but with a serious sort of play: dove racing. The "dove-milkers," as they were called because of their enthusiasm for the sport, rose at around six or six-thirty, for the precious birds had to be taken by train to northern France and released. In 1907 alone, six million doves were transported this way on Sunday mornings, to the displeasure of those who considered dove racing a waste of time and money. In fact, not only did it cost good money to feed, transport, and train doves, but all kinds of wagering over the races went on each Sunday morning in local cafés. Some women, wrote Claes, complained about more than the money, saying that their husbands looked more longingly at the doves than at them. And more than a few pastors were unhappy that the doves typically were expected to return right in the middle of High Mass, or mid to late Sunday morning, so that men and boys were outside the church, eyes to the sky. But the dove-milkers themselves felt like the boy in Stijn Streuvels's story "Sundays," who thought there was nothing lovelier than a white dove against a blue sky, and who knew all the different colors of doves—white, snow white, scalloped, blue, hail blue, pink, speckled pink, gray, black spotted, striped, and more.

This was the case too with Sander Candeel, who lived near Ernest
Claes. Sander was a member of the parish choir but also a great lover
of dove racing, and the two interests conflicted. As a choir member,
Sander never had time to fish on Sunday mornings, nor watch the fire-
fighters practice, nor gossip and smoke pipes in cafés after early Mass.
But most of all he never had time to watch his own son's prize doves
come home. Usually Sander accepted this situation, but one Sunday in
June there was an especially important competition, for which the
doves would be released from a location even beyond Paris and for
which large purses were promised. This brought him to a crisis.

Sander's son Lowie had two prize doves in the big race: the "famous shell-blue female" and the white male. Interest in general was
so great that almost no men attended High Mass that morning,
just women, schoolchildren, one or two "old-fashioned fellows" who
thought dove racing childish, and of course the men of the choir. Never
had Sander regretted his fine voice as much as he did today. In fact, as
he stood there frustrated, high on the roodloft with the other choristers,
he decided that he would resign at the end of the year. All through the
service he "mumbled and groaned" that the Mass was moving too
slowly, and did the organist really have to play such long interludes?
More than once the organist gave him a stern look, to which Sander
could only hiss, "You try being serious when there are three hundred
francs at stake!" Through a single windowpane high in the church,
Sander could just see the roof of his house, where Lowie's doves were
supposed to return, and on this Sunday he kept his eyes fixed on that
spot.

It came time for Sander's solo, during the *Credo*. As an experienced
chorister, he could sing it with little thought. But that Sunday, in the
middle of his second repetition of *"cum gloria,"* and with his eye still
on the roof, Lowie's shell-blue landed: Sander interrupted his solo to
yell out "By God, there's our Lowie's blue!" And this so loudly that the
other choristers jumped in surprise, while everyone seated below
turned to look. The organist saved the day by "loudly playing ten
notes at once" and the choir went on as if nothing had occurred. Some
people laughed about it afterward, but most found it scandalous. And
Sander never had to resign after all because he was dismissed from the
choir. Was it worth it? Lowie earned 160 francs for the shell-blue that

Sunday (an Antwerp dressmaker earned three francs a week, men in the textile industry about fifteen a week).

Not every pastor, or organist, was against doves, however. One of Claes's pastors attracted people to church on Sunday through his famously short Masses. "A good Mass must be short, ask anyone," wrote Claes, and this pastor's particular motive for being short was known to all: he wanted to see the doves come in. Indeed he was so fast with Sunday Mass that one of the village's ubiquitous pious women reported the pastor to the bishop, who felt obligated to summon the man. Fortunately, the bishop was an old friend from the seminary, and the pastor took care to bring along a basket of his best apricots, plus a rabbit supplied by the church custodian, a well-known poacher. After some mutual flattery and casual chitchat, the bishop proposed that they go to his chapel and see just exactly how fast the pastor read his Mass. The pastor complied, proceeding at his usual pace, "for he was an honest man," while the bishop sat there with a watch. When it was finished, the bishop declared, "I can do it three minutes faster." The pastor replied, "With an empty stomach, so can I, Eminence." After that they never talked about fast Masses again, and the pastor continued to get out early enough on Sunday morning to see the doves.

After early-morning dove racing, or fishing, came early Sunday Mass, just as in centuries past.

In Belgian villages, where a common saying held that "Sunday without Mass is no Sunday at all," church services were still heavily attended. A "proper person had to go to Mass, it simply couldn't be otherwise," recalled Ernest Claes. As he remembered it, one could "write on half a piece of paper those who never came to church."

Bells rang on Sunday in his village and others well before starting time, as in the Middle Ages, and then again more steadily about fifteen minutes before. Those who preferred early Mass were often servants (who had to work at least part of the day), younger children (too noisy in High Mass), housewives (too much to do the rest of Sunday), the hungry (who wanted to break their fast from the night before as early as possible), and the energetic (who wanted more free time during the

rest of Sunday). Families who lived close by the church often sent a few
members to both early and high Masses, so as not to overcrowd the
place at either time for those who journeyed from outlying farms.
Women typically sat in the middle of the church, while men sought the
side aisles, farther removed from the action up front. The prosperous
had their own special chairs, with red or green velvet on the seat and
the owner's name engraved on a copper plate, assuring themselves of
a prime place even if they arrived late. Before sitting, all turned the
chair toward themselves and knelt upon the seat. Between the *Gloria*
and the Gospel they turned the chair again and sat down; then for the
sermon—which some complained went as "long as twenty minutes"—
they turned their chair sideways toward the pulpit. The very poorest,
who wished to avoid the small rent charged for any chair, and the least
interested, who wished to show it, simply stood in the back. Often this
group chatted about doves, cycling, or the weather, and shuffled out
quietly when the sermon began in order to get a drink at the café, before filing back in again for the final blessing. If there was too much
noise in the back or elsewhere, the "suisse" or custodian, who walked
around conspicuously during Mass, would shush people. Except for all
the bustle around the chairs, it much resembled a scene in a medieval
church on Sunday.

Mass itself proceeded much the same. The pastor, assisted by a few
altar boys from the parish, celebrated Mass in Latin, while facing the
altar and thus away from the audience. The High Mass remained more
elaborate than early Mass, as scriptural texts were usually sung, a
choir provided fine music, and the whole sometimes lasted a full
seventy-five minutes. Something else in either high or early Mass was
also familiar: pastors complained that at the first sign of the blessing,
or the concluding words *Ite missa est,* people disappeared quickly out
the door.

But of course much was new at Mass as well, thanks to intervening centuries, mostly in details and characters. It was toward these especially that Claes turned his eye. Now regularly in village churches
were choristers, such as Sander Candeel, who on every other day were
ordinary working people. But on Sunday they "stood a little higher,"
literally and figuratively, than everyone else in rural villages because
everyone knew that the quality of religious life in the parish depended

greatly on them. Some, wrote Claes, fought for the chance to join, or tried to impress current members with their "strong throats" during informal auditions in cafés on Sunday nights. "When the peasants on Sunday heard Seppe Landuyt draw out his deepest bass notes" so that the pane in the farthest window of the church, right above the baptismal font, started vibrating—which Seppe himself knew very well, for he proudly kept one eye on it while prolonging the note—"they nod to each other and say, 'There's Seppe, what wind!' " No wonder that when Mass was finished in Claes's village and the choristers went to visit the nearest café or two to slake their thirst, people readily offered to buy them drinks and pressed half-franc pieces secretly into their hands.

Also newly present since the Middle Ages at Sunday Mass was the chair-setter. In Claes's village this was a woman named Mieke Waegemans, who lived in a small house on the corner of the market. For arranging the church's chairs each Sunday, and for collecting the chair rent during Mass, she received a paltry income of twenty-five francs a year. She also kept a small candy store, popular with the children after High Mass, where they liked to spend their "Sunday cent" on syrup balls, sugar hammers, and more. Still, altogether she earned very little. And so one Sunday, when she learned that the men of the church council were now drinking wine during their meetings at the church's expense, she went on strike, seeking thirty-five francs a year. The next Sunday during Mass, Mieke didn't come around with the basket: she simply stayed seated in front and cried. Everyone knew why. Hence, "they all believed the pastor a little less that day" when he preached on the Good Shepherd and the Lost Sheep.

As present as seemingly ever on Sunday, according to Ernest Claes, were a number of older pious ladies who kept a stern eye on things, but new since the last couple of centuries were local nuns who ran a school or hospital. It was best when the pastor got on well with the nuns, but often they were rivals. One of Claes's pastors did not shy during Sunday Mass from sprinkling scandalous amounts of holy water their way. Those children who could make it through service remained a common sight at Mass, but Claes paid them more attention than did most. His most popular character, named *De Witte,* or Whitey, regarded Mass as a time to play marbles on the church square afterward or to stand in front of the candy store. But the service itself was a matter of sheer endurance. Like so many children at church, Whitey sought to amuse himself during the sermon, and once he tied together the chairs of a boy and girl seated in front of him: when the sermon was finished, and everyone stood to turn their chairs, the tied chairs made a huge commotion, mortifying the shy couple, who never sat together again. Whitey and his friends also enjoyed looking at the burning candles during Mass. Some suspected that this was a sign of the boys' deep piety, but in fact they were watching closely to see how far down the candle was burning: when it was a small enough stump, they could take it to play with and no one would notice, but they couldn't let it burn down too far either. Hence their rapt attention. The prioress of the local convent once complimented a boy's father on how devoutly his son fixed his eyes on the image of the Virgin, which amazed the father himself.

Villages had always housed skeptics or the other-believing, who distinguished themselves on Sundays through indifferent or conspicuous nonattendance at Mass. By Claes's time they went under the names "Liberal" or "Socialist." The example Claes remembered best was a man named Jef Leirs. He seemed not so much a convinced socialist as someone who liked to annoy the pastor. This Jef Leirs accomplished by singing irreverent songs in praise of skirts or Napoleon, by standing during Mass in the back of the church with a smirk on his face, and by raising troublesome questions in response to the pastor's sermon. His most aggravating effort came right after the pastor had preached on the miracle of the wine at the wedding in Cana. According to Jef's calculations, there were seventeen liters of wine per person at Cana. "They must have all been pretty sauced," he said to the pastor. The pastor fumed at such irreverence and countered with a more modest figure. "Well, that would still be three liters per person," replied Jef, "and that was Our Dear Lord's wine, much stronger than pastor's wine!" The exchange continued in this fashion, and so bothered the pastor, who was not a learned man, that for some time he drank no wine at all, even though "he liked a glass as much as anyone else."

And so Claes went on, describing character after character in his well-filled village church on Sunday.

———

After High Mass, the rest of the day seemed like an endless landscape of possibilities to a young boy such as Ernest Claes.

Right when he came out the church door, there often stood a singer, who composed and performed songs on all recent popular subjects—murders, disasters, love scandals—and held up for sale the sheet music to those songs. Parents ordered their children to walk right past such scandalous fare "with an aristocratic Sunday face," but the curious stood around in a circle. He also saw the shopkeeper open briefly to sell sandwiches, especially to those who had traveled far to get to church. And of course café doors went open too. These were really more taverns than cafés, for they were far removed from the chic places of Paris. Here the men and older boys sat to tell news, comment on the pastor's sermon, enjoy a pint, and play cards for a while, until the Angelus rang at 11:55 and all went home to their Sunday meal.

For Ernest Claes, this meant that rather than the usual lunch of porridge or soup, plus boiled potatoes, steamed vegetables, applesauce or rhubarb, a bit of herring, and some bacon, blood sausage, or pigs' feet and ears, there was today a pork cutlet, plus rabbit, chicken soup, or horse meat. There was nothing special about the usual onion sauce that accompanied it all, but there was about the rice pudding with brown sugar, or the steamed pears, yellow vanilla cream, or jam tart that came later.

After lunch there remained a couple of duties at church, but these could be enjoyable. Some people attended "Lof," or Adoration, an early afternoon prayer service at around two or three. Then the occasional Sunday procession, meant to be solemn, might provide as well a good deal of fun for young people, accompanied as it was by the local brass band, colorful flags on houses, plenty of vendors, and opportunities for socializing. For teenagers there were youth groups that met for an hour or two. And, of course, for those children about to take first communion there was Sunday afternoon catechism.

If catechism was less than exciting, it was at least in the mind of Ernest Claes made bearable by the pleasant event that it anticipated: "not so much communion itself but a series of sparkling Sundays with a new suit, hat, gloves, and church book, and two weeks without school" after Easter. In fact for many villagers, even more than for bourgeois Parisians, a fine Sunday outfit, superior to one's everyday clothing, was mostly what made Sunday an extraordinary day. Ordinarily villagers wore wooden clogs on their muddy roads and fields, but on Sunday they wore real shoes or boots, bordered with beige or light gray material. Men and women usually owned a special Sunday coat, worn for years, made of impossibly sturdy material. Women wore black cloaks and hats with lace, which hardly matched the finery of Paris but represented their best. On Sunday a man's weekday cap might be traded for a genuine hat, made of felt. Boys and men wore a white handkerchief in their pocket, which on weekdays was too dirty for such a thing. And they especially wanted a fine suit, rather than their everyday worn-out version.

What Claes's character Whitey worried most about was whether he would get a brand-new Sunday suit or have to make do with a suit already worn by his older brothers, hanging now with much care in the left corner of the armoire. When he thought about that old suit, all the pleasures of Sunday disappeared, for it was completely out of fashion now. When he was between suits, young Ernest Claes himself looked at his mother every Sunday with hopeful eyes, but most of the time she simply gave him her pained expression: not this week. Then one Saturday the news would finally come: tomorrow he would go into town with his father and shop for a new suit. During peak periods, such as before Easter, tailors and fabric sellers worked late into the night, and on Sundays, because that was when most of their clients—working-class people and farmers—could visit.

After catechism, Sunday afternoon was wholly for recreation. This was a favorite moment for village fanfares to perform, and Ernest Claes played the drums in his. Louis Morin's negative opinion about this rage of the late nineteenth and early twentieth centuries was shared by plenty of others. In Claes's village, many mothers and fathers, even a few priests, despised the local fanfare because the young men neglected Sunday afternoon Adoration, made "more racket than ever," got into more mischief, drank more beer, and caused more arguments over their "incessant need for money" to pay off instruments and cover other "expenses."

But the young people of Belgium felt otherwise. Like the church choir, the fanfare was partly about the music and largely about the prestige and privilege of belonging. This was evident most of all on

Sunday, when the fanfare participated in music festivals in one town or another, the train stations full of "shiny instruments and marching peasants." The biggest supporters of the fanfare turned out to be the café bosses, who profited nicely on Sunday after such thirst-inducing marches, and of course the village girls, who admired the musicians, mostly young men and teenage boys. Boys of fifteen and sixteen, wrote Claes, who once needed to be in bed by nine, "now courted girls with confidence late into the night because they played second bugle or third cornet in the fanfare." The young women, who "stood around jabbering and talking foolishness with anyone in the fanfare," rarely attended the young ladies' congregation on Sunday afternoon anymore. And although the young women still went along on Sunday processions, none came home with consecrated candles, "just some frill like a silver ring or brown comb." All because of the fanfare.

Late Sunday afternoon might also, in Claes's village, be a time for the occasional outing on the steam train to Brussels, the nearest big city, but most villagers spent Sundays closer to home, where things were cheaper. There were interesting woods and plenty of inland waterways that froze in winter and became crowded with ice skaters. And most of all there was the Sunday favorite, since the Middle Ages, of the café, not only at midday but in late afternoon or evening too.

For rural "cafés," Sunday remained the biggest and often only day of business. Usually simply the front room of someone's house, they popped up in homes where "the wife didn't object" and some extra income was needed. Because many rural households fit these criteria, villages often had several: in fact, Belgium had one café for every ninety people in 1840, and one for every thirty-five people in 1907. Gaining approval from the local burgomaster wasn't terribly difficult, nor was setting one up. A few wooden tables, wooden chairs, a counter with copper rings, a buffet for glasses behind the counter, a coal stove, and a spittoon would do the trick.

This rural Belgian café was mainly for men and older boys. Save for the lady of the house, or sometimes her daughter(s) who waited on customers, women were few. Indeed women had fewer opportunities generally on Sunday in the countryside, bound as they were to kitchen, children, and even parents. Many of them went to early Mass so that they might have a bit of time to themselves in the morning, when they might place their weekly orders in the village stores, or drink a cup of coffee and eat pastry at the baker's. But they usually were not in the cafés on Sundays, which were akin to men's clubs.

Claes's favorite was run by the local blacksmith and his wife Melanie, the "only fashionable woman" in the village. From all around, the "menfolk came together there on Sundays, to drink beer, talk, tell stories, play games, and sing. It was so crowded that you were pushed right up against someone else and you could chop the tobacco smoke." Behind the house was the terrain for ninepins, where there might be two francs in the betting pot. A "couple of famous players went home on Sunday night often with more money in their pocket than they'd gotten from their wives for spending money after Adoration." The younger boys were busy with their own games. The men who had already drunk too much to play stayed in the tavern arguing and "stoking each other up over pigs and cows and women." Young men of around twenty often sat next to the canal along the main road, right next to the smith's house, chatting about girls and teasing one another so secretively that "anyone could guess that unedifying things were being said."

Melanie stood behind the counter and served, while the smith took care of those out back playing ninepins: a whole pile of empty and half-empty glasses stood on the bench next to the pigsty. In winter there could be no thought of ninepins, and then the café was really crowded—some playing cards, old men with their feet on the stove smoking pipes, some telling stories of ghosts and witches—and always warm given the crush of people. But it was the singing that Ernest Claes remembered best, especially on winter nights. One man, whose nickname was Spider, "didn't know one song when he was sober," but "after his seventh or eighth drink somehow he knew twenty-five and could not be shut up."

The biggest songleader was the smith himself, who when it was his turn stuck his chaw of tobacco in his vest pocket, took a swig of beer, and yelled out, "We'll sing about Malbroek!"* Here was one of the

---

*This is the Flemish name for the Duke of Marlborough, the eighteenth-century English commander who led armies against Louis XIV.

smith's great heroes, and he launched right in, through endless verses and refrains, allowing others to join in only on the refrain.

Yet Malbroek wasn't the smith's favorite song. Instead that was the song about the "French doll." He sang this less often because his wife Melanie didn't like it, for as the most sophisticated woman in the village, she rightly suspected that the song was "just a little bit about her." Still, if she were out of the room, and no young boys were present, then the men would egg on the smith until he finally "would set himself a little more firmly on his chair" and then begin singing about the alluring and sophisticated "French doll." Everyone was allowed to join in on the refrain and also on the last tragic verse. When that big moment arrived, the smith always looked toward the kitchen door to make sure Melanie wasn't nearby, then signaled the others to join in. They sang that verse with a face "as if they were sitting in a Requiem Mass," lamenting he had ever married the French Doll.

These were the possibilities that made up the Sundays of Ernest Claes and many other villagers seeking a bright spot amid the dreariness and poverty of everyday life. They were not the Sundays of all. Here as in other countries were plenty of people who did not enjoy Sunday—those who had to work, those who didn't have enough money to join in popular recreations, or those who didn't know what to do with themselves when not working and thus were literally driven crazy by the stillness of the day, as in Stijn Streuvels's story "Summer Sunday." And now even those who had been able to see Sunday as a bright spot were about to regard the day otherwise as well.

The invasion of Belgium commenced along the eastern border, as expected, where overconfident German forces charged the forts of Liège with wave after wave of infantry. At least 25,000 German soldiers were mowed down in these early days by Belgian machine guns and cannons, but when the Germans brought in their big guns, the ragtag Belgian army proved no match for this strongest army in the world. Within three weeks the German army had taken Liège, Namur, Dinant, Leuven, Brussels, and all of the east on its way into France. The French, who would suffer monstrous losses of troops during the war, soon criticized the Belgians for offering apparently feeble resistance. But neutral Belgium had not wanted this fight, yet fought anyway at great cost—for as Germany had promised, there was to be retribution for resistance. When the German advance was finally halted just outside Paris, part of the German army stayed in France to hold its position while another part returned to Belgium to finish the work of conquest and take it over. All talk of just "passing through" was forgotten: the goal now was to achieve total domination, or as German generals put it, to squeeze Belgium dry, "slowly like a lemon."

On October 9, the German army took Antwerp, one of the greatest port cities in the world. By early November most of the rest of Belgium had fallen too; only a small, westernmost sliver of coast was saved thanks to the centuries-old remedy of opening the dikes around the Ijzer River to hinder further advances. Now virtually all of Belgium was in German hands. And then the war bogged down: it would not be over by Christmas after all, as many had thought. Instead, from December 1914, the combatants dug in on either side of a lengthy, immovable front stretching from the Belgian coast all the way across northern France and south to Switzerland. French, English, and Belgian armies were on one side of that front, mostly in France but also in the thirty-by-ten-kilometer sliver on Belgium's extreme west. The German army was on the other side, occupying the northernmost part of France, all of Luxembourg, and almost all of Belgium. The situation would remain much the same for the next four years of horror and wretched Sundays.

Two basic themes ran through these new Sundays. First, all-consuming war usually made Sunday just another day of struggle, violence, and tedium. And second, people nevertheless tried to carry out familiar rituals meant to preserve something of the old Sunday. These two themes played out differently according to all the usual Sunday variables, such as social and economic considerations: those with more money, for instance, could find old Sunday luxuries on the black market. But what stood out especially as a difference-maker in one's Sunday experience was geography, especially one's proximity to the front line. The more distant from the front, the greater the chance that some semblance of the old Sunday remained. Soldiers and civilians closest to the front had very little Sunday, the few who remained in tiny Free Belgium had little more, while the vast majority of around seven million in Occupied Belgium had a slightly better chance at Sunday. But even in occupied regions, the sense of loss was profound.

SUNDAY IN TRENCHES

In the front trenches, the old Belgian Sunday practically ceased to exist, even as a dream.

This was due not only to the obliterating horrors of war but also to a new scheme of time for soldiers: four days in the front line, four days in the nearby second line, then four days of "rest" in the more distant third line. In 1917 this scheme was changed to six days in the front two lines and six days of rest in the third. Either way it made Sunday—or any other day—a secondary marker of time: what mattered most to soldiers were those four- or six-day cycles, of which Sunday might or might not be part. The ordinary week, and the names of days, meant little. Indeed, soldiers wrote in their journals that one of the things they noticed was that all days seemed the same to them now.

When trench warfare began in December 1914, some 52,000 Belgian soldiers occupied the westernmost front, down from the 117,000 who had begun the war. Their equipment was backward, their uniforms were ruined, their ammunition was depleted, they wore wooden clogs rather than boots, and they were quite lucky the German offensive stopped when it did. But the Belgian army stabilized and recovered, counting 168,000 better-equipped troops by the war's end. This was partly because the Ijzer front, where Belgian soldiers were stationed, was less lethal than elsewhere; the Germans on one side of the flooded Ijzer and the Belgians on the other were generally content to hold what they had rather than wage such suicidal offensives as those at Ieper or the Somme, which cost upward of a million English, French, and German lives. Yet despite suffering fewer offensives, the Belgian soldiers in the trenches still led an existence often as nightmarish as their counterparts on all sides.

While extending as the crow flies over a mere thirty-kilometer stretch of territory, Belgian trenches wound about in mazelike fashion to an actual length of four hundred miserable, wet, insect-ridden, rat-filled kilometers. Within this maze, Sunday and every day were domi-

nated by the regular routines of war, which ranged from long periods
of boredom to episodes of brutal and terrifying fighting. As the German soldier and Expressionist painter Otto Dix summed it up (for life
in the German trenches was much the same), it was lice, rats, barbed
wire, fleas, shells, bombs, underground caves, corpses, blood, liquor,
mice, cats, artillery, filth, bullets, mortars, fire, steel, the work of the
devil.

Above all else, almost every day on the Belgian front was wet; the
ground was so close to the water table that trenches had to be built up
with sandbags rather than dug down, and rain fell regularly all year
round. Yet for all the wetness, little water was suitable for drinking or
washing. And when things got especially wet, buried bodies floated to
the surface everywhere. So much dampness and contaminated water
helped spread disease: one-third of those who died on the Belgian front
succumbed to typhus, dysentery, bronchitis, and the flu.

Likewise present every day was the possibility of fierce fighting—
even on this "quieter" portion of the front, even on Sunday. In fact
Sunday fighting was an old habit by now. As strict as the Old Testament Israelites had been about their Sabbath, for instance, they still
made some allowances for war on that day. And although the eleventh-
century "Truce of God" among Christian knights banned fighting on
Sunday, it permitted defensive fighting. Because almost all combatants
considered themselves to be on the defensive one way or another, Sunday battles were predictably frequent. The famous Battle of Bouvines,
in France, was waged in July 1214 on a Sunday, among participants
who were quite aware of the fact and took care to justify it. Over the
next centuries, Christian Europe rarely gave even a second thought to
Sunday battles, and by Waterloo, and then World War I, there was no
thought at all. As the Scottish poet James Grahame cynically lamented:

> *Of all the murderous trades by mortals plied,*
> *'Tis War alone that never violates*
> *The hallowed day by simulate respect,*
> *By hypocritic rest.*

But if Sunday fighting was an old habit by World War I, it was more
horrific than ever. High-explosive gunpowder, rapid-fire rifles, machine

guns, poisonous gas, flame-throwers, and long-range artillery shot over miles at unseen targets—all products of the recent industrial age—amplified the usual terror and made slaughter more efficient than ever. For instance, at least twenty thousand British soldiers alone fell on the first day at the Somme. Perhaps stronger than the fear of death was the fear of maiming, for the new weapons were particularly adept at blowing off limbs, an especially frightening prospect among those many skilled and unskilled soldiers who in peacetime made a living with their hands. A Belgian chaplain named Van Herck noted one Sunday a soldier's complete dismemberment by a direct artillery hit: "first we found his splattered brains, then a hand, then a broken piece with two ribs," until eventually they gathered five sacks of remains. Such scenes, and the deafening roar of guns, helped to make psychological shock, often called "shell shock," another constant presence. So was smell, which some soldiers remembered perfectly years later, from the rotting corpses of men, horses, mules, and rats, all mixed with excrement, lingering gases, and the acrid odor of artillery shells. And this was not to mention the fiery throats, burning chests, and sweat dripping from beneath iron helmets that accompanied fighting on any day.

As terrifying as the fighting was, even more likely in the first line every day was outright boredom. Shelling with large guns was sporadic—now overwhelming, now quiet. Shooting of small arms might be more frequent, even daily, as small patrols popped up briefly from the other side to gather intelligence. But still more time was spent simply waiting. As Henri Barbusse, a famous French author on war, observed, soldiers were machines of waiting: one waited while leaning against the trench, one waited for relief from new troops, one waited for letters, the next round of shelling, soup, daylight, and finally death.

To relieve stress and boredom, soldiers might engage in temporary and usually implicit truces with enemy troops to "live and let live," quite against official policy on both sides to "kill or be killed." These truces were most famous and explicit at Christmas rather than on Sunday, but they might occur on any day in more subtle form: not shooting artillery at breakfast time so that both sides might eat, not shooting at the enemy during cold weather when he was out gathering straw because you would have to do this yourself, shooting past targets, beating out rhythms of popular tunes with a machine gun to entertain others

while satisfying the commanders' demands to fire, using mortars to lob
beef tins to the other side. All were the result of soldiers coming to realize that they had more in common with their counterparts in the other
trenches than with their own high command. One reason commanders
on both sides kept issuing orders for suicidal offensives was not mere
stupidity but the knowledge that the more opposing soldiers understood each other, the less inclined they would be to fight: offensives kept
the juices of hatred and anger and fear flowing.

Better-known ways of relieving daily tension and tedium on the first
line included playing cards and reading. Especially as the war bogged
down, demand for reading materials increased. Some 278 different
newspapers for Belgian soldiers appeared during the war, and the favorites were decidedly not the few "official" newspapers, despised by
soldiers for their unreliability and for encouraging fighting to the awful end. Flemish-speaking troops were also supposed to be equipped
with the *Mass and Prayer Book of the Flemish Soldier.* Other edifying
books were directed at them as well, condemning loose women, the
French *philosophe* Voltaire, or the common soldierly habits of looting,
drunkenness, and making light of religion. At least as common as devotional materials, however, was erotica, including not only ribald
songs but especially printed and written material, whose presence most
chaplains naturally blamed on French allies.

In addition to reading, soldiers in the front lines might write letters,
especially to so-called "war godmothers," young ladies from various
Allied and friendly countries who volunteered to write to Allied
soldiers—such as this American example: "Noticing your appeal in the
Tribune of October 4th for American Girls to write to Belgian soldiers,
I am writing you for three or four names. There are four girls in our
family and we should each be glad to cheer any soldier of the 'Allied
Army' and especially a Belgian, the most wonderfully courageous
country of loving people in the world, with the exception of America,
of course." Eight thousand such godmothers were writing to nine
thousand Belgian soldiers by the end of the war.

One activity in first-line trenches was indeed more common on Sunday than on other days: Mass. Chaplain Van Herck found it an unforgettable experience, celebrated as it was inside a place where "one
could hardly stand erect, and only meters from the Germans." Another

chaplain noted with gratification those soldiers who knelt in the trenches every Sunday, sometimes in the mud, to receive the Holy Sacrament. But Mass lasted but a moment in the trenches, and not at all if fighting was heavy. Even when Mass was possible, another chaplain complained that at its conclusion he had nothing to do the rest of the day except spend his time in "lazy trifles," so that it didn't seem like Sunday at all.

Life in the second line of trenches was similar to life in the first: slightly more removed from enemy lines but easily within range of big guns, and thus full of the same mixture of boredom and tension. More obviously different for soldiers, including on Sunday, was the third or "rest" line. This meant that soldiers now moved back to barracks or private homes in nearby towns of Free Belgium and northern France, and that they might have up to half of their Sunday for genuine rest and diversion.

Soldiers still in training camps on the third line spoke of "Sunday hours," which meant Mass, the occasional inspection, maybe a class, and much free time, as most of their training occurred during the week. Often they spent Sunday in a café or on a terrace, reading newspapers, strolling around town, visiting the barber or dentist, eating at their "usual restaurant," and invariably running back to barracks at night to meet curfew.

But this rather relaxed schedule changed once soldiers joined the fighting. Then they were back on the third line for just an occasional and busier Sunday, including marching in straight lines, which those who knew the trenches found to be a ludicrous waste of time. They found just as ludicrous required Sunday afternoon classes on such subjects as "Long Live the King," instructing them always to obey and never to murmur, and concluding with patriotic songs that caused the battle-hardened to "double over with laughter."

Usually a busy third-line Sunday also promised a somewhat ordinary Mass. This might occur in a still-standing village or an urban church, but just as often took place in a barn: scores of genuine churches, their towers regarded as potential lookout points, were destroyed early on by long-range German shelling. Chaplain Van Herck wrote that he cel-

ebrated nine o'clock Mass one Sunday in a barn, where the three horses
to the right of the altar listened "with great interest."

At least as likely to be visited on Sunday was a café, just as in peacetime. But now the beer was bad, as were the food and tobacco, and the
places tended to stink. Still, soldiers went anyway, and it was no coin-
cidence that those who got in trouble with their own military police for
being "uppity" often did so on a Sunday, when the cafés were fullest
and the drinking went on longest. Various journal keepers noted that
in the towns of Free Belgium and northern France, the military police
often had to raid taverns and confiscate strong drink, because too
many soldiers were becoming drunk, especially on Sunday. There were
also "chic restaurants" in some villages, but most soldiers could not afford these and thus stuffed themselves more cheaply along the "frites
boulevards" ("frites" were soon called "French fries" in English but
were actually invented in Belgium).

Another old urban ritual that continued during the third-line Sunday was visiting libraries, art exhibits, and other cultural opportunities, but these were now directed especially at soldiers. The town hall
of Alveringem, for instance, hosted over the course of three weeks an
exhibit of pieces created by soldiers themselves: no less than four hundred soldiers and civilians attended on any single day, with a high of
twelve hundred one Sunday. The exhibit reflected the soldiers' world
only too well: a miniature bomb-thrower, constructed from metal
found in trenches, that could shoot seventy-five meters; small torpedo
shells that actually exploded; a small field cannon with bombs; a lady's
pin in the shape of a bayonet; and all sorts of airplanes, paper cutters,
ashtrays, and more. There were also such paintings as "The Louse
Seeker," "Landscape of a Bleak Front," "Helmets," "The Bridge at the
Farm," "The Spy," "Sublieutenant Machine-Gunner Coninx," and a
mother having her children pray for their father at the front. Drama
and music were perhaps the two most important cultural activities on
the third line, and as before the war, Sunday remained the most important occasion for them. The army organized an orchestral symphony
and various string quartets, and the soldiers' Masses inside third-line
churches became well known for their remarkable singing: it helped
them to forget their misery for a moment, said stretcher-bearer Vols.
There were also language classes and reading classes, for as many as

10 percent of Belgian soldiers were still illiterate, compared to 5 percent of French.

Finally, soldiers on the third line tried a variety of other old favorites, if in new form. Some fished and swam. Others picked vegetables in the soldiers' garden and had a decent salad for once. Some walked to half-ruined towns and tried to amuse themselves despite the dilapidated state of things. One Sunday the French general Poincaré gave one thousand francs to soldiers in the Belgian town of De Panne to throw themselves a party. Occasionally soldiers were granted a genuine vacation—longer than a four-day break on the third line—to Paris or Le Havre, some even to London. The army medical doctor Joseph De Cuyper spent part of his Sunday there walking with the English in Hyde Park. Paris was the most popular destination, reputed among soldiers as a city of 300,000 women, and a chief purpose of this trip was indeed sexual. There were no official brothels in the Belgian army, as in the French and German, but there were plenty of unofficial such places behind the front lines. These, combined with trips to Paris, resulted in venereal diseases for about 7 percent of Belgian soldiers by 1917.

FREE SUNDAY

The few civilians who still lived in the tiny unoccupied part of Belgium shared Sunday with soldiers on the third line, for civilian towns and villages *were* the third line. They therefore shared many of the same experiences as well.

A big part of this was because most of Free Belgium soon came within range of the war's powerful new guns. When the shooting began, German guns had a range of twelve kilometers. But a new German gun called Long Max reached to forty-seven kilometers—nearly thirty miles—with shells over six feet long and weighing more than two thousand pounds.

Thanks to these guns, plus the novelty of airplanes dropping bombs, civilians even thirty miles removed from either side of the front were likely to spend at least part of Sunday, like soldiers, dodging shells. The closer a town was to the trenches, the more likely it was to be fully destroyed, but just about every nearby town incurred some damage. Indeed both sides could have devastated even more villages and towns than they did. This knowledge caused great tension on every line, especially during the eternal moments between the shooting of a gun and the actual explosion of its shell. Just as terrifying was the silent and often deadly release of poison gas, such as at Armentières on a Sunday in July, when civilians fled into their cellars at the news of gas; more than one thousand were poisoned anyway, and three hundred were killed. Over time, civilians near the fighting, like soldiers, learned to distinguish the sorts of shells being fired and the likelihood of one landing near them: several women in Poperinge, for instance, sat outside their doors sewing even while the shelling went on just blocks away, because the shells had never come closer than that. At each explosion they simply crossed themselves, said, "May God punish Germany," and continued sewing.

Just as fighting might come to civilians on Sunday, so might other dirty business of war, such as executions of deserting and traitorous soldiers. Judicial executions of all sorts in previous centuries often were deliberately *not* performed on Sunday, but during World War I, Sunday was common enough for such matters, especially as the war went on and more and more soldiers deserted. Because civilians had more free time on Sunday, even during war, a Sunday execution was also more public than usual.

The Belgian chaplain Cyril Verschaeve spent a long Sunday in October 1914 "dragging his soul along the ground," consoling a deserter to death. At six A.M., Verschaeve entered the prisoner's room—an unsettling sight for the man, because the appearance of a priest signified the end. And the man seemed little interested in talking about religion, either in this room or as they rode in a car to the execution ground. Pastor Verschaeve wondered whether he was "talking too high," as priests called it. At one point the condemned man needed to stop and relieve himself and did so chained to his guard. But he shook so badly that when finished he could not get his clothes straight again without help. Finally the car stopped near a cemetery and church, and the man's face went pale gray.

Pastor Verschaeve hoped that the execution would at least be finished before Mass let out. But the guards were slow to settle on a spot, and people began streaming from the church while looking at the big car. Within fifteen minutes the crowd had learned the news and there-

fore stayed put. Boys pointed their fingers at the condemned, and soldiers stood warily watching at a distance, for they knew that such punishments were meant partly as a warning to them. Verschaeve asked
the crowd to please give the man room in his last moments, but another hour passed before all was arranged. Those in charge settled on
the back wall of a tavern, not far from the church. To reach it the entire party had to walk through the crowded tavern, whose patrons
stared hard. The prisoner was blindfolded as the priest said the last
words, then let the man kiss the cross. Finally came the order
"Chargez," the click of the guns, and the command to fire. It was quarter after nine on Sunday, not long after early Mass, when the man fell
dead against the wall.

Sunday was also an "ordinary" war day in the hospitals of Free Belgium, where the stream of wounded from the not-so-distant trenches
was constant and heavy. As the famous German novelist Erich Maria
Remarque said, "only in hospital does one begin to understand what
war actually is." Each Sunday the Belgian nurse Jane de Launoy assisted at the operating table, worked heroically long hours, and engaged in such selfless actions as exposing herself to typhus, tetanus,
and other diseases borne by wounded soldiers—just as she did every
day. Except for a few patients attending chapel, and except for a short
break, Jane's Sunday routine was indistinguishable from that of other
days. As she so succinctly put it one night when too weary to record
details, she was "always working without a break and wrestling
through difficulties."

Another night she summed things up at greater length: shells flying
past, new patients constantly coming in (often dead), serum drop by
drop, oxygen, bandaging, washing, combing, delousing, clipping,
making beds, imposing order, feet like lead, contending with mercurial
doctors who might upset an entire medicine chest because it was not
in order, rotating stations too frequently to see patients all the way
through. Not to mention comforting civilian girls who came here to be
near their wounded boyfriends, then watched the boyfriends die. Or
hearing people say that nurses chose their occupation out of morbid
curiosity, or paternalistic snobbery, or simply to get a husband.

But just like third-line soldiers, Jane de Launoy and other civilians
tried to make Sunday as different as possible. She too attended Mass

on her Sundays off or during her two-hour Sunday break, but this was
no peacetime Mass. When stationed in the once-glittering Belgian resort town of De Panne, Jane went to the same church as King Albert I
and Queen Elisabeth, who enjoyed a good reputation among their people for staying so close to the front. One Sunday in the royal church,
shelling commenced on the town at 9:20, twenty minutes into the service. The church's windows shook from a nearby explosion, and some
inside the church were in a panic to rush out; police guarding the door
drove them back. Jane ran beneath an arch, thinking that if the ceiling
came down, she, as the only nurse present, had to be prepared to help
others. The king himself, seated in his usual place in the left aisle,
didn't move a muscle, aware that every eye was turned on him. He
looked a bit pale, said Jane, but otherwise continued following Mass,
which seemed a bit "otherworldly now, even an out of body experience." She would never forget that Mass, she said. As soon as it finished, she rushed to the hospital to help with the inevitable stream of
wounded: in fact, 127 of them were waiting, including officers, soldiers, women, and children.

More often Sunday Mass was less dangerous in Free Belgium and
even an emotional rallying point. For it was at such moments in ordered, purposeful gatherings, near enough to battle but removed from
the awfulness of dying alone in a trench, that heroic resolutions were
easiest to make and seemed most possible to fulfill. Twenty-year-old
Jeroom Leuridan noted the overwhelming guilt he felt during Sunday
Mass while kneeling amid Belgian soldiers: they were just his age, and
he had not yet enlisted. The melancholy deepened as he noticed the
broad scar on the pale cheek of the rifleman standing next to him, and
soon after that Sunday gathering he enlisted as well. This sense of resolve was only heightened by the stirring music of military choirs in
khakis, boots, and spurs beneath lacy choir robes, by the military
trumpets blaring out dramatically at the moment of consecration, and
by the inordinate quantities of lovely flowers (which Jane de Launoy
often took back to the hospital to decorate the rooms of the wounded).

Even less elaborate Masses, held in taverns or barns or partially ruined churches, full of refugees with tattered clothing and beaten-down
faces, could stir emotions. Jozef Simons attended a shot-up church one
Sunday in Poperinge, where about fifty could gather inside and where

only parts of the stained-glass windows survived, but the sunbeams that glided through the remaining glass and threw their lights over the altar and robes carried "fantastic colors." In such settings, the music too might be more striking than usual, with the soldiers' "thundering bass" reassuring all while cannon boomed in the background, and deeply bowed heads conveying resolve.

Because of Mass, Sunday remained as in peacetime the biggest day for priests, whether at the front or on the third line. Indeed, at times there were more Masses than usual on war Sundays: a chaplain Van Walleghem said anywhere from eighteen to twenty-five Masses some Sundays, whether in barns, in the open air, inside churches with birds flying in and out of gaping holes, or even in churches filled with wounded soldiers. Bells did not ring for Mass on wartime Sundays, because it would announce to the German army that everyone was in church—as if they needed that intelligence—and in fact a number of priests and civilians died while at Mass. Thus priests read Mass quickly, to get everyone out as soon as possible. The English Protestant clergy in Free Belgium were likewise busy on Sunday, holding their services almost always in fields rather than in proper churches. But this was not only to avoid collapsing roofs: although military allies, these English clergymen were also religious rivals to Belgium's Catholic priests, who were reluctant to allow Protestants the use of any Catholic church still standing. And so English Protestants almost always worshiped in fields—which had the decided advantage, however, of granting the worshipers immediate access to the usual match of English football that followed. Like churches, these matches could be targets for bombs: one Sunday in May 1917 saw more than twenty footballers wounded by shelling.

Sunday Mass offered another attraction in wartime: one could see not only Belgian soldiers up close but also Allied troops from France, England, and Russia. (Americans arrived in 1917.) Relations among these troops fluctuated, as did relations between the troops and Belgian civilians. But Sunday Mass was the moment when some of the most favorable impressions of other soldiers occurred. The Russians seemed exotic, and the English well behaved.

More complicated were the French, for whom Belgians as always reserved their most mixed sentiments. Ernest Claes once noted that the

Belgian clergy had long taken the lead in condemning France as "spoiled," "sinful," a "giant Sodom and Gomorrah," something "like hell itself," for here was the land of the church-smashing French Revolution, the land that separated church and state, the land that chased monks and nuns. Yet in the next breath, these same teacher-priests took great care to fill Belgian students with French language, literature, science, spirit, and culture, so that "we were completely Frenchified and our young minds a well-prepared field to receive that spoiled sinfulness of Godless France." Most Belgians doing the condemning had never been to France. Neither had Claes, but his association with French prisoners during his own wartime imprisonment in Germany convinced him that they were "no worse than we are," and in fact perhaps the opposite was true, for he had seen French soldiers during Sunday Mass, praying fervently and approaching the altar for the Holy Sacrament. Certainly some French distinguished themselves through their brutality and immoral chatter, but so did some German and Belgian soldiers, reminded Claes. There was a "naturally spontaneous good-heartedness" in the French that you have to love, he concluded. There was no pretension. And though they stood upon some point of trivia like it was life and death, they were "rainbows in full summer."

Outside of church services, civilians, like soldiers, tried to spend the day as much as possible in the old style. The people of Poperinge, determined to have their Sunday, went out walking along the town's pockmarked boulevards. During sunny afternoons in March and April 1915 there was bombing but also much promenading, and even concerts between the shelling.

Jane de Launoy noted the crowds that walked along the beach of De Panne on Sunday, equally determined to have their special day, even while shells sometimes exploded above their heads. Once Jane herself and a friend were so walking one Sunday when debris from antiaircraft guns began falling around them; they simply moved a few yards into the water, colder but safer. On another busy Sunday, a great crowd of people swam in the ocean, including two of Jane's girlfriends, when suddenly an English plane crashed just behind them into the water. The wave from the splash swamped the girls, while the two surviving pilots bobbed up and down nearby. One pilot removed his jacket, shirt, and shoes to swim more easily, and began to remove his pants as well—until he saw the girls, whose heads were already spinning. Would the pilots choose drowning or honor? mused Jane. Because it was Sunday, a large number of British soldiers were strolling along the beach at that moment and happened to see it all: determined to aid the pilots, about twenty stripped naked and swam out. Jane's two friends, still stunned and looking at the plane, were unaware of the "modern Adams" about to descend upon them. The pilots were saved and the crowd on the beach broke into laughter and cheers, while the poor girls simply floated on their backs as the swimmers passed by. Even the hospital emptied to see the scene, and on the beach a naked British soldier wearing only a helmet snapped as many pictures as he could.

One purpose of Jane's Sunday walks down the beach of De Panne was not merely to relax or tempt fate but to visit her family at home during her two-hour break in the afternoon. More than once while at home she fell asleep during dinner, in front of her plate, while everyone ate quietly so as not to disturb her. When she had an entire Sunday off, she sometimes spent it at the family home sleeping. Once she took a hard-earned vacation to Paris, and on Sunday made sure to ride a boat on a lake in the Bois de Boulogne.

Jane mentioned two other peacetime forms of Sunday diversion still attempted during war. One was the skits she and a friend were persuaded to stage in honor of the king and queen, which Jane thought Queen Elisabeth in her pink golf pants and satin blouse thoroughly enjoyed. The second was Sunday musical concerts, which she did not organize but certainly attended, noting the baffling mixed variety of prize-winning classical violinists and bawdy soldier choruses.

All the concerts, plays, and promenading were brave attempts to make Sunday, and life, normal, but even the steel-nerved Jane de Launoy admitted that these went only so far to soothe the turmoil within. After one memorable Sunday shelling, she wrote of herself and fellow nurses, "How can we all be normal women after this?"

OCCUPIED SUNDAY

If Sunday was absent in the trenches and somewhat present in Free Belgium, then surely it was saddest in Occupied Belgium, where eight in ten natives still lived—but now under foreign rule.

Experience varied here as well of course. In general, occupied villages and towns lying near the front endured much the same sort of anxiety on Sunday as those in Free Belgium, while villages and towns lying deeper in Belgium suffered less from actual fighting than from boredom, malaise, and hunger. Experience also changed over time. Conditions became critical from winter 1916 on, so that by the end of 1917 almost three million people, some 40 percent of the population, were in serious need; such basic items as building supplies and diapers, to name but two, were nonexistent. Occupied Belgium was indeed being squeezed dry (one recent historian prefers the more violent metaphor of rape) and was seen increasingly by German command as the sole source of support for the entire German war operation.

Most in the occupied areas experienced the war and its emaciated Sundays as they had more pleasant Sundays in old days: in villages and small towns.

Stijn Streuvels, a well-known novelist of Belgian rural life, left a particularly detailed wartime account of his own village, Ingooigem, population 1,569. Only miles behind the active front, it knew little actual fighting but instead much waiting, uncertainty, and deprivation, just like most villages. More than most witnesses he included reflections in his massive journal on how war changed Sunday.

When the war was just a month old, he wrote that Sunday was no longer "the great point of change in the series of weekdays, when one thinks of going out or of diversion." That world was already gone, and one stayed at home instead, "reading the papers." There was no more music on Sunday, and no desire for it, because it now sounded "sour in our ears" under the prevailing mood of seriousness: all trivialities were forgotten, and one especially feared that making merry with music might offend those villagers who mourned a brother or father or husband in the army. The old "festiveness of Sunday morning" now contrasted mightily with the quiet anxiety of waiting for news, "like the ceasing of life's breath." In short, with thoughts so riveted on war, hardly anything else, including Sunday, mattered. Indeed, doctors in the village noted that since the war had begun, there was almost no illness: people had no time or inclination to think about how they felt. When Kermis Sunday rolled around in October, no one thought of observing it, but instead wanted like every day to climb a nearby hill and hear the cannon better, in order to guess the progress of the battle. War did not observe Sunday, concluded Streuvels.

This change in mood made Sundays uncharacteristically boring in villages, a "dead day." Indeed it was on Sunday that sorrow weighed the heaviest, and loneliness was least bearable, because Sunday's customary easing and granting of relief from the worry and drudgery of the week had vanished. Sunday had always brought variety and hope, but now the calendar "was a long strip of paper filled with the same sort of numbers: no more of the red-lettered Sundays and feast days" of time past. Without a real Sunday, there was in fact less sense of time, period. Occasionally villagers realized, like soldiers in the trenches, that they had no idea what day it was. And yet Streuvels himself always knew when it was Sunday. Things got so bad that he actually found himself wishing, in a most uncharacteristic Belgian fashion, that it would never be Sunday at all, because disappointments were then all the greater, the contrast with old Sundays more obvious. "Compelled worklessness" during the week meant merely boredom; but compelled inactivity on Sunday meant sitting there and suffering deeper sadness and anxiety than ever. He wrote of Sunday passing in the "blackest loneliness," of how odd it was that on lovely summer Sundays now not one person was to be seen over the whole landscape, of how people didn't bother to wear their Sunday best on Sunday any longer, and of how people had not even a piece of fat for their Sunday dinner. True, there was no excess, and no brawling, any longer on Sundays, yet he missed even these because they at least signaled variety and life. War simply "leveled and erased" Sunday.

In this setting, the "slightest tremor of excitement" on Sunday stood out like a massive shaking of the earth. One Sunday a street organ unexpectedly played outside Streuvels's door—an "insane contrast" to the quiet of a dead parish, and the sound made him melancholy. Sunday visitors were rare, and indeed it was a "romantic surprise" when someone knocked at the door on Sunday, just to talk. Even with complete strangers, conversation flowed, if always about the war, in contrast with the old days, when people "split hairs" to keep conversations going. But even these conversations were too rare on Sunday.

Just as in Free Belgium, the old ritual of Sunday Mass continued in occupied territory too, if even more strongly colored by war. Churches

on the occupied side of the front hardly resembled themselves anymore, if they were still standing at all. One pastor noted that an unusually chilly Sunday in April 1916 meant an icy first communion for
the local children, because all of the church's windows and part of the
roof were gone; the children stood in the covered choir, but the altar
where the pastor prepared the Holy Sacrament was exposed to the
heavens, and snowflakes fell into his chalice. Sunday services were also
held at less convenient times now. Unlike in Free Belgium, where
Catholic pastors had authority to deny the use of their churches to
Protestant allies, occupied Belgian villages were simply told by the local German authority that services for Protestant troops would be held
at one hour and Catholic services at another; sometimes German
Catholic soldiers also had a separate service.

None of these services were announced by church bells. German authorities wished to save them for emergencies, or feared that bells
could be a signal to revolt. But most often the bells had simply been
shipped to Germany, where they were melted down and fashioned into
cannons and other armaments. Such an empty-sounding Sunday was a
strange experience for a country accustomed to living by the rhythms
of its bells. The emptiness was accentuated when, bells or not, fewer
people came to Mass: some studies have argued that attendance increased because of war, others that it declined. There is some consensus now that overall attendance did decline during the war, but at
crucial moments—the initial invasion, various offensives—it picked up
dramatically.

Surely the sermons at Mass contributed as well at times to the
empty feeling of Sunday. After the initial shock of occupation wore off,
and soldiers and villagers reached a working understanding of what
was allowed, the pastors began climbing back into the pulpits. They
preached on plenty of the old topics, even if many seemed hopelessly
irrelevant now. But more common were topics directly related to war,
and these had a far better chance of inducing sadness.

One of the favorite themes for Sunday sermons in Streuvels's parish,
as in many others, was that war was a punishment from God because
of the "looseness of morals" in the land (and of course in France). The
only sure way to end their suffering, said pastors, was through penance
and virtue. On the way home from such a sermon, Streuvels walked

with a man who fretted that "God divides up these punishments so badly!" The man had three sons in the Belgian army whose fate he didn't know, the German soldiers in the village had just taken his cow, and what would he feed his wife and daughters this winter? Yet he had done penance his entire life "through my poverty and have never harmed one child." He could therefore not understand why God might send the plague of three dead sons upon him, as the pastor suggested. Streuvels wondered quietly how in the world pastors could speak of penance and punishments to "such simple good people forced to give up their sons."

He heard as well of other pastors who from their Sunday pulpit took upon themselves the role of Jonah among the Ninevites, predicting which sinful cities would fall next. Fashionable Antwerp was already ruined, so that Brussels and the port city of Oostende now stood at the top of the list. Streuvels concluded from such sermons, and from repeated condemnations of worldliness and pleasure-seeking generally, that although many pastors had worked among their flocks for years, they hardly understood their needs and mentality, but merely sought to "control people through threats." Who in this poor village, he wrote, was preoccupied with exaggerated desire, luxury, and worldliness and thus deserved chastisement from God? And did priests have no "luxury or ease" themselves? Then how dare they criticize those who had none?

Ernest Claes felt the same about the Sunday sermons he heard: did pastors really need to emphasize that sorrow and misery were punishment from God for sins? Most people, he figured, reasoned more simply: all that misery came from Germany. One pastor supposed that the tears he saw after such sermons were tears of penance, but in fact they were tears of discouragement after trying so hard. Certainly people always fell short in something, and so their troubles could always be linked to punishment from God. But this wasn't persuasive to the likes of Streuvels or Claes or even to less articulate villagers.

Another common topic for the Sunday sermon was the memorial for the local dead, when the sobbing of friends and relatives conferred an even more somber tone than usual. On the other hand, such memorials became common enough in Streuvels's village that people not immediately affected grew casual: he saw singers in the choir giggling, for instance, making the whole proceeding seem a "mere bunch of words." Sometimes it seemed so to him as well: such common terms in sermons as "heroic courage," he decided, were too often merely an invention to motivate people to do things they would never do on their own, another way of "using lovely words to cover horrible things." There were also sermons on being kind to refugees who regularly tramped through the villages of western Belgium while fleeing shelled villages near the front—Allied guns could shoot at long distances as well. People in Ingooigem felt for these refugees, because who knew when they too might be next on the road to nowhere. But that did not mean they always helped them; indeed they grew weary of them, and such Sunday sermons rang hollow over time.

Some of the sharpest rebukes during the Sunday sermon were directed at profiteers, who saw not ruin but opportunity in war. The shoemaker Felicien Vanhove reported in his journal that his pastor repeatedly sermonized on the need for storekeepers to post prices rather than invent them for each customer who came in, and to mark items up at most by 20 percent above cost rather than the exorbitant amounts he saw. Here at last was a wartime sermon many people liked to hear, for most did not keep stores and favored low prices. But Vanhove the shoemaker was sensitive to it. He could not deny that war had given him more business than ever before, thanks largely to the German troops who needed his services, but he did not wish to be seen as a profiteer. Thus even as he complained in his journal that he worked most Sundays and therefore "had no Sunday," he also gushed about the phenomenal sums of money he made on that day, sums he had never approached in peacetime. To assuage his conscience, or to put himself in good stead with his neighbors, he also noted that he smuggled out large sums of money to support troops fighting in Free Belgium.

Even sharper than the rebukes of profiteers in Sunday sermons were those directed at the alleged sins of women, but now in the context of war. Streuvels did not hear many such sermons in Ingooigem, but others near the front recorded them often, such as the loquacious physician Jules Git. Priests in his village saved their best thunder for girls who lingered near the doors of cafés full of German soldiers, and for married women whose husbands were often fighting in Free Belgium.

"Your husband or brother is fighting, and you lead a loose life!" railed more than one pastor on Sunday, some going so far as to say that such women were unworthy of the names "Belgian" and "Christian." "Sadly," reported Jules Git without explaining details, some women "deserved this." But the doctor was not necessarily in favor of the "charivari" or upside-down serenade, used for centuries to publicly condemn those who violated social mores: it was not coincidentally a Sunday when one young woman in his village, who had spoken too long to soldiers, was "serenaded" by more than a hundred young people, constantly whistling and hissing at her for fifteen minutes while escorting her from the village.

Related Sunday sermons noted the "light and wolfish clothing of our women," with one pastor urging people to spit on women who went into the streets with "exposed neck and chest." Dr. Git noted with some regret that rarely had people responded so immediately and literally to a sermon, as afterward some schoolgirls did just that. The doctor himself was scandalized more by the finery of women than by their exposed necks: one Sunday he was so bored that he merely stared out the window, and in so doing was stunned at "what women could wear after twenty-two months of war": sheer stockings, silk blouses, colorful dresses, and shiny "doll shoes." The "American stores," so called because Americans played a major role in the Committee for the Relief of Belgium, even put up signs saying that there would be no food for those who dressed too fashionably. Still other sermons warned women not even to think about approaching the communion table on Sunday with an exposed neck.

Whatever the extent of familiarity may have been between women and German soldiers, it suggested a wider phenomenon present especially in villages, and certainly in Streuvel's Ingooigem: namely, that as the populace got to know the soldiers firsthand, either through living under the same roof with them or seeing them on Sundays at church, they felt less enmity than expected. They even came to see that German soldiers were much like them.

A good part of that realization came during Sunday Mass. Just as those in Free Belgium undid some of their prejudices toward foreign Allies through attending church with them on Sunday, so did people of Occupied Belgium encounter during Sunday Mass the unexpected thought that their avowed enemies were decidedly human. Plenty of Belgians long resented and feared the mostly Protestant Prussian soldiers in the German army, but soldiers from Bavaria were mostly Catholic and often worshiped alongside the Belgian locals at Sunday Mass, where they made a big impression.

It was at Sunday Mass that the heroine of Ernest Claes's *The Mother and the Three Soldiers* first felt sympathy for the three German soldiers who had for some days been billeted in her barn. Early in the Mass she prayed for her two sons in the Belgian army with her whole heart, "that they might return home soon from the war." But then she saw "her" three German soldiers standing in the rear—one skinny, one scarred, one coughing—"in their faded uniforms, and now they too were mixed up in her thoughts for her own soldierly sons. "The Mother had the impression that they all resembled each other, as if they were more or less one, all those poor soldiers." After Mass a neighbor friend chatted with the Mother, ranting about how evil the Germans were and asking whether there was news from her sons. Usually the Mother liked speaking with the neighbor, but not after this comment: no, she had no news. And she no longer spoke with the neighbor, who considered all German soldiers evil. Henceforth each Sunday during church the Mother prayed not only for her two boys but also for "her three German soldiers and their wives, children, and mothers."

Claes did not see such things firsthand, for he spent the Great War in Germany as a prisoner, but the story does reflect that gradual change in sentiments that many surprised villagers experienced. It also suggests, however, through the neighbor woman, that this change was neither complete nor universal nor simple. For even while sympathy emerged, fierce resentment against the German army persisted, especially because before the war, wrote Stijn Streuvels, many Belgians regarded Germany as a doting older brother. France was the place of decline—"overcivilized, rotten, godless"—and England was an "egotistical, sly oppressor." Then war began, and suddenly the French and the English were their best friends, while the Germans were the caricatured officer with the monocle and a horrible scar over his cheek, loud and arrogant.

Streuvels, who himself quartered German soldiers, summarized the complex reality: some soldiers were indeed big and bad, but others were not. Some were delighted when locals spoke German, others were angry when they did not. Most German soldiers looked like middle-aged fathers, quite ordinary without their pointed helmets. By the end the feeling in his village was that the Germans here, left to their own devices, wouldn't harm a cat. Such willingness to see German soldiers as fellow humans won Streuvels some harsh criticism from more fiery Belgians, when excerpts from his journal were published even while the war was raging.

But again he was hardly the only one to feel this way. Many knew the names of "their" soldiers staying with them, and counted how many came back from the front after rotation. They sat at the fireplace with them, learned about their families, and realized that the early stories of Germans cutting off the hands of countless children were exaggerated. Now they saw German troops treating children kindly and sharing rations with their host family. One journal keeper had a better memory of the Germans who lived with his family than of the English soldiers who later freed their village. And many commented on how piously German soldiers worshiped on Sunday. In the early stages of the war, news that Bavarian soldiers had confessed and communed went far toward calming Belgian villagers. And when villagers saw these soldiers in person, reported a pastor named Edmond Denys, praying piously, thumping their chests three times during the elevation, and bowing their heads deeply while taking communion, opinions immediately changed.

A new Sunday ritual in villages that probably hurt goodwill between the sides was the public reading of official decrees from local German authorities, performed right outside the main door of the church after Mass, while people exited. Often these involved the requisitioning of goods, which Stijn Streuvels noted faithfully for his village—almost fifty separate items, several repeated frequently. The decrees also dictated which crops people should plant and when, plus other farming matters, thus filling the Sunday air with great anxiety, as people feared what would be required next. Would all cattle be ordered to market by eleven the next day, or an entire harvest demanded? Villagers filled the air with grumbling too, especially when it was announced that strong drinks in taverns were for the umpteenth time prohibited.

But sometimes the decrees provided comic relief. To Streuvels's Ingooigem came word that all art objects must be turned in: people looked at each other quizzically, causing him to speculate that this was the first time the phrase "art objects" had been uttered in the village. Regularly the decrees revealed the German authorities' failure to grasp local conditions—such as the order to "plant every bit of their field" when they already had, or to plant more oil-bearing crops such as sunflowers, which brought even more laughter from the audience, for "real farmers never take flowers seriously." Equally humorous was the ban on all cockfighting, for the announcement was made in summer, and cockfighting, as everyone knew, occurred only in spring. But whatever laughter the Sunday announcements brought, it did not make the day much easier or relations better.

After Mass and the announcements, most villagers had little else to do on routine Sundays. Streuvels has already noted the reluctance to play on Sunday, at least among adults. But young people had a greater desire for release and relief. Teenagers in the village of Jules Git argued that just as the bow could not always be taut, so could they not always sit there crying and wailing about the war. One Sunday they therefore began singing loudly in a café, where they were arrested by German police for disorderliness. Adults were willing to celebrate first-communion Sundays for their children, but these were problematic too: the pastor in Git's village asked the more prosperous not to overdo new clothing for such days and to use any excess funds to purchase clothing for the first communions of poor children. Adults were also willing to hold parties to raise funds for Belgian prisoners of war, but pastors protested when such parties were held during Sunday Mass!

Here was how people in Occupied Belgium coped psychologically when they did decide to hold Sunday festivities: by linking the festivities to the relief of suffering. This was the stated purpose behind almost all concerts and plays that villages put on. The physician Jules Git was also an amateur playwright, and he was more delighted than anyone when a concert and farce, to benefit Belgian prisoners of war, were performed one Sunday afternoon in his village. "The actors even understood what they were doing!" he rejoiced. Especially "the local coiffeur, Gustaf," contributed to the high quality of the performance, which was enthusiastically attended and applauded. Still other Sunday shows were for the benefit of "The Clothing Work," and there were numerous soccer matches for some war-related cause.

Some Sunday activities, however, could be linked to no noble cause and were frowned upon no matter what. People avoided concerts and activities sponsored by German troops, usually held on town squares. Belgian priests denounced dancing at all times, especially during war and most especially if it occurred with German soldiers. The same was true of swimming: a Pastor Slosse could not refrain from expressing his disappointment that a policeman, church councilor, and two or three men from the local confraternity were only too eager to swim on Sunday, or at all. These were signs of the loose morals of the times, he concluded. The new cinema, especially popular on Sunday, met with mixed reactions: if the content was suitable, then priests did not object, but most were glad that children under sixteen were barred when such German movies as *Bride for One Night* and *The Bathing Maiden* were shown.

One acceptable old Sunday activity that disappeared completely now was dove racing—not so much because it was offensively exuberant but because there were no more doves. That long-favorite sport of working people, in England and Germany and any number of countries besides Belgium, was literally destroyed there by German authorities, who suspected that doves were being used to carry military intelligence. Thus in village after village the order went out that all doves must be killed. Those who did not comply were fined, even imprisoned, and in a few cases shot. The six million doves kept in Belgium before the war were slaughtered in huge numbers—"what heartache and tears," said Dr. Git. "Who would have thought that doves were so loved here?" This wasn't all sentimental: plenty of café bosses stood to lose much income from the betting that went on in their establishments on Sunday.

The café itself still opened on Sunday, but with painful limits and changes. Streuvels noted that after the initial shock of invasion wore off, people in his village started frequenting cafés again on Sunday for a pint of beer and to hear any news. But over time only a few bothered to engage in the old ritual, for there was only one topic of conversation—war—and no reliable news about it. Instead there were only rumors and speculation, and people in villages were prepared to believe anything.

Jules Git reported that the café in his village was still a place on Sunday to drink a glass of beer, play some cards and billiards, and smoke a pipe, but many stayed away because the German police liked to come inside and check personal identification cards that day, and who carried such a thing around on Sunday? Those who did go, however, like those in Streuvels's Ingooigem, traded stories and gossip and the wildest rumors about the war: the latest in June 1916 was that Germany had sold Belgium to the United States, and thus if Belgium wanted its independence it would have to negotiate with the Americans. Most of the conversation centered on how long people thought the war would last. But part of it was for reminiscing on the old Sunday, as suggested by the exiled Abraham Hans. Wartime Sundays only sharpened his memory of freshly scrubbed houses in his village and the glorious prospect of a long, free summer Sunday. The farms on such a day now all seemed to have white gables, green doors, and shutters, the farmers were smoking pipes at the door, boys were tumbling and playing and laughing and crying, girls were strolling along flowery paths with suitors, fields were gleaming, and weathervanes stood still.

Another well-known Flemish writer, Virginie Loveling, provides a glimpse of a wartime Sunday in town—specifically, the important provincial city of Ghent, in western Belgium.

Ghent's population of nearly 200,000, and its location within range of Allied airplanes, made it a far more important target than a village such as Streuvels's Ingooigem. On Sunday or any day here, the now elderly Loveling (seventy-nine when the war began) was likely to be shaken from a good night's sleep by bombs, so that she had to feel her way in the dark, barefoot, sarge over her shoulders, and thoughts racing. Over time such unsettled nights became common enough that she chose to stay in bed or didn't even hear them, or occasionally put her head out the window to watch.

Like Streuvels, Loveling too pondered the loss of Sunday, which to

her had meant especially companionship: Sunday without friends was
no Sunday at all, she decided. For more than twenty years, the never-
married Loveling had spent every Sunday with a woman friend whose
home was always warm and "the centerpoint of a circle of friends."
They all looked forward to the Sunday gatherings, and the time spent
there always went by too fast. But now that friend was dead, and war
made gathering more difficult, and so Sunday dragged on, forever and
sadly. She concluded that during war there were various days "destined for dejection and woe, but among these are mostly Sundays." It
was still something of a rest day for laborers, but for artists such as
she, who "controlled their time," or for the retired and unemployed,
Sunday was a day that weighed down. "The empty Sunday exercises
tortuously its power over you, with no prospect of certain joy or companionship." Even when Loveling had once been on a long journey at
sea, where all days seemed the same, Sunday still touched the "empty
void." Now she could only ask, "Where have you gone, my joyous
Sundays?"

With her longtime Sunday group broken up, she nevertheless soon
tried to get out on Sunday as before. Although a sporadic churchgoer,
Loveling noted that Sunday church was the only meeting not forbidden by German authorities, and thus many people attended if only to
see others. One week Loveling decided to attend because she had heard
talk that a certain pastor was unusually frank in his sermons and dared
to speak the truth in the presence of German officers. In fact, the sermon was disappointing, she wrote, as he spoke in the "most general
terms about disasters that try people" and simply urged people to
prayer. But the occasion did bring her face to face with German soldiers, who in cities lodged less frequently in people's homes than in villages. Exiting their own Mass when she arrived, they walked past in a
sea of gray, topped by "mostly pious faces" so praised by local clergy.

She also tried occasionally to visit others on Sunday for dinner or
talk, and she hosted visitors as well, even if it brought less joy than
Sundays past. The small family dinners were full of conversation, as
usual, but inevitably about war—such as the shocking execution of the
British nurse Edith Cavell in Brussels, or the death of Pierre Pirenne,
son of the famous historian Henri. Or they noted that another histo-

rian, Paul Fredericq, greeted the news of his impending exile to Germany by saying, "How nice to go to Germany at German expense, and what an opportunity to trim my weight!"

Even when conversation lasted long on wartime Sundays, food never did. It was in short supply from the start, especially in cities, for densely populated Belgium always had to import grain, unable to grow enough of its own. Hence when Germany sealed off Belgium in late 1914, it sealed off most of Belgium's food supply as well. To compound the shortage, much of the food the Belgians did grow was sent to Germany. This was where the Committee for the Relief of Belgium came in: by November 1914 it began shipping what would become one billion dollars (or five million tons) of food, all "without noteworthy corruption." Yet even this was hardly enough to bring people above the bare minimum of existence. Vast numbers went to soup lines every day, including for their Sunday meal, especially in towns like Ghent and Brussels. Some better-off recipients of relief received it in the form of "discreet charity": these well-heeled people could not get themselves to queue up for food and so food was brought to them instead, or separate eating halls were designated for them.

Yet lack of food rarely kept Loveling from visiting on Sunday. She might go to the home of a wealthy friend to play cards, or visit another friend who, to Loveling's distress, proudly showed off an unexploded bomb her husband had brought home. She might receive visits on Sunday as well, once from a German officer, who informed her that relatives in the United States were seeking information about her. Chatting longer with the man, and with other German soldiers who visited in official capacities, she couldn't help but see, as Stijn Streuvels did, the human side of her conquerors, especially because she had German family. (Her cousin, however, the equally well-known novelist Cyril Buysse, who spent the war in the Netherlands, had nothing good to say of any German.)

On Sunday afternoons, Loveling often followed the other people of Ghent in making the usual promenade, even when the weather was not ideal. Promenading was hindered somewhat in 1917, when the "evening clock" was ordered, meaning that it grew dark early and thus people sat in their homes from four P.M. on doing nothing—especially painful on Sunday, she noted. Still, while there was light, many went

out. Loveling sometimes wondered how many of the people out walking were "cowardly" enough to listen to the various German concerts
offered that day on squares around the city. She also pondered that except for the constant rumble of guns from the front, one might not
even know, from appearances, that it was war at all. Flowers bloomed,
boys pulled wagons with small chidren in them—indeed the whole
population of Ghent seemed to be out walking. Who would have
guessed that "they were prisoners of war" in their own city?

In the parks, where she preferred to walk, everything seemed on the
surface the same as ever: countless roses and buds in summer, and
countless ladies and girls walking by, even better dressed than the
ladies who shocked Jules Git in his village. "Coquettes with hats,"
Loveling called them, "big white collars against both cheeks, their
necks daringly bare, dark jackets, narrow dresses that impeded forward progress," flesh-colored or white transparent stockings on
straight and crooked legs alike, and white or gilded shoes on heels
"like pins beneath their feet." Children wore red, pink, blue, and yellow, the braids of young girls swung wildly across their backs, boys
pushed hoops, dignified burgers moved forward silently next to each
other, and lovers on shaded benches in secluded corners of parks inclined their heads. A mass of people went in and out of the waffle
house in the park. Heavy carriages pulled by three horses, with German uniforms inside barely visible, drove past.

At last, another crowd of people walked on to the cemetery, busy
even on peacetime Sundays but especially now, while people crowded
in to read names and stepped over a host of freshly dug graves.

Any account of Sunday in Occupied Belgium must include at last its
capital city of Brussels.

Not only did Brussels's museums, squares, Jubilee Park, narrow colorful streets, broad tree-lined avenues, arches, lakes, surrounding
forests, and spoken French lead visitors to regard it as a small Paris, but
its Sundays did too. This all changed with war. Within three weeks of
the German invasion, Brussels fell without resistance. At least it, unlike
Ghent, was removed from the fighting, so that one heard the muffled
sounds of big guns only in the still of night. And Brussels was probably

the best-fed city of the entire occupation, even if women were seen begging on its streets as early as September 1914, and Cardinal Mercier
was soon asking wealthy women to dress down on Sundays to church,
so that young women who owned only clogs might feel welcome. In
fact, for those who lived outside the city, Brussels, for all its sorrow, still
held a certain allure. German officers wished to be stationed there, regarding it as the next best thing to Paris. And on Sunday, notable natives from surrounding villages put on their best suits and gloves and
endured the maddening obstacles put in the way of anyone now trying
to travel in order to visit even a diminished Brussels. Some Dutch too
tried to continue their old habit of traveling there on Sunday.

For most who lived in Brussels, however, life was more like slow
death. Natives tried to meet war with their characteristically spicy humor, calling the big guns they heard in the distance "church music," or
hanging up maps of Belgium crossed by two red strips of paper and the
words "closed for remodeling." On Sundays some Brusselaars still
tried to reach the countryside, as in the old days, but now with new
purpose. At first these were sober pilgrimages, but then people burst
out of the trams that stopped at the edge of the city, laughing and
drinking, spreading out in fields to look for cartridges, exploded shells,
uniform buttons, and other remnants of war, while inspecting recently
flattened villages. Crosses marking fresh graves were scattered across
the landscape, a beret suspended from a cross here, or flowers there,
and people sat near them to eat a Sunday picnic without even uncov-
ering their heads.

In the occupied city itself, the boulevards for a time were still black
with well-dressed Sunday walkers, but there was an ominous silence
now, as if, reported the journalist and poet Karel van de Woestijne,
everyone were going to a funeral. He heard no newspaper sellers, no
other hawkers, no screeching brass bands emerging from the trains of
Brussels's three stations. The favorite Sunday bird market, on the famous Grand Place, was almost nonexistent because its most popular
attraction, doves, had been banned.

Van de Woestijne's own Sundays in Brussels became increasingly
dull. On some he just sat in his garden with a blank mind, feeling old,
although barely in his forties, and that time was passing by, for there

was no end in sight to war. Neither Sunday, nor the budding of spring, brought any of the usual hope to life. On other Sundays he imagined the ugly scene near the flooded rivers Leie and Schelde, where soldiers were fighting and suffering like mudmen. He should hardly complain that his own room was damp, and that the windowpanes were losing their clarity through all the condensation. One winter Sunday in 1915 he watched his sick wife emerge from bed to look out the window— there was sun, but almost nothing on the street, contrary to past Sundays. A German soldier walked past, carrying freshly pressed whites for an officer, but then the street was lonely again. On stormier Sundays the streets felt even emptier, so that there was an "infinite sadness" in the air. Sunday in Belgium had meant liveliness, and without liveliness there was no Sunday. Moreover, the lack of employment and of hope were felt more keenly on Sunday, and so people shut themselves in and plunged into dreams—dreams of King Albert "marching into Brussels at the head of the victorious Belgian army," or dreams of revenge upon German soldiers. As in Ghent, most inhabitants of Brussels did not get to know their occupiers well, and thus felt little sympathy for them.

One beautiful spring Sunday in 1916 it seemed to Van de Woestijne that the old Sunday had returned, for all of Brussels headed to the countryside, dressed up and optimistic. But on closer look it was clear that these were last year's clothes, that the families' packages were full of bad bread and no butter, and that people were recreating for the sake of health, not for amusement in the old fashion. It wasn't quite Sunday, in other words, even though the old rituals and forms were tried. Sunday wasn't merely a series of activities, but a condition of mind and spirit. The animation of old, the exuberance, the joy, the careless folly of "happy hours of leisure" were all gone thanks to war, however familiar the activities themselves might have seemed. "How could one possess joy when one heard cannons?" he wondered. It only made him recall Sunday two years earlier, before the occupation: the civic guard had paraded colorfully about, village brass bands marched in and out of the stations, religious processions traversed the streets, the royal family and its entourage went to the afternoon races, military concerts were held in parks and woods, musicians and singers circulated from guinguette to guinguette—it all seemed a fable now. "To smoke a cigar among friends while drinking a bottle of Geuze beer"— for a Brusselaar this was only a memory of past Sunday splendor.

Some other familiar Sunday activities likewise promised normalcy, then likewise disappointed. In smaller streets one could still find aggressive hawkers of magazines, books, cloth, wax, royal portraits, caramels, and so forth, but their numbers thinned now on Sundays. On some Sundays, life came from young children; girls from all schools in the city stood on street corners, offering roses, wildflowers, and more flowers for sale, but even this was tainted by sadness, because the proceeds were to benefit war orphans. German soldiers circulated among this burst of life and color, yet "they passed by without a word, neither buying nor being offered flowers, as if all understood." Another Sunday, children sold bonbons to benefit "discreet charity."

There were also open-air concerts on many Sundays, but these were sponsored almost exclusively by German authorities now, and most natives did not bother, or dare, to attend: doing so was regarded as disloyal by fellow Belgians. Indeed when German authorities organized a major Sunday concert at the magnificent Brussels Munt theater, bringing in a choir and orchestra of 350 from Cologne for the occasion and posting blue signs everywhere weeks in advance announcing special prices to lure natives inside so that the world would imagine all was normal in this conquered capital, the Brusselaars cleverly resisted: some wealthier citizens bought up half the tickets, then stayed away, so that the hall was half empty. And if the ladies of the evening still strolled along the boulevards of Brussels in the evening, including on Sunday, they no longer wore colorful dresses but instead low-cut rough material, as if to blend in with the meaner times.

An exception to Sunday malaise in wartime Brussels occurred in the old theaters and new cinemas. At first people made resolutions to attend neither, as long as the prevailing mood was sober and numerous families mourned sons and fathers and husbands. Yet despite "melodramatic vows" these theaters and cinemas gradually came to life again on Sunday. Karel van de Woestijne took his son to the theater on a Sunday in December 1914, where he sensed that the public, weary of dull Sundays, was simply glad to refresh itself and was therefore overly kind to the most mediocre players. All theaters were busy enough even in the stark winter of 1916 that on one Sunday in November they earned an astonishing twenty thousand francs. Van de Woestijne, in favor of such diversions generally, did wonder whether in these lean and sober times especially the "disrobed revues" offered by some theaters were fitting. The number of cinemas mushroomed dramatically during the war, even though Sunday and recreation generally were on the decline. Fifty million tickets were bought in Occupied Belgium from June 1916 to June 1917 alone—many of them on Sunday, of course—reflecting the popularity of the new medium, whatever the circumstances.

Despite all these, the mood of Sunday in wartime Brussels became more somber over time. By August 1917, even in good weather, Sunday, according to journalists, was always mournful. Change in "the physiognomy of Brussels" was most apparent on Sunday, for though there was little commerce anyway during the week, on Sunday the streets were "like a tomb, like a sleeping village in a distant province," with scarcely any pedestrians, with most people staying at home. Not even a lovely sun and warmth, the usual sure remedies to get Belgians outside, were enough. Another journalist went to promenade in the countryside on Sunday, August 5, and saw no one, which was a striking difference from the year before. All exuberance was gone, the guinguettes of the suburbs were empty, and there was no more bread or special Lambic Geuze beer anyway. Only "the nouveaux riches, who had earned their money dubiously" during this war, could be seen in suburban cafés.

Somberness was likewise the mood at churches in Brussels, which nevertheless resonated, like the churches in Free Belgium, with stirring renditions of the "Brabançonne," the Belgian national anthem, at the end of each Mass. At some churches three patriotic songs were sung: the Flemish "Lion of Flanders" at the beginning of Mass, the French "Valeureux Liègeois" at the end, and then the "Brabançonne" to top everything off. When the occupying authorities banned the playing of the "Brabançonne" on the organ, crowds in churches sang it unaccompanied and even more resolutely, so that despite the efforts of the clergy to clear out the churches to allow in the next group for Mass, people sang to the bitter end, and were joined by the voices of those waiting outside.

Perhaps the most dramatic Mass of all in Brussels occurred the Sunday after New Year's Day 1915, when Cardinal Mercier's famous letter, "Patriotism and Endurance," was read from the pulpit, to the displeasure of German authorities. So bold was the letter that other Belgian bishops refused to sign it, believing that Mercier would bring punishment upon them all. In essence, the letter instructed Belgians that they owed no inward loyalty to the new regime: they were occupied but not conquered. They would comply with their bodies but not their souls. Despite the opposition of fellow bishops, Mercier distributed the letter through seminarians who were going home for Christmas, with instructions that it be read the following Sunday in all churches. General Von Bissing, the governor-general of the occupied lands, considered the letter an incitement to revolt. He organized efforts to seize copies from the printer on the Sunday night before it was delivered, and he considered arresting Mercier. Emissaries did show up at the doors of most parish priests on Sunday, January 3, 1915, and ordered the priests not to read the letter aloud during Mass, but most did anyway, for copies enough had survived. Still more were prepared and sent out prudently in sugar crates, which as a valuable commodity could be shipped anywhere.

Thus went the tense, tedious Sundays of Brussels during the war, Sundays that were mostly obscured and even at times completely lost.

SUNDAY RESTORED?

On the last Sunday of the war, November 10, 1918, chaos seemed to reign, and the old Sunday seemed further away than ever.

In Brussels, a series of events broke out that would have been unimaginable even a week before. The day began calmly, although with much anticipation, as everyone awaited details of the armistice that was to commence the next day. Then a few hours later, after a long line of German troops departed the city, rumor spread that Brussels was in the hands of a revolutionary Marxist government, run by German soldiers who had rebelled against their commanders. Several red flags were indeed spread around in German barracks, and several high German figures fled in automobiles. Around one P.M. a pack of German soldiers formed in the main streets, holding red banners, while around three another big noise emerged near the station, celebrating the return of French and Belgian soldiers from the front. Crowds sang the "Marseillaise" and the "Brabançonne," while the German soldiers watched, amused. Then the flags started unfurling from the windows—Belgian, French, English, and American—while German soldiers waved red flags, perhaps hoping that Brusselaars would forget this horrible war and cry out to them "Comrade!"

But they were wrong. There was angry yelling between the Germans and everyone else, the German sentinels who guarded the occupied government buildings were disarmed, and soldiers began tearing the distinctive markings from their uniforms, then arresting their own officers. Everywhere among native Belgians and Allied troops were choirs and orchestras, performing especially national songs, and by evening a mixture of patriotism and savagery lingered in the air. It was no ordinary day to be sure, but it was no real Sunday either.

West of Brussels, in Stijn Streuvels's village of Ingooigem, untouched during almost the entire war, there was turmoil at last on this final Sunday: Allied troops had begun their march into Belgium and were driving German troops backward. Ingooigem lay right in their path, and so the writer's fine home, a bit worn but still standing, was after all this time summarily ruined, by troops from both sides. Departing Germans shot up the village; incoming English and French soldiers "made themselves at home" and pillaged what they could. Away from his village the past few weeks, Streuvels went on this final Sunday on foot for twenty-five kilometers to see the ruin for himself. Thousands of refugees were on the road with him, to Antwerp and elsewhere, and the sight that greeted many at home was no better. It took months for order, and thus Sunday, to be restored just in his village.

Far to the east in Belgium on this last Sunday of the war, Kaiser Wilhelm of Germany, who happened to be in the country, was trying to flee, terrified of the revolutionary fervor among his troops in the big cities. His goal was the neutral Netherlands, to the east, and so he left the old Belgian resort town of Spa early that Sunday, in seven salon railway cars and two baggage cars. When rumors reached him that the revolutionary troops would not allow him to pass through Liège, the entourage transferred itself to a line of Mercedes and sped the final thirty kilometers toward the border. The stunned German guards there opened the gates, and the Kaiser suddenly stood on neutral ground. But that did not mean that he could cross into the Netherlands. He was forced to wait all day long by the Dutch government, which quickly gathered to consider his request for asylum. While the Kaiser waited, word of his presence spread among Belgian refugees and Dutch citizens nearby, who came down to yell insults and shake their fists, for they blamed the entire war on him. Upset, he retired to his car and spent a miserable Sunday. The government's favorable decision finally came days later: the Kaiser was allowed to cross over, and he would pass the rest of his days in a castle in Doorn, in the northern Netherlands, dying there in 1941.

But with the Kaiser gone and the war over, Belgians had their beloved Sunday back, if only partially and only gradually. Sunday returned slowly to Streuvels's weary Ingooigem, to Claes's impoverished Zichem, to the streets and parks of Loveling's Ghent, and to the boulevards of Brussels, and even more slowly to obliterated Poperinge and Ieper, near the otherworldly devastation of the trenches. Belgium was not the same after war, nor was its Sunday. Of course Sunday would have changed over time even without war. But war dramatically threw every habit and institution into disarray and accelerated change at an uncomfortable pace for many. As Jane de Launoy said at the end, "Too much sorrow overwhelms the joy, too much mystery remains unclarified, too much deception. Confidence is gone. We'll never be certain of anything again." War had made even Sunday uncertain.

6

First Man (bored): It makes you sick. I hate Sundays.

Second Man (ruffling his newspaper): So do I, but there's one a week and there always has been and always will be and there's nothing you can do about it.

First Man (grouchy): It's not like this on the Continent. It's their big day over there, all the cafés open and football matches and race meetings and everybody's gay, and . . . not over here though. Everything's shut up.

Second Man (annoyed): I wish you would.

First Man (sighing repeatedly): Oh dear. Oh dear. Oh dear.

From "Sunday Afternoon at Home," *a BBC Radio Program by Tony Hancock*

England, Especially London, Between Wars

Just as Sunday returned to Belgium after war, if in new forms and settings, so also to everywhere else it had been obscured—including in
England, where Sundays were famously still.

Yet even the seemingly fixed Sunday of England was no longer the
same after the Great War, thanks to at least two influences. First was
the sharpened appetite for pleasure, on Sunday or otherwise. This developed not only from four gloomy years of horrifying war but from
disillusionment with old, Victorian ways that were now seen as having
contributed to war. More than one English observer soon asked, why
should youths submissively follow the wishes of their elders on *anything*, when those same "wise" elders had made "their sons fight seven
days a week for four years"? Such questions eventually rippled out to
the old, strict Sunday: millions could be willingly sent to slaughter, but
a more relaxed Sunday was somehow wrong? Not that anyone
thought the venerable English Sunday would vanish overnight. As one
proponent of a more relaxed Sunday put it, fear that the dreaded
"Continental Sunday" would conquer England was no better grounded
than "our grandparents' fear of witches." But desire for some sort of
change to Sunday was real after the war.

A second influence on Sunday was an increase in the amount of free
time generally, when one might feed the new appetite for pleasure. This
increase was about not merely more time to rest from work, but the
growth of a "leisure culture" that offered more choices in how to use
all that free time. The initial expansion of leisure occurred even before
the Great War, with the establishment of the free Saturday afternoon
by the 1880s. Soon one Englishman could claim that the free half-
Saturday was "part of our religion."* Further expansion of leisure
came just after the Great War, with the reduction of the workweek

---

*The push for the free Saturday afternoon was begun by the secular Early Closing
Association, founded in 1842. But industrial bosses eventually supported the free
Saturday afternoon too, in the hope of more productive workers. Churchmen came
to support it because they believed it would free workers to recreate and run errands
on Saturday, not Sunday.

from fifty-five to forty-eight hours.* By 1920 most people therefore had free time on all of Sunday, on Saturday afternoon and evening, and on weekday evenings.

This reorganization of the week was less radical than the attempted ten-day week of French Revolutionaries during the 1790s, or the Russian six-day week begun in 1931 (and abandoned in 1940). But it had far greater impact on modern timekeeping, including outside of England: foreigners first called the free Saturday afternoon "the English week," the English themselves after 1880 called Saturday and Sunday together "the weekend," and after the Great War more and more countries adopted both the term and the practice of a "weekend."†
The new workweek also had a big impact on England's famous Sun-

---

*Certain socialists and utopians argued that the workweek could have been even shorter. They calculated that in an industrial economy only three hours of work per day were required to produce enough necessities for all: the vast majority of a day could therefore be given over to constructive leisure pursuits of one's choice. At the other end of the spectrum were those economists, employers, moralists, and clergy who resisted any expansion of free time because they doubted the ability of the working classes to use it wisely. But according to some historians, there was another reason that the reduction in working hours remained modest: the rise of consumer culture. The newfound ability of industrialized economies to produce far more goods than once thought necessary helped create an unprecedented desire for goods, redefining "necessities" and requiring long enough work hours to feed it. Gary Cross contends that during the 1920s and 1930s, Britain, France, and the United States all could have chosen leisure culture but opted instead for consumer culture and the related work ethic required to sustain it. In other words, leisure culture certainly expanded after 1920 but was still subordinate to consumer (and work) culture and could have expanded much further. Each society chose to work more than was "necessary" in order to produce more goods than were "necessary," rather than devote even more time to leisure.

†Technically, of course, it was wrong to call the seventh day (Saturday) and first day (Sunday) together the "weekend." Calendar makers long recognized this, as Sunday still generally appeared as the first day. But with Sunday now firmly established as a day of rest, it was hard conceptually to think of resting on the first day without having first worked. Placing Sunday at the end of the week might also speak to the percolation of the sixteenth-century argument that the seventh-day Sabbath had been transferred literally to Sunday. Certainly the incorporation of Sunday into the weekend now made it harder to think of Sunday as the first day.

day more specifically, mainly because it led to the latest tug-of-war over just exactly what that Sunday should be.

Those English who wanted to keep Sunday quiet insisted that the very reason for the free Saturday afternoon was to make recreation, play, and business unnecessary on Sunday. But those who wished to broaden the English Sunday held that, despite an increase in free time, new leisure opportunities and facilities were not enough to accommodate everyone who wanted to take advantage of them, unless these were available on Sunday too. Sunday had to be a part of wider leisure culture, not separate from it. Besides, these people were tired of their notoriously quiet Sunday.

THE OLD, OLD REPUTATION

The reputation of England's Sunday was, like most cultural reputations, built mainly with foreign materials. Visitors had a look around on Sunday, compared things to what they knew at home, then disseminated their damning or praising reports. Most such reports are not necessarily wrong. They simply tend to lack nuance: the foreign place becomes wholly this or wholly that. And in the case of the English Sunday, it was portrayed as wholly tame, for better or worse. So deeply rooted was this idea among foreigners that they found it hard to see an English Sunday any differently, even after the Great War.

These old foreign views, already apparent in the sixteenth and seventeenth centuries, had practically calcified by the nineteenth. Berliners of the 1840s, who according to Friedrich Engels made Sunday "the merriest day of the week," were alarmed when the local Protestant clergy took steps toward establishing an "English Sunday," an institution "most repugnant to the feelings and habits of all continental nations." Commenting most frequently on the horrors of the English Sunday were surely their closest continental neighbors, the French. In 1863 Louis-Auguste Martin urged his fellow citizens to visit impressive London, but not on a Sunday: for instead of a busy manufacturing and commercial city, on that day "you will find a vast necropole of hermetically sealed buildings, top to bottom," with iron gates protecting stores in funereal fashion. It was worse when it rained, but rain or shine, one must "keep the hand from games, the lips from song, the fingers from keyboard and embroidery." In his experience, only reading was permitted. Emile Gigault de la Bedollière wrote similarly in 1860: whereas Sunday in Paris was a day of widespread pleasure, in London it was "as if life has been suspended."

Such views persisted after the Great War. One travel guide noted that the quiet of an English Sunday still caused great anxiety in foreigners. The French "go all to pieces, and pace the floor mournfully; Italians think it must be the Revolution or Doomsday." Not even Americans, who supposedly coped better with English Sundays, were thrilled, as reflected in George Gershwin's satirical song "Sunday in London Town," from his 1923 musical *Rainbow Revue*. In this, English characters sing disapproval of "frivolous" French Sundays, stroll in the park until it starts to rain, read books, feed ducks, "solemnly walk up and down," and twiddle their thumbs. Running the dog in the fog was "excitement enough for the day," a "trip on the bus is a riot for us," knitting was thrilling, and every churchly oration was blessedly "full of damnation." And yet, unbelievably to Gershwin, this to the English was "the best day of all." Even travel guides that claimed that an English Sunday now offered more than it had before the war seemed unconvincing, listing things to do that would hardly have impressed anyone who had been to France: walking on Sunday's less crowded streets, visiting museums and galleries now open in the afternoon, attending "uncommonly interesting services" at the city's famous churches, hearing concerts at Albert Hall in the evening, and riding the many buses that at least drove *past* a number of interesting sights, such as Whistler's house in Chelsea, where his mother had once chastised him for painting on Sunday.

Another group of foreign visitors, including many Americans, valued the quiet of the English Sunday. Like certain seventeenth-century Dutch preachers, they saw it as an inspiring model, worthy of imitation in their own countries. Washington Irving, in London during the early nineteenth century, praised the "rest and repose of Sunday" there: smoke was gone, the rumbling of carriages and pattering of feet ceased, a salutary hush reigned, and the sun was not dull but merely sober, pouring its "muted yellow radiance" into blessedly quiet streets. Other American, Swiss, and even French visitors (usually Protestants) of the nineteenth century likewise lauded the day's calm, praising especially its insistence on no work.

Obviously everyone who visited agreed that an English Sunday was quiet, before and after the Great War. The only point of debate was how desirable such a Sunday was.

THE OLD, OLD STRUGGLE

If foreigners were practically unanimous that the English Sunday was tamer than other versions, so that the Sunday-observing world still seemed to be divided between England and nearly everyone else, it was also true that among the English themselves things weren't quite so simple, especially after the Great War. There never was universal agreement here as to what Sunday should be.

Serious, large-scale debate in England over Sunday was as old as the Puritans, of course, as noted in Chapter 3. And the debate had almost always centered on the question, how much play should there be on Sunday, and what sort? Opponents of expanding Sunday fun and games relied on two main arguments over the centuries. First, more play always led to more lawlessness and disturbance, wholly unbecoming the day. And second, more play always led to more work, to serve those who were playing. Especially the second was more than a minority opinion and eventually became a linchpin of the English version of Sunday: better to shut things down and risk that some people might not get sufficient recreation on Sunday than to risk that someone might have to work.

This view gained momentum in the late eighteenth and early nineteenth centuries, when the Evangelical religious revival included the revival of a strict Sunday. It found its greatest champion in the Lord's Day Observance Society (LDOS), founded in 1831, which through the rest of the century consistently and often successfully opposed any new outlets for Sunday recreation. Better organized and more influential than twin organizations in France and elsewhere, it confidently denounced crowded stations and steamboats on Sunday, light conversation, and even Sunday walks (on the grounds that some might assume you were being frivolous). It hammered on old theological arguments: the Sabbath had been clearly transferred to Sunday, and the commandment clearly said to labor six days and rest all of Sunday, not merely part of it.* It repeated arguments based on custom: one should never even utter a "sportive word" much less play sport on Sunday, and although the Sabbath was a "most happy day," one should never laugh. The LDOS wielded new scientific arguments: various bits of evidence suggested that the Earth itself was naturally susceptible to a seven-day week and a weekly period of rest. It applied the most rational economic arguments: the expansion of entertainments would mean the expansion of working hours too. It fell back on patriotic arguments: the journal *King & Country* insisted in 1902 that it was an English duty to rest on Sunday in the English way, and that those who did not were simply traitors. And at last it turned the Sunday lens, so often and so unfavorably focused upon the English, back upon Continental countries: the many French who worked on Sunday catering to amusements aged prematurely, most stabbings in Rome occurred on its licentious Sundays, and even the heirs of Calvin and Luther in Protestant Geneva, Sweden, and northern Germany had suffered the consequences of excessive work and play on their rotten Sundays.

If all of this sounded harsh, the LDOS and its supporters repeatedly insisted that they were moderates. To prove it, they often measured their views against an even stricter play-free Sunday: the Scottish. For although Sabbatarian tendencies had been bred in England, they had found fullest expression in Scotland, and perhaps Wales. Long before the nineteenth century, a Scottish Sunday was generally reputed to be more severe than an English, even by the Scots themselves: it was supposedly marked by little conversation, much study of the Bible, not a single trifling word, the locking-up of swings, sharp rebukes for whistling, and especially long sermons. If foreigners commented more on the English Sunday than the Scottish Sunday, it was because more of them went to London than to Edinburgh. The English, however, knew the Scottish model well, and because of it English Sabbatarians tended to see their own Sunday as a happy medium between the excesses of their neighbors both to the north and on the Continent.

Moderate or not in the past, the LDOS did indeed begin to revise its

---

*This of course then raised the question of whether working on only part of Saturday, or until only the late afternoon on weekdays, also violated the commandment.

goals after the Great War, when its opposition to all Sunday play became unfeasible. It would now allow some recreations rather than lose the entire battle over Sunday. One Anglican vicar, although still opposed to organized games on Sunday, did support "honest" games that day: "A ball is not inflated with evil . . . I would rather see boys playing a vigorous game than fooling about in the streets." Others would now allow the opening of museums on Sunday, but with caution, for in their eyes the benefits of limiting amusements (quiet and no work) were preferable to the price of expanding them (more work, more noise, and dissipation). Hence despite concessions the LDOS was still more comfortable with a Sunday that included merely reading, light walking, music, contemplation of nature, and time with family and friends.

In fact, many ordinary English people after the Great War also favored a restrained Sunday, if not quite as restrained as the LDOS version. Surveys conducted informally by the sociologically interested group Mass Observation found that of one hundred English people interviewed in 1945 for the project *Meet Yourself on Sunday,* two-thirds still preferred the relatively forced confinement of the English Sunday, mostly because it meant they did not have to work or engage in their usual routine. And this after the deprivations of the recent war. About half of the respondents simply wanted to change certain details of the day, such as allowing a few sport and entertainment venues to open. A thirteen-year-old girl might have expressed this sentiment best, in summing up her own Sunday: "Nothing particular ever happens, and yet I would not call it dull."

The English song "That Sunday Morning Feeling" reflected nicely the popular sentiment for a restrained Sunday, quite in contrast to Gershwin's ridicule:

> *Sunday morning feeling,*
> *Not a thing to do,*
> *. . . Shall we do the crossword?*
> *Or take a bus to Kew?*
> *. . . There's nobody in the Strand,*
> *And Piccadilly looks deserted for the day,*
> *But please don't misunderstand,*
> *It may seem rather funny, but we like it that way.*

Indeed, was it Gershwin's song in particular that caused his musical to be coolly received in London? Or that provoked one actor on opening night to step out of character for a moment in order to blame "a decline of morals" in the English theater on American influences?

Stacey Aumonier's short story "One Sunday Morning" likewise showed affection for the native Sunday. The hero, Jim, rises at seven-thirty, not happily, but "then, oh joy! his conscious brain registered the abrupt reflection that it was Sunday. Oh, happy thought. Oh, glorious and soporific reflection! . . . Oh, Sunday, glorious and inactive day!" The great "charm of the situation" lies in the fact that there was no hurry. He gets breakfast in bed, reads the paper from cover to cover, shaves, bathes, and dresses as slowly as he pleases. He hears his wife bustling about in the kitchen and so goes out to walk, where he sees a great number of men also out walking. The quiet streets have their "Sunday look," which he finds "wonderful." He looks forward to a good meal, then some port, a cigar, and another round with the Sunday newspaper.

If many foreign visitors found such fondness for a restrained Sunday incomprehensible, it was another foreigner, a travel writer, who might have explained it best: "It has been remarked that the British take their pleasures sadly, and this is attested by the crowds at the beach who merely sit and stare." In other words, even if many English looked grim on Sunday, perhaps that was how they preferred it. Engaging enthusiastically in "fun," as Louis Morin showed for France, could after all be draining.

Another group of English, however, were long less sure of the virtues of their quiet Sunday, and looked with longing at Continental models. They could not take this too far, of course. Like Sabbatarians, most claimed to be moderate, and insisted they merely wished to rid the English Sunday of its relentless bleakness and to borrow only the most reasonable things from Sundays in Europe.

There was no shortage of native volunteers willing to condemn Sunday's past and present bleakness in England. Charles Kingsley's *Alton Locke,* from 1850, has the working-class hero remember without the slightest hint of sentimentality the two "unintelligible, dreary sermons" he was forced to hear each Sunday as a child, the terror in church "lest a chance shuffle of my feet or a hint of drowsiness" should result in punishment at home, and books "of which I could not understand a word." Charles Dickens's Sundays were even grayer than his other days, the streets in *Little Dorrit* "melancholy in a penitential garb of soot," and everything "bolted and barred that could possibly furnish relief to an overworked people." There was nothing "for the spent toiler to do, but to compare the monotony of his seventh day with the monotony of his six days." Dickens's *Sunday Under Three Heads* asserted that only a "truly iron-hearted man" would be against opening such potential sources of pleasures as the British Museum and the National Gallery, and that religion "should not be incompatible with enjoyment." Were a few more pleasures allowed, then people would no longer dread Sunday. Others recalled the Victorian Sundays of childhood with "an extraordinary mingling of affection and horror," or that they "seemed to include a refusal to enjoy oneself and stopping others from enjoying themselves too." And the criticisms were multiplied in *Punch* and other magazines, in efforts by the new Sunday Evening Association, and most simply eloquent of all in the riots of 1855 at London's Hyde Park, which supported the expansion of Sunday pleasures.

After the Great War, such homegrown criticisms of the English Sunday continued. One-third of the Mass Observation respondents of 1945 wished to change Sunday significantly, not merely in its details. "I don't like Sundays much. It's all right for the rest, but there's not much to do," said a female shop assistant. Working-class women interviewed expressed resentment of the extra work that a "restful" Sunday entailed for them: "I simply can't bear Sundays; it's a day which everyone regards as a rest day except for me. They all go out; my man sleeps in a chair; and I'm left with a load of dishes to wash up. I hate Sundays. I dread to see it coming. It's the one day you're supposed to rest, and yet with a family how can a woman rest?" Mass Observation concluded its study with this pessimistic assessment: "It has grown into a day of negatives and emptiness."

Some of the clergy also jumped on the bandwagon for a freer Sunday after the Great War. The Reverend Henry Carter, director of the

Methodist Social Service wing, supported a Sunday bill that would mean "final liberation of the British people from as dismal, irksome, and unnatural a prison as any civilized race has ever submitted itself to." The Bishop of Croydon, E. S. Woods, stated that "the church should say plainly that Sunday is not an unsuitable day for some forms of recreation." He worried especially that vast sections of the population had few opportunities for Sunday recreations in summer, and in winter were without a comfortable room, fire, book, or wireless set. Were they simply to stay inside? And so in regard to the latest debate over Sunday opening, he concluded, "There are occasions when the church must set itself against the whole world. This is not one of them."

The crowning criticism of the English Sunday, however, was a radio episode called "Sunday Afternoon at Home," by the comedian Tony Hancock. It aired in the 1950s, but every activity (and inactivity) it describes was present and familiar in the 1930s, when Hancock was growing up. Perhaps the dullest Sunday ever imagined, it opens with a series of yawns and "Oh, dears" as a small group of adults in a suburban living room watch the time drag by. "What time is it?" asks the first man irritably. "Two o'clock" is the reply.

> *First Man:* Is that all? Dear me. I'm fed up.
> *Second Man:* Shut up, let me get on with my paper.
> *First Man:* Well I'm fed up . . .
> *Second Man:* We're all fed up.
> *First Man:* Are you sure it's only two?
> *Second Man:* No, it's one minute past two now.
> *First Man:* Doesn't the time drag? I do hate Sundays. I'll be glad when it's over. It drives me up the wall, just sitting here looking at you lot. Every Sunday it's the same, nowhere to go, nothing to do. Just sit here waiting for the next lot of grub to come up.

More impatient exchanges follow, including a disagreement over who gets to read the Sunday paper next. Suddenly the sameness is broken: it's begun to rain! "That's all we wanted," says the first man. "I think I'll go to bed."

Woman: You've only been up an hour.

First Man: Might just as well be in bed, nothing else to do. . . .

Second Man: Why don't you sit down and relax! It's a day of rest!

First Man: Oh, dear. What a life. It's Sunday. Had a rotten dinner. It's raining. And I've got nothing to do.

Woman: Plenty of odd jobs around the house.

First Man: Oh shut up, it's a day of rest.

With nothing to do and nothing to discuss, the first man begins asking the time again. It's now two-fifteen. Miserable, he calculates that nine and three-quarters hours remain until Monday. "Depressing isn't it? Don't care very much for Monday either. I mean Saturdays are always spoiled thinking about Sunday. You know I sometimes think, what's it all about? What are we here for?" Here he is displaying that old inclination stirred up by Sunday's break from routine: the setting in of big, overwhelming, transcendent, uncomfortable thoughts. Rather than really ponder the question, however, he quickly takes a favorite alternative path among Sunday-dreaders: look for something less overwhelming, anything less overwhelming, to divert attention. He therefore begins noticing faces in the pattern of the wallpaper and pointing them out to others.

And so goes the afternoon. He wants to sing, but the key to the lock on the piano is lost. He suggests going to the cinema, but it doesn't open until three-thirty, and the only movies playing are old ones he has already seen. How about the pubs? Open only at seven. They wonder about visiting a friend in the hospital, an ideal Sunday activity praised for centuries. "Why don't we go see him this afternoon? We've got nothing to do," says one. But they finally conclude, "Well it's a long way, isn't it. He's probably asleep; he wouldn't want to see us anyway." Someone suggests a game of Monopoly, but the board has been lost.

More glances at the clock—and suddenly, the memory that daylight savings begins that night, and thus they may put the clock forward a whole hour! Now time is flying. One man takes a pencil and begins filling in the o's, d's, p's, g's, and q's in the newspaper—what he always does when there's nothing to do. Someone suggests playing the gramophone, but it winds down, out of power. The nut bowl contains only shells and a banana peel. "If we had a dog we could take it for a run." That did it for the first man: "Oh I give up. I'm not coming downstairs next Sunday. I'll have one of my pills on Saturday night, and I'll wake up on Monday."

These examples on both sides of the centuries-old debate in England over what Sunday should be are only a few from a multitude, but they are enough to illustrate that even in England opinion was hardly uniform.

CLASS ON SUNDAY

The same was true of actual experience. Assorted patterns can be found, but there never was a single sort of English Sunday.

One's experience was shaped, as always, by geography, age, gender, beliefs religious and otherwise, ethnicity, personality, and more. It's especially worth taking a look here at a variable already seen at work in France but emphasized even more by the English themselves: social class.

Before the nineteenth century, Europeans spoke of social "rank" rather than social "class." Typically these ranks included some configuration of nobles, clergy, bourgeois, and peasants, who despite differences ultimately cooperated with one another. After the French and Industrial revolutions shattered this configuration, Karl Marx popularized a new version filled with *competing* social classes: in his terms, aristocracy, bourgeoisie, and proletariat, or in popular English more often upper, middle, and working classes. These classes did not cooperate, said Marx, but were inherently at odds with one another and sought to control economic and political power at the others' expense. Naturally, there was much variety within each class, but contemporaries recognized easily enough the basic distinctions.

These distinctions held on Sunday too, in England just as in France or anywhere else.

Charles Dickens recognized what had already been apparent in other periods and countries as well: the "pampered aristocrat" and "gloomy" churchman simply could not understand what Sunday meant to "those who lead working lives." This still held in England after the Great War. Enough working-class accounts of Sundays have survived to confirm the day's lasting importance to those who labored physically on every other day, in often arduous conditions. To many workers, Sunday was more about rest from work and enjoying a little recreation than it was about wild, Continental-style play. Whether this was due to preference, restrictive laws, or lack of money, their Sundays remained relatively quiet.

Two especially whole accounts illustrate nicely the general layout of working-class Sundays. The first was written by Phyllis Walden, of Keston, who outlined in agenda-like fashion one of her Sundays in 1937.

7:15 A.M. She wakes up laughing about a scene in a film from the day before.

7:30 A.M. She brings tea and digestive biscuits upstairs to have in bed with her husband, a ritual she always enjoys because most days she gets up at 6:00 to see her husband off by 6:45. When the children make too much noise the husband shouts, "Shut up, it's Sunday." Phyllis feels very lazy for deciding not to rush out and get milk from the dairymaid, who is done by 8:00.

8:30 A.M. Her husband says he will have his breakfast of bacon-fried potatoes and fried bread in bed.

9:00 A.M. Phyllis washes, makes more tea, cooks breakfast, and serves it to all. Her husband helps clean the dining room and upstairs because their daughter has some kind of "skin complaint" that needs to be dressed.

10:30 A.M. Dinner preparation begins—including roast beef, potatoes, beans from the garden, and apple pie and custard.

11:30 A.M. Phyllis makes coffee and her husband stops working in the garden. She worries that dinner will be late because they rose late.

2:15 P.M. Dinner is finally on the table, long after the usual time of 1:00. Everyone enjoys the meal. Afterward the oldest son cycles to visit some cousins.

3:30 P.M. Everyone cleans up together, then the children play in the garden and Phyllis makes scones for tea.

4:45 P.M. Phyllis sits down and reads the wireless schedule, then turns it on at 5:00.

6:00 P.M. She wakes up from an hour nap, taken while listening to the wireless; her husband is preparing tea. She goes to wash and change.

7:30 P.M. The children go to bed and Phyllis and her husband sit and listen to the wireless.

8:15 P.M. They listen to the church service from St. Martin's in the Fields, which they don't usually do, because neither of them attends church. Phyllis enjoys the peacefulness and "shut-inness." She wishes she could have many days like this Sunday.

9:00 P.M. She and her husband fix supper.

9:15 P.M. The oldest son finally returns from visiting family.

10:05 P.M. Everyone goes to bed.

The second account is by another Phyllis, her last name Willmott, who wrote at greater length about Sundays in a working-class neighborhood of southeast London. Here too, and in other working-class neighborhoods she knew, Sunday was mostly a day of relaxing at home (except for her mother), mixed with the occasional outing.

After Saturday night's ritual bath and Epsom salts, Sunday morning itself was a time of "delight and of lazy, good-humored calm." Phyllis and her siblings awoke first and ran into their parents' bedroom, where they were told to keep quite awhile longer. They lay there whispering, staring at the wallpaper and the smashed bugs that stained it. The "fusty" odor of the house "blended pungently with the smell of Dad's bucket of pee" under the double bed. On Sundays particularly, the bucket's contents gave out a decidedly beery odor, an inevitable result of his Saturday night's hard drinking "up the pub." The "great Sunday morning treat" was when her father brought tea for everyone in bed. Each week it was something different, based on what he had grabbed in the pub the night before: sometimes "chocolate biscuits, gigantic round arrowroot, or the pink and yellow finger wafers."

After ten or twenty minutes, Phyllis's mother went downstairs to fix breakfast and her father returned to his deep sleep. The children eagerly followed their mother, for during the week they were required to stay mainly upstairs. And, on Sunday, downstairs was more exciting than usual: like a number of working families, the Willmotts' household included a set of grandparents, and on Sunday morning plenty of aunts and uncles and cousins came to visit. During these visits the fam-

ily decided which route to follow for the Sunday morning constitutional toward the heath, and which pubs to visit along the way. The
children did not have a say in this matter, but they looked forward to
the walks "as a time to be with the men," to get treats, and to play.
When the group stopped at the chosen pubs, the men went inside while
the children waited outside for biscuits and lemonade. Phyllis's parents
actually disapproved of other parents who did this to their children on
weeknights—but on Sunday it was acceptable because of the more familial atmosphere on the streets.

At the heath, the children ran and played fetch with the dogs. Sometimes they rode on paddleboats in the pond or tried their model sail-
boats. They always ended up at an "ex-servicemen's club on the heath
where the men drank beer and the children went inside to drink lemonade" (as it was a private club). The whole journey was well over a
mile, but "it was understood" that the children would not complain
about the long walk. On the way back home in the early afternoon,
they had to stop a few times to relieve themselves after so much drinking. It was easy for the males to find urinals, but Phyllis as the only girl
was told to just "go behind a tree" or "up the alley."

If the group came home early, or skipped the weekly walk to the
heath altogether, then Phyllis and her brothers went to the local Anglican service with their mother. Their father came along only on special
occasions: he never openly mocked religion, but in his view "Christianity made no more sense for the ordinary workingman than some
of the more primitive religions he had noted on his travels." Phyllis's
grandparents never attended at all, "deliberately giving the children
the impression" that they were old enough to be excused from such
duties. And although their mother took them to church, she seemed to
enjoy the occasion more for social reasons than out of "deep personal
conviction."

When Phyllis and her mother attended church together then, they
dressed together and added such special touches as some lipstick and
powder or a new feather for an old hat. In this world fashionable
teenage girls wore white gloves and flowered straw hats on Sunday in
the front pew of the church. Most of the boys, including Phyllis's
brothers, joined the choir by age eight—as much for the promise of oc-

casional cash as anything else, for her brothers were neither very reverent nor religious; they whispered and ate sweets during church, but were careful not to misbehave too much or they would be kicked out of choir. When the services concluded, Mrs. Willmott, not wishing her dressing-up to be wasted, often went to join her husband at the pub or the ex-servicemen's club. She felt uneasy about it, for she had been raised a Methodist and therefore learned that God did not approve of drinking and that "the pub was as sinful as the church was righteous." She also worried that the curate would see her turning down the road toward the pub rather than the road for home. The children, to the contrary, were expected to go directly home, precisely so as not to mess their Sunday best.

In the meantime the monumental Sunday dinner was being prepared at home, usually by Phyllis's grandmother, who cared neither for church nor for the family's walks. The meal consisted of the usual "superior piece of meat," roasted potatoes, and boiled greens. After dinner the children washed their faces and put on caps or berets before going off with their cousins to Sunday school. Phyllis usually liked this time, but extremely vivid missionary stories told by enthusiastic teachers frightened her. Most of the adults took afternoon naps while the children were gone. On the way back home, the children usually dawdled, because once home they were not allowed to play outside. Here as elsewhere the streets were practically empty of traffic and seemed to "exude a special brooding atmosphere."

Another afternoon ritual on Sunday was waking their father, weary from the morning's exertions, for tea. After this came the "high spot" not only of Sunday but of the entire weekend, when their father would go out once again, with his brothers and friends, to "get in the beer" at a nearby pub, while Phyllis and her brothers waited impatiently upstairs to be invited down with the cousins. When that moment finally came, the children were the center of attention, singing a song or reciting a poem. But inevitably her grandfather would break in with a bawdy song of his own, or a funny story. Later, when all the men returned from the pub, "the front room was as awash with people as the overfilled glasses were with beer." One of the uncles played the piano for still more singing: at first the selections were from old music halls or the war, but the evening always concluded with hymns and psalms, and "Onward Christian Soldiers" was the signal for the children's bedtime.

As pleasant as these Sunday evenings were for the children, Phyllis's mother did not enjoy them. She was irritated at how much money was spent on alcohol, and how her live-in mother-in-law was always "queening it" over her sons. At first Mrs. Willmott simply delayed coming downstairs on Sunday, but after some years she wouldn't come down at all. One of the children was always sent to get her, but she clung stubbornly to the "guerrilla war" with her mother-in-law. In the end their mother spent most Sunday nights with her husband at the working men's club instead of in the front room. And if Phyllis's parents were not at home, then she and her siblings were not allowed to join the party in the front room, which made for "a very dull Sunday evening." When they grew older, the children were sometimes allowed to go along to the working men's club for dancing on Sunday evening, if they had behaved themselves that day. During church Phyllis prayed for God's help to be good, because she wanted so badly to attend the dance.

A final unpleasant Sunday ritual in the Willmott home was the evening quarrel between Mother and Father. After a few hours at the pub, her father's normally dignified personality grew surly, and the arguing and swearing would begin. Her father would be silent the next day, or brusque, then try to make things up by playing the piano, proud of the latest song he had learned. But Phyllis's mother simply said to her daughter, more than once, "Your father is a very peculiar man." True, her husband's job may well have included a manager who was a bully, and one had only to talk back wrong in order to be fired and face the misery of unemployment—even worse during the 1930s. He therefore regarded Sunday as his grand day for unwinding. But his desire on that day to be his own man could also result in harsh treatment of others. That too was part of Sunday.

And so Sunday went, in working-class family after family. A mill family in a northern town rose late, had their best meal of the week at two; at three the children were washed and properly dressed for a walk in the streets or park; by five all were back for high tea; at six the church bells rang; at eight they returned home to entertain friends and relatives who dropped by, while the younger members of the family sought what amusement there was in the street. More gloomily, the miners of the "grey villages of Lancashire" sat on Sundays "on their haunches against the walls, their hands between their knees," a white whippet on a lead in the center of each group, the men smoking and looking at the highway. Whatever the particular details, the general pattern was to stay at home more than usual, break up the day with a visit to a pub or with friends on the street, and spend little. This routine was sometimes spiced with the sort of elaborate outings discussed later in this chapter, but only sometimes. As one working-class woman wrote, "You make a splash once, yer tied up for months," and the temptation was especially strong on the free Saturday and Sunday.

In some ways the middle-class Sunday overlapped with that of the working class. A big dinner, some socializing, possibly Sunday school, naps, a walk, and other elements were apparent as well in Eileen Elias's middle-class childhood Sundays. But differences were obvious too, usually in regard to money and style.

On Sunday Eileen's family rose late, in time for her mother to warm the rolls she had made the night before. Like many middle-class households, the Eliases had a maid, but she did not come on Sunday; thus middle-class mothers resembled working-class mothers in having more work than usual that day. After breakfast everyone prepared for church at eleven: the act of attending church, especially the Anglican Church, was a sure sign to all that one belonged to the respectable middle class. Even more important to Eileen, however, was that it was the one day of the week when she, and so many other young girls, wore white.

In her mind, each day of the week stood for a color: Monday was dull pewter gray for it followed the brightness of Sunday, Tuesday was silvery blue, Wednesday was azure, Thursday green, Friday golden-brown, Saturday scarlet, and Sunday white. This was what helped to make the day delightful to her. She knew that technically Sunday was the first day of the week, but the act of wearing her best dress and hat always made it seem like the week's climax. Most of the other young girls wore the same kind of white dress as hers, with a high neck, laced edges, narrow ribbon, many tucks, and most important, the sash. This was the only item that wasn't white, and deciding which color sash to wear was a crucial part of the Sunday routine. Her preparations culminated with brushing her father's silk top hat, which was no simple matter. He wore it every Sunday, saving his ordinary bowler for weekdays. He also regularly repeated to them, "Slack in dress, slack in morals"—a good middle-class prejudice if ever there was one. Even when top hats were out of fashion, he insisted on wearing one partly out of nostalgia and partly out of a belief that current standards in all respects were inferior to those of the past—another good middle-class article of faith. Yet another of her father's beliefs was that "peace at all cost was the rule on Sundays," and that no matter what, she was not to disagree with her father or any other family member on that day.

On the way to church Eileen's family walked past all the closed shops. Only the pub was open, and then only during midday and the evening. To "honor the Sabbath," her family would not go inside it, and Eileen herself even looked away while walking past. Still, she tried to breathe in the smell of beer anyway. At church she also tried to look away from the ladies' fine hats and other fashions, to concentrate on spiritual things, but it wasn't easy. The family rented a pew up in the gallery in the second row; from here she could see others in the gallery but could not quite see over the rail to look at people below. The service seemed to last forever, "really quite tedious and the prayers incomprehensible." And her mind wandered to think about such things as why they said "Ah-men" at church rather than "Ah-women," and wouldn't someone just once object when the vicar announced a marriage and asked for objections? Afterward, families and friends mingled, and boys watched for opportunities to walk home with girls under the guise of family conversation.

With worship over, attention shifted to a good meal and an afternoon nap. As in working-class homes, it was the best meal of the week, and practically every house on the street had the same: roast meat, vegetables, special trimmings, and dessert, on an immaculately set table. Eileen could never understand why afterward the adults wanted to waste the best part of the day with an afternoon nap, but that was what they liked to do. While everyone was sleeping, Eileen memorized the Collect from her prayer book, since her mother required that it be recited word for word every Sunday afternoon. Unlike so many other parents, Eileen's mother did not send her children to Sunday school but read to the family instead, usually from novels: *Little Lord Fauntleroy, Alice, Daisy, Swiss Family Robinson,* and plenty of Dickens, Scott, Thackeray, and Conan Doyle. Her brother tinkered with some bit of machinery, and Eileen painted while her mother read and they all snacked on sweets. Afternoon tea always interrupted the reading. In Eileen's family, Sunday was not a time for visiting, as in many other families, but for their family alone. "So the caller who happened to look in on a Sunday afternoon sometimes received a chilly welcome." Thus Sunday tea was usually a family-only affair in her middle-class home, with the best cups and saucers (the second-best were used for Saturdays, even when there were guests), a damask tablecloth, a vase of flowers in the middle, a huge fruitcake made by her mother, piles of bread and butter, and jam in a glass dish. When the tea was cleared away on Saturday, family and friends would gather around the piano to sing all sorts of songs, but on Sunday the family alone sang only hymns, which "we children sang with straight backs and open mouths, making as much noise as we could." The last hymn sung was always "The Day Thou Gavest, Lord, Is Ended."

Eileen's Sunday, especially the finer clothes and table-setting, suggests the essential difference between the middle- and working-class Sunday in England, seen already in France: middle-class activities and style required a good deal more money.

Little need be said about an upper-class Sunday, for the usual reason: although it was in some ways like a middle- or working-class Sunday, most distinctive of all about the upper-class version was that it looked much like other upper-class days.

Except for a brief interlude at church, or the occasional aristocratic family that allowed no Sunday games, the upper-class Sunday in England was, according to critics, simply "the easiest day of seven," little different from the others. If not that, Sunday was at least part of a leisurely upper-class country weekend, which began Friday afternoon and ended Monday morning. (Before the Great War it might run from Thursday through Tuesday.) Moreover, this weekend was set not in a featureless or run-down neighborhood but in a large country house, often loaded with guests. *Every* day of such a weekend meant sleeping until nine, dragging breakfast throughout the morning, engaging in afternoon activities organized by the hostess, and enduring long meals and conversation at night. Novelists depicted three sorts of country-house weekends: (1) the weekend of piercing soul-study, "inspissated gloom, and tenebriferous melancholy"; (2) the weekend that began with "a flogging scene at some famous school," followed by loads of brilliant young people arriving at home and discussing the Hollowness of Life, the Comicality of War, and the novels of D. H. Lawrence—all amid absinthe cocktails and lunches of foie gras, quails, persimmons, and pomegranates; and (3) the weekend with no deep thinkers or verbal wit but instead a licentious scene featuring slim young women exquisitely gowned and well-dressed vacuous men all seductive, all seduced, a "weekend of wooing, white shoulders, starry eyes, satiny chemises, and tiger-skin divans."

Such events were not only foreign to middle- and working-class persons on any day but were as likely to occur in upper-class homes on a Saturday or Monday as a Sunday and thus to diminish the distinct quality of Sunday. As elsewhere, Sunday in England was really about the working and middle class, and it is on their growing assortment of Sunday activities that one ought to focus.

LYING DOWN AND EATING UP

Certainly the English list of "things to do" on Sunday after the war remained shorter than any such French list. The broad portraits above of working- and middle-class Sundays were dominated by decidedly unremarkable activities, the very sorts of things that confirmed in many minds the old reputation of the quiet English Sunday: sleeping late, "chinwags" with friends and family, much time at home, much time preparing and consuming meals, Sunday school for children, reading, perhaps church, some music, a walk or two in the park or street, and visiting the pubs. But what these portraits did not mention, and what especially foreigners did not see, was that there was also a proliferating number of new activities available on Sunday after the war, including more sports, social clubs, and excursions than ever before and the hugely popular cinema. Many of these took greater effort and money in England than in mainland Europe, where Sunday tended to be publicly organized and celebrated. But just as a few guidebooks promised, an active Sunday was more possible than ever in England, if one was willing to make that effort.

Still, one must start at home. If the English Sunday between the wars meant more time than usual at home, then sleep and food were two of the main attractions.

The sleepy Sunday of England was not merely figurative. Almost all reminiscences from the time mention how people looked forward to "lying in" on Sunday morning, beyond the usual six or six-thirty of the weekday. The early morning lie-in was less true of church-attending English Catholics, of course, as many of them opted for an early Mass. But church-attending Protestants could lie in as easily as anyone, for Protestant services tended to begin as late as eleven or eleven-thirty.

The afternoon nap or "lie-down" was mentioned nearly as much as lying in, although certainly not by pleasure-seeking adolescents and other young people. Charles Harper noted in 1927 that his own home-bound Sunday included morning church, a walk in the park, dinner, and a "heavy stertorous sleep on the sofa." Others mention falling asleep in a chair all afternoon. Even busy housewives might find an hour to nap in the late afternoon. The Sunday afternoon nap also proved to be a favorite time for sex among married couples—in surveys at least as popular, if not more so, than Saturday night. Couples from the disguised northern town that Mass Observation generically labeled "Worktown" (later identified as Bolton) confirmed that Sunday afternoon was definitely their favorite time: some in the survey called it the Sunday "mattinay." Here was another reason to send children to Sunday school, even among nonbelieving parents.

Another prominent at-home activity on Sunday was eating, featuring the traditional Sunday dinner but occupying much of the rest of the day too. This was due not only to more time on Sunday to prepare food but also, at least in middle- and working-class homes, to more time to eat it, so that meals became more of a ceremony. Sunday often meant four separate eating times, with especially breakfast and dinner superior to weekday meals. Stacey Aumonier wrote of the "solemn rites affecting the Sunday joint," representing "the core of English life." A London railwayman noted that breakfast on Sunday was bacon and eggs and tomatoes rather than porridge or shredded wheat, while Sunday dinner always featured meat, vegetables, Yorkshire puddings, and bread and butter or milk pudding for dessert (as compared to the sponge-based cake preferred among middle classes). George Orwell wrote in *Down and Out in Paris and London* that workhouse food too was better on Sundays, with meat, bread, and vegetables to spare, although this did not extend to prison food. In working-class homes, much baking for the week was also done on Sunday—cakes and jam tarts for weekday tea, especially—so that the working-class housewife on Sunday might have to care for morning tea, breakfast, more tea, dinner, supper, and evening tea, with baking in between.

Upper-class meals were lavish and expensive all weekend long. Breakfast was a large, protracted enterprise, lasting from nine-thirty to as late as eleven-thirty, ending perhaps a bit earlier on Sunday to allow attendance at church. It might include honey and marmalade, coffee, cold meats with parsley and jelly, an urn of porridge, eggs, hot kidneys, sausages, bacon, mushrooms, kipper, ham, tongue, and game pie. Lunch after church could be just as lavish but also informal and drawn out, so that the usual array of guests could come and go as they pleased. It often featured eggs to start, a main course, cold meats, dessert, and cheeses, with everyone helping themselves. Tea in the afternoon could be a more serious occasion, and dinner a couple of hours after that certainly was, with people expected to dress rather formally—women in knee-length dresses, men in dinner jackets, the host in a smoking jacket, and in very grand houses, the men in coats with tails. In the 1930s some such families followed the fad of coming to dinner in pajamas, but formality was the rule. For dinner too the spread was lavish, this time served by the household staff and accompanied by long, elaborate, idiosyncratic conversations often loaded with "national pride, chauvinism, and xenophobia," the "treachery of liberals and foreigners," and, at least after the ladies departed, many rounds of port, old brandy, and cigars.

In 1920 church remained an important part of the English Sunday—
partly as an actual activity but mostly as a cultural force. Almost every
autobiography written between 1900 and 1930, regardless of the author's class, mentions the prominence of formal religion and morals in
his or her upbringing and the supreme importance of Sunday church
in conveying both. Still, by 1920 churchgoing was far from universal.

The long-standing image of church attendance in the West, and
more specifically in England, held that churches were full on Sundays
until at least the Industrial Revolution and perhaps even to World
War I. Then secularization, urbanization, a shortage of churches, and
disillusionment brought on by such a horrifying war led to mass disaf-
fection. But scholars now doubt this image, especially the "secularization" that supposedly always tagged along with industrialization, for
various reasons.

First, the churches of nineteenth-century England were most successful in gaining new members right during the Industrial Revolution,
not before: overall membership did not decline but grew steadily from
1800 to 1910.

Second, church attendance tends to go in cycles rather than suffer
everlasting decline or enjoy eternal increase. For instance, during the
nineteenth century, church attendance peaked for the Church of England in 1851, and for nonconformist churches in the 1880s. Decline
followed, but between 1945 and 1958 church membership, baptisms,
communicants, Sunday school attendance, and church marriages all
increased significantly again.

Third, despite legal requirements before the nineteenth century to
attend the national church every Sunday, attendance had never been
universal and beliefs never homogeneous, in England or elsewhere. Up
to half the people in towns of the old Dutch Republic, for instance, belonged to no church at all. Figures for Easter communion in England
never approached the near-universal figures of some Catholic countries; in 1633 in Great Yarmouth, more than twelve hundred people,
half the congregation, did not fulfill their religious and civic obligation
at Easter. And even in areas of France and Belgium where almost all

people did indeed attend Sunday Mass, religious understanding was not where officials wanted it to be. In other words, church attendance could be sporadic in the old days too, and orthodoxy certainly was.

Finally, even though attendance peaked in English churches during the mid- to late nineteenth century, virtually none were full on Sunday before World War I. Typically they were more empty than full, at about one-third of capacity. One scholar, Robin Gill, has called this misperception the myth of the (newly) empty church. In fact, churches were mostly empty long before World War I, and not much emptier thereafter. The chief reason, said Gill, was overbuilding: especially in smaller towns and rural areas, churches of the later nineteenth century competed for members by erecting new and attractive structures, yet many members and potential members were already moving away from such places because of economic forces. Heavy migration toward big cities made already superfluous small-town churches even emptier, thus feeding the impression of a "decline in religion." That empty churches continued to stand as monuments even after they had closed down—unlike failed businesses, they were not demolished or sold—confirmed the image of religious decline and secularization.

But that image is misleading, alleged Gill. In 1902 overall church membership in England was actually still increasing. In the 1920s and 1930s overall church attendance, at about 12 percent each Sunday, was only slightly less than it had been before the Great War, hardly the drastic decline long supposed. Moreover, churchgoing *increased* slightly after the war among suburban, educated, middle-class people—precisely the group most exposed to the new "secular" thinking. As for supposedly disaffected working classes, they still made up the bulk of most every congregation. In fact, church attendance declined at a faster rate among the upper classes than among the working classes in numerous parishes around London.

The figure of 12 percent attending church weekly is hardly inspiring, but its meaning is no more self-evident than that of other trends. One scholar reads the figure this way. First, the 12 percent who attended on any given Sunday in the 1920s and 1930s were not always the same people: far more than 12 percent attended occasionally. And second, most people of the early twentieth century "were believing without attending."

Certainly some among the English left all churches because they stopped believing. But most English still accommodated religion one way or the other, even if they did not attend. About half did this by formally belonging to a church. Others sent their children to Sunday school and held views—reflected in legislation and new opinion polls regarding birth control, divorce, obscenity, and the undesirability of the Continental Sunday—derived originally from religious sources. As another scholar put it, "Britain was a Christian nation before 1950 because the majority had at least some faith, not because the minority had strong faith."

Randolph Churchill, son of the famous prime minister, came to similar conclusions, preferring to see nonattendance at church as a shift in religiosity rather than a decline into irreligiosity. By not attending regularly, modern people were "doing precisely the same as our ancestors did: namely, keeping some parts of our traditional heritage, while rejecting others" and building a new heritage. The broad preservation of basic religious beliefs represented the keeping, and the tendency of most to miss church weekly represented the rejecting. But this was a natural process, repeated every generation and neither inherently good nor bad. In fact, it is better understood as: some things lost, and some things gained. If a certain number of churchgoers were lost, for instance, how many of them used to attend out of fashion or convention or legal obligation? Those who attended now were more likely to do so out of honest conviction, and that could be counted as a gain. Churchill figured, very unscientifically, that the English Sunday probably gained and lost in about equal proportion each generation. The difference between the English Sunday of "today" and that of "our fathers" is "more reflective of the general difference between the two periods rather than an alteration of conscious intent specifically for Sunday."

Complicating the problem of identifying religiosity in England, continued Churchill, was that there were probably as many varieties of spiritual life among churchgoers as among nonchurchgoers. In other words, any set of attendance figures takes one only so far in getting at "religiosity." Some churchgoers kept the bond between themselves and the church as "an act of symbolic attachment," while some nonchurchgoers may have had deeper religious beliefs than regulars in the Sunday pews. Indeed, one could not say that Sunday attendance in any era, in any religion—even in the fully Catholic Middle Ages—necessarily meant full belief.

These rather abstract arguments take on more life through numerous statements of both churchgoers and nonchurchgoers, unavailable in such quantity before the twentieth century and its opinion surveys. Among the nonattenders, certainly some expressed hostility and disbelief, including condemnations of "clerical domination" and "rigid dogma." A Mrs. S also came close to unbelieving: she couldn't remember why she stopped attending, but she thinks it was because she concluded that life was "much harder than what parsons tell you: where would you be if you always turned the other cheek?" Yet more common were reasons that suggested other motives. One woman declared in 1930, "You don't have to go to church. I mean, you can live a decent life without all the rigmarole, can't you? Strikes me that half the people who go to church are humbugs anyway, Sunday Christians. No, I don't think He'll hold it against me. When I get to the pearly gates He won't hold it against me, I'm sure of that. And if He does, I'll tell Him straight. I was too busy on Sundays getting dinner and tea for you bloody lot to have time to sit on my arse in church." Mrs. M was likewise devoted to working for her family on Sundays but stopped attending mainly because of an unkindness at church. Mrs. F, also busy with family, added that in any case she didn't have any proper clothes, and people "are so quick to notice if anyone is shabby." A barmaid named Miss R, offended by all the talk of sex in the staff room, believed "profoundly in the Christian doctrine" but did not attend because she disliked the current parson. And so it went.

On the other side of the coin were those who did attend but not necessarily out of deep belief, or even any belief. A number said they quite enjoyed singing in the choir as boys but that didn't necessarily make them "religious." A Mr. R in Rowntree liked music in the great cathedrals on Sunday, but "don't make the mistake of thinking I'm religious." Mr. D attended on most Sundays to please his wife. Mr. V was "fat and lazy, drinks and eats too much, bets heavily on horses and cars, has a mistress, and attends the Church of England" every Sunday. Mrs. X was a rather unconvinced member of the Church of England but went to church as a "matter of form"; during the services she made so many "mental reservations" that in private she could hardly consider herself a Christian at all. Mrs. R. was neutral toward religion but went to church as an example to others. Similarly, Mr. P, an undertaker, attended because people expected it, but he didn't take the services seriously: he had "put many in their coffins but none of them yet told me they were still alive."

Others admitted to attending out of a desire to socialize. This was not necessarily an irreligious motive, given the importance since ancient times of fellowship on Sunday. But it could take on less than devout forms. An Edwardian maidservant of a bishop, for instance, remembered Sunday as a pleasant day because only "essential work" was to be done that day, and because the service was enhanced by "the young fellows from the town" in the back of the church, "smiling and making eyes at the female house staff." Indeed, the possibility of romance helped many young women look forward to Sunday services. "All our religious observance, which played so large a part in our lives, became more thrilling and exciting when we could peep across at the lads under cover of our hymn-singing, and later we joined up with them for a few delicious moments on our demure walks over Crowhill Road after evening service." Here was another reason to dress up for church, besides the sheer thrill of nice clothing expressed by Eileen Elias earlier. Henrietta Isleworth from Preston wrote that she loved the white silk dress she got every Good Friday and then used often on Sundays through the year. Isabella Jones in the same town wrote that she enjoyed attending church four times every Sunday while growing up, because it allowed her to dress in her best all day long. Kate Langholm attended Catholic Mass with her friends, Protestant services with her mother, and then Sunday school in the afternoon, all of which she loved for the same reason: she got to wear her best clothes the whole day. The French endimanchée lived in England too.

Many more such examples of variously believing attenders could be cited, if never calculated with mathematical precision. But perhaps the story "Sunday Morning's Dream," from 1930, best captures their spirit, and the want of devotion that might prevail in church on Sunday. Thanks to a vision, the main character is able to see beyond the visible prayers and faces of the congregation and into their thoughts and hearts. A small child's prayer ascends exactly as spoken. But the thoughts of most people wander, contradicting the apparently pious expression of their bearer. Members of the choir discuss the next hymn with one another. One woman peers over her prayer book and thinks, "How shamefully late Mrs. Slack always comes, what an awful example to set to her family! Thank goodness no one can accuse me of that sin!" "New hats again already!" thought Mrs. Slack in response. "How can they afford it, and their father owing all his Christmas bills yet? If my girls look shabby, at least we pay our debts." "Ah! There's Tom S," nodded a young man to his friend in the opposite gallery, "he is growing quite religious. At church two Sundays running: how long will the devout fit last?" One man "composed in his mind a letter he intended to send" without recollection of the holy place where he stood. "Some young girls rehearsed scenes with their lovers; some recalled the incidents of their last ball. Careful housewives planned schemes of economy, noted warning to their servants, or decided on the most becoming trimming of dress or hat."

If it's clear enough that devotion is notoriously difficult to measure, for those who did bother at least to attend, there were plenty of new attractions in old forms to appeal to their spirituality. Methodists still had an abundance of hymns, including all six thousand of Charles Wesley's. Every English church benefitted from new English hymnals pioneered by Ralph Vaughan Williams and Gustav Holst, full of tunes ancient and modern, English and French and otherwise.

In London at least, sermons could be so appealing that special guidebooks were devoted wholly to them, listing the virtues and styles of each church and preacher, including such celebrities as the Reverend Dr. John Short, and Dr. Dick Sheppard, for whom people queued up hours in advance. On Sunday afternoons at St. Martin-in-the-Fields, the Reverend Geoffrey Studdert Kennedy, affectionately known among soldiers of the Great War as Woodbine Willie, spoke soldierly language in his popular sermons, peppering them with slang and even expletives, all to chasten and arouse his audience to what he felt was the essence of Christianity: relieving the suffering of others. People did not necessarily mind being chastised this way for their sins: the well-known Catholic Fr. H.F.B. Mackay of All Saints' Margaret Street in London said that one of the reasons for the popularity of John the

Baptist was that he called those around him a "generation of vipers. There is nothing that society likes better than to be scourged in general terms." And the guidebooks ecumenically suggested countless other possibilities, from the Salvation Army, to tent revivals, to Liberal Jewish synagogues, all in a wide variety of languages.

Some did not like all the new possibilities for Sunday church, nor the new tendency to develop broadly appealing, ecumenical services, or services so easily reconciled with the world. As the loquacious Scottish theologian A. M. Fairburn put it, "I am grateful that my childhood was nurtured on the Book of Psalms rather than on the jingling verses that celebrate the 'Sweet Savior,' or protest how I love 'my Jesus.'" Penny Hunt, in a 1931 tract, was weary of such teachings as "Jesus was a very nice man and we ought to be living in a very comfortable world." He wanted something stronger, a recapturing of the Christian Sabbath "to gird up the whole nation," and he simply expected people to attend church and endure it. Both Fairburn and Hunt would likely have condemned as too colloquial the *Chats with Chums: 24 Sunday Morning Addresses to Boys and Girls,* published in 1928. They certainly would have detested the efforts to turn every once-worldly action of the church into a sacrament, reflected in the sanctification "even of church bazaars": "such breath-taking liturgical inventiveness should not have been beyond devising a form for the blessing of Bingo or for the concelebration of Canasta."

But reduced or not, attended or not, or even attended imperfectly, churches still cast a wide net across an English Sunday.

THE GOOD BOOK(S)

In the 1920s and 1930s, attendance at traditional Sunday schools was declining at a faster rate than attendance at church. Yet the Sunday schools were still fuller than churches, and a familiar institution for vast numbers of children.

The tradition of these schools went back at least to the Reformation on the European Continent, but in clearly recognizable form in England to the late eighteenth century. By 1800, at least 200,000 working-class children alone in England were enrolled. And by 1888, an impressive three-quarters of all English children attended Sunday schools. That number fell by the 1920s, but masses of children still attended.

Scholars like to debate whether Sunday school was a means for middle-class organizers to control working-class children, or to what extent working-class children and adults ran things as they pleased. But the children themselves, at least in later reminiscences, tended to think of Sunday school more concretely. They recalled especially certain hymns, prayers, and visual images that stayed with them forever, such as John Johnson's vivid color illustrations of Babylon, replete with forbidding clouds, brooding evil, and Mount Zion draped in light. Their memories weren't always fond. But because Sunday schools gave parents a break; promoted respect for the Sabbath, prayers before bed, grace over meals, orderliness, punctuality, and cleanliness; and organized sports and dancing and singing classes, many sent their children anyway.

If Sunday schools began to decline during the 1920s, it may have been due just as much to the existence of rival educational and social institutions as to the usual explanation of declining belief. Alongside or instead of Sunday schools were now boys' and girls' clubs. Some eighty thousand boys between eight and twenty-one in greater London belonged to boys' clubs, originally created to encourage attendance at Sunday church but now more general-interest in nature. A "really good" boys' club of any sort, including Boy Scouts, might on a Sunday meet for a morning church service, then hike or run in the country during the afternoon, with reading and quiet games from seven-thirty in the evening. Girls' clubs, including the YWCA or Girl Guides, began with similar purposes as boys' clubs, first offering Bible classes, then extending to such areas as French, handicrafts, singing, cooking, or dressmaking, several of which were suitable for Sunday. About 73,500 girls belonged to Girls' Brigades around London from 1923 to 1933, and even more belonged to Girl Guides.

Among the working classes especially, another rival was the Socialist Sunday School (established in 1892), Adult Education (established in 1903 by the University of London), and the Sunday Evening Association (established in 1883 to promote general cultural activities on Sunday). The National Council of Labour Colleges and the Plebs League organized education on Sundays, as well as on Saturdays or weeknights. Working-class adults pursued here further education in their trade or in general knowledge, while children at Socialist Sunday Schools encountered an adaptation of the churches' Sunday schools. The Socialist version tended to reject the idea of personal sin as the cause for human suffering, and blamed instead the "rotten social system" that resulted from free enterprise capitalism. It was not necessarily secular or Marxist, as many directors of Socialist Sunday Schools claimed that their theories came straight from the New Testament. Traditional church people were not convinced, however, especially not when they heard such hymns as "We're a Band of Little Comrades."

Church people would have objected less to Socialist lessons based broadly on Christian ethics, including "Gambling," "Happiness," and "Companionship," but they would have again been mistrustful upon hearing the Socialist Ten Commandments, starting with the first: "Love your schoolfellows, who will be your fellow-workmen in life." Or the seventh: "Whoever enjoys the good things of the Earth without working for them is stealing the bread of the workers." The catechism followed the church's question-and-answer format but with a new purpose: "Why is Socialism necessary? Because the present system enables a few to enrich themselves out of the labour of the People." Like traditional Sunday schools, the Socialist version declined after World War I, so that only thirty-four remained by 1935.

Although all sorts of Sunday schools declined after the Great War, literacy and reading increased. In fact, the two trends were probably related. Reading was possible at any time of the week, of course, but the still limited choice of activities on Sunday made that day a favorite. The biggest boom was observed among children, who had such Sunday-flavored publications directed at them as *The Boys' Own Paper* and *The Girls' Own Paper,* featuring fiction, illustrations, and hobbies along with religious messages. Adults had even more Sunday periodicals from which to choose, the most famous of which was *Sunday at Home,* begun in 1854 to promote the "sanctity of the Sabbath" and continuing until it folded in 1940—because, as the paper itself stated, fewer people were spending Sunday at home reading by now. Numerous other works suitable for Sunday emerged from the Religious Tract Society and then its successor, the United Society for Christian Literature, such as *Light in the Home* and *True Catholic.*

But people read far more than religious publications on Sunday, of course. Most people interviewed in surveys said they read more for escapism and relaxation than for knowledge or piety. Critics of popular literature were not exactly thrilled with the increase in reading, given the sorts of things people preferred. Favorite authors of boys were Captain W. E. Johns, Richmal Crompton, and Enid Blyton, and such periodicals as *Adventure, The Rover, The Wizard, The Hotspur,* Orwell's *Boy's Weeklies,* and more. These were younger versions of serial magazines and pulp fiction—the favorite sort of reading material among adults, and the favorite target of critics. People of all classes also enjoyed light fiction, detective stories (Arthur Conan Doyle, Agatha Christie), westerns, adventure, romance, and humor (especially P. G. Wodehouse), while working-class people had a taste for nonfiction, including history, biography, crafts, and arts. More serious literature, some of it banned, came from Thomas Hardy, T. S. Eliot, D. H. Lawrence, T. E. Lawrence ("of Arabia"), Aldous Huxley, and the poets W. H. Auden and Stephen Spender. But lighter fare prevailed: what one Scotsman said about Glasgow—"Getting drunk is the nearest way out of London, so reading is the quickest way out of Glasgow"—applied to certain English cities too.

The only sort of Sunday reading that can be spoken of with certainty as mostly a Sunday activity was the Sunday newspaper. "More people read more newspapers on Sundays than weekdays," concluded the Hulton Readership survey in 1948, confirming a long-standing trend. "Out of every 100 people in England and Wales, 26 read three or more Sunday papers, 36 read two, 30 read one, and only 8 read none at all." Stacey Aumonier put it more poetically: it is "strange how much more interesting and readable a Sunday newspaper is than a daily paper. A daily paper is all rush and headlines. . . . The Sunday paper was conceived in the interest of breakfasters in bed. . . . Everything seemed interesting; even political speeches were not too dull, but divorce and criminal cases were thrilling." This thrill obviously wasn't universal, however: the Sunday paper petered out in France and Belgium, partly because it was eventually made illegal, but surely as well because there was too much else to do.

As Aumonier suggested, it wasn't only greater length that distinguished Sunday papers but the stuff inside. This tended to concentrate on the juicier bits of news—the "exclusive and entertaining," the scandal, and the gossip—rather than the more serious. *The News of the World* was the best source, read by every second person, but *The People* and *The Sunday Pictorial* were also favorites. Sunday papers also contained more sport than usual; this was partly because so many matches and games were played on Saturday, and people wished to learn the results. As one observer wrote, "One of the chief differences between the Continental Sunday and the English is that on the Continent, people often go to church first and play football afterward, whereas we seldom go to church at all and read about yesterday's football in the papers." The papers also gave extra attention and drama to the Sunday accounts of sport, such as the cricket headlines "England in Peril!" and "Can We Avoid Disaster?" *Sunday at Home* condemned the Sunday newspaper partly for its attention to sport, but especially for its emphasis on crime and scandal; such condemnation was in line with the Sabbatarian tradition that if secular reading on Sunday was sinful, then the papers were the biggest culprit, for they "have still the air of naughty little scapegraces playing truant from church." They were full of film stars, actresses, wayward clergy, murderers, the doings of the Prince of Wales, the Loch Ness monster, and the latest mind-bogglers from Freud and Einstein.

George Orwell understood well the exceptional nature of the Sunday paper. In an article in *The Tribune* entitled "The Decline of the English Murder," he wrote, "It is Sunday afternoon, preferably before the war. The wife is already asleep in the armchair, and the children have been sent out for a nice long walk. You put your feet up on the sofa, settle your spectacles on your nose, and open the *News of the World*. Roast beef and Yorkshire, or roast pork and apple sauce, followed up by suet pudding and driven home, as it were, by a cup of mahogany-brown tea, have put you in just the right mood. Your pipe is drawing sweetly, the sofa cushions are soft underneath you, the fire is well alight, the air is warm and stagnant. In these blissful circumstances, what is it that you want to read about? Naturally, about a murder."

He didn't say what caused this sudden fascination on Sunday with the criminal and lurid, but one other observer thought he knew. Surely, he suggested, it was because so much crime and scandal could be found in another old Sunday reading favorite, which therefore served as a model for modern newspapers: the Bible.

STAYING IN

It's clear enough by now that the quieter, sleepier, reading sort of English Sunday meant a lot of time at home. Some seemed to enjoy the chance to do nothing there for once (although women were still usually doing something). Others such as Tony Hancock felt there was no choice but to stay home. And still others lacked the energy, imagination, or means to find something to do somewhere else.

A man interviewed by Mass Observation said that he stayed home on Sundays because the day was dull and miserable and he found more "enjoyment" at home. Yet this man also recognized that by staying home he contributed to the day's general dullness: "I never go out at all on Sundays if I can avoid it. I have occasionally wondered why I have this habit of staying indoors on Sunday—and I really don't know the answer." He had no religious connection to the day. His father, an agnostic, had always stayed home, while his mother, even less religious, rested on Sunday because she worked long hours at her grocery store six other days a week. Thus this man, now grown, stayed home as well, and clung to the idea of "peace, a bright fire, and hours of reading." He heard others say frequently "Oh I hate Sunday," "Sunday is a miserable day," and so forth, but when pressed for reasons, it turned out they usually stayed at home and were miserable because other people stayed home. In fact some, like Tony Hancock's character, threatened to "stay in bed all day." One man interviewed about his Sundays stated that a "central London Sunday is, broadly speaking, a hangover."

Yet plenty of people tried to entertain themselves while at home. Besides eating, sleeping, and reading, other domestic activities included the old standbys of singing and playing parlor games. Adolescents or young adults might be found playing "Postman's Knock" or "Film Stars" on Sunday or otherwise. The latter required little imagination, as demonstrated by a group in Bolton one Sunday night: the young men sat on couches and chose the name of a film star; the young women came in one at a time, said the name of a film star, then sat down next to the young man who'd chosen it. When all were matched up, the lights went out. Upper-class households, especially country estates, might be busy with parlor games every day of the weekend, such as bridge, backgammon, the new rage of mah-jongg, jigsaw puzzles, new crosswords, or the family's own made-up, often arcane games that alternately embarrassed or bored uninitiated guests. Children there might play sardines and murder over and over, or even dance.

Phyllis Willmott and Eileen Elias have already noted the importance of singing in their working- and middle-class homes on Sunday. The Methodist Philip Oakes had the same recollection of his middle-class upbringing: his family was full of singers, and his treble voice "joined the chorus every Sunday" when his lay-preacher father gathered friends and relations around the piano to sing hymns. They also sang sophisticated pieces from *The Messiah* or *Judas Maccabeus,* selections from the *Indian Love Lyrics,* and the (for them) less reverent "Camp Town Races" and "Drink to Me Only"—everything punctuated by the scent of "pipe tobacco and lavender water." His mother also served the guests "potted-meat sandwiches and biscuits and cups of Camp coffee which came in a bottle bearing a picture of a British officer in India sitting in front of his tent," and his father used the occasion to showcase some new line of pottery from his firm.

No one can say how many families sang on Sundays, but if the number declined between the wars, it probably had something to do with the advent of a new at-home choice on Sunday, and other days: the radio, or "wireless." Radio for entertainment, and not merely for advertisements and news, began in 1919, and by 1938 more than 90 percent of English households had at least one radio.

The heart of British radio was the BBC, founded in 1922, which many English believed was the finest network in the world. To the disbelief of Americans, it operated without commercial interruptions. The company's founding director, Sir John Reith, imposed such rules as requiring announcers to wear dinner jackets during evening broadcasts, and most programming fit that dressed-up image: weekdays were marked by classical music, the dramatization of novels and plays, and assorted programs, while Sunday offered more classical music, more drama, and a lot more religious programming. Sunday also featured the notorious "great silence" during the morning, to avoid conflicting with religious services. The Sunday lineup long went something like this: general religious programs from 9:30 to 10:45, the great silence until 12:30, serious music and talk until the 8:00 P.M. church service (later modified to 5:30 or 6:00), and another dose of serious music until 11:30 P.M. From 1933, as churches began to realize that live broadcasts actually increased the general appeal of their congregation, a morning service was sent out as well.

Many people liked the Sunday lineup. Some postponed Sunday lunch to listen to a series called *This Symphony Business,* while others waited for the BBC Dance Orchestra on Sunday evening. And in fact such programming allowed more people to hear classical music than ever before. But others found the Sunday offerings growing stale: by 1935 the Radio Manufacturers Association was urging more "light entertainment" on Sunday and the abolition of silent hours. When the BBC was slow to change, people switched to a growing number of competitors. Radio Luxembourg captured two-thirds of the Sunday audience at certain times of the day by the 1930s, and Radio Normandie from France was popular as well, thanks to its lighter music and programs—far preferable to what some English called the BBC's "Sunday Horrors." A study in York showed that on Sunday morning, working-class people switched on Radio Luxembourg and left it there all day, at least until the evening church service on the BBC at eight. In fact, many working-class nonchurchgoers had their only contact with organized religion through the BBC's Sunday evening service, with its "congregation" of five million.

Despite complaints, the BBC stayed with this basic schedule until World War II, on the assumption that the nation was Christian and Sunday was the Christian's special day. Its stated intent was not to promote a single Christian church but rather Christianity generally. Hence an Anglican service was broadcast one Sunday, services of other denominations on other Sundays, and nondenominational services every second Sunday, with the message to be "thorough-going, optimistic and manly," unconcerned with narrow dogma. Some critics called it "Emasculated Christianity," while others thought it all less ecumenical than it might have been, as some groups were excluded altogether—including Fundamentalists, Free Thinkers, Christian Scientists, Spiritualists, Mormons, and Jews (the latter on both Saturday and Sunday). Thus the Sunday programming was more than an "Anglican vehicle," but it was still not as inclusive as it might have been. The emphasis on religion on Sunday remained the most controversial aspect of all the BBC's programming decisions during the 1930s. Alternative secular programming on Sunday evening began only in 1940.

One of Mass Observation's many volunteers, William Bradley, recorded his own listening habits on Sunday in September 1937, and they included no religious programming at all. At 12:30 he and his roommate listened to Haydn Wood's *A Manx Overture* on the BBC. After the program, they napped, read, and played with the cats until 2:00, when they listened to another wireless program. Next they listened to records of Dvorak and Brahms on the phonograph, then after dinner tuned in to the BBC again, to a program about the cinema. A recital of Beethoven's *Waldstein* Sonata and some Chopin followed. They then shut the radio off to avoid the BBC's evening religious service, turned it back on for the news, and at last heard the final act of *The Wind and the Rain* by the Sheffield Repertory Company.

AFTERNOONS OUT

For Tony Hancock and many other English, Sunday ended right there at home, as uneventfully as foreigners suspected. But for those who bothered to get out, Sunday could by now look quite different from how it had in the past.

Although some English still regarded museum attendance as unseemly on Sunday, for instance, more and more found it respectable. The British Museum, "the history of the world under a single roof," had been open on Sunday afternoons since 1885, and the National Gallery and National Portrait Gallery from 1896. On the way to such destinations, some window-shopped; indeed, some streets in London were known for their lighted Sunday displays.

Probably busier on Sunday afternoons than museums and streets were England's parks, much as in Paris or even war-torn Belgium. These were swollen on summer Sundays, far more than on other days, with family groups and young couples on benches, swings, and walkways. Hyde Park, the model for Paris's Bois de Boulogne, was especially popular. Together with Kensington Gardens, to which it was connected, it counted more than six hundred acres, and represented on Sunday, as did the parks in Paris, a green alternative for those who could not afford longer excursions to the seaside or country. Although edgier than Kensington and a favorite site of protests, Hyde Park on Sunday was more likely to feature walking, riding, swimming, boating, resting, and the famous Church Parade. This last began when church let out between twelve and two and was an occasion for "all the fashionable people" walking through to separate themselves from everyone else "by some natural law of classification." Mr. A. Milton recorded his impressions of a Church Parade in 1923: "The place was like a beehive. Besides the innumerable strollers, there were hundreds of men and women seated on the Park benches and chairs, watching them. Rotten Row, the road reserved for horseback riders, was full of these." Hundreds of carriages and motorcars also joined the slow parade.

On Sunday Hyde Park was also home to picnic baskets filled with sandwiches, bread, cheese, and lemonade, not to mention a cricket bat and wickets. One guidebook commented that the mother in such scenes inevitably looked ten years older than she really was, because of her ceaseless working, but at least on Sunday she looked radiant. Boys played in the park's Serpentine pond on Sunday outside of church hours, thus between six and ten A.M. and then from two to six in the afternoon, but girls were not allowed at all. The state apartments at Kensington Palace were open on Sunday from two to five between April and October, while at the other end of Hyde Park was the famous soapbox. There on Sunday one could usually hear an anarchist or Socialist or clergyman, or perhaps a Cockney teenager speaking about his bitter experiences in the Salvation Army, and always someone from a temperance group. At various places in the park, "surreptitious games of football," formally not allowed on Sunday, were played behind the policeman's back—at least until he saw them and told them to stop. Then, about twenty minutes later, the game would resume.

Kew Gardens, outside the heart of the city, was another popular park destination on Sunday, and newspapers spoke of the "Sabbath hush" that prevailed there. The sights and sounds of frogs, swans, and other birds filled the air, but a certain eighteenth-century formality, and the beauty of the gardens with their waist-high flowers, subdued everything. Families brought lunches or an easel and paints, and everything seemed peaceful, as "quiet as a church"—which was meant as praise.

Other popular destinations on Sunday, for those with time and money, were the country and the seaside, just as in France.

This could be to escape not busy streets, as in Paris, but instead urban gloom. A certain Gladys always left London on Saturday, for instance, because on Sunday "it's almost a city of the dead, not quite: it has a strong back-on-Monday look about it." In contrast, Tristram Coffin noted that in the village of Iffley, people loved Sunday, as they set up tables beneath chestnut trees next to the schoolhouse, and the band played, drawing working people even from Oxford.

Sunday visitors to other villages described similarly idyllic scenes. People there ate dinner slowly, read the Sunday papers, and attended cricket matches on the village green, grouped in families under the shade of an elm tree. "A middle-aged man in flannels and sports jacket stands smoking a pipe and watching the match; a spaniel pants at his feet." Two boys on his right followed the game, two girls were uninterested but lay about on the grass and giggled. Near a tandem bicycle, a man in khaki shorts and a white shirt "follows the play intently from his seat, a woman knits in the grass and faces the road." Most people wore their best clothes, even if they didn't attend church, and some worked without a second thought, especially farmers.

Toward evening the villagers entertained themselves by watching the "day trippers" and sightseers tear back through the village for home. "Cyclists pour through the village in squads of bare legs, white shirts and shorts," while the locals "loll against windowsills, hang over gates, or lean out of upstairs windows watching the traffic." The pubs reopened at seven and were soon packed with men and women drinking soft drinks and beer, while outside the pubs the ground was quickly littered "with sweet and ice cream papers, empty cartons, paper bags, cigarette packets, matchboxes, debris of the day." This wasn't terribly different from the suburban Sunday described by Louis Morin in France.

Like Morin, those on excursions into the country would also have bumped into cars along the way, or ridden in them—and far more than ever before. About 250,000 cars were sold in 1919 in Britain, then 1.5 million in 1929. And the Sunday excursion was a primary purpose: indeed the Sunday drive and the Bank Holiday traffic jam were institutions by the 1930s. Agatha Christie had Miss Dorothy Pratt and Mr. Edward Palgrave leaving town on a Sunday drive "just like everybody else." Some Sabbatarians objected to the Sunday drive because it forced chauffeurs to work, but as driving became more common and fewer chauffeurs were used, then the only objection was that Sunday driving was not a sufficiently sober recreation.

One did not need a car to reach the country or coast on Sunday, thanks to an increase in bus and rail service on that day to serve the crowds leaving town. On a summer Sunday in "Worktown," bus stations were filled with people headed toward the sea. These excursions had been popular since before 1900, despite the Sabbatarian argument that if buses and trains would cease on Sunday then the working classes would have no choice but to stay at home and attend church. But after these early battles, Sunday rail and bus service attracted ever larger crowds. These thinned temporarily during the Great War but picked up rapidly afterward. Since the paid vacation was not invented until the 1930s, and then usually lasted only one week per year at best, it is not hard to imagine how important these Sunday excursions were in the popular mind.

At the seaside as in the country, Sunday was a lively day. One travel writer stated, "The brightest Sundays are summer Sundays, especially those days spent in the country or at the seaside where there is an air of luxury and exuberance which can tempt thousands out of town." A Mass Observer described a July Sunday at a "South-coast seaside resort" that looked much like a scene described in France by Louis Morin. The deck chairs were full by ten-thirty, young men and women eyed each other, some read the newspaper, some swam, some played fetch with eager dogs. The observer watched a middle-aged man, "heavily built, very hairy chested, waddle down to the sea," while a young woman nearby said, "He's got some flesh round his middle. I reckon he's got a nerve to want to show off a figure like that." Young children pranced about in feathered paper hats, people ate ice cream and drank fizzy lemonade, and English, American, Norwegian, and Indian sailors conversed on all sides in their different languages. Around four, an audience of four hundred working-class, middle-aged people gathered to hear an orchestra at the pier, the "light, popular music of the Tea for Two variety." Most of the men read newspapers throughout the show, while the women knitted; some leaned over the pier and gazed at the fishermen there. A middle-aged woman approached her husband: "I've just had my fortune told. It says I'm going to meet a tall, dark and handsome husband (playfully puts hand on husband's cheek) and you're not tall, and not dark, and you're not handsome." Here at the beach was an English Sunday "at its noisiest, most crowded," and for some most fulfilled. But as one participant noted, it also "cost a pretty penny," and again was a rarity for many.

Also out on Sunday in England, just as in France, were cyclists. The first Cyclist Touring Club was organized in 1883, and by 1933 had thirty thousand members. Naturally there was some discussion of the propriety of cycling on Sunday, as there had been of motoring or riding the train—not to mention discussion of women cycling on any day. Some believed that for women cycling was unhealthy and indecorous, caused gynecological problems, and so forth, but by the 1920s English clubs were quite mixed. Moreover, although Sabbatarians argued that cycling forced repair shops to open, cycling itself tended to have a more savory reputation than rougher sports, and thus it thrived. Those who bothered to defend it said that cycling fit the basic Christian ideal of athleticism, and was better than simply "lounging at the river."

According to a Mass Observation account, one club began its Sunday outings at ten in the morning, right during Protestant church services, when anywhere from six to twenty young cyclists gathered. All were in shorts, unless the weather was cold. The boys occasionally wore black berets, while the girls had a "friendly rivalry" to see who could wear the brightest and most unusual beret. The cyclist leader usually picked the pub for lunch. Everyone brought their own sandwiches, and the young women and men ate together either inside or outside the pub, the men drinking beer and the women something lighter. They all returned home around seven or eight. If it was not a hard day of cycling, then the homeward pace was leisurely, with stops at fairgrounds, pubs, or cafés in neighboring towns. Sometimes groups of eight or nine people broke off and attended the cinema that evening or ended up at a member's house—at least if the parents were not home—where they held impromptu parties with an "emphasis on flirting, mild necking and generally enjoying themselves."

Another old country pastime, walking, was also increasingly popular on Sunday and the entire weekend. It long had a supposedly middle-class flavor, based on the assumption that such people enjoyed little exercise or fresh air during the week. But by the early twentieth century plenty of working-class people walked in the country as well, leading to the formation of hiking and "rambling" clubs. The latter usually involved an afternoon walk, while the former was more ambitious and could last an entire weekend. Walking per se was harder to condemn as a Sunday activity than cycling, motoring, or beachgoing. Most complaints about it occurred when a walk conflicted with Sunday services; sometimes "entire choirs" were off hiking on Sunday, and had the nerve to post the announcement on the church door, where they also gathered.

One of the earliest such clubs was the Sunday Tramps, formed by Leslie Stephen, father of Virginia Woolf, in 1879, but the real explosion in the popularity of hiking and rambling occurred in the 1930s, especially among the numerous upper-working-class and lower-middle-class. The clubs had different purposes, often ecological or sportive, and also political, such as "freedom from the artificial, the sophisticated, and the obsessions of the everlasting cash nexus." But walking was their common activity, partly or wholly on Sunday, and participants sometimes covered twenty to thirty miles in a day.

As Sunday walkers grew more numerous, so did their conflicts with landowners over rights of way. Here was a less idyllic Sunday scene than was supposed to reign outside of London. Conflicts also multiplied with the growing horde of "motoring demons" who ruined Sunday walks. One T. W. H. Crosland wrote a six-point guide for dealing with motorists in the country: pack a good supply of splints and surgical bandages to dress yourself when knocked down, carry a pocket book and sharpened pencils for taking numbers of cars that run you over, jump quickly into a ditch when you see a car approaching, stay close to a hedge or wall in turning a corner lest you be struck, do not swear at those who run you over for they are genteel people, and if you succumb to injuries remember that you are dying in a glorious cause: giving pleasure to wealthy brewers, Members of Parliament, record-breaking drivers, and all their ill-bred wives, sisters, and aunts.

Another walker, Clare Cameron, followed the increasingly common pattern of initially finding the rural idyll on Sunday, then having it dashed by crowds. In a village near York one Sunday, the roses, orchards, and ivy on stable walls helped her to feel peaceful and to "forget all of the cruel, ugly, urgent, and unjust things of life." But in York itself her sense of Sunday gloom returned, simply because it was a city. It was "no more romantic or engaging in the bleak hours of early Sunday morning than any other English town, however great her age or venerable her architecture." Cameron's new and undesirable surroundings, her below-average breakfast, and the noise of motorcycles and cars flooding past to get a good place on the beach caused her to "muse upon the hated English Sunday of the provinces, prim, restrained, mincing, bleak and unutterably ugly, which puts a leash upon activity and a fetter upon the spirit; wherein the hours are marked by that slavish regard for formula, which expresses itself in preparations for heavy feasting throughout the day, in due attention to the commands of the doleful bells which ring out, it seems to me, with but one message always: 'O come to church, good people, come to church to die!' "

Despite such dramatic disappointments, enthusiasm for weekend walking was undeniable. In *The Call of England* (1928) the travel writer H. V. Morton caricatured the most enthusiastic sort of hiker, the "Peak Walker," who on Sunday climbed the Lake District's various offerings. He was outfitted in khaki pants, a tweed jacket, stout walking boots, and windblown hair. Ordinary people during the week, on Sunday they set out, thanks to specially priced train tickets, to conquer mountains. Among them could be distinguished the "ordinary rambler" and the "storm fiend." The former ventured out on Sunday when the weather permitted, but the latter rejoiced in hardship and went out regardless. He or she liked "nothing better than to drop down from the moors into Manchester or Sheffield, as the shades of night are falling on the already thick gloom of Sunday, looking as though he or she had been blown up, flung into a stream, dragged through wire netting, ending up with a triumphant victory over sixteen gamekeepers and a dog." Afterward the men among them drank beer and the women tea, while they all ate eggs and tinned pineapple and sang songs.

The religious sentiments of these walkers were usually not explicit. Some surely were indifferent to religion and went walking because Sunday was a free day. Others perhaps followed the pattern of the Irish Catholic walker who easily reconciled a proper Sunday with vigorous walking. First he attended Mass. Then, "having spent the early hours of the Lord's Day as it should be spent," he and two companions were free to begin their ascent of a mountain. The weather was fine, the day so inspiring that he thought of Psalm 117, "This is the day which the Lord hath made; let us be glad and rejoice therein." Then he made sure to come home in time for evening Rosary, a sermon, and prayers.

EXPANDING SUNDAY SPORT

Similar reconciliations with Sunday devotions were occurring in the realm of sport.

Thanks to the film *Chariots of Fire*, Eric Liddel's refusal to race on Sunday during the 1924 Olympics became famous. But it must be remembered that Liddel, running for Britain, was Scottish and not English, that some English considered him a traitor for putting himself ahead of his country, and that opportunity for Sunday sport in England was expanding anyway at this very time.

Certainly some opportunity had always been there. Although many Puritans wanted to eliminate all Sunday games, some were played anyway, both legally and illegally. In the Middle Ages, for instance, English kings had ordered the practicing of archery on Sunday, Kings James I and Charles II had both sanctioned suitable games, and people had long diced or played versions of football despite prohibitions against them. The real question was therefore *which* games. For their number to expand, they would have to become more respectable generally and more compatible with Sunday in particular.

The biggest steps toward the widespread respectability of modern sports were taken during the Victorian Age. At this time, especially ball games, such as the latest forms of football, tennis, and golf, grew dramatically in popularity and stature. There even emerged a sense that sport was not merely about play or a needed break from work but could be the bearer of moral virtues. This was at least as explicit after World War I. Sir James Marchant said in 1927 not only that "we have invented most of the good games" but that "it is no accident that the Englishman expresses his deepest moral convictions in the terms of a game." In other words, sport was more than sport: it was an expression of English values. A later observer called sport "the Englishman's religion" and said that it provided more pleasure "than religion itself, politics, literature, science, and art." After West Ham United was defeated in the 1923 football cup final, many team members attended a Congregational church the following day, Sunday, and heard the minister sermonize on the beneficial lessons that could be learned for life from football: team spirit, discipline, unselfishness, and more.

These ideas did not necessarily make sport acceptable on Sunday, of course: the old English assumption that more play on Sunday for some meant more work for others still held. But the increasing moral legitimacy of popular sport helped lead to more specific ideas and solutions for sport on Sunday.

These ideas were voiced more forcefully than ever after the war. H. W. Pearson of the Workers' Sports Association emphasized the health and social benefits of Sunday sport: "Our games keep us healthy, and mean abstaining from habitual drinking, late hours, etc. The alternative to Sunday games is walking about the street with little to do, which we feel is much more conducive to drinking, bad company and various other things which might lead a youth astray." More explicitly religious arguments were articulated by Lord Snell of Plumstead in 1933. He considered himself a religious man and thought religion a good thing for all, but he blamed Sabbatarians for making Sunday so solemn and dark that people wished to rebel against religion altogether. Precisely in order to keep religion healthy, he wished to allow the expansion of Sunday sport. Certainly Sunday should be for rest and the healing of mind and body, but he disagreed with Sabbatarians that their particular formula for rest suited one and all. For young people especially, "exercise *is* rest," and Sunday was their main day for it. He also criticized Sabbatarians for distorting the image of the Continental Sunday in order to drive fear into English hearts: Lord Snell had himself traveled widely in Europe and had never seen the widespread drunkenness and immorality that Sabbatarians held up as an inevitable result of more Sunday play. What evidence was there that "to kick a ball or to row a boat on Sunday would lead to wholesale demoralization"? He likewise rejected the usual arguments that Saturday afternoon alone provided sufficient time for play: there simply were not enough parks available on Saturday to accommodate all who wished to play football, for instance. And if a few more park keepers should have to work on Sunday in order to make it possible, then "let the Sabbatarians remember that they ride the trams and trains on Sunday, and use the services of police, doctors, and firemen," and that in their homes either servants or wives cook and labor so that the Sabbatarian may have a comfortable Sunday. Someone would always have to work on Sunday, play or no play: the question to him was, did the benefits outweigh the cost? Eric Liddel himself allowed Sunday sport under certain circumstances. During World War II, while imprisoned in the Japanese internment camp where he would eventually die of a brain tumor, Liddel broke his seemingly unbreakable principle of no sport on Sunday by organizing and refereeing games for young people. Left to their own devices, the participants usually ended up fighting, until Liddel intervened and organized them—demonstrating that he too had priorities higher than not playing on Sunday.

Certainly some were still unconvinced about sport's ties to religion and morality: a recent book about sport newspapers entitled *Babes, Booze, Orgies, and Aliens* suggests the long-standing association of the "unholy trinity" of sex, drink, and gambling to sport, on any day. But advocates of Sunday sport were saying that it didn't have to be that way.

Whether one favored Sunday sport on physical, social, or religious grounds, the practical solution proved to be the same for all: organize things privately. Here was the key to Sunday sport, or Sunday anything else, in England.

Privately organized sport emphasized participation, where all the physical and moral benefits of sport were said to occur. These could therefore be allowed. Spectator sport, in contrast, was offensively pub-

lic, charged admission, and caused many to work. These were still unacceptable. After the war, almost all professional teams continued to
prohibit or discourage Sunday matches because they were public and
charged admission. Even some amateur sports avoided Sunday, including football, the most popular sport in England by now. But many amateur sports and the clubs that promoted them began to flourish on
Sunday.

Liverpool in the early 1930s, for instance, boasted among the working classes alone 1,000 football clubs, 500 tennis clubs, 400 cricket
clubs, 200 hockey clubs, 200 bowling clubs, and 100 cycling clubs.
Those who had their own grounds could play as they pleased on Sunday. The football clubs, which needed extensive space, usually did *not*
have their own grounds and had to rely on public parks, where poli-
cies varied greatly. As late as 1937 in Manchester, for instance, the city
council rejected games and recreations in public parks on summer Sundays, while London in 1933 removed all such bans in its parks. Suffice
it to say that the Lord's Day Observance Society still had its best success in obstructing games on publicly owned grounds, and anywhere
there was an admission fee or a strong commercial element.

As the list of clubs in Liverpool suggests, few sports were exclusive
to any class. But some were dominated more by one class than another.
Middle- and upper-class sport on Sunday often included croquet, tennis, or golf, usually played on club grounds or at country estates,
shielded by hedges. Tristram Coffin left an account of a Sunday croquet match with the dean of an Anglican cathedral on a Sunday afternoon in 1925, attended by a good crowd—but because there was
nothing commercial about it, no one objected. More formally organized were tennis clubs, which mushroomed after the war, numbering
2,900 by the mid-1930s. But more controversial on Sunday were golf
clubs.

The earliest golf courses were etched out along the coasts of England and Scotland, yet by 1900 groomed inland courses were boom-
ing as well, and Sunday play was soon, not surprisingly, an issue. One
problem was that the vast size of any golf course, public or private,
made it highly visible, still controversial on Sunday. A second was the
problem of requiring caddies to work that day. And a third was golf's
lack of widespread social approval: it was mostly for elites, and there

was no teamwork, no heroic physical challenge, and no leadership, thus how could it be useful in real life? Still, of the twelve hundred golf clubs opened by 1920 in Britain, about one-third of them advertised Sunday play, with only a few of these, incidentally, in Scotland or Wales.

Part of golf's acceptability on Sunday was that the game enjoyed reverential attitudes: P. G. Wodehouse was not alone in regarding a golf course as "Nature's Cathedral," and how much better to be there than in an actual cathedral on Sunday? Donald Cameron, a Scottish character in A. G. Macdonnell's *England Their England,* found golf a much more interesting religion than the Presbyterian Church of his native land. Other enthusiasts combined the two, as at St. Nicholas Church, in Wallasey, where the vicar held early Sunday services for a few minutes in the presence of men wearing golfing clothes, who had left their clubs on the church's front porch. But growing Sunday play was also made possible by efforts to solve the chronic problem of Sunday caddies, in one of three ways: allowing them to volunteer their services (surely in hope of later reward), allowing golfers to play without caddies (which caused the caddies to protest), and attracting caddies by offering to pay them anyway, despite prohibitions. In fact, Sunday became the caddies' most profitable day. As one explained it: "It's all very well for Professor Browning to sit in his easy chair on Sunday after lunch and think how lovely it is to go to church, but please remember he isn't half-starved and he isn't dependent on a round of golf for a meal." That many caddies were not churchgoers to begin with was one reason many golfers agreed to pay them. But Sabbatarians wondered whether willingness to caddy on Sunday wasn't precisely the reason for the lack of churchgoing among that group.

Some more popular Sunday sports included billiards, angling, the inevitable pigeon fancying (dove racing), and even public skating rinks and pools. But as popular as any, among all classes, was cricket. This game was by now long respectable because of its lack of betting and its supposed character-building qualities, even on Sunday. Most sports had their religious-like rituals, but cricket was more explicitly connected to formal religion in its emphasis on good conduct, honor, and other virtues; some even saw it as synonymous with Christian morality. For that reason some Anglican clerics themselves supported Sunday cricket. The model priest of the Oxford Movement, John Keble, from the 1830s to the 1860s used to lead his congregation out to play on summer Sundays after Evensong, so ennobling did he think the game. More recently, the Archbishop of Canterbury even made the radical suggestion that people should decide for themselves whether to play cricket on Sunday.

In the end, more cricket was played on Sunday in southern England than in northern. Opponents could not accept that the game's obvious moral qualities were enough to justify Sunday play. A Mr. F, a working-class man interviewed by Mass Observation, even quit his club when it began playing on Sunday. For amateurs, however, it was often hard to avoid Sunday, because matches tended to run over several days and the weekend suited the game's unusually lengthy time frame best. Indeed, even with modifications by the 1920s, it still usually required a weekend, or at least an entire day, to finish a match, and Sunday remained best for that. Professionals typically began their games on Mondays and usually finished before Sunday, but not always: if they ran over, they were, despite the public and commercial quality of their game, reluctantly allowed to continue.

Far bigger and far more controversial exceptions to the usual rules against public sport on Sunday included boxing and greyhound racing. Boxing regularly occurred on Sunday between the wars, before paying audiences of all classes. Was this growing acceptance on Sunday due to the sport's growing respectability? Such popular preachers as Pat Mc-Cormick at St. Martin's-in-the-Fields flung about boxing similes in sermons, much as some of his medieval predecessors had done with wrestling; such talk held the men's attention raptly, and the women liked it "because their men pay attention." "Think of the energy put into training for boxing, and what happens when you haven't trained? When you have, you know just where to get your blow in. Give yourself to God, as a boxer gives himself to training. You must train, get your punch in. Give yourself to God at least as much as a boxer or runner gives himself to a corruptible crown."

Perhaps the most surprising public sport allowed in England on Sunday was greyhound racing. Whereas most sports—certainly on Sunday—claimed to be primarily about the game itself, or to promote this or that virtue, greyhound racing was blatantly about betting, every day. More expensive horse racing almost never occurred on Sunday in England, but many greyhound tracks—where betting was cheaper, the locations more accessible, and the whole enterprise clearly aimed at working people—operated every day of the week. The races became such a notorious threat to people's financial solvency that the term "going to the dogs" derived directly from this sport. First organized in the nineteenth century, greyhound racing by 1933 drew some 6.5 million people annually to more than sixty tracks. Tracks licensed by the National Greyhound Racing Society did not race on Sunday, but many did not belong to that organization. Usually there were eight races each day, of five minutes each, spread over two and a half hours: most of the intervening time was spent organizing bets. Illicit greyhound racing and betting also occurred on the London marshes on Sunday, where the interested brought their whippets to run.

Although England's most popular sport, professional football, was not yet played on Sundays, between the wars its enormous presence was felt on that day in at least two ways: the growing number of Sunday football leagues among amateurs, and the birth of wildly popular football pools.

Unlike cricket, football long suffered an unfavorable reputation among the great and middling in English society. Edward II in 1314 ordered the Lord Mayor of London to forbid football in the fields of the city not only because it interfered with archery practice but because it was a public nuisance. With the Reformation it was less acceptable than ever to play football, much less on Sunday. Richard Conder, a champion footballer during the 1620s and 1630s, marked his conversion to pure religion and a true Sabbath to the time he quit football, mostly because it was always played on Sunday. And Shakespeare's *King Lear* made it an insult to call someone a "base football player." In the late nineteenth century, English football went in two directions: rugby and "soccer" (which retained the name of football). Rugby became more the game of the upper classes and elite schools, while football maintained broad appeal among the masses. In fact, it grew into the preeminent mass spectator sport of the early twentieth century: 111,000 watched the English cup final in 1901. It also was soon the most popular amateur sport. And for long, both professionals and amateurs played their matches on England's free Saturday afternoon.

After the Great War, more and more amateurs wanted to play on Sunday. Some ministers and Sunday school teachers remained big critics of football because of this and because the game was still associated with betting and drinking. But many others by now found that the game's new civilized form made it acceptable, and churches themselves often sponsored teams. Crowds did their best as well to improve the image of the sport, singing "Abide with Me" as part of the Cup final ritual in 1927; reporters described the singing crowd as "one huge congregation," reflecting the "depth of religion in the national character." Such could only help the sport's image, which by the 1930s had improved drastically. That was also when the biggest pressure came to allow more Sunday football.

Early instigators included the Communist British Workers' Sports Federation (BWSF), which, unlike the dominant Football Association, had no problem with Sunday play: soon after London allowed football in its public parks in 1933, the BWSF boasted 130 teams in its Sunday league there, and some 585 nationwide. Still, this paled next to the 35,000 teams and million players of the mainstream Football Association, which stuck to Saturday afternoons. Organized amateur Sunday football became more widespread only after World War II, and professionals began to play on Sunday only in the 1980s.

Far more common on Sunday between the wars was *talk* of football, which became livelier than ever thanks to the excitement created by the new football pools. During the mid-1930s almost seventeen times as many people bet on professional football as watched it, thanks to the pools. In the larger picture of gambling, the football pools were not dominant: they attracted only one-fifth the money of horse racing and even less than greyhound racing. But culturally the pools may have been more important than either, involving a tremendously wide spectrum and number of people, and commanding great attention on Sunday.

Public, legalized, mail-order football pools came to England right after World War I. The courts decided that *forecasting* the results of football matches was a skill, not a matter of chance, and thus the usual laws against betting did not apply. The various companies that ran the pools also took other steps to distinguish themselves from ordinary betting. They gave no odds, but simply took a percentage of all money bet. They required people to send in their forecasts one week, and the money to be bet only the next week; those who failed to send money were blacklisted. And they required bets on numerous matches, to keep the fixing of matches to a minimum.

The pools quickly gained appeal, partly because they were remarkably free of fraud, partly because they required only small amounts of money to participate, and especially because they offered the sense that even nonexperts had a chance at winning. Newspapers provided evaluations of the upcoming games, but everyone knew that "studying form" was usually no better than sheer luck. Also appealing was the sense among most that the pools were not gambling at all: The Mr. F mentioned earlier, who quit his cricket club when it started playing on Sunday, did not think twice about betting on the pools, even though he opposed gambling. And a Mrs. R interviewed by Mass Observation resented her husband's gambling losses at the horse and greyhound track but regarded his football coupons as a "harmless flutter." About 10 million people participated in the pools each week, and during the Depression the total amount bet rose from 10 to 40 million pounds per year, with the average weekly bet around three shillings—modest even for a lower-working-class family.

What the pools had to do with Sunday began on Thursday. That night, a person or family typically filled in their coupon(s) listing Saturday's upcoming matches. Each coupon contained only ten to fifteen of all the matches to be played that day. The bettor had to be at least twenty-one years old and bet at least six pence per coupon, one pence per match. A participant received a single point for a correct home forecast, two points for a correct away forecast, and three points for a correctly forecasted draw. Winning a large dividend usually required guessing at least ten of the matches on a coupon correctly, but winning a small prize by betting on only a few matches was easier. This was what most people did—in one survey, 85 percent had won something, usually a few pounds—and the regular small prizes kept them going. In any case, Thursday was the day for filling in the forms, Friday for sending them in to the pool company of one's choice, Saturday and

Sunday for awaiting the results, and especially Sunday for brooding or glorifying.

The first papers announcing the results appeared on Saturday night after the matches, but some appeared only on Sunday. One Miss L, a spinster over seventy, was a devout churchgoer who would never think of gambling, but she played the football pools eagerly—and she and her companion never looked at the results until after Sunday morning matins at church. But however many learned the results on Saturday night, almost all spent Sunday fretting over or exulting in their choices. Among the winners, Sunday involved still more anticipation—for the dividends. These depended on how many people had bet that week and how many big winners there were, and all this was announced only on Monday. In working-class pubs, the pools were discussed exclusively on Saturday nights and Sundays. A Nottinghamshire collier and his wife reported that "before we started coupons, football was never mentioned in our house. Now it is *the* topic on a Sunday." And Randolph Churchill wrote, "A sorrowful feature of the English Sunday is the sound of thousands of men cursing their luck as they check their football pools." Sunday was also spent in reading closely about next week's matches, in early preparation for Thursday night's betting, when the cycle would begin again.

The Football Association was supposedly against the football pools, to halt the "cancer of gambling." But when it tried to interfere with them, the country went into an uproar, "more than it did after Hitler's decision to invade the Rhineland." Guardians of morals contended that many larger crimes started "with having a shilling or two on" a football match. Yet especially the working classes defended the pools, saying that they never bet much, and besides the wealthy always had plenty of places and money to bet—including at the stock exchange. And a person ruined on the stock exchange "brought others tumbling to ruin with him . . . Tell me that the poor working man who spends six pence a week is ruining the country!"

This defense of the pools was elaborated by John Hilton in his study *Why I Go In for the Pools*. From three hundred responses, Hilton concluded that 90 percent of the population could not, through hard work and thrift alone, make enough extra money to set aside some savings, and so they tried additional means, especially the pools. They were looking to provide for their children or for elderly parents, to begin a business, or to add some small comforts to their homes. One laborer wrote that he and his wife took an hour or so each week to fill in coupons, in the amount of ninepence a week, with the hope of one day winning a sum "which would remove the sense of insecurity that is always hanging over our home. We sit and think and puzzle of some way of getting out of the rut; but so far only the Pools have presented a hope, very slight I admit." An unemployed dockworker said, "The reason why I and thousands of other unemployed have a modest six pence or shilling which we can ill afford on the Pools each week is that one day we may have the luck to win a decent sum and so put an end to this strangling existence which we lead." Or as another put it, "Filling in the family coupon makes a bit of excitement. That may be a good thing, for work and bed day in and day out gets monotonous."

Many also saw the pools as a mutual aid society. They were happy when someone else without much money got at least something. One man wrote that pool winners were always rightfully Tom, Dick, and Harry, that the pools reflected the brotherly principle of sharing without great expense to anybody, and that they were even a force for peace. "We in my family risk two shillings a week between us, money we cannot afford, in the hope of getting that fortune drop out of the blue. At least someone gets a chance of getting something different from the present state of affairs." Whereas in insurance one pooled risks, in the football pools, concluded Hilton, one pooled hopes. And the peak of that hope, at least for winners, came on Saturday night and Sunday.

EVENINGS OUT

For those who wished to get out on Sunday evenings during the 1920s and 1930s, there existed as well a few new opportunities, from music and dance to the cinema and the pub.

James Nott recently concluded that music and dancing, although long popular in Western history, were in England more popular during the 1920s and 1930s than ever before. This was largely because of new mechanized music and the rapid spread of dance halls. More than

780,000 gramophones were manufactured in England in 1930, and sixty million records were sold the same year, with the biggest musical influences being American jazz and dance. How often these recordings were heard on Sunday varied from house to house. As for dance halls, the Mecca group alone owned more than two thousand by 1938. Although closed on Sunday to the public, dance halls were now so popular that many private clubs of all sorts rented them for the day. Other people organized less formal dances in their homes. Mass Observation interviewed a working-class person who belonged to a darts club, but on Sunday nights the darts club came to his home for dancing, with their wives and daughters. Ranging in age from thirty-six to forty-eight, the adults drank beer and danced the latest craze, the Lambeth Walk, to piano and accordion music, preferring songs that had some connection to their lives, including "Up Goes the Price of Meat," "What Does It Feel Like to Be Poor," and so on. At least one Catholic priest, taking the pragmatic route, hosted Sunday evening dances in the hall under his church in order to keep teenagers and young adults off the streets and out of the pubs. Working-men's clubs and ex-servicemen's clubs, like that visited by Phyllis Willmott, might do something similar.

The single most popular form of entertainment to emerge between the wars was the cinema. It was popular even before "talkies" began in the late twenties, and by 1934 admissions had reached 963 million a year. Most moviegoers were young working-class people, but the upper and middle classes soon overcame their early mistrust of it. Originally organized for Sunday showings in the typically private way, film became so popular that more and more towns decided to allow public shows on Sunday, thus making the cinema one of Sunday's few public, commercialized activities in England.

Naturally this change did not occur without the usual storms of debate. Opponents resisted Sunday cinema on religious grounds, insisting that there were church and social organizations enough on Sunday to satisfy needs, and that the cinema would cut into attendance at church. Some cinema owners themselves resisted, believing that opening on Sunday would decrease profits during the rest of the week, for who would go on other nights if they could go on Sunday? But support for Sunday films was wide and strong: manual laborers emphasized how exhausted they were after a week's work and that there was little more relaxing than a warm, soft chair in the cinema on a Saturday or Sunday evening. One eighteen-year-old said that those his age simply would not stay home on Sunday night, no matter what; they wanted excitement, and wouldn't the cinema be a better choice for them than the pub? "If we can't have it one way, we'll have it another." He explained that he himself had begun drinking only lemonade, but it was soon beer and then whiskey, all because he had nowhere to go on Sunday. Open cinemas would help solve this problem. An organization known as the Brighter Sunday Movement gathered speed in the 1930s, reasoning that if hotels could offer entertainment on Sunday, and cities could hold concerts in the park, and theaters could host charity concerts, and the better-off could play golf and fish and boat in their clubs, then why couldn't working people attend the cinema?

In 1932 Parliament agreed, passing the Sunday Entertainments Act, which allowed local authorities to have the final say on Sunday cinema, under certain restrictions: namely, that employees were not to work a seven-day week, that viewing should begin only in the late afternoon, and that a portion of every Sunday's profits should go to charity. The English Church was split over the Entertainments Act, and even those in favor insisted that only films of a wholesome character be shown on Sunday (explaining perhaps why Sunday films long tended to be proven repeats). People both old and young happily welcomed the Act, claimed one historian: the old because in walking to church on Sunday they could feel smug that their old world had been superior to this one, and the young because they had their films. The cinema became especially a suburban and neighborhood recreation, alongside pubs, and communities took pride in them. They often built several theaters, bearing such lofty names as Regal, Palace, Majestic, Roxy, Granada, or Astoria, and decorated them with velvet seats, gilded handrails, and carpeted stairs—like the medieval church building, a far nicer place than one's home.

Probably the simplest form of public Sunday entertainment outside the home, aside from walking, was the aptly named pub. There was little new about the tradition of Sunday taverns, cafés, and pubs, of course.

The pub's importance lay in the fact that it remained after the war the leading social institution of the working classes, even on Sunday. People spent more time in pubs than anywhere but home or work. Pubs were more numerous, held more people, and were entrusted with more money than the church, the cinema, dance halls, and political organizations combined. In Worktown, among whose 180,000 people some of the best studies of pubs were done, there were 200 churches, 200 policemen, 30 cinemas, 24 prostitutes, and 300 pubs.

Certainly the English pub suffered some decline in patronage after the Great War. This was due partly to crusades against pubs, but largely to increasing disapproval among the working classes of drunkenness. Both contributed to less drinking than before. A Mass Observation survey in 1934 noted that in 620 pubs around London, men before the war regularly drank two to three pints of strong beer on each visit, whereas now they drank one to one and a half pints of mild. Still, beer remained a basic attraction of the pub. Numerous establishments and individuals touted its presumed healthy qualities, with signs that read "Beer Is Best" and "A healthy appetizing drink that will help to keep you fit. The best refreshment." One respondent to a survey about drink wrote, "I drink beer to keep me fit, it do's the stummick good and there is only one good reason I Drink Beer, it is because I cannot eat it." The most enthusiastic response came from a sixty-six-year-old man, who said, "I drink Beer because it is food, drink, and medicine to me, my Bowels work regular as clockwork, and I think that is the Key to health."

But the pub was always much more than a place just to drink. The Worktown survey revealed that most people said they drank for health reasons, while 35 percent drank primarily for social reasons. After all, according to Mass Observation, many working-class people didn't typically invite one another home but simply met at the pub, making it the center of their interactions. Standing or sitting, they planned activities, forgot their cares, socialized, talked about betting, sport, work, people, beer, the weather, and politics. They smoked, spit, played games such as dominoes, darts, or quoits, placed clandestine bets and received winnings or paid out losses, and sometimes sang; certainly they drank beer too, often taking turns buying rounds, but usually drinking slowly. Indeed, drunkenness while at the pub was now very rare.

Making pubs different on Sunday from weekdays were shorter opening hours (usually from noon to two, then again from around seven to ten) and a more sociable, even more familial, atmosphere than usual. On most days the crowd was usually male and working class, but Sunday brought in more women and finer dress. On a weeknight, a working-class man in the vault might wear a cap, a scarf around his neck, a coat, trousers, and a nonmatching waistcoat, while some even wore their workclothes; but on Saturday night and Sunday the dress improved.

Partly because of the dress, there was even less distinction of classes on Sunday in a pub. One Mass Observer noted a certain fifty-year-old police inspector who went into a pub every midday and enjoyed two or three halves of bitter without company. "He treats nobody, and nobody treats him—a matter on which there is a complete understanding." But on Sunday midday, the police inspector "drinks as many as nine halves of bitter, buying rounds for others and being treated himself." Sunday afternoon was "the only time he is able to behave as he would like to in this bar."

The most obvious difference on Sunday was surely the increase in the number of women. A typical pub had three rooms: the vault, the game or tap room (for dominoes and cards), and the lounge or main room. The women who came on Sunday typically sat in the main room and drank bottled beer rather than draft beer. Men preferred draft beer because it was cheaper, and because they liked to watch it being drawn, knowing that it was tempting for the waiter to mix stale beer with the fresh in the barrel. Men stayed in the vault, reserved exclusively for them, only part of the time on Sunday. While there, they always stood, which interested Mass Observation because most of these men had been on their feet all week at their jobs, yet it seemed no burden. Men also felt freer in the vault, even spitting on the floor if they wished—it was like a club but without the requirement to pay extra dues to belong. On Sunday, however, men left the vault for a time to sit with their wives or girlfriends in the main room, which was much cleaner, without ashtrays, saliva, beer-stained bar, spittoons, or sawdust on the floor. Some liked to say that "in the vault men are men, and in the lounge men were women's men."

Perhaps for that reason, some men still believed that women should frequent pubs really only on Sunday night and perhaps Saturday night. After the Great War, as pubs increased slightly in respectability and drunkenness declined, women might appear more often on other nights as well, if not to everyone's pleasure. On Friday night they should be shampooing their hair, thought some men, and on Sunday afternoon they should be home making dinner. Middle-class views did not allow young single women to go to pubs at all; if you went, said one woman, "you were a prostitute in those days; nice women didn't go." Yet this stark division of presumed roles neglected the fact that 44 percent of the women in Worktown worked outside of the home, and that at work they suffered discrimination in wages, not to mention unwanted sexual advances. These women had little leisure time, less than any other group, and surely some expected that they might be allowed some time at the pub, even when it wasn't Sunday—especially when the church in 1920 was saying that it must "frankly acknowledge that it has undervalued and neglected the gifts of women and has too thanklessly used their work."

There was another reason, however, why men resented the presence of women in pubs other than on Sunday, and this one was far more practical: the pub was cheap entertainment, yet still not cheap enough for two. Many men could not afford both his and her beer more than on Saturday night or Sunday. And the expectation of buying rounds for others—including your wife's friends—didn't help. Plenty of women knew the experience of having their husband, in the vault, order a cheap beer for them on Sunday. Such a woman would then ask the obliging server to bring her a finer beer instead, making up the difference with money she had saved from the household budget.

For some men or women, the pub essentially took the place of church on Sunday. Plenty of people interviewed said that they took their entire family to the pub that day. (The children would play in the corridor or hide in the cellar if a policeman paid an unexpected visit.) So important were pubs on Sunday to others that they referred to the "sad dreary hours" of the afternoon when pubs were closed. Some even thought it a more religious atmosphere on Sunday: more drinking was done on Saturday night, but more talking was done on Sunday night, when pubs were actually busier. The ever-assiduous watchers of Mass Observation, who were counting the mouthfuls and the con-

versations, attributed the calmness to "the influence of Sunday, as its
special nature seems to be enough of an influence to reduce 'over-
drinking' even for those who are not religiously minded." The pub
owner himself, said one study, should be not only an authority in
sport, good at cards and dominoes, and affable but orthodox in religion, or at least not antireligious—in fact, he should be much like a
preacher, with a good relationship between himself and the customers.
The vault room was more like a church than anywhere in the pub, said
another observer: the bar separated the pub owner from the customers, as the altar separated clergy and flock; bottles were arranged
carefully on shelves, windows were often ornate, handles stuck up
from the barrels of beer like tapered candles, plus there were rituals of
toasting, buying rounds, glass-swigging, and more. This went on at
least until the pub owner called out in the vault "Time Gentlemen
Please!" or sometimes "Empty Your Glasses Please." That was the signal to return home and face the prospect of another week of work.

It was only fitting that the interwar period in England should have
ended on a Sunday, just as the Belgians felt the first shock of war on a
Sunday. Clearly it was a popular day, among so many other things, for
ultimatums.

On Sunday, September 3, 1939, a disappointed Neville Chamberlain announced that Britain was at war. As one contemporary put it,
"The war came at eleven o'clock on a quiet Sunday morning in September. It was announced by Mr. Chamberlain in the tones of an elderly dove whose olive branch has been snatched by rude eagles, and
no sooner was his speech over than the sirens wailed in London and
everyone said, 'Here they come!' But they didn't." And unlike the on-
set of WWI, there was "no singing, no marching soldiers, no splendid
brass bands, no appeals to King and Country," but only "an air of
anti-climax over England" on that Sunday, which marked the end of
peace for the next six years.

As in Belgium and France during the Great War, bells soon stopped
ringing for church, and the relatively quiet English Sunday became
more sober still under the pressure of war. But in 1942 Winston
Churchill decided, despite war, to reinstate the ringing of church bells

on Sunday before services, because he missed that familiar sound of an English Sunday, even if he rarely answered their summons himself. At least the ringing helped restore something of the Sunday that had emerged before this latest war—a Sunday beloved by some, dreaded by others, and more varied than supposed by many, with its quiet and familiar home rituals, but also a more active side. Sunday activities would expand even further after this war, if too slowly for the likes of Tony Hancock.

7

SUNDAY ALL MIXED UP

The United States in the 1950s

During the 1955–56 television season, over several Sunday afternoons, NBC aired an innovative program entitled *Wide, Wide World*. The innovation lay not in the program's now primitive (and even offensive) commercials, nor in the live (if canned) interviews and commentary. Rather it lay in the deployment of some sixty-four cameras and seventeen hundred technicians all around the country, in order to offer a bird's-eye view of the spectacularly varied American Sunday.

Organized around such themes as "Sunday Driver," "Sunday with Youth," and "Sunday in Autumn," the program covered a staggering array of activities. These included a wide assortment of traditional religious services, at the Catholic San Fernando Mission in California, a suburban Protestant church in Chicago, university congregations in

New Orleans and Berkeley, an Air Force base in Nevada, and two accommodating Jewish synagogues in Rhode Island and Texas. But this was only the start. Also included were an amusement park and an equestrian school in California, a high school pep rally in Ohio, a 4-H meeting in Wisconsin, the Intermountain School for Indian children in Utah, a big-dance recording session in Detroit, an amateur hot-rod racing strip near the San Fernando Mission, water-skiing feats by co-eds in chiffon capes near the University of Miami, underwater ballet at a Florida resort named Weekiwachee, training exercises at an Air Force base in Ohio where it was never Sunday because they "must be alert at all times," a cable car in San Francisco, commercial fishing in New England, the quiet campus of Princeton University, steel plants near Cleveland with furnaces operating at 2,900 degrees even on Sunday, a Nebraska cornfield, a speedboat on Nevada's Lake Mead, the Texas State Fair with more than 300,000 people in attendance that Sunday, tourists in the Grand Canyon, the Rockettes performing at Radio City Music Hall down the street from NBC, and more.

It's an impossibly long list, but it could have been longer still. For although variety had marked Sunday in any number of places and times, the U.S. Sunday by now was arguably most varied and lively of all. Surely this was simply an extension of American cultural variety more broadly, resulting from the nation's vast geographical expanse, its immense population of 160 million and growing, its many regional cultures, its diverse ethnic and religious makeup, and the presence of sometimes conflicting cultural models from both England and Continental Europe. Trying to get a handle on at least one aspect of American culture, namely, the nation's countless religions, the historian Robert Ellwood has used the metaphor of a "spiritual marketplace." Such a metaphor is also a useful way to try and make sense of the American Sunday.

On the American Sunday marketplace of the 1950s would stand not only an overwhelming number of churches but also every element of a literal marketplace, including commerce, food, drink, entertainment, and plenty of noise. Of course every Sunday-observing country had such a marketplace in one form or another, from busy France and Belgium and the Dutch Republic to quieter England. But what stood out about the American version of the 1950s was the exuberance evident in *every* part. In other words, not only did Americans of this decade play as much on Sunday as any other Sunday-observing nation, and probably do more business, they also went to church more too. Here was a rare combination.

FOUNDATIONS

How such a hybrid Sunday came about deserves a bit of explanation.

In many ways it was the product of forces already seen at work elsewhere. One early and lasting influence on the American Sunday, for instance, was the Puritan tradition. Although not far from the English mainstream, the Puritan Sunday was stricter, after all, and in New England, rather than in "lax" Holland or Old England, colonists were free to establish their vision of the perfect "Sabbath." Indeed, the Sabbath's importance as a motive for leaving England and Holland made it one of the foundations of Puritan identity in the New World.

But the Puritans were hardly alone in the New World, or all agreed among themselves, so that rival versions of Sunday were also important here. Such dissenters as Roger Williams, for instance, despised the idea of any civil enforcement of religion, starting with Sunday laws, because in his mind they were "unchristian," even a form of "spiritual rape." Other early versions of Sunday came from Anglicans, Presbyterians, Baptists, Dutch Reformed, and more. In "Reformed" New Amsterdam (later New York), the famous Dutch willingness to put business first and thus accommodate all sorts of peoples led to the sort of moderate Sunday seen back in the Dutch Republic. The Puritans hadn't quite escaped the lax Dutch after all. This more moderate Sunday also came to be typical in New Jersey, Pennsylvania, Delaware, and the Carolinas.

Certainly some visitors, including English visitors, thought Sundays in the colonies generally more severe than those back home, even part of a fledgling American identity. But the increasing variety of peoples and cultures made it unlikely that a single version of Sunday would prevail, particularly after the U.S. Constitution of 1787 went further than the Dutch Republic in refusing to designate even a "public" religion, much less an official religion. Still, long before this date, Sunday was in flux and subject to debate in the Americas, with some decades and centuries more heated than others.

That old trend continued in the nineteenth century, due largely to some other familiar influences: industrialization and urbanization. In 1790 barely 3 percent of Americans lived in cities; by 1890 the proportion was up to 33 percent—with some predictable issues for Sunday. Now that many homes lay more distant from churches than the Puritan ideal of one mile, should those without their own transportation walk to services on Sunday, and grow weary, or use public transport and require others to work? If one could not afford an icebox large enough to avoid a Sunday delivery from the ice truck, during sweltering urban summers, was it permissible to buy food that day? Should new urban institutions, such as libraries and museums and parks and spectator sports, now available for the first time to mass numbers of people whose free day from work was always Sunday, open that day? And what of new telegraphs, telephones, and electricity, which consumers would soon expect to have available at all times, including Sunday, but which would then require someone to labor at all times as well? The industrial parts of industrialized society seemed to require seven-day-a-week operation.

Another huge influence at work upon American culture and its Sundays, far more than in Europe, was massive immigration. The U.S. population grew by more than 70 million people in the nineteenth century, an increase of 1,300 percent, most of them immigrants from Continental Europe without English or Puritan backgrounds—and thus with very different ideas of what Sunday should be. Catholics grew five times faster than the rest of the population between 1800 and 1850, constituting about 5 percent of all Americans by the latter date, then exploded in number during the second half of the nineteenth century. Some early Catholics had promoted Sabbatarian ideals, believing that such were typically American. But after the Civil War, Catholics from southern Europe, Germany, and Ireland came in massive numbers and brought their more recreation-oriented Sunday with them (although the Irish version tended to be less so).

Under these pressures, Americans commenced yet another furious bout over Sunday, and this one lasted longest of all. In fact, the Sunday question was the longest of all national debates during the nineteenth century, preceding and outlasting even more heated debates over temperance and slavery. Those Americans in favor of a Puritan-like Sunday relied on plenty of age-old arguments, such as the English notion that more play meant more work, or that as Sunday went so went the nation, or that a spate of recent "natural" disasters was in fact supernatural punishment for violating the Sabbath. Little more original, though now in an American context, were assertions that lax Sundays were part of Satan's effort to destroy the burgeoning land, and that God granted extra material prosperity to those who had faith enough to rest from worldly labors once a week—how else to explain the prosperity of those trading giants, England and the United States? Some blamed the temptation of a lax Sunday on new industrial inventions, such as trains and steamboats, which people used for excursions on Sunday, or the bicycle, portrayed by one minister as the vehicle for an "army of young people wheeling away from the house of God with the devil leading the run and an imp on every wheel." But plenty more, forgetting their own origins, simply blamed the latest immigrants, the "influx of foreigners with their European Sunday customs," who came in the tens of millions after the Civil War. The Continental Sunday (which *Harper's* magazine defined as "beer, flowers, kisses, and display of bodies") prevailed in the U.S. by now, lamented one critic, and if it should continue to prevail then "farewell to our loved Christian land."

Other Americans of the nineteenth century (most of them also Christians) did not regard a strict Sunday as inherently American at all. Indeed in some respects, especially when it involved compulsion, they found it anti-American. This side too brought out old theological arguments: Sabbath rest was for the Jews, the Sabbath wasn't Sunday, the New Testament abrogated the Sabbath requirement, and so on. They argued that new trains actually promoted Sunday rest, because while speeding along mail and people, they required no work of animals and very little of humans, in fact far less than when everyone transported themselves to church on Sunday. In their more modern arguments, they sounded like European counterparts. "Rational observance," which said that what was good on Sunday was to be measured by what was good for the body and soul, rather than by some fixed list drawn up under different circumstances and times, should be the measure of Sunday activities.

In this same spirit, Elizabeth Cady Stanton wrote that Sunday at home was fine for the wealthy, in their virtual palaces full of private libraries, paintings, food, and other needs and entertainments. But to expect children in tenement housing to stay home all day Sunday was asking too much. And by organizing no healthy Sunday activities for them, society was encouraging especially boys to stand about idly on street corners and drift toward the forbidden. Finally, American anti-Sabbatarians, like English anti-Sabbatarians, concluded that a Continental Sunday wasn't so bad after all. H. W. Bellows, a Unitarian minister from Boston, argued in 1872 that such a Sunday, with its promise of recreation, was not frivolous. Instead it was a natural extension of an already fulfilling week, one often spent more religiously than was typical in America. In Bellows's view the strict American Sunday was the result of too many American Protestants spending their week in highly secular fashion, in "fanatical pursuit of money," from which rut they felt the need to make Sunday dramatically different—even a day to purify themselves.

By 1900, Sabbatarians were steadily losing ground, and Sunday recreations, including mass entertainments, were gaining. Widespread skirmishes over Sunday persisted into the 1920s, but thereafter were reduced to local debates. The World's Fair was more than once accompanied by debates over Sunday opening, but the side in favor of opening won often. New seaside resorts and amusement parks were now packed with visitors on Sunday. And the Metropolitan Museum in New York, open on Sunday from 1891, attracted 900,000 visitors from June through December that year—200,000 of them on Sundays.

If recreation was one large presence in the new American Sunday after 1900, right alongside was its twin, commerce. In many parts of the United States the Sunday marketplace was real. Just as the English feared and the French seemed to accept, when some people recreated on Sunday, others had to work. The American workweek as a whole was, as in Europe, actually becoming shorter, and new restrictions on Sunday labor were in place. But these did not apply equally to all sectors of the economy. In the leisure sector, Sunday work was steadily growing.

In the U.S. as in England and France, the economy was moving from manufacturing industries toward service industries. This trend culminated in 1956, when for the first time there were more white- and pink-collar American workers than blue-collar. Those in the leisure industries were a big part of this shift, and with Sunday still the favorite day for leisure, they earned much of their living that day. Factories might close on Sunday, and farming could be kept to a minimum, but it was much harder to close restaurants, shut up amusement parks and ballparks, or clear the airwaves—not when Americans with more money in their pockets were trying to spend it that day. Not when competitors were eager to provide the same service. Not when such gradually emerging suburban enterprises as supermarkets, department stores, auto dealers, and real estate brokers found that a large percentage of the week's sales (sometimes 30 or 40 percent) occurred on Sunday. Not when it was realized that closing on Sunday meant some sales would never be recovered—these did not spill over into other days but were simply lost. Not when American consumers were more and more inclined to regard shopping as a leisure or recreational activity, even an "exciting pastime," for which Sunday was always a favorite occasion.

Naturally, the degree of Sunday-opening varied around the U.S., but it was hard to resist for both customers and owners, given the added number of shopping hours and higher profits. Studies of trends in Sunday commerce after the 1950s have found that general economic activity is in fact higher in states with fewer Sunday-closing laws: the old Puritan calculus, that Sunday closing brought greater economic prosperity, was therefore wrong, at least in industrialized America. Sunday-open states tend to have higher incomes, without the exploitation of seven-day-a-week labor once feared by unions: for when more people are employed, fewer work every day, and the average number of hours worked per person per week actually declines. Whether the increased prosperity was worth the Sunday price was of course another question, open to the usual furious debate.

One might easily conclude from this crash course on the evolution of the American Sunday before 1950 that in all their recreating and enterprising, Americans forgot about religion, as many religiously minded critics alleged.

These critics saw in the increase of Sunday business and play a reflection of the wider processes of "secularization" and "decline" and "loss of belief" already discussed for England. One American observer in 1926 implied just such a decline in his lament that "our forefathers called it the Holy Sabbath; our fathers called it Sunday; we call it the week-end." This observer would have also deplored the results of a survey of recreational activities one Sunday in Brooklyn in 1921: 200,000 people went motoring that day, 200,000 attended the cinema, 150,000 visited the park, 50,000 entered dance halls, 20,000 watched vaudeville shows, and 2,000 played golf.

But a theory of religious or cultural "decline" is little more helpful here than it was in England for explaining how Sunday was changing. The problems of using attendance statistics to gauge spirituality have already been noted, but it is striking that even while opportunities for Sunday recreations were increasing, Americans were also going to church in steadily increasing numbers. And while at the founding of the republic not even two in ten Americans belonged to churches, by 1950 six in ten did. In other words, the Brooklyn survey failed to track how many recreation seekers also attended church that day. More important, believing Americans were attaching new meanings to the sorts of recreational and technological activities that the Brooklyn survey did mention, as well as to Sunday work. Such activities were not necessarily signs of indifference toward religion, but could be made compatible with it.

A study from 1945 sought to explain how Sunday activities once seen as objectionable by religious-minded people might become acceptable. H. S. Jacoby's *Remember the Sabbath Day? The Nature and Causes of Changes in Sunday Observance Since 1800* concluded that this process was *not* the result of declining, or increasing, morality. Rather, Sunday changed when the world around it changed. As Americans experienced changes in transportion, industry, urbanization, and leisure, they were bound to experience changes in their Sunday activities as well, and to see those activities in new ways. Along the way morals were reconfigured, not lost. Jacoby illustrated this phenomenon by showing that during every Sunday debate in America between 1800 and 1940, each succeeding generation regularly saw once-condemned Sunday activities become accepted as "normal" and "traditional." And this occurred in a context of increasing association with formal religion, not less.

Thus when streetcars first appeared in 1859, there was great opposition to their running on Sunday. But in 1904 even Sabbatarian advocates had no problem with Sunday streetcars, mostly because they seemed a "normal" part of the world into which they were born; Sabbatarians themselves now relied upon them for such "good" purposes as getting to church. Early American Blue Laws said, among other things, that there was to be no traveling, cooking, making beds, sweeping homes, running, walking in the garden, or cutting hair on Sunday, and also that no woman should kiss her child that day, but many in later generations found these activities acceptable and regarded themselves as no less moral for it. Lucy Wells composed in 1847 a list of Sunday rules as long as the Mississippi, but over time fewer people regarded most things on that list as objectionable. In fact, wrote Jacoby, almost every Sunday activity once protested by Sabbatarians eventually came "to be socially and legally accepted on Sunday."

Other scholars have gone beyond Jacoby to show how certain Sunday activities not only became acceptable but were transformed into something positively virtuous. The term of choice here is "sacralization," or making something sacred. Examples from recreation were legion. While unbelievers had no need to think twice on religious grounds about visiting amusement parks on Sunday, for instance, believers did, and without believers the crowds would have been much smaller. An owner of a New Jersey hotel on the Boardwalk understood this and built an open-air church for those who wished to have church amid their Sunday recreations. Applegate's pier in New Jersey became known for concerts of sacred music on Sunday nights, and McShea's Ocean Pier sponsored church services at the merry-go-round. Similar examples in sport will appear later. In other words, cleaned up into new forms, a great number of leisure activities might for believers become more than recreation, but worthy Sunday activities.

Even the realm of Sunday work could be sacralized. In the United States, as in England, a work ethic, and the prosperity believed to result from it, was valued more than a leisure ethic—and this had consequences for Sunday. Witold Rybczynski has even contended that the presence of a strong work ethic in a country actually makes extensive Sunday commerce more likely, not less likely, while countries with a stronger leisure ethic are more likely to restrict Sunday commerce. This went beyond Saint Benedict's ancient notion that Sunday work was merely preferable to Sunday idleness; instead, it elevated work to a virtue, if it was necessary to one's sacred livelihood and was a boon to one's community. The famous American retailer J. C. Penney, a devout Methodist, was a perfect example. During the 1930s he justified doing business on Sunday in an American mining town because he felt that he was doing good, more than if he had observed the traditional Methodist Sabbath. Thus even his retail business might involve an element of service.

A sacralization of earthly things had occurred often enough within Christianity; why not in certain earthly endeavors as well? Ordinary wood and brick were turned into sacred houses of worship. The ordinary wafer of Catholicism turned into the body of Christ itself. Ordinary folk songs were transformed into hymns. Clement of Alexandria told ancient Christians that riches were not necessarily bad but could be transformed to something holy. And war itself, with all its horror, and despite the commandment not to kill, was more than once sacralized in America and Europe. Then why not work too? Of course people needed rest, but in the new economy only some would work on Sunday, and they would have other days to rest instead.

Some Americans would never accept that things they once considered profane could simply be redesignated as acceptable, or even sacred. To them, the process could be seen only as the succeeding generation's acceptance of lesser moral standards. It is possible that someone may yet devise an objective scale on which to measure the morality of one generation's Sunday habits versus another's. But it is also possible that changes in those habits were the result of changes in understanding and context rather than a "decline in morals" or "loss of faith." Otherwise, how to explain that the following statements have been repeated so often over the centuries? A Sabbatarian minister in 1865: "There has never been a time when Christianity has been assailed by more formidable weapons than at present, referring specifically to the Sabbath." A Sabbatarian in 1879: Christians were no longer sure, as they certainly once had been, about what was right or wrong on the Sabbath. And the laments of the Sabbath committee of the Southern Presbyterian Assembly in 1939: "We live in a time when everything is being reconsidered. Nothing is accepted because it is old. The general idea is that whatever is, is probably wrong." Any of these sentiments might have been expressed in 1100 or 1500 as well, for they reflect an uneasiness with emerging ways and the threat they present to familiar ways. Put another way, older generations tend to regard coming generations as morally inferior because of, among other things, changes to the older Sunday, but many of the older generations' own acceptable Sunday activities had, often unknown to them, once been condemned by earlier generations.

However the changes over time should be understood, by 1950, even by the 1920s, the American Sunday had been, in the words of Alexis McCrossen, shaped into its "enduring forms"—in other words, those forms still recognizable to present-day Americans. These included a good deal of worship but also widespread rejection of the Puritan ideal that Sunday was for worship only. Like the French and other Europeans, Americans had already concluded that Sunday rest should include Sunday recreation and play too. Both church and play were only accentuated in the 1950s.

AMERICAN RELIGION ON SUNDAY IN THE 1950S

Like previous decades, the 1950s witnessed changes in the context around Sunday, and these inevitably had an impact on Sunday itself.

After the Depression of the 1930s and the restraints of World War II, the 1950s seemed to exude prosperity and confidence. Personal income tripled, and the workweek was reduced to forty hours. Disneyland opened in 1955, Ted Williams received $125,000 in 1950 to play baseball for the Boston Red Sox, and the ultimate consumer nation emerged: with only 6 percent of the world's population, the United States used up 33 percent of the world's goods and services. But then, that's what all the work was for, and why one writer called the U.S. the "Consumer Republic." Construction boomed and especially suburbs sprawled: more than one million people left New York City for affordable and roomy suburbs, where 29 percent of Americans would soon live. Although not invented in the 1950s, suburbs flowered then, and exerted an influence even beyond their numbers through their new style of living, beginning with such new home conveniences as vacuum cleaners, refrigerators, air conditioners, washing machines, and televisions, and ending with that suburban hallmark, the automobile. In the suburbs, a car was a necessity, not a luxury. About 68 million cars and trucks, roughly one per household, were on the road now.

But alongside this context of prosperity there were struggles old and new. Such famous suburban models as William Levitt's "Levittowns" in Pennsylvania and New York—featuring concrete slabs, street pavers, precisely arranged buildings, trees twenty-eight feet apart, no laundry on Sunday, rules for regular lawn cutting, and chimes rather than buzzers for doorbells—also contributed to ulcers, heart attacks, and other tension-related disorders. The presence of the Cold War against the Soviet Union added to that tension. Suburban planners spread out living space partly to spread out the risk of destruction from atomic bombs: condensed cities would mean easier targets and more deaths. Fear of nuclear destruction was also evidenced in regular evacuation drills at school, numerous backyard bomb shelters, and frequent nuclear tests. A 1954 survey revealed that 78 percent of Americans believed that all citizens should report to the FBI any neighbor believed to be Communist. And beyond the physical and psychological burdens of the Cold War were those of a Hot War, in Korea, where 1.8 million Americans went into combat.

Increasing racial and ethnic struggles also marked the decade—not everyone benefited from increased prosperity or high American ideals of equality. Anti-Semitism lingered, and resentment grew against increasing numbers of Latinos and Asians. And although Simon Montgomery became the first black pastor of an all-white church in 1955 in Mystic, Connecticut, and although *Brown v. Board of Education* legally ended segregation in U.S. schools in 1954, and although Adam Clayton Powell, representative from New York, declared optimistically in 1955 at an international conference that "racism in America was on the way out," serious tension remained through the decade and beyond.

And these are only some of the best-known examples. All of them, plus still other social, economic, political, and cultural changes, showed up on the Sunday marketplace too, including in the churches.

Historians have called the 1950s the "Fourth Great Awakening" in
American religious history, for during this time an unprecedented proportion of Americans belonged to churches or synagogues and attended religious services.

The nearly six in ten who in 1950 claimed religious affiliation increased to seven in ten by 1960, more than ever before in American
history. Related to this rise was the tremendous increase in church-
building: $26 million was spent on new church construction in 1945,
and $935 million in 1959 (and only part of the increase was due to the
rearrangement of resources after World War II). No other Western culture was as churchgoing or church-oriented as the United States by now.

The breakdown of church membership by religion varies according
to which sources one consults, and of course to how one arranges the
impossible number of specific denominations in the U.S. into parent
groups. But in 1960, when about 125 of 178 million Americans belonged to churches, it looked something like this:

Catholic	42 million
Baptist	20 million
Methodist	12 million
Lutheran	8 million
Jewish	5 million
Presbyterian	4.2 million
Episcopalian	3.3 million
Orthodox	3 million
United Church (Congregationalist)	2.2 million
Disciples of Christ	1.8 million
Mormon	1.5 million
Assemblies of God	.5 million
Reformed	.4 million
Seventh-Day Adventist	.3 million
Other Protestant (many)	millions

Not evident from this list is that every group grew in size during the
1950s, even those longest in America (Episcopalians, Presbyterians,

Congregationalists, Jews), which had steadily been losing ground to Catholics and more recently Evangelicals. Still other religions, outside the Jewish and Christian traditions, existed in the U.S. as well, of course, but these would take on greater importance in future decades.

Beyond membership and building figures, a 1955 Gallup Poll showed that 97 percent of all Americans considered themselves to be "religious," that 94 percent believed in God, 95 percent in prayer, and 90 percent in the divinity of Jesus. Tellingly, it was in 1955 that "In God We Trust" was added to U.S. coins and in 1954 that the phrase "under God" was added to the Pledge of Allegiance. The church as a whole was the most trusted institution in the U.S., the Bible a regular best-seller, and the evangelist Billy Graham, the liberal Protestant minister Norman Vincent Peale, and the Catholic archbishop Fulton Sheen major media stars. The latter's television program even displaced Milton Berle's as the most watched in the country.

All of this believing and all of this Sunday churchgoing was astonishing to those who saw the U.S. as a product of the Enlightenment and its supposedly antireligious sentiment. The U.S. never had an official church, and yet the longer time went on, the more interest in religion seemed to grow. How to understand it? Some foreigners and scholars attributed American interest in religion precisely to the lack of an established church: a "free religious market" was the key. Others pointed out that unlike democratic movements in Europe, which were directed against the established order and thus against established churches, the rise of the American Republic was cast in religious terms from the start, with talk of "sacred rights" and an absence of large-scale sentiment against religion per se. By the 1950s, thanks especially to the Cold War and the "Red Scare," this old tendency toward Americanized religion was stronger than ever, and in no small way connected to the sense that American values included religion and that Communist values did not. Hence the need to display those values through belonging to a church and spending part of Sunday inside it.

A sense of patriotism was obviously not the only motive to join a church and attend on Sunday, but it played an important role. It was important enough that Dwight Eisenhower had himself baptized while president, made sure everyone knew that his cabinet meetings opened with prayer, and openly endorsed the value of religion in general, without ever getting too specific. Every Friday, American children who watched the *Howdy Doody* television show were reminded by Buffalo Bob to attend the church or synagogue of their choice that weekend. The "I Knew a Church" series in *Good Housekeeping,* offering sentimental recollections of Sunday worship by an assortment of believers, likewise reflected the effort to promote religion generally.

NBC's *Wide, Wide World* devoted one Sunday episode exclusively to images of various worship services among America's "Three Faiths" (Catholicism, Protestantism, and Judaism). Belonging to any of these faiths and attending services, the episode implied, was an American thing to do. The episode naturally focused on aspects of each faith that were most broadly American. A priest at a Catholic home for troubled boys stated, "We take care of all faiths, we're all brothers," while a Sister of Charity at a foundling hospital in New York said the same. The oldest synagogue in the United States, in Newport, Rhode Island, founded in 1658, showed off its colonial roots and patriotism simply by gathering on Sunday rather than the traditional Saturday, but also by the rabbi's expressing thanks for America's lack of religious persecution. At another Sunday-gathering synagogue in Houston, a rabbi emphasized cooperation with Christian churches in the area. At a student congregation near the University of California, a minister could not stress enough how important his ministry was among so many young people studying nuclear energy, crucial to the nation at the moment. And at Ellis Air Force Base that Sunday, Catholic, Protestant, and Jewish chaplains were presented as equals, and F100s took off to the strains of adoring choirs, sanctifying the planes with the singing of "Lord God Protect the Men Who Fly." Finally, the episode included a tribute to Thomas Jefferson, held up as *the* model of American religiosity, for his emphasis on variety and freedom in worship rather than on a specific creed.

Wide, Wide World was right on the mark in its suggestion of an American religion. Pastors were appreciated if they were gifted speakers, but at least as important was being good at the American pastimes of business and Rotary Club, and being able to mix the languages of theology and commerce. The Presbyterian minister Clare Tallmann's Founders' Report of 1955 exhorted his suburban Chicago congregation to give freely, saying, "Blessed are those who use the offering

envelopes, for their contributions shall be recorded, and shall be de-
ductible from their income tax. Blessed are the systematic givers, for
there shall be order in their lives and in their quarterly statements." At
an Episcopal church in rural Nebraska, the congregation of "real dirt
farmers" of varying economic standing had the sense that the U.S. represented the highest pinnacle of human civilization and had been ordained to it by God, while the clergy were well versed "in the value of
real estate and how to emcee." Such smaller denominations as the
Greek Orthodox in America, or such increasingly prominent groups
as Evangelicals (whose most famous figure, Billy Graham, saw anti-
Communism as a basic tenet of Christianity), likewise followed the
pattern of Americanization. Catholics integrated themselves more fully
into American culture than ever before, reflected in Archbishop Sheen's
30 million viewers of various faiths, who each week listened to such
common-ground topics as "How to Have a Good Time," or Communism and secularism. So did American Jews, who saw a decline in anti-
Semitic attitudes, evidenced in such conspicuous actions as Ronald
Reagan's resignation from a country club that refused to accept a Jewish applicant (the source of Groucho Marx's famous quip that he
wouldn't join any club that would accept him as a member).

Certainly the churches were not completely homogenized. Protestant and Catholic relations generally were at a low point around 1950,
for although united by anti-Communist sentiment, they were divided
by the questions of government aid to parochial schools, the establishment of an American embassy in Vatican City, efforts to convert each
other's flocks, and the candidacy of John F. Kennedy for president.
More liberal Protestants looked warily at less-educated Baptists, and
older churches tended to be suspicious of America's countless smaller
religions.

And then there was the problem of depth. America's churches were
criticized for a lack of genuine spirituality and for their devotion to
this-worldly values of business and "success." Just as any decline of
Sunday churchgoing in England did not necessarily prove a decline in
spirituality, so did the rise of Sunday churchgoing in the United States
not necessarily prove a rise in spirituality. One Protestant critic suggested that a typical Sunday service was more a charade than an encounter with God: there were invocations, hymns, and sacred texts,

but the prevailing mood was comfortable, humorous, pleasant, chatty, and even cute. One study suggested what clergy had always feared but never quite wanted to believe: namely, that what they said on Sunday didn't much matter to the flock. Many attended church because of social pressure and as a "leisure time activity" rather than as a spiritual way of life.

A famous summary of such criticisms appeared in 1955: Will Herberg's *Protestant, Catholic, Jew.* This book argued that churchgoing in the U.S. was now more a matter of social belonging than religious faith. Members of each religious group were more American than anything else, and simply represented different manifestations of the same commonly held values: the supreme dignity of the individual, merit in activity rather than passivity, self-reliance, a high standard of achievement, optimism, and idealism—or what he summed up as "the American way of life." In one sense, this resembled what had occurred in the Roman Empire of the fourth century: something above paganism and Christianity had to exist to unite all Romans. In the U.S., with its numerous faiths, some uniting point had to be found as well. It was simply that to Herberg and other critics, the result wasn't necessarily genuine religion, no more so than participating in Roman civic rituals had been to Augustine. In each case, the main goal was to conform to the world around them.

Criticism of the American religion was narrowed further: it was said to reflect only the values and lifestyle of the middle class, in their new suburban churches on Sunday. One observer quipped that nowadays it seemed God spoke only in the suburbs. More seriously, the scholar Martin Marty noted that there was no sin in being middle class: the sin was in assuming that the particular idioms, forms, and language of one's class were "normal" and thus applicable to all.

The new church buildings reflected those idioms. Interiors often included traditional stained-glass windows, but also brick, blond wooden pews, and a vaulted ceiling—simply a larger version of a suburban American living room, but for Sunday. And Sunday "success"—attendance figures, money raised—tended to be connected to notions of quantifiable success taken from the middle-class world of business. Hence just as rural living influenced religion and Sunday in the Middle Ages, or industrialization did the same in the nineteenth century, so suburban living affected the style of American religion and Sundays in the fifties.

Obviously it is no simple task to define religion in the U.S. during this decade. But 97 percent of Americans considered themselves to be religious, and going to church on Sunday was an important way to demonstrate it. Indeed, by the 1950s, Sunday worship was the "most common mode of ritual participation in the U.S."

CATHOLIC SUNDAY IN AMERICA

The tendency to Americanize was stronger in some faiths than others on Sunday. But just as striking as the theme of Americanization at Sunday services was the great variety of worship. If the inclination toward the great melting pot was present on American Sundays in churches, so was the inclination to maintain the great American salad bowl, the ingredients of which didn't always blend so easily.

Although most Americans were Protestants in one form or another, the largest single denomination in the U.S. was Catholicism, with over 20 percent of the entire population. Alan Ehrenhalt has constructed a memorable portrait of St. Nicholas of Tolentine parish, in Chicago, which he describes as one of the prominent and confident Catholic parishes in America during the 1950s. In St. Nick's, as it was called, belief in tried and proven ways was strong, and these were certainly present on Sunday. But even here some accommodations to American culture could be seen that day.

By 1950 more and more parishioners were closer to the dream of American assimilation: like other urban parishes, St. Nick's was filled with second- and third-generation immigrants from every European ethnic group, who were eager to achieve the status of middle class. Perhaps more than others, they also packed the church on Sundays. The eleven hundred seats in the main sanctuary were filled every hour on the hour, from seven A.M. to noon, meaning that the vast majority of parishioners attended each week. In these years before the reforms of the famous council, Vatican II (1962–66), Mass was still much as it had been in the Middle Ages—still focused on the actions of the priest, with parishioners stepping forward for communion, kneeling on a red cushion, and receiving the wafer safely on their tongues while an altar boy "hovered next to them" with a silver platter to catch any consecrated crumbs. And after the Gospel reading, parishioners still heard the usual brief sermon, which was still shorter than most Protestant sermons. This is explained in the "Question & Answer" section of the *American Ecclesiastical Review*, a Catholic publication for priests, which noted that there was no ideal length for sermons, but a pastor would do well to remember a common saying: after ten minutes a sermon becomes an anesthetic. In addition to the sermon, the pastor might add friendly suggestions for family relationships, remind parishioners which books and movies the League of Decency had declared unsuitable for Catholics, or warn against laxity in prayers or confessions. But whatever the topic, the emphasis on Sunday was sin, which was everywhere.

When imagining sin, some devout parishioners certainly had in mind a specific place: the favorite local hangout, Hoffman's Tavern, just down the street from St. Nick's, open at noon on Sunday. Here too was a still-lingering medieval tradition. Within minutes after the eleven o'clock Mass let out, the tavern began filling with parishioners. Some on their way to the morning's last Mass, at noon, skipped it altogether, saying they were going to "High Mass" at Hoffman's instead. At this "typical corner saloon," "long, narrow, dark, and smoky," with a scent "halfway between bourbon and perfume," patrons could play cards or bet on horses or just feel at home. Sometimes the crowd imitated the pastor in good fun, and sometimes younger assistant priests dropped in for drink and conversation.

Instead of the tavern, or in addition to it, the men of the parish could choose to join the Holy Name Society. This group traced its origins to the thirteenth century, but was now meant to help keep men connected to the church, in the face of what many saw as an ongoing "feminization" of religion. The men of St. Nick's liked their Society and its director, Father Joseph Lynch, an assistant pastor, in no small way because he too enjoyed cards and sports. He got them to attend Mass together and take communion together and perform other devotions, but just as important he went along on golf, bowling, and baseball outings. The monthly communion breakfast, on a Sunday, linked all of their interests perfectly: some five hundred men gathered to take communion, eat breakfast, and listen to a talk by a Notre Dame athlete, or some other Catholic celebrity or politician.

The women of St. Nick's could belong to an old-fashioned altar and rosary society, which was more work than entertainment, including on Sunday. And the women attended Sunday Mass in greater numbers than men: as in many blue-collar parishes, about two-thirds of the regulars were women. They kept the old devotions going, even when newer priests and some parishioners called them into question as remnants of "immigrant Catholicism." These same priests and parishioners were more enthusiastic about the pope's decision in 1956 to increase lay participation during Mass, or to experiment with reading Mass in English as well as Latin, which made them feel if not more American at least more modern.

The head pastor, Monsignor Michael Fennessy, wished to change little at all. In service here for more than thirty years, he liked the old ways, and his presence dominated the parish every day, if most visibly on Sunday. Dressed "day and night in a black cassock that reached his shoe tops," he was everywhere in the parish, like a medieval lord of the manor, and on Sunday night when he appeared at a parishioner's door, he expected to be let in for conversation. His Catholicism was not any kind of homogeneous Americanized religion. He "frightened the altar boys" with his intensity, he laid hands on the shoulders of the ailing and assured them they would recover, and he believed in social action but not in any form smacking of Socialism.

Like other pastors in Chicago, Monsignor Fennessy had a team of priests to help him. More severe than the pastor himself was Father Lynch, the classic "bad cop" assistant pastor. Respected rather than loved, he preferred "invoking rules and issuing orders," just as he had done as a marine during World War II, and he was determined to root out wrong regardless of whatever rights of privacy he might violate. On Sundays, when he stood at the altar with his back to the congregation, he still seemed to know what people were doing. If someone had an itch to leave Mass early, he might "wheel around and humiliate him" and tell him to get back to his pew, because he had more to say— including requests for more offerings, and of course if it was autumn, he would urge all to attend the parish school's football game after the last Mass.

To Father Lynch, as for many other football-loving Catholic priests, American football was simply "an extension of the religious service."

For that reason there was little hesitation about Catholic elementary schools playing on Sunday afternoons in Chicago in the 1950s, and little thought about Father Lynch pacing the sideline during each game, protesting the referee's calls and "passing around a cigar box for donations that had somehow escaped him during morning service." Father Lynch was the team's spiritual adviser, but he took this to mean "demanding that they never lose." In fact they rarely did, as a case full of trophies proved, but when they did, Father Lynch was there the next morning, taking the best players from class and scolding them. He also expected nearly all girls of the eighth grade to be at the game too, as cheerleaders.

Not every Catholic felt this positively about football, or sport. And not everyone in St. Nick's admired Father Lynch. But just about anyone who grew up actively Catholic in the United States in the 1950s knew someone like him, present every day in busy parishes but most obviously on Sunday, in church or on the sports field.

This image of a Catholic Sunday as a day to both accommodate and resist American culture at the same time was true beyond St. Nick's.

Expanding recreation on Sunday, made possible by a shorter work-week, was not objectionable to Catholic leaders as long as it did not interfere with Mass. When one reader of the *American Ecclesiastical Review* inquired about Catholics who missed Mass on Sunday because they were hunting and fishing, the lengthy response came that recreation in the U.S. had certainly been taken too far and that it was a sin to miss Sunday Mass, but "reliable theologians" had assured that under certain circumstances such activities might be justified. Another questioner wondered whether a young married man who wanted to build a house himself, but was free only on weekends and needed to finish before winter set in, was allowed to work on Sundays too. The answer came that it was acceptable as long as Mass wasn't missed, because it was a good cause, as accommodations for young marrieds were scarce, and such scarcity led to such undesirable things as "domestic dissension and birth control." And what of building a less necessary vacation cottage? The answer: if one could not pay to have it built, then building it even on Sundays, after Mass, was fine—for although the builder might already own one residential house already, "it is a great boon for a family to have a vacation house in the country or at the lakeside." Some of the Sunday Mass questions would be solved in 1964, when the church announced that Saturday night Mass was a permissible substitute for the Sunday obligation. Critics contended that the church was caving in to recreational interests, but the church quite rightly, if perhaps conveniently, pointed out that ancient Christians had also celebrated Saturday night services.

Recreational opportunities were therefore present enough for Catholics. Frank Sullivan, writing in the 1954 *Good Housekeeping* series "I Remember a Church," looked back fondly on his Catholic childhood. This was partly because of Sunday Mass—the flowers and lighted candles on the altar, the vestments of the priest, and the clouds of incense and the aromatic odors "always stirred my imagination." But it was also because Sunday evening services included a strong social element and the chance to go out on Sunday night, for then the "Catholic, Methodist, Presbyterian, and Baptist boys and girls went to the services at their churches, and afterward we all met downtown at Curtis' confectionery for a hot chocolate or a soda." Or they gathered at someone's home where the girls made fudge, then all gathered around the piano to sing "Bedelia," "By the Light of the Silvery Moon," "Arrah Wanna," and other favorites.

J. F. Powers's gruff but sympathetic priest, Pastor Joe Hackett, similarly alternated on Sundays between old Catholic rituals and new American habits. He also reflected another important and often ignored Sunday theme: the burdens upon the clergy that day, their biggest workday. Father Joe, laboring in the suburbs of Minnesota in the 1950s and 1960s, told his new assistant pastor on their first Saturday night together, "Better turn in early, Sunday's always a rough day," with plenty of Masses and disgruntled parishioners.

Even Sunday afternoon, when Masses were finished and Catholic priests were free to unwind and enjoy some "priestly fellowship," could be rough. Father Joe, his assistant, and a monk named Father Otto, who came to help each week with Mass, had all afternoon together if they pleased—but their interests didn't always run in the same direction. Father Joe liked to keep the paper tidy, for instance, while Father Otto had a weekly wrestling match with it, causing Joe silently to fume and to begin sequestering the sports section so that he could at least read it "intact."

Here was another point of irritation that upset good fellowship: Joe loved sports, especially the American pastime of baseball, and liked to watch the Twins on TV on Sunday afternoon. But Father Otto, when he watched at all, was a "clumsy viewer." He offered "no insights" to the game, complained Joe silently, but merely repeated the obvious: after a strikeout, he lamely cried "Strikeout!" and punched the air. And to punctuate his incompetence, the monk often left the game at crucial moments in order to use the bathroom. Joe tried taking Otto to some home games on Sunday, in the hope of sparking deeper interest, but the monk's ignorance and his rather amused attitude toward the whole experience were unacceptable and spoiled Joe's Sundays.

At least the new assistant pastor shared some of Joe's interests, and would play a serious game of catch with him after the Twins had finished. Or if the assistant was gone that Sunday, Joe would pitch alone against his stadium-green garage door and its white-lined strike zone, imagining himself on the mound at Fenway Park—smelling the popcorn, peanuts, hot dogs, cigarettes, cigars, and grass, and hearing the respectful cheers for the portly, middle-aged priest. When finished with his vigorous workout, Joe took a bath, went over to the church to read his breviary and pray, ate dinner, and dropped off the monk at the bus station. Then he liked to end Sunday with an old movie on the TV in his study.

The Sundays of one of American Catholicism's biggest icons during the 1950s, the Trappist monk Thomas Merton, looked much different from those of Father Otto, or Pastor Joe, or the parishioners of St. Nick's in Chicago. This was partly because of the physical setting, in the monastery of Gethsamene—one of the most medieval, least modern institutions in the Western world, seemingly out of place in the republic of the United States. But it was also because of Merton's stubborn resistance to the American culture of prosperity and success, and what he saw as modern Catholicism's tendency toward it. He was not alone in this: other Catholics complained about the "gracious living" of certain Catholic priests and thus the "abdication to Yankee standards." Still others were offended by those pastors who, like Father Joe, sometimes seemed most interested of all in baseball. Yet Merton, who rarely left his monastery and was sworn to long periods of silence, was arguably the most famous internal critic, and this came out on his Sunday.

The main Sunday activity for one and all at the monastery was the same as on other days: contemplation and prayer. Merton made the first Sunday of each month his special day of recollection, when he noted his strengths and weaknesses. He also reflected on the world immediately around him, in the green hills of Kentucky, the "curtains of mist hanging over the Knobs, pigs garrulous in the lush wet grass and a dove in the cedar tree." From there, Merton reflected on American society, and then the Catholic Church in America. For all his abhorrence of Communism, he found that the single-minded denunciations of it prevented Americans, Catholic or not, from reflecting on their own shortcomings. As for the American Church, he concluded one Sunday that it had become "largely Protestant." Not that Protestantism was evil, but that Catholicism had to be true to itself to work, rather than promote an "All-American cult of good humor," productivity, and prosperity.

What made Sunday stand out even more for him and the other monks was a uniquely Sunday activity at the monastery: the ancient tradition of weekly "chapter," a time for announcements, business discipline, and instruction. More than one of Merton's Sundays, full of lofty thoughts, were ruined by chapter. More than once he noted that he "came out of chapter slightly angry as usual on Sunday." Chapter always included a sermon, some better than others. But far worse were announcements of the latest news and rules. Each Sunday five to ten new rules were announced regarding the common chant. Some of the news they heard of the outside world pleased him, such as the progress of their new branch monastery in Utah. But more offensive were the delighted reviews of sales figures for the monastery's various products. "I am assured that the sales of cheese and hams will run into six figures, into the hundreds of thousands," wrote Merton, but "I cannot conceive that the Holy Spirit is behind this big cheese business." Equally offensive to Merton was the "relish" with which the superior announced that a U.S. satellite was now flying over Russia, because to Merton it reflected a popular view of religion that associated America with God's church.

Finally, Sunday chapter was, for Merton, filled with silly theology, silly thoughts, and silly devotions. On March 25, 1958, the monks were all told that "Adam and Eve ate the apple on a March 25th," based on someone's calculus. Another Sunday they received a "nice little sermon on seeing the bright side of things and not always the dark side," which he found both sappy and obviously aimed at him. He felt dishonest and cowardly for not openly objecting to such things and instead only stewing and venting in his journal, but what was he to do—send an exposé to the press? At times his remedy was to flee to the woodshed, in the rain, to recover, and then that Sunday would be "no worse than usual." Another remedy was to take "strong coffee" or find the humor in the proceedings: rather than cry over a sermon which declared that the medieval monk Saint Bernard "didn't come to the monastery with his head full of baseball, football, and track," Merton would instead chuckle and remember his own shortcomings, or listen to the soothing sounds of the sparrows in the woods.

These were not common Sunday thoughts in the U.S. or even in Merton's monastery.

PROTESTANT STRAINS ON SUNDAY

The theme of the clergy's burdens on Sunday was evident among Protestants too, as it was for John Harper at St. John's Episcopal in Washington, D.C., who worried about his sermon, met with couples wanting to marry, mollified parishioners who complained about the church's decor, felt obligated to attend cocktail parties, called at the hospital, let his thoughts wander to the Redskins game during his sermon, or tried to cope with the unrealistic expectations people had of him generally.

But a more common theme running through a certain brand of Protestant Sundays was a lingering, unaccommodating desire for a strict Puritan sort of day. Those who sought this actually accepted many other American values but simply could not agree with a recreational and commercial Sunday.

When the states of North and South Carolina conducted National Guard drills on Sundays in 1959, Baptist conventions protested. The commanding officer explained that these drills were necessary in order to avoid a third world war, and that guardsmen were able to attend church on Sunday even when they were in the field—besides, "the Puritans went to church with blunderbusses on their shoulders." Still, certain Baptists were unconvinced. Similarly, the Reverend J. Douglas Gibson of the First Methodist Church in Conyers, Georgia, urged President Eisenhower and the secretary of defense in 1958 to send up the nation's new rockets on days other than Sunday. An official from the Department of Defense who was assigned to answer that letter responded that the day was indeed sacred but that the moon was close enough to earth only four days a month for a rocket launch: "If all conditions are met on a Sunday, we must proceed, asking the Lord's forgiveness for this rude imposition on His day." Surely, God would not frown upon what they were doing, because it was necessary "to secure the blessings of our way of life." Here, in other words, was an even higher priority than a strict Sunday. Yet even this commonly held American sentiment did not persuade many Methodists.

Another Methodist, Lyn Cryderman, titled the memoir of his youth in the 1950s and early 1960s *No Swimming on Sunday,* reflecting the impact of the day's Puritan tone upon his entire childhood. The son of a missionary, and then eventually a Methodist minister himself, Cryderman felt that his entire life revolved around Sunday services. As a child, he predictably loved Saturday, because it meant baseball and catching snakes in the swamp. But Sunday was even more dreadful than schooldays, characterized not only by long services at church but by "inspirational music on the hi-fi, the hissing of the pressure cooker, the aroma of pot roast"—all signs that "another perfectly good day was about to be ruined."

Sometimes he feigned illness to avoid church, even putting the family's thermometer close to his lamp to heat it up, but this trick backfired when he wasn't allowed to play that afternoon, due to illness. Sunday "play" wasn't terribly enticing anyway, he decided: it included board games, naps, and taking walks—no bike riding, no sports, no television, just "a sorry game of Sorry." Still, usually he went along to church, starting with Sunday school, which wasn't always as bad as he thought it would be. After a teacher pulled on the thick rope that rang the church's bell, the children filed in row by row, divided by gender, while parents sat in the back. During these "opening exercises," a Sunday school "superintendent" was in charge of trying to get the children to calm down: here in the sanctuary, one had to be especially reverent. There were announcements, including birthdays, and everyone sang "Happy Birthday" to those called to the front, who were given an unsharpened pencil as a present. Pencils were also handed out to those who had brought friends along, to the friends themselves, and to anyone who had memorized the assigned Bible verse for the week.

Bigger prizes were reserved for those who distinguished themselves with perfect attendance at Sunday school throughout the year, in the form of lapel pins. Each succeeding year could bring another pin, so that on "rally day," which kicked off every school year, it wasn't unusual to see at least one old person in the congregation walk proudly forward with a chain of pins hanging below the waist. Attendance was a major preoccupation, reflecting a society that was beginning to measure everything. Close attention was paid not only to one's personal attendance but to setting new local records and to outdoing other Methodist Sunday schools around the country. An attendance thermometer always stood just to the side of the platform, so that all could see the figures for themselves. Grown men led cheers to surpass other congregations, and Sunday school board members talked often about sending one of their number to Los Angeles or some such place to make sure other congregations were not cheating. Countless pencils were handed out as motivation, and Lyn and his friends got in the habit of thinking "Whom can I invite next week?" to make the thermometer climb higher. When enthusiasm waned and the thermometer stabilized, the minister brought out the "big weapons": he would promise to kiss a pig, or wear a dress, or take a pie in the face. And in fact this almost always motivated them: for beyond their ordinary churchgoing friends, almost everyone had "a pagan friend or two" for such crucial times. It wasn't easy to get them to come along: the usual promise of a pencil wasn't enough—it might even get the inviter beaten up. Instead it required digging into one's personal collection of baseball cards or some other treasure. There was one Seventh Day Adventist boy in town, whom they were sure would come if invited (and whom they all envied because he could play baseball on Sunday), but the last thing they wanted to do was to pay him back by attending his religious services on a Saturday, thus taking up the whole weekend with church. In 1959 the local Sunday school finally won a big competition, and the way they celebrated was enough to cause any witnesses to think that they had "backslid."

Besides motivations for attendance, opening exercises included such activities as adults donning costumes and acting out "hilarious skits," the pastor telling dramatic Bible stories, and kids reciting Bible verses. Especially women storytellers liked to use colorful flannel pieces of blue sky, meadows, pigpens, prodigal sons, and more on the inevitable "Scene-o-felt" to illustrate their stories. Depending on the humidity, the age of the pieces, and the angle of the easel, the figures sometimes fell off the board, always at the wrong time, such as when Jesus fell off the cross too early in a depiction of the crucifixion. But the presenter of the day deftly used the mistake to begin the story of the resurrection.

A final highlight of opening exercises, in thousands of American churches on Sunday, was the small plastic or cardboard church near the pulpit in which children were encouraged to deposit coins for this purpose or that—often the upkeep of their own building. They paraded forward to do so, while the piano played "Bringing in the Sheaves" or "We're Marching to Zion," and the adults followed behind them with larger sums.

If some parts of the opening exercises were fun for Lyn, classtime was better still. While the adults stayed upstairs for their own class, the children marched downstairs into the damp, dark, and cold basement and entered smaller classrooms full of fun, at least as he remembered it. Teachers were sometimes less enthusiastic: one wrote, "There is no breed of human more perverse, plaguing and pertinent, than the junior boys' class in any Sunday school." Young Lyn Cryderman, however, liked the activities, always connected to Bible stories, and consisting mostly of cutting and pasting and coloring. He and his classmates liked tasting the glue, and its smell, but their round-nosed scissors made it hard to fashion precisely their lambs of paper and cottonballs, or stars, or all the animals for Noah's ark, or the flags of countries where visiting missionaries had been working. They also made get-well cards for sick people, and pencil holders for all of their attendance pencils, and Nativity scenes out of Popsicle sticks and scraps of cloth. When they were a bit older, their teacher, a high school science teacher, showed them what "likker" did to their brains and demonstrated with various magical bottles of fluid how Jesus washed their hearts with his blood: the teacher held up clear liquid, then poured in black liquid to represent sin, then poured in red liquid that turned it all clear again.

The main service, which followed Sunday school, was far less interesting to Cryderman, partly because back in the sanctuary one had to whisper; any shouting up here and people worried that "you were going charismatic." The opening hymn he liked fine, which always seemed to be Luther's "A Mighty Fortress," played heavily on an old Hammond organ. The choir director stood near the board that listed the hymns for the day, the sermon topic, and the amount of money collected the Sunday before. Then came responsive readings from the King James Bible, including many "thee's and thou's and verily's." Weary of standing, Lyn leaned over the pew in front of him, only to have his mother pull him back by the shirt collar. Then came more hymns and a long prayer by Pastor Verdon Dunckel, whom everyone called Uncle Dunk. The prayers tested everyone's patience most, for Uncle Dunk regarded them as an art form and an opportunity to mention anything he'd accidentally left out of his upcoming sermon. He began within "our little town," then moved out to the entire world, filling in anyone who'd missed all the gossip that week by mentioning not only specific sins from which sinners needed saving but a few names as well. If Uncle Dunk heard a few "Amens" (never ah-men, like the liberal churches) during the prayer, then he "hammered even louder" on that point, which usually involved condemning liquor or Hollywood. People had distinctive responses during prayer, including "Ooooooooh, precious Jesus!" or hallelujahs and groans. But this congregation was not "charismatic"—if they were, their pastor would have ended each word with an extra syllable sounding like "uh," or they might have spoken in tongues or engaged in healing, but they regarded all that as "going backward." When finished, Uncle Dunk would announce the potluck dinner Friday night at the fire barn sponsored by the Junior Missionary Society.

By the time the hour-long sermon rolled around, the children in the audience were, like Ernest Claes's Whitey and the audiences of the ancient and medieval worlds, done for. They quietly played hangman, or

tic-tac-toe, often on the back of offering envelopes, until parents con-
fiscated them. Or they might undo one of the screws holding the hymn-
book rack in place, but if they went too far and the rack fell, there was
trouble. Lyn's mother made up quasi-religious activities, such as seeing
how many words they could make from the letters of a Bible verse, and
she allowed them to read their Sunday school take-home paper, but no
comic books. He later learned that some of the high schoolers in the
congregation irreverently spent the sermon randomly opening the
hymnal and adding "Between the Sheets" to whatever title appeared.
It was too wicked to do this for any title that had Jesus in it, but it was
fine for titles such as "Glorious Things of Thee are Spoken" or "Love
Divine."

When Uncle Dunk finally said "In conclusion . . ." they knew that
only ten minutes remained in the sermon, but by now even parents had
given up. Kids were folding any scrap of paper into airplanes or coloring empty spaces of the bulletin, while dozing men jerked upright
when wives or mothers elbowed them. At 11:45 on Sunday morning,
the greatest challenges to the Christian were "hunger, boredom, and
fatigue." At last came the final hymn, all five verses, then a benediction
by Uncle Dunk, repeating what he'd said already in the sermon. The
last "Amen" meant only another half hour until pot roast.

After dinner there wasn't much to do besides take a nap, do a jigsaw puzzle, or play the board games already mentioned. A late afternoon meal, smaller than at noon, usually included toasted-cheese
sandwiches, then it was back to church for another round of singing,
praying, and a sermon—just like the seventeenth-century Puritans and
Dutch Reformed. The Sunday evening service included more singing,
with the song leader sometimes inviting anyone from the congregation
to shout out the page number of a favorite hymn. Younger members of
the audience mischievously requested the most obscure, putting blank
looks on everyone's faces.

Another interesting feature in the evening was the testimony service,
during which members were free to speak as moved. The bad thing
was that this usually ran right through the new *Wonderful World of
Disney* on Sunday night television; the only redeeming element was if
someone with a "real bad sin" broke the silence and held them all cap-
tive with a litany of indiscretions, usually including drinking and

smoking, maybe sex or gambling. Still, if given a choice, Lyn would have rather been home watching *Bonanza, The Wonderful World of Disney,* or *The Ed Sullivan Show.* Only once, when he was twelve, did his mother let him stay home to watch TV: when the Beatles appeared on Ed Sullivan. His arguments for *Bonanza* and *Disney* never worked—"all my friends get to," or "church is boring"—but his "once in a lifetime" argument bore fruit at last, as it did for many of the other 78 million Americans who watched the Beatles on that Sunday night.

This Sunday in the family of a Methodist missionary resembled in some basic ways the extended-worship Sunday of their colonial forebears. Later in life, when Lyn Cryderman was a preacher, he was glad that many old Sunday ways had disappeared and that kids could now play basketball on Sunday and that seats in church were now padded. But like some others who regretted much of their tedious childhood Sundays, he still wished that something of them had been preserved.

Lucy Forsyth Townsend's girlhood Sundays in the Presbyterian faith were likewise strict, more so than for many of her fellow Presbyterians by now.

On July Sundays in her small town in eastern Kentucky, she climbed into her grandfather's Studebaker with her four siblings and mother, and sometimes her father, to go to the local First Presbyterian Church. Outside, men and women chatted on the sidewalk and shook her gloved hand as she walked up. In retrospect, she remembered only the sunshine and the "sweet smell of gods and goddesses in clothes," with herself as the "embodiment of southern girlhood"—carefully curled hair, creamy skin, patent leather shoes, and a pink rose corsage cut from the garden pinned to her Sunday-best dress. The only highlight she remembered from the service was singing "Glory Be to the Father, and to the Son, and to the Holy Ghost." Sunday dinner consisted of roast beef, cut-up potatoes and carrots in gravy, lime Jell-O with canned pineapple and mint, green beans, corn on the cob, tomatoes and cucumbers from the garden, rolls with butter, milk to drink, and ice cream at the end.

Although other local Presbyterians weren't terribly strict on Sunday by this time, her lower-middle-class mother still was—not harsh, but just careful to focus the day on worship. The dinner, and free time afterward, were dominated by religious talk. Her mother expressed contempt for the local church's habit of catering to the rich (specifically to the local country-club set that dominated their congregation) and of looking down on the neighboring Baptists for their supposed lack of refinement. Her mother also conducted long discussions over dinner about church history and theology, including various Protestant sects and "the authoritarian Roman Catholic Church." Sometimes they visited other churches personally, and often their mother called them in from hot summer afternoons to hear Bible stories, which she made more interesting than had the teachers at Sunday school.

Members of still other faiths experienced, or promoted, similar sorts of restrained Sundays. Organizations such as the Lord's Day Alliance continued to push for the restricted Sunday they believed had once dominated. The Reverend Norman Guy sounded terribly Puritan in 1964 when he warned against those "who say we are not bound to obey the Sabbath." Many Baptists (and not only Seventh-Day Baptists, who worshiped on Saturday) also engaged in Sabbath-speak and observance, refusing to accommodate changing trends.

Mormonism, a small, American-born denomination that claimed ties to neither Catholicism nor Protestantism, lay near this part of the Sunday-observing spectrum as well. Its first leader, Joseph Smith, was born into a New England world that simply assumed Sunday was the Sabbath and that observing it was strictly a self-evident need. For all of his other innovations, there was nothing new about his promotion of a stricter Sunday. And that Sunday continued when the faith moved to Utah in 1847.

By the 1950s, the Mormon Sunday, still focused in Utah, looked much like Cryderman's Methodist Sunday, if slightly more relaxed. Mormon teenagers in the 1950s might drive to Dairy Queen or such places on Sunday evenings, after all. But in church, Mormon sermons, like Methodist or Baptist sermons, or like the sermons of Gregory of Tours from the Middle Ages, often included stories of good or ill fortune that followed good or ill Sunday observance. Many stories were drawn from the faith's pioneer past, including the trek to Utah; the pioneers did not travel on Sunday, for instance, and this was meant to encourage a modern Sunday free of work, commercialism, and unseemly amusements. One such story was the skeptical farmer who decided to test the Sabbath commandment by planting a field and working it *only* on Sunday, to see what would happen. Surprisingly, it proved to be an excellent crop, the best grain on his farm, and so he put up a sign for all to see: "This crop was grown on Sunday." But one day lightning struck his field and burned it completely—except for the sign, a witness to all who passed by of the dire consequences of ignoring the Sabbath. Quotes from Brigham Young, the church's second leader, also persisted into the fifties: those who "go skating, buggy riding, or on excursions on the Sabbath day are weak in the faith," and Sunday was "a holy day, not a holiday."

Similarities to the Methodist Sunday were also evident in the day's basic structure: a series of church services throughout the day and family time at home in between. Indeed, church leaders had said in 1928 that it was "unnecessary for families to go beyond their own homes or those of their kindred." Certainly by the 1950s Mormons were making even greater efforts to assimilate into American culture: a new temple in Los Angeles bore less specifically Mormon symbols and looked more like the Beverly Hills mansions nearby it, the Mormon Tabernacle Choir continued its famous Sunday broadcasts and became the chief exponent of American patriotic hymns, and the Utah legislature, dominated by Mormons, twice failed to pass Sunday legislation, largely on the old American grounds of individual choice. But for many Mormon adults, Sunday itself looked much like a Puritan Sunday. As one believing woman put it, the definition of a Mormon was "someone who is in a meeting, going to a meeting, or coming from a meeting," especially on Sunday.

ETHNIC AND RACIAL STRAINS

Despite certain common themes in the churches on the Sunday marketplace, then, there were clearly differences as well, which led to different sorts of Sundays. Another variable affecting one's Sunday was ethnicity or race, which in the increasingly diverse U.S. is especially worth a closer look.

Massive immigration from Europe halted in the 1920s, thanks largely to American legislation that, some felt, was meant largely to stem the tide of poor European Catholics. By the 1950s most European immigrants were, like those at St. Nick's parish in Chicago, therefore into their second and third generations and moving toward middle-class respectability. These older immigrant groups still encountered problems and prejudices, but in the 1950s at least three other ethnic groups stood more conspicuously outside the melting pot: Jews, Latinos, and African Americans. Native Americans and Asian Americans stood there with them, but a look at these then prominent three will illustrate the common tensions.

Tensions not only spilled over into Sunday but were arguably felt more acutely that day than others. In one sense, Sunday could be a day for relieving everyday social tensions: those not easily assimilated into American society spoke often of the solace that came from worshiping together each week, a refuge from the pains of the past six days. But in another sense, religious worship on Sunday could be a poignant or even bitter moment, when issues of assimilation or exclusion seemed sharper and more unjust than ever—precisely because of ideals which were held up as available to all yet which seemed to contradict the experiences of these particular groups.

One can begin to understand the strains of an American Jewish Sunday in the 1950s through Anita Block's short story "Sunday Morning."

It is rightly situated in New York City, home of the most concentrated population of Jews in the world, numbering 2 million of the city's 8 million inhabitants. There a Mr. Levy visits his son, daughter-in-law, and grandchildren each Sunday, and each Sunday he is filled with strongly conflicting emotions. Because the son married a gentile woman, custom said that the father should not even acknowledge the couple—but the father wished to visit anyway, and besides, his gentile daughter-in-law treated him more kindly than did his son, who emerged in his Wall Street suit only for dinner and superficial conversation. The father was also pained at how his son had Anglicized the family name: many American Jews did so, but did his son have to take it so far, from Levy to Leighton? As Mr. Levy sat talking each Sunday with the daughter-in-law he could not openly recognize, he was proud of his son's fine job and apartment here in New York, with seventeen rooms, housekeepers, and governesses, and of the grandchildren who made him feel welcome, but it dispirited him too. He could not discuss any of it with his friends—not his son's good looks and success or his fine grandchildren—while his friends incessantly bragged about their own offspring. And for part of the Sunday visit the grandchildren were away at church: a Protestant church. The thought caused Mr. Levy to study his hands and think: "Two little Protestant children, two little Leightons who go to church with their Protestant mother. And David Levy, son of Israel Levy, who is now David Leighton." For this Jewish man, Sunday was the loneliest and saddest day, for it was then, when he saw his son and grandchildren in the flesh, that all the tensions and strains were most apparent.

Eli Evans's work, *The Lonely Days Were Sundays*, suggests the same sentiment, which was perhaps felt even more acutely outside of New York City. Evans's grandmother, who lived in the South, once said that the sight of her neighbors going to church on Sunday, combined with the reality of being in a tiny minority, made her feel like an outsider and thus to "have hunger in her heart for her own people." Especially outside of large cities, she suspected, many American Jews must have similarly experienced this loneliness of soul on Sunday, despite their generally improved position in American society.

Loneliness came not only through disappointing visits to over-assimilated children, not only through feeling like an outsider while almost everyone else went to church, but also when Jewish merchants were forced to close their stores on Sunday by local laws. Sunday opening had been one of the most public points of conflict for Jews since their arrival in the New World in the seventeenth century. Although Jews tried to assimilate where possible, various "Blue Laws" (so-called, say some, because of the blue paper on which they were first printed, or, say others, because blue characterized the sober tone of such codes) regulating Sunday commerce and recreation generally were always a sticking point. They were not necessarily aimed at Jews, but the impact was most obvious among them. Jewish merchants worshiped on Saturday and thus closed their stores that day. Non-Jewish competitors of course remained open. Jewish merchants wished in compensation to open on Sunday, which to them was not a holy day. But the Blue Laws of most states prevented it.

In the late nineteenth and early twentieth centuries, some reforming Jews sought, for economic and cultural reasons, to move traditional Sabbath observance to Sunday, thus blending with the rhythms of wider American society. But most American Jews felt that this went too far, and Jewish merchants therefore maintained their usual practice of closing on Saturday while seeking to open on Sunday. For long the major strategy was to seek specific exemptions from Blue Laws rather than to challenge their constitutionality. But this had mixed results: sometimes exemptions were granted, sometimes they were not. Sometimes Jewish merchants opened anyway and the laws were not enforced, but sometimes they were. The very unpredictability was a source of strain on Sunday.

According to a recent study, Blue Laws were never perfectly observed or enforced, by Jews or other Americans. Civil disobedience in the form of Sunday opening among people of various faiths was the rule rather than the exception, in all periods of American history. This was due partly to indifference toward Sunday opening among authorities, and partly to how convoluted and arbitrary the rules could be. Yet Blue Laws had great symbolic meaning, and states, who had jurisdiction over Blue Laws, were reluctant to drop them altogether, and therefore made occasional raids on violators. Religious supporters feared that if Blue Laws disappeared, then so would Sunday and so would the United States. Unions also wanted to keep Blue Laws because of the shorter workweek they promised. Opponents, including Jews and Seventh-Day Adventists, looked for even competition. But before World War II, these opponents of Blue Laws were often labeled as un-American, even secularist, atheist, or Communist, for wanting to open on Sunday. That Christian and other merchants who opened as usual on Saturdays had an unfair advantage over Jewish merchants, who closed two days a week, usually went unmentioned.

During the 1950s the tension continued, as sporadic enforcement of the laws always threatened to upset the Sundays of Jewish merchants who dared open. In fact, in 1955 Manhattan's police department cracked down over several Sundays on the sale of prohibited items. Soon afterward a group of Jewish merchants and other proponents of Sunday opening decided to go beyond seeking exemptions from Blue Laws and to challenge them openly, on constitutional grounds—specifically that they violated the first amendment's ban on the state's establishment of religion. By favoring Sunday closing, the state was implicitly endorsing Christianity's holy day. The key case proved to be *McGowan v. Maryland,* argued in 1961 before the Supreme Court. The court held that even though Blue Laws were originally motivated by religious forces, they could be kept as long as states found convincing secular reasons to justify them, such as the desirability of setting aside one day a week for repose and recreation. Moreover, such laws had to be broadly desired, nondiscriminatory, reasonable, and most of all uncomplicated, without all the usual arbitrary exceptions. This put an end to such laws as Pennsylvania's, for instance, where one could buy tricycles on Sunday but not bicycles, or Philadelphia's, where one could buy seat covers for a car but not slip covers for a couch, and a real football for teens but not a toy football for kids. Or New York's, where one could sell food, beverages, ice, tobacco, flowers, confectionery, souvenirs, newspapers, gasoline, oil, tires, drugs, medicines, and surgical instruments, but nothing else. Or Massachusetts's, where one could dig for clams but not dredge for oysters. Still, if a state could meet all the required tests, then it could still pass Blue Laws—and in 1961, 49 of 50 states still had such laws in some form.

This could have been bad news indeed for Jewish merchants, but by the time of *McGowan v. Maryland,* Sunday opening was common anyway in the United States. Other non-Christian merchants were indifferent to Blue Laws, but so were a growing number of Christians, who did not see Sunday closing as necessary to their faith. Jews themselves were more often open on Saturday than ever before, so that the entire weekend had a commercial presence. The clincher for all was suggested earlier: greater profits. Sunday opening meant more sales than Sunday closing, and even more fundamentally one had to keep up with the competition or else. One superstore president said, "The competition forces us into it," and many others said with their deeds the same thing. And there was additional motivation in the fifties: more Americans now saw entrepreneurial commerce as one of the most important distinctions between themselves and the state-driven Communism of their new rival, the Soviet Union. Suburban stores now tended to open on most Sundays. Downtown stores, further away from popular suburban living areas, had mixed feelings about Sunday opening, with smaller stores tending to oppose it and larger stores wishing to compete with suburban rivals. Labor by now was also split about Sunday: some industries, including J. C. Penney's retail stores, still had people working seven days a week, which workers didn't like. But other industries simply hired a larger workforce to spread the hours out, and paid higher wages on Sunday, which some workers favored.

Hence the 1950s were an odd decade for Blue Laws: confirmed in theory and present in almost every state, they were nevertheless increasingly limited and ignored, as the old American value of commerce came to be prized on Sunday too. For Jewish merchants, the decline in Blue Laws certainly removed at least one of their Sunday headaches.

Another group experiencing tensions on Sunday in the U.S. were Latinos, who with the decline of immigration from Europe after 1924 became the leading new immigrant group in the country.

Growth in the Latino population went from 4 million in 1950 to 6.9 million in 1960, and then 19.5 million in 1970. That growth was mostly urban: in 1920, 75 percent of Hispanics lived in rural areas; by 1960, 85 percent lived in cities. Thus a Hispanic Sunday in the U.S. in the 1950s was in the first place an urban Sunday.

One of the prominent Latino groups in the 1950s was Puerto Ricans, who, because they already enjoyed U.S. citizenship, were free to move anywhere in the country. There were 302,000 Puerto Ricans on the mainland in 1950, some 82 percent of them in New York City. In 1960 the total had grown to 888,000, with 69 percent in New York. Hence a Puerto Rican Sunday was not only urban, it was usually situated specifically, like a Jewish Sunday, in New York City.

Yet not even New York, with its sixty or so ethnic groups and long tradition of immigrants, was a world into which ethnic newcomers could move easily, not even on Sunday at church. More established ethnic groups were trying to leave behind their immigrant roots for middle-class America, both at home and at church, and often had little patience with or understanding of newcomers. A moving account of this tension, and other aspects of Puerto Rican Sundays, may be found in Piri Thomas's autobiographical *Savior, Savior, Hold My Hand* (1972). Born in 1928 in Spanish Harlem to Puerto Rican parents, Piri was the oldest of seven children. In his late teens he became a drug addict, and in 1950 he received a six-year prison sentence for armed robbery. This book recounts his attempt to reenter civilian life in 1956, with Sunday playing no small role.

Piri was not an eager churchgoer, especially not after his first week home, when all the smiling attention paid to the returning "ex-bandido" embarrassed him to the depths. Still, Piri occasionally went anyway to please his aunt, with whom he now lived and who, unlike most Puerto Ricans, was not Catholic but a member of the Spanish Mission Pentecostal Church. He also might attend due to his interest in a neighbor girl named Nita, who made Piri "feel like a poet" just looking at her. But his "rotten self" also told him that Nita was too good for him, and so he rarely went to church anyway.

One Sunday night he tried church again. The congregation was proud of its modest concrete-block building, paid for by countless bazaars and small donations. Above the doorway a hollow cross with a lightbulb inside flashed the church's name through stenciled openings. On one wall was a painting of the cross and a Bible inside a crown of thorns, on the other a painting of a white dove, representing the Holy Ghost. Carefully lettered verses from the Bible adorned every wall. Everyone smiled at him as usual, but he liked it now, and that they called each other "Brother" and "Sister." He also liked Pentecostal music, and "the way everybody really swung in the worship of God." Some of the people looked peaceful, but most reflected "a kind of self-awareness, the kind that one can only get after having gone through one kind of hell or another out there in the world and then finally discovering some sort of refuge by becoming a part of the church." The plate offering was passed, and every person, "poorer than a ghetto mouse," their clothes "straight from La Marketa," came up with something, "from a penny way up to a quarter." Piri thought that maybe God wouldn't mind if they kept their coins sometimes, but it was pretty clear that "there was nothing except for real in a lot of the church members, like they were singing for real . . . praying for real . . . loving for real . . . and well . . . just asking God to give them courage, strength, love, and mucho faith so as to be able to walk the rocky roads of the harsh reality of the living hell out in them streets."

In other words, they were not here to perform a Sunday ritual so that they might feel more American.

This atmosphere moved Piri to seek his own religious experience, and it came during another Sunday service. After hearing moving stories, and some speaking in tongues and song, Piri stirred. A war started inside him: he worried that "his boys would know he was on a God kick." He worried that he was going to find himself "hung up in the middle again," trying "to keep your down rep on the street while trying to be a down Christian. . . . Your boys gonna start seeing you going to church regular-like and walking them streets with a Bible under your arm instead of a pistola." But finally he stood up and walked forward to make his public acceptance of Jesus, looking neither right nor left, just dimly hearing the Praise Gods and Hallelujahs and thinking that "I was gonna be somebody after this long walk." He knelt down and answered the question "Do you accept Jesus Christ as your personal savior?" with a cry of "I do!" And he did feel good, but he wondered whether he felt as good as old Brother Rivera or some of the others.

After that Piri was a regular on Sunday. He began studying the Bible hard, joined a Young People's Society, and directed some of its service. He bought a secondhand guitar in a pawnshop and started writing spirituals, including his first, "Savior, Savior, Hold My Hand." He testified at street corner meetings about his transformation from prisoner to believer, and he wasn't sure exactly what he wanted to say and he wasn't exactly sure what Jesus had done for him, but he was trying, and "trying beats a blank."

Sunday now also meant seeing Nita, who taught Sunday school in the basement. Piri stood outside the door sometimes to listen, hearing her try to explain why Jesus had said "Suffer the little children" while the kids "yakked away in Spanish and English about school and baseball." Piri finally went in and asked to speak a minute with her, while the suddenly silent kids made knowing side glances and kissing sounds. Two hugged each other in exaggerated fashion; one put his hands over his heart and rolled his eyes. Piri asked what time he should visit today, since she had told him that Sunday was the day for visiting at her house. She said to come in time for dinner. That visit, and many other Sunday visits, went well, even though Nita's dog sniffed him annoyingly; eventually Piri and Nita married.

Together they were stalwarts of Sunday services, especially after Nita gave birth to their son Ricky. One Sunday Victor, Piri's best man, was teaching Sunday school about the responsibility of being a Christian and overcoming temptation. This put a smile on Piri's face, and he made a little batting motion, because he knew Victor was going to Yankee Stadium that afternoon to watch the game and that the church elders would not have approved—causing Victor quickly to add that what was sin to one person might not have been to another. But Piri was at church weekly, and he started a club for teenagers with a Christian missionary named John, who wanted to work with "hard gang kids." This meant among other things driving around on Sundays to pick the kids up for church. They took them not only to Piri's modest neighborhood church but also to a big rich church run by fellow white Pentecostals. John had arranged for the big rich church to "open their doors" to fifteen Puerto Rican kids during Sunday school. And here things began to look different for Piri.

On driving up to the church that first Sunday, the kids were impressed, calling it a church and a half. Piri was likewise impressed but also wary. As they walked, they didn't make a squeak, thanks to expensive wall-to-wall carpet: it was a "golden temple," and the brothers and sisters inside dressed the part. "Our kids were mucho awed by it and talking in hushed whispers, smiling back at all the hundreds of smiling faces." They walked past many filled rooms, figuring they'd be shown into one, but instead they got an empty one of their own. Everyone was a little uncomfortable, but a man stood in front of them "making brotherly sounds," to "welcome you in the name of Jesus Christ," and "This is your church and we can worship our God in Christian fellowship together." This helped ease the tensions. They sang some songs everyone knew, "What a Friend We Have in Jesus" and "Nearer My God to Thee," then had a lesson, a prayer, and left. They felt great, the welcome mat had been rolled out, and then they were smiled out of sight—"we almost felt wanted in the Great Church." Weeks later, as the kids started to feel comfortable, talking and laughing freely, the "sssshhhh's" started coming from the regulars. Things grew a little worse when the kids sang "What a Friend We

Have in Jesus" in "five-part harmony on a fast upbeat à la street scene." That brought disapproving frowns, and Piri sensed some of the people didn't really want that kind of religion there at all—didn't think of it as religion even.

Precisely these Sunday encounters caused Piri to feel a previously unrealized distance between himself "and a certain brand of Christianity." All that contact with the big rich church made him notice things he hadn't noticed before, or hadn't wanted to notice, about white-ghetto relationships, at church and otherwise. They weren't equal after all, despite all the religious talk. The big church was full of the chosen ones, "sent to save us, on their terms." People mostly stared at the kids, or ignored them, but never made them feel equal. The inside of the church was like Madison Square Garden, the pews and wood-work and pulpit all from Tiffany's. People wore gold cufflinks and were afraid to put a wrinkle in their clothes. His church was "poor in bread, but really rich in spirit, and this was just rich in pesos. Maybe I'm wrong, I thought, but they're here in God's house acting like it was some kind of business appointment." They looked at each other "with a kind of Who's Who attitude." Piri knew all Christians were not like this, but "those that are sure were muffing it for the nitty-gritty ones. They even say Amen like they're counting money."

Piri tried to explain these sentiments to the missionary John, who was not Puerto Rican. If they were part of the Sunday school, then why did they need their own separate room? asked Piri. John urged him to be patient, but Piri felt, "It's like we always must give in, must do right, must follow, must bow and scrape." Piri calmed down after a while, and still hoped for better relations with the Great Church, but then came more disappointment. He was mad that Saint Paul "dug slavery," as he learned at Bible camp from white kids; Piri remembered that Paul was supposed to have some big thorn in his side, "maybe this was it, believing in slavery." Even at his own church, he was no longer sure: one Sunday, sitting with Ricky and Nita, he watched the middle-aged lady next to them study Ricky's thick-textured hair (Piri was more black than white, and so Ricky had even curlier hair than Nita).

Soon Piri was staying home from choir practice, then from church itself, and Nita wondered whether he was "getting cold in the Lord." He didn't answer, but finally let it out. He wasn't cold, "just frozen to

death by hypocrisy. What's the point of my going to church seven days
a week and praying and singing while our Barrio is swinging with all
kinds of miseries?" He didn't want to wait until heaven before life was
right. "I believe the true salvation of us ghetto people is when we get
together in one solid fist and smash down the walls of bullshit
hypocrisy. Honey, I've seen more brother- and sisterhood in our nitty-
gritty people than in any of those great golden temples. . . . We got
some missionaries to El Barrio who wheel and deal in souls because
they know so many of us want to believe in something other than this
hell we're living in." But you "can't listen to the words of Christ on the
cross and be nailed to it yourself at the same time. The ghetto is our
church and the only way we're gonna make a heaven out of this hell is
by getting together." Nita understood, but didn't quite agree, and left
for church. Piri could only think that there "must be a million ghetto
crosses out there."

The sort of difficulties experienced by Piri Thomas were evident in
other U.S. churches as well. In fact, a truly integrated congregation,
whatever the ethnic groups or denominations involved, was the exception in the 1950s. Some congregations actively excluded certain
groups, but even those who tried to include them often experienced
failure through misunderstandings.

The Catholic Church, for instance, was certainly making efforts
in New York to integrate Piri's fellow Puerto Ricans into existing
parishes. But the obstacles were formidable. The established American
Catholic clergy was made up mostly of second- and third-generation
Irishmen, while Puerto Rican newcomers seemed even more exotic
(and threatening) than southern European immigrants, spoke a language
foreign to most clergymen, and settled in inner cities rather than increasingly popular suburbs. Catholic priests had long worked among
poor immigrants, but because earlier immigrant groups had assimilated and the clergy was becoming suburban middle-class itself, this
new wave of immigrants after World War II was in many ways a shock
for them.

The middle-class American values of the church and the clergy were
not understood as merely that, but rather as orthodox and self-evident,
which often got in the way of understanding Puerto Rican religiosity,
and vice versa. For example, nonverbal language was almost com-

pletely opposite between the established and new cultures, so that there were misunderstandings and irritations before the talking even began, with neither side understanding why. But the misunderstandings ran into more substantive areas as well, such as how to approach authority, sin, ritual, and the miraculous. American sexual mores, for instance, were relatively strict, influenced by long-standing Puritan values and Irish immigrants; Puerto Ricans had known neither experience, and their society had long accepted consensual unions as a preliminary step to, or even substitute for, marriage, and had regarded fidelity and stability as more important than the church's official sacrament.

Overcoming these and other barriers was complicated, despite sincere efforts on both sides. Cardinal Spellman of New York genuinely wanted to integrate Puerto Ricans into the American church "and ethos." To him and to other bishops, segregation was a bad thing imposed especially on black churches, and they wanted to remove it for all groups. But most leaders sought integration by expecting Puerto Ricans and others to adapt to established American ways, which were regarded as the norm or even as "neutral" truths. To many Puerto Ricans, integration at church therefore meant losing their identity and, more specifically, their way of expressing themselves religiously. That was why Catholic Puerto Ricans into the 1970s preferred on Sunday to attend one of their two ethnic parishes in East Harlem rather than the typical Spanish-language Sunday Mass in the basement of a neighborhood parish. If forced to integrate, many Puerto Rican poor would stay home on Sunday, or like Piri's family join a more independent evangelical church, where they could worship within their traditional culture. More dramatically, they might quit church altogether, and in New York there was extra temptation to do so: 58 percent of New Yorkers in 1957 claimed no religious identity, making them much less churchgoing than most Americans.

It wasn't institutional Catholicism, then, to which many Puerto Ricans were loyal, but Puerto Rican spirituality. No one wanted to be told they could not belong to a congregation on ethnic grounds, but no one wanted to be forced to belong to one either. The desire for integration into American society didn't necessarily extend to church on Sunday, for worship, unlike what the established clergy of any church often believed, was expressed in specific cultural forms. Irish-American Catholicism was not neutral either, but likewise influenced by cultural practices and values: it simply might not have seen them that way.

All this tension dismayed pastors who meant well by their attempts at integration. A few, such as Ivan Illich, were more successful than others: arriving in New York in 1952 from Austria, he learned the language of local Puerto Ricans, lived among them, and especially learned such values as unquestioning kindness to strangers. They were not without values, he realized, as some American clergy believed, but simply had different values from middle-class America, and even saw many middle-class values as selfish. He also realized quickly that many Puerto Ricans failed to attend the local parish's Mass because it started exactly on time: for Puerto Ricans, punctuality meant rigidity, and putting clocks ahead of people. For most Puerto Rican Catholics, full religious integration meant full cultural integration, and that was giving up too much.

Much the same dynamic was true among the even larger Mexican-American population of the U.S., especially concentrated in the Southwest. Like other Hispanic groups, their numbers increased rapidly from 1930 to 1960, in Texas, Arizona, New Mexico, and beyond. Here too the cultural gap was noticeable between existing church and immigrant believer. The champion integrator in this region was Archbishop Robert Lucey of San Antonio, who for years fought racism against Mexicans and blacks alike, even ordering all Catholic schools in his territory integrated within six weeks of the famous *Brown v. Board of Education* decision in 1954. But he too failed to appreciate how important the obstacles to integration were. Once he walked out of a confirmation ceremony, disappointed in what he saw as a lack of preparation among the candidates; but Mexican-American Catholics saw this as a humiliation and even neglect, and could therefore never consider him a true shepherd.

Without much mutual understanding, it was little wonder that 1965 surveys showed that Mexican-Americans used five words to describe their pastors, only one of them good: scolder, grouchy, money-grubber, proud, kindly. Collection envelopes and bingo, two of the temporal props of the American church, seemed more monetary than apostolic

to Mexicans, who preferred shepherds' plays or foot-washing ceremonies.

Thus, in some American churches, Sundays were also a day when
misunderstandings between clergy and flock, or between established
flock and newcomer flock, were only accentuated.

If European immigrants of the late nineteenth and early twentieth centuries, or Latinos of the 1950s, found integration into established
American congregations difficult, then the overwhelming majority of
black Americans found it nearly as impossible as ever.

Present in significant numbers since the eighteenth century, blacks in
America remained far more numerous than Latinos, totaling 18.9 million by 1960. Some 64 percent of them were Baptist and 23 percent
Methodist or African Methodist Episcopal, with a smaller number
who were Catholic. Despite efforts of some churches to integrate
American congregations during the 1950s, 95 percent of blacks continued to worship separately on Sunday—just as they did much else
separately both before and after the Civil War.

Partly because of this, Sunday always had great meaning among
black Americans as a day of refuge. Indeed, William McClain has recently written that although Sunday was an organizing point for many
peoples, it had been especially so for the black church and community.
"People talk about losing the Lord's Day, well black people never lost
it!" Sunday was long the moment when black Americans found "hope
and sanctity and blessing from a week of loss and indignities." It was
a day not only of the usual rejuvenation, high-heeled shoes, pressed
dresses, and suits and ties found among many groups, but especially "a
testimony of God's ability to sustain life in the midst of trial." Sunday
always came, Sunday always endured. Although McClain did not
mention the French and Russian attempts to eliminate Sunday, their
failures would have confirmed his sense of Sunday as a symbol of endurance.

During slavery, Sunday was a free day, which some former slaves recalled made it better than Christmas, for Sunday came weekly. During
the eighteenth century, much of that Sunday began to be spent at

church, because by the 1780s slaves had joined established Christian congregations in large numbers: about one-fifth of all Methodists by 1800 were black slaves, while Baptists also numbered a good proportion of blacks. These denominations might have done what the new nation did not: recognize all people as equal—at least on Sunday. But for most Americans it was still unthinkable: slaves were soon segregated into the Black Pews, or Slave Balconies. Eventually many walked out to establish their own congregations, including the African Methodist Episcopal Union in 1790, and later the Black Baptist Union. Some recalled walking barefoot fourteen miles or more in Sunday clothes to reach their new churches, carrying their shoes so as not to ruin them, then putting the shoes on once inside the building. With so much travel, and lengthy services, attending church ended up taking all of Sunday. Still, to many this was better than a weekday. In fact a common motif among black slaves was imagining, like the poor Belgian boy Ernest Claes, a future time when every day might be Sunday.

Sabbatarian attitudes against certain Sunday activities could be found in some black churches, before and after slavery. In the later nineteenth century, a former slave recounted that "I never sleep away my Sunday now," because of an experience she once had while taking a Sunday nap. Just after falling asleep, she felt someone pull her dress; she supposed it was her children, and said "Go way!" But just when she nodded off again, she felt that pulling again, and she opened her eyes to see no one there. "So I knew then it was the Master; and, says I, 'Lord, I won't sleep your day away'; and I have never lain down to sleep a-Sunday since." She also used to count chickens and bring in eggs on Sunday, but one Sunday morning she got halfway to the chicken coop when a voice told her, "This ain't the day!" She stopped and heard it again, and said, "Sure enough, Lord, this ain't the day," then turned around and never went out again on Sunday to care for her chickens. Major Taylor, a black champion cyclist of the late nineteenth century and a Baptist, refused to race on Sunday, a fact those opposed to the integration of the sport used to their advantage in trying to keep him out.

But strict Sabbatarianism was not a central feature of black Sundays. Instead the emphasis was on celebrating Sunday by attending church. Services there were hardly uniform in content or style: some middle-class black congregations were embarrassed by the "undignified" ways of numerous storefront churches that dominated cities, for instance. But generally speaking, even the most staid services tended, like Latino services, to include more emotion and music than were present in established white churches.

One black preacher has explained this more specifically, identifying four distinct characteristics of black worship. First was a personal approach to Scripture: in other words, although most black churches were regarded as evangelical, they usually avoided making statements about biblical inerrancy and focused on the immediacy of Scripture in one's life. Second was ritual, which included robed choirs, grand processionals, starched uniforms for ushers, and responding "spontaneously to the spirit"—formally called "call and response" or more casually "shoutin'." Third was music, especially that directly connected to black experience: if "A Mighty Fortress" inspired a Lutheran congregation, then "Precious Lord, Take My Hand," did the same for black congregations. And fourth was preaching, based on the Bible but again linked explicitly to black experience: this was more poetic than logical, more a dialogue than a monologue, and especially "more prophetic than pastoral," like Isaiah calling into question a nation's ethics and mores, or Nathan rebuking the errors of his own king David.

This last, the charismatic preacher, might have been the centerpiece of black worship on Sunday, and by the 1950s there were plenty of famous examples around. Joseph Harrison Jackson was pastor of Olivet Baptist in Chicago, with fifteen thousand members; after 1953 he was also president of the National Baptist Convention and its five million members and thirty thousand affiliated churches, the largest black organization in the world. There was also C. L. Franklin, who like many Baptist preachers received his calling at age fifteen or sixteen, and who had his own radio show starting in 1952, when his congregation overflowed the church building in Nashville. People lined up outside to get in for the Sunday night broadcast, and to hear his daughter Aretha, who began singing publicly at age fifteen, then toured with her father until 1960, when her own career blossomed.

Among such luminaries, the preachers at Dexter Baptist in Montgomery, Alabama, were long just another star in the firmament, but then all the more instructive in illustrating the nature of black Sunday.

In theory, black and white could have worshiped together at Dexter Baptist on Sunday, or anywhere else in the South, because churches were private institutions. But within the context of a long tradition and myriad laws that prohibited blacks and whites from playing checkers together in public or riding together in a taxi, and that established a floating line in buses with blacks placed behind whites and required black people to pay their fares at the front of the bus then exit and get on again through the rear doors while in the meantime the driver sometimes drove off, and that justified segregation on moral grounds, the environment for worshiping together was less than inviting. Not that churches in northern and western states were much different in practice. Some there tried to integrate, but many made black believers feel unwelcome or denied them equal status. The British journalist Alistair Cooke, then a correspondent in the U.S., was struck by how Northerners ridiculed the South's institutionalized racism yet were blind to their own shortcomings: the "dignity of equal contact" existed in the North, and that was something, but "this is not intimacy" or true integration. Northern cities were simply cold. Or as Ralph Ellison put it in his famous novel, a black male was an "invisible man."

Dexter Baptist was born in 1877, its first minister was a former slave, and its church was located on land where an old slave pen had stood. Built of reddish brick and topped by a copper roof, by 1950 it was one of the last wholly black properties in the downtown area of this capital city of Montgomery, thus giving it some status—all the more noticeable on Sunday, when the church was busiest. Dexter Baptist had known a good many preachers, perhaps because of its reputation as a "deacons' church," meaning that lay officers were more in charge than the preacher, whose appointment they controlled. But despite the dominance of the deacons, certainly the office of preacher here, as in any black church, was a distinguished one, the only white-collar position open to black men during slavery and by the 1950s still one of the most prestigious.

In the years before 1950, Sunday services at Dexter Baptist often featured a public clash of wills between deacons and preacher. One of the strongest-willed was Reverend Vernon Johns, a grandson of a hanged slave. The congregation, proud of its restrained style of worship, found much to like in Reverend Johns. They approved of his opposition to "shoutin'," as he would not tolerate even the quietest "Amen" during a sermon. They also liked his poetic sermons. But the congregation did not like Negro spirituals, and he did: during Sunday services he often tried to sneak one in, announcing the hymn number casually, but the organist would refuse to play it. The flock also disliked the preacher's tendency to treat controversial subjects in his sermons, such as segregation. One Sunday in 1949, just after a local lynching, he posted on the church's marquee that week's sermon topic: "It's Safe to Murder Negroes in Alabama." The deacons were mad at him for drawing unwanted attention to their respectable church, but this only made the preacher rail against respectability: there was too much fashion show and not enough religion in the congregation, he announced. And so Reverend Johns stubbornly posted on another Sunday the sermon topic "Segregation After Death."

Yet for all of the preacher's bluntness, what the deacons may have liked about him least was his penchant for doing business, including during and after Sunday services. This congregation with middle-class pretensions was trying to show that, like white Americans, they could achieve the economic dream. Yet here was their preacher telling them to take pride in physical labor and then performing it in public on Sunday right under their noses. To supplement his income as preacher, Reverend Johns sold hams, onions, potatoes, watermelons, cabbages, and sausages from the back of his pickup just outside Dexter Baptist, plainly visible to all the white Methodists walking past on Sunday. He chastised his critical congregation for buying into the white premise that underlay slavery—namely, that labor was demeaning. What was demeaning was oppression, he insisted, not labor. He also regularly discussed gardening during his sermons, pulling out an onion or cabbage from the pulpit not only to make a metaphorical point but at times to announce special prices. He even dared to sell fish, citing examples from Scripture to defend himself against critics who knew that socially fishmongers had always been the lowest of the low.

Vernon Johns was no backward man: people still came from all around on Sunday to hear his moving sermons and watch him pound the Bible, and so despite his offenses he survived for long. But in 1952 the conflicts grew so strong that he resigned five times, until finally the deacons turned off the electricity, then the gas, and finally the water in

the rectory, to drive him out. His friends urged him to be a pastor, not
a prophet—it was much safer that way. But to no avail. Finally in 1953
he left the rectory for good. In December of that year the position was
still open, and one Sunday a young candidate whose friends called him
Mike King arrived from Atlanta to give a trial sermon. It was rather
blandly entitled "The Three Dimensions of a Complete Life."

The deacons had first heard about Reverend King through an asso-
ciate in Atlanta, and they liked what they heard, because the young
man sounded more conventional than Vernon Johns and was only
twenty-five; thus he would be, they reasoned, less headstrong. Reverend King was the grandson of Alfred Daniel Williams, who had built
Ebenezer Baptist, in Atlanta, and the son of Michael King, Sr., who
had enlarged Ebenezer's congregation from two hundred to four thousand. Reverend King, Sr., was successful enough that in the summer of
1934 he asked his large congregation to send him on a summer tour of
Europe, for cultural and religious reasons. He was so impressed by the
sites involving Martin Luther that he changed his name from Michael
King to Martin Luther King and thus changed the name of his son as
well, whose friends continued to call him Mike; but the change of legal name made both men feel higher expectations of themselves.

Hence before he became a legendary activist for civil rights, Martin
Luther King, Jr., was a preacher, and his day, like centuries of preachers before him, was Sunday. Given his heritage, Sunday had always
meant church and especially preaching. He learned his style in the first
place simply by breathing it in, like most black preachers of the time,
but then he refined it with education, as urged long before by Booker
T. Washington, who complained in 1890 that three-fourths of all black
Baptist preachers and two-thirds of black Methodist preachers were
morally and intellectually unfit. This was due in part to no requirement
of formal education in black churches and in part to obstacles facing
blacks who did wish to obtain such education. As late as 1933, 80 percent of the black clergy were not college graduates. Martin Luther
King, Jr., went against that grain and pursued higher education at
Morehouse College in Atlanta and at the already integrated Crozer
Theological Seminary in Philadelphia, and he finally received a doctor-
ate in theology from Boston University. All this helped him to develop
in his preaching an unusually interesting combination of spontaneity,

high polish, perfect diction, and formal thought. He also reflected an ideal promoted by Benjamin Mays, president of Morehouse College, who wanted young black men to think logically and profoundly and also to drive a good car, wear good clothes, and have money in the bank—much like the ideal white American man of the 1950s.

The young man whom the congregation of Dexter Baptist saw standing before them on that Sunday in December 1953 was indeed determined to be the best in both the black and white worlds, which was why he had pursued his graduate studies in the legally integrated North. At Crozer he graduated as valedictorian, and at Boston University he proved himself to be among the brightest of his class. Yet his greatest gift lay not in originality of thought but in synthesis, application, and especially presentation of thought—or in other words, preaching. While engaging at the university every tradition of Western thought, he also perfected his preaching style. He and his friends read every volume of *Best Sermons of the Year*. He came to understand that preachers were measured more in the hearing than in the reading. He mastered the basic sermon models passed down through the centuries or recently developed by preachers before him: the Ladder (climb through increasingly complex arguments to a strong conclusion), the Jewel (hold up a single idea from different angles), the Skyrocket (a gripping human interest story leading to a cosmic spiritual lesson), the Surprise Package, the Twin Sermon, and so on. He and other black students jokingly contrasted these with homespun models: the Rabbit in the Bushes (if you feel a stir, keep shooting at it) or Three Points in the Palm of a Hand. While still at the seminary, he already spoke with an authority that made people forget he was only five foot seven, he already realized that audiences liked big words because they made them feel bigger too, and he already criticized preachers who used undignified tactics and said they had to "shout" in order to "get Aunt Jane." King wanted to get Aunt Jane without theatrics. And that was how the congregation at Dexter Baptist preferred it.

By the time he preached there in December 1953, he had also developed a number of sermons that he would use the rest of his life, including "How a Christian Overcomes Evil" (not by the Ulysses model, who stuffed wax into the ears of his sailors and strapped himself to the mast to resist the Sirens, but by the Orpheus model, who simply played better music). This audition sermon would remain another favorite. He explained in his dignified baritone that the complete Christian life included three dimensions: length (caring for one's self by being the best one could be), breadth (caring for others), and height (caring for God). It was an impressive sermon for the occasion, more solemn than later passionate versions. That suited the deacons just fine. They offered him the job in early 1954. After some hesitation, King accepted, and immediately became the highest-paid black minister in Montgomery, at $4,200 a year. This was the same year that Ellis Island finally closed, and that *Brown v. Board of Education* was decided by the Supreme Court.

From his trial sermon, or even his first months in Montgomery, the deacons would not have realized that Martin Luther King, Jr., was as inclined as Vernon Johns to devote his Sunday sermons to the sensitive matter of civil rights. As an undergraduate, "Mike" King had been a fun-loving "Morehouse gentleman." His first sermon as resident pastor of Dexter Baptist, on a Sunday in September 1954, was no soul-stirring message of theology or civil rights: instead he reviewed the church's finances and insisted that all members of the congregation register to vote (only 5 percent of blacks in Alabama were registered at the time). Even during the months after his official installation on October 31, the same day Martin Luther formally posted his list of protests against certain Catholic practices, his willingness to speak out was not yet clear. His sermons in those early days were more pastoral than prophetic, as his congregation preferred: "The Answer to a Perplexing Question (Why Is There Evil?)," or "Rediscovering Lost Values." And there was no gospel choir in Dexter Baptist, no call and response, and no spirituals, but instead *Gloria Patri* and organ preludes by Handel, Mendelssohn, and Bach.

In fact, in many ways Reverend King was a typical, educated preacher. Like his father, he could become preoccupied with Sunday attendance, and if out of town would even call home to ask about it. Word on the street said that he was a good but not great preacher, and the church was only half to two-thirds full his first year. But this soon changed. More than his father, who stood up courageously when personally confronted by racism yet did not like to preach on it, and at least as much as Vernon Johns, young Reverend King soon showed his inclination to engage in serious Sunday sermons about race. This was sparked partly by his own unpleasant experiences, but also by the ideas percolating inside him since his days at Boston University, and about ready to explode: these included not only the nonviolence of Mohandas Gandhi but also the ideas of Reinhold Niebuhr.

Niebuhr's *Moral Man and Immoral Society,* published in 1932, argued that individuals might well be persuaded to change through the use of reason, justice, and love. But institutions (nations, corporations, labor unions, colleges, social groups, even churches) were inherently selfish and designed primarily to perpetuate the institution itself. They would therefore not respond to reason, justice, and love, but instead only the ultimate language of institutions—power. Thus, to change institutions, one had to dirty oneself in politics and speak their language. Using power did not necessarily mean using violent force, however, which was where Gandhi's ideas came into play.

These ideas of Niebuhr and Gandhi began to emerge in the Sunday sermons of Reverend King at Dexter Baptist. The congregation, already appreciative of his formal, polished style, now sensed his "controlled heat," and his reputation as a preacher spread. Invited to preach elsewhere, he brought down the house at more than one black church around the U.S., and by November 1955, his one-year anniversary at Dexter, his own church was full every Sunday. Some in the congregation complained that he was too busy and away too much, even though they were proud of him. But his guest preaching was only the start of his fame: it truly skyrocketed beginning in December 1955, when Rosa Parks, a seamstress in Montgomery, was arrested for refusing to move to the back of a local bus, and the local NAACP, with the cooperation of Reverend King, decided to take public, nonviolent action. Such incidents had occurred before, even in twenty-seven cities in the late nineteenth century. But this became the best-known incident, and this was in no small way due to the preaching skills, honed over so many Sundays, by the Reverend Martin Luther King, Jr.

The community meeting that was organized to protest the arrest of Rosa Parks was held at Dexter Baptist, on a Monday night, December 5, 1955—thus not a Sunday, but in fact, the meeting and the civil rights struggle that followed had everything to do with Sunday preaching and church. People on both sides of the segregation issue in the

South were churchgoers, and claimed the stamp of divinity for themselves. Meetings and marches on both sides often began in churches, and included a hymn or two, a sermon, and a prayer—all bulwarks of Sunday services since the ancient Christian world. King's "sermon" on December 5 catapulted him into the wider public light. Ironically, although his own congregation did not practice call and response during his Sunday sermons, the address this night could be nothing other, given the high pitch of emotions—and he did it without a second thought. People in the audience, who vigorously participated in the sermon, spoke later of his transformation before their eyes. "We are here this evening for serious business," he began in a speech that ignited the crowd, setting out the plan for a nonviolent boycott of Montgomery's buses. Now he turned for good from the pastoral to the prophetic, now his life would be about far more than Sunday sermons, and his Sunday sermons would be more than ever about everyday life. *Life* magazine did the first national story on King in 1957, and soon after that he moved to Atlanta, taking over at Ebenezer Baptist—to the sorrow and relief of his congregation at Dexter, who as usual had mixed feelings about their now famous preacher.

By the end of the decade, issues of legal and cultural segregation in the U.S. were still far from being solved, including within churches: feelings about segregation varied in many denominations and congregations, or were even ignored. As a result, people still worshiped mostly apart on Sunday in America.

SACRALIZING SUNDAY SPORT

As *Wide, Wide World* has already made clear, just as prominent as church on the American Sunday marketplace was a seemingly infinite variety of other activities. Any number might be elaborated, many of them resembling activities already seen in Europe, but perhaps most distinctive about the American Sunday was the development of mass spectator sports and entertainments on Sunday—even especially on Sunday—right alongside growing attendance at church.

Some Americans resisted this trend of Sunday sport and refused to join in, on religious grounds. Some joined in because they were indifferent or hostile to religion. But because a steadily growing percentage of Americans belonged to churches through the 1950s, most who joined in considered themselves religious. In one way or another, they therefore went through something like the sacralization process mentioned earlier, applied specifically to sport.

According to Alexis McCrossen, author of the most authoritative study of the American Sunday, Americans began engaging in sport and other recreations on Sunday not so much because they ignored religion as because they brought these activities, once regarded as "worldly," into the realm of the sacred. Sanitized "theater, sports, and music could rightfully join sacred activities such as singing hymns" that day. This did not mean that every aspect of sport had to be made sacred, or every participant made a saint, but simply that sport's potential virtues were detected and emphasized. The process was similar to what occurred to sport in England between the wars, but went a step further. Whereas increasing respectability for sport there made possible at least privately organized activities on Sunday, Sunday sport in the U.S. was long a massive public spectacle, suggesting its even more elevated status.

Sacralization of sport occurred in connection not only with traditional religion but especially with the broader American religion discussed earlier. Just as Americans in the 1950s might attend church on Sunday because it was an American thing to do, so they might engage in or even watch a sport, particularly when the sport took on a specifically American form such as football or baseball, or was accompanied by its good friend, business. Even professional sport could be sacralized in this way, transformed from irreverent diversion or money-grubbing to the mass celebration of such favorite American values as prosperity, individual choice, and healthy competition—all opposed to the dreariness and oppression said to characterize Communism. In this context, watching too was a form of participation.

One early step toward sacralizing sport in general was the sponsoring of athletic teams by American colleges. More than privately organized sporting clubs, colleges enjoyed widespread respectability and were often linked to one religious denomination or another.

A second early step was the establishment of the YMCA in 1866 and its promotion of "Muscular Christianity." Intended to counter the perceived feminization of religion mentioned earlier, the YMCA promoted the desirable moral virtues of sport and physical play, such as improved character or "Christian courtesy," mentioned in 1897 by Luther Gulick, Jr., of the YMCA. "Christ's kingdom should include the athletic world," he declared. Another virtue was promoted by another muscular Christian, Amos Alonzo Stagg, in the prayer he uttered with every pitch he threw in baseball: "Help me do my best."

The biggest virtue sacralized by Muscular Christianity, however, proved to be winning. This was linked closely to the culture of success present in that other sacralized American endeavor, business. Success in either was easily visible and measurable, with a clear outcome—and of course professional sport, one of the great new leisure-time industries, was itself a business. Sport certainly didn't need Christianity to promote the idea of winning, but if winning could become a Christian virtue, then believers could find God in their desire to conquer all foes on the athletic field, even the professional field, long condemned by purists for emphasizing winning and overtraining at the expense of fun and sportsmanship.

This approach gave such people as Stagg, who claimed to love both the ministry and sport, the mental tools he needed to reconcile the two passions: winning was a virtue, not merely an outcome. In fact, more than for "doing his best," Stagg became famous for his unabashed pursuit of winning, even at the expense of other possible Christian or American virtues. He was credited, after all, with inventing the hidden-ball trick in baseball, which many opponents deemed un-Christian. He also was credited, in football, with the famous "Notre Dame shift," a tactic meant to confuse the opponent, which some regarded as at least unsporting and perhaps unfair, though Coach Jesse Harper of Notre Dame said that he got the "shift" from Stagg and Stagg got it from God. With a pedigree like that, who could argue? Stagg was also notorious for irregular recruiting when he coached at the University of Chicago. Most explicitly, he coauthored an early book on football in which he stated that the objective was to win, not merely to engage in pleasure. Stagg simply had a different definition of what it meant to be Christian: it was not about the cultivation of passive virtues but about winning at whatever one did. Didn't Saint Paul speak of winning the race, not merely of trying to win? Christian sportsmen should therefore also want to win. Like his friend James Naismith at the University of Kansas, Stagg held pregame prayers and employed all sorts of Christian language to motivate winning, right into the terminology of various games. Baseball had its sacrifice bunt, and football would eventually have its Four Horsemen and Hail Mary. Critics of baseball pointed out less religious terms, such as "stealing" bases, but these were ignored by those looking for sport's virtue.

The growing appeal of all aspects of Muscular Christianity was reflected in how certain ministers of the early twentieth century used it to attract young men and boys to Jesus, "the captain of the team." It was reflected in the reimaging of Jesus: Luther Gulick foreshadowed Billy Graham by saying that Christ was a perfect man—not only in mind and spirit but also in body, just like an athlete. And it was certainly reflected in the attitude already apparent in Father Lynch of St. Nick's in Chicago toward football, an attitude that preceded him by decades. His model for fusing sport and religion was Notre Dame football, sacralized long before by Father John O'Hara: "Notre Dame football is a new crusade; it kills prejudice and it stimulates faith. . . . It is a red-blooded play of men full of life, full of charity, of men who learn at the foot of the altar what it means to love one another, of men who believe that often play can be offered as a prayer in honor of the Queen of Peace." Such an endeavor was no mere diversion but a way to express virtues of competition, toughness, and especially victory— all meant in a specifically Catholic context, but ultimately fully American too. For Notre Dame engaged American culture on its own turf, the football field, and showed that the Catholic version was best: what was more Catholic yet also more American than that? Or than the manner of measuring success, namely in the *Religious Bulletin* circulated at Notre Dame, which correlated fifty years of football scores with communion statistics? Father Charles Coughlin, the well-known radio priest of the 1930s and 1940s, included Notre Dame football as part of his promotion of such typically American middle-class values as capitalism and visible success.

But Notre Dame and other colleges played their games on Saturday. Just as in England, the growing legitimacy of sport did not lead universally or instantly to Sunday play. Some prominent lovers of sport remained against it. More explicit support for sport on Sunday did, however, emerge during the 1910s and 1920s. This will be further evident in the separate discussions of baseball and football below, but was reflected more generally in such events as the inclusion of a "Sports Bay" in the rising Episcopal cathedral of St. John the Divine in New York. Fashioned in 1928, the bay portrayed scenes in stained glass not only of biblical sport—Jacob wrestling with an angel, David fighting Goliath, Paul racing—but modern sport, to make the link explicit. Soon after the bay's completion, Bishop Henry Potter suggested that sport could be beneficial on any day, through his statement that "mental or physical recreation and exercise" on Sunday was up to the individual. He also labeled the Puritan Blue Laws, outlawing sport on Sunday, as "mistaken views" of "old religion." Another Episcopal bishop of the time, William Thomas Manning, took it further: he wanted happiness and gladness on Sunday, and if that came through tennis, golf, and baseball on that day, then so be it, as long as one attended church in the morning. Sports had "just as important a place in our lives as prayers," God was as interested in games as he was other aspects of life, religion must be in touch with the whole of life, and a "beautiful game of polo was just as pleasing to God as a beautiful service in a cathedral." He added only one qualification: like many English, he did not want commercialized Sunday sport, only active participation in Sunday sport.

Lay believers were coming to similarly positive conclusions. Fred Manfred's *No Fun on Sunday,* a novel set in the late 1920s and early 1930s, illustrates beautifully the process of sacralization and the sorts of tensions that usually led up to it. The young and promising Sherm wants to play professional baseball, but his mother is against it because it means he would have to play on Sundays. He discusses it with his brother John, who warns him that the church would be against it too. Sherm responds, however, with some theology of his own: "the church ain't always right. In the Academy, I studied a little church history, and there I found out that our church fathers changed their minds a couple of times. So that tells you something. It's mostly ordinary human beings like ourselves making up our church rules and not necessarily God. Though our preachers like to tell us that God only talks through them. And not us." He emphasized his reinterpretation of church history with another thought: "I intend to be such a good shortstop, and a moral one to boot, that no one will question whether or not I have the right to play ball on Sunday." Yet Sherm continues to have doubts about playing on Sunday, and this time it is his brother John's turn to do the reconciling between profane and secular: "Listen, bud. The good Lord wouldn't have given you the talent to play baseball the way you do if he hadn't intended that someday you could play in heaven. That God-given talent wasn't given for nothing. He must've had a reason for it."

Here in these exchanges was a typical process that believers went through when they decided to play on Sunday after all: the reality of the Sabbatarian tradition, doubts about its origins and current relevance, and the sense of responsibility to develop one's God-given gifts, which might then turn even Sunday play into a virtue. In the end, Sherm's professional prospects were ruined by a farming accident: some people, he was sure, uncharitably regarded this as God's judgment, to prevent him from playing baseball on Sunday, but Sherm could only think: Then what about all the other Christians God was allowing to play baseball at that very minute, in the big leagues?

He was right about that. A real-life big-league player went through much the same process in the 1950s. Vernon Law grew up in a Mormon household that, like the church generally, didn't approve of Sunday play. When he signed with the Pittsburgh Pirates out of high school in 1948, it was with the understanding that he would not have to pitch on Sunday; as a pitcher, he didn't play every day anyway. This understanding was honored for one year, but then the team's leadership changed, and Law was simply informed that baseball was an everyday job and he would have to be ready if called. When Branch Rickey, who famously refused to attend the ballpark on Sunday as either a player or a general manager, moved over to lead the Pirates, he did not reverse that policy, despite his own views. Law was therefore in a bind.

His church leaders eased it by urging him to play, mostly on the basis that he had signed a contract and should keep his word, suggesting that an even higher value was at stake than avoiding Sunday play. Here was also a chance, on this giant stage, to shine a spotlight on his religion—again, a higher value than not playing on Sunday, and reflecting that watching sport was no passive activity but a form of participation in something big and meaningful. Wasn't that the ideal at a church service too? Law added a final reason: baseball was his job, his livelihood for his family, and thus itself a sacred obligation. And it was an honorable job; sometimes it just happened to occur on Sunday. "There are a lot of farmers, they have to get up and milk those cows on Sunday, they have to take care of their animals. That's their work, that's their livelihood. There are lots of gas stations, lots of guys have to work that pump. And in my particular profession, it was baseball." Vernon Law grew up on a farm, and had he stayed in farming he would have been working on Sunday too.

If Vernon Law's Mormon religion was willing to acknowledge exceptional cases, it usually remained closer than most other churches to the Puritan tradition by discouraging Sunday play. But fewer and fewer churches did so by 1950, and instead preferred to reenvision Sunday in such a way that it might include sport. By this time, the National Council of Churches, made up of thirty-four Protestant denominations plus Orthodox Christians, felt that strict Sunday observance—including the absence of play—was less important to one's Christianity than many other factors. And most Americans in general by this time, most of them religious, did not include Sunday closing laws, or anti-recreation laws on Sunday, among their chief wishes. The National Council therefore ceased taking a stand on Sunday laws, and left to individuals the decision about what to do. Here was a modern expression of one ancient Christian approach to Sunday: namely, that to the Christian every day was holy. Whether something was right or wrong depended not on the day of the week but on the deed and the context, and these were best left to individuals to decide.

Baptists, Episcopalians, and Lutherans, all of whom had at least known some Sabbatarian strains in America, were similarly inclined to allow more individual discretion on Sunday. Some Methodists (not J. C. Penney, whose stores were open) worried about the day's commercialization. Presbyterians too, who in early America were one of the many faiths to vigorously "safeguard the Sabbath," now altered their views. Even the stricter Southern Presbyterian Assembly, while expressing displeasure around 1950 with the spread of a "continental Sabbath," admitted that "a large section of the lay mind" wondered whether New Testament and early church practices and even traditional Presbyterian habits regarding Sunday ought to be transposed to a modern context. If they were not, the old strict Sabbath might actually work against modern Christianity. The Assembly urged Presbyterians to use the Sabbath as a day of worship, instruction, rededication, family activities (including games and refreshments), rest, and Christian service—all quite traditional, but to be determined by individuals, not the church. Moreover, the Assembly lamented the "dull and dreary series of do's and don'ts" likely to emerge in attempts to legislate Sunday. It wanted a decent Sunday, but no strict rules dampening it. Finally, the Assembly concluded in 1960 that it would no longer ask states to censor this or that on Sunday, but simply support voluntary Sabbath observance as more genuinely Christian than forced observance.

Churches that still promoted a stricter Sunday accused Presbyterians of being lax, and concluded that this simply reflected the decline of commitment in America to religion and churches. But Presbyterians themselves saw their position simply as a decline of commitment to the old Sunday, not to Christianity: like ancient and medieval and early modern Christians, they were reshaping their faith and expressing it in the context in which they lived. More liberal-minded Unitarians of Boston in 1958 went so far as to try a daring experiment: they moved their traditional Sunday meeting to Thursday night. For although they desired congregational worship, they regarded family and individual recreational time—invariably focused on Sunday as ever—as even more sacred, so why shouldn't the congregation worship on another day and leave Sunday to families?

Such statements did not explicitly promote Sunday sport, of course, but through their general questioning of old habits and through leaving choices up to individual discretion, they certainly allowed it. Stronger if still implicit support for Sunday sport from obviously religious circles came from Billy Graham, through his endorsement of so many well-known (and thus winning) professional athletes who were Christians. His wife Ruth had told him when they were dating, "Saturday nights I dedicate to prayer and study, in preparation for the Lord's day." Yet Billy Graham made these Christian athletes, who inevitably played on Sunday before large crowds, an important part of his crusades, and they regularly spoke on topics such as "Who's coaching you in the great game of life?" Thus he helped to sacralize professional sports.

Graham was enthusiastic about sports himself, especially golf. He liked to discourse, along fairways at fine country clubs, to "ball-bearing manufacturers and textile-mill magnates on the exhilaration of prolonged Bible study." He once exclaimed about heaven, "Boy I sure hope they have a golf course up there!" He also advocated a more "manly" image of Jesus, asking a producer of a film about Jesus to please "get a man with great strength in his face. I have seen so many pictures of Jesus as a weakling that I am sick of it. He was no sissy and he was no weakling . . . He must have been straight, strong, big, handsome, tender, gracious, and courteous. . . . He was a real he-man, talk about your football players. . . . He was physically the strongest man on earth." This astonished such listeners as Alistair Cooke, the well-known English broadcaster working in the U.S., who could not recall any such descriptions of Christ in the Bible—only the Isaiah texts that portrayed Christ as a tender plant, a root out of dry ground, with "no form nor comeliness that we should desire him," and a man acquainted with grief. But despite Isaiah, Graham's depiction certainly meshed with the more positive image of sport among believers and as embodied by professional Christian athletes.

Also crucial in the 1950s, especially among those of more evangelical leanings, was the birth of the Fellowship of Christian Athletes in 1955, which extended to thousands of amateurs but starred professional athletes who especially played on Sunday. Brooklyn Dodger Carl Erskine spoke at the opening banquet; like Jesus, he used parables taken from his immediate world, and so they were drawn from sport rather than agriculture. His young son inadvertently but tellingly prayed on another occasion, "In Jesus' name we play." The Fellowship's creed was "My sweat is an offering to my master, my soreness is a sacrifice to my savior," and the Bible was "God's Playbook." Erskine himself admitted that a sports locker room was still no place for the uninitiated, and hardly full of piety, but as in the general population, many athletes were Christians after all. Prominent members of the FCA included the Olympic pole-vaulter Bob Richards, the NFL quarterback Otto Graham, the college football coach Bud Wilkinson, the Yankees' announcer Red Barber, the baseball owner Branch Rickey, and of course, the fiercely Christian Amos Alonzo Stagg. Most of them, even the ballpark-avoiding Rickey, were connected to Sunday play, but all believed that sport could be a vehicle for Christianity, on whatever day it was played.

Such attitudes toward sport were not unique to America. Others, including the English, had before the 1950s already stressed manliness, male bonding, the need to vent aggression in healthy ways, the relationship between sport and character, the idea that Jesus was perfect in body and spirit, the superiority of physical to intellectual development, and patriotism through sport. But now they took on a particular American twist, by holding up *American* sport and *American* values as a sort of religion in their own right, valid on any day. In fact, says Charles Prebish in an article called "Heavenly Father, Divine Goalie," a religion of sport had certain advantages over traditional religion. The latter knows internal patience, cheek-turning, long-suffering, and other immeasurable and often invisible virtues, while sport holds up visible success, drama, and the simplicity of a clear winner versus a loser—even good versus evil. In other words, sport was about more than sport; it was a conveyor of appealing American values, desirable even on Sunday. In fact, what better day to hold up a society's dearest values than its holy days? Certainly this was evident in the two most popular American games of the 1950s, football and baseball.

THE SUNDAY GAME

If football and baseball were the two biggest spectator sports in America during the 1950s (with basketball still a distant third), what was it that made them so, and why especially on Sunday—*the* day for professional football, and the most heavily attended day for professional baseball?

Part of it was simply that they were American. The U.S. Immigration Service tried to prove one immigrant-alien was a Communist by having a witness testify that the alien liked soccer more than baseball. "What an insult to the country," said the witness. He would have likewise been insulted by the visiting Frenchman who found baseball to be a game played by "ridiculously attired young men" running "like lunatics" and whose meaning "escapes the profane." The French visitor had no kinder words for American football, one of the "most brutal and ugliest sports in existence." Naturally, foreigners in any country might find native sport puzzling, but their comments do cause one to pause and consider why a nation's sports take the forms they do. In other words, what about football and baseball spoke to Americans and their values and thus made each sport popular enough to be favorites on Sunday too?

Ted Morgan theorized in 1993, in *The Settling of North America,* that American life and sport were shaped by two contrasting concepts: frontier and hinterland. Football is a frontier game, because it has to do with the conquest of territory. The aim is to invade the other team's land and settle there until the goal line is crossed. Thus football is a metaphor for land hunger, a "ritualized reenactment of the westward movement" back to colonial times. The field is marked off like a conquered wilderness, divided into "ranges and townships and sections," on which players act out the conquest of the frontier. Baseball, on the other hand, is a game of the hinterland, "gentrified from the start." There is no need for an "unnecessary roughness" penalty, because baseball is a game of the civilized, established for "men of high taste." There is no fighting over territory, "because the convention has been established that the teams will take turns occupying the same field." There is no "time anxiety," whereas in football the clock made it a game of seconds, much like life and death on the frontier. In baseball, games are called on account of rain, while football is still mostly played in frontier weather conditions of rain, snow, and ice. Both the frontier and the hinterland appeal to Americans. Yet Morgan speculated that because football harkened back to the more "epic qualities of the frontier" (or as scholars say about the appeal of ancient games, more obviously involved a "cosmic struggle"), it ultimately became most popular; something deep in the American psyche admired that original frontier spirit even more.

Certainly all metaphors can be taken too far, and the triumph of American football over baseball took many decades, but Morgan's ideas offer some insight into why these sports have not only been popular but generally acceptable as mass spectacles on Sunday: because they give tangible form to such American spiritual values as know-how, craftiness, toughness, subtlety, refinement, and more. They were expressions of American life, not merely games, even for those "merely" watching. Certainly other sports, including cricket and European football, could make similar claims. But the point here is the peculiarly American forms and their desirability to huge audiences, even on Sunday.

Titles of some recent football books reflect an apparent paradox between the game and religion, including *Violent Sundays, Violence Every Sunday, Mean on Sunday,* and *Sunday Mayhem.* Violent football might easily enough be reconciled with the rough frontier, but how with Sunday and religion?

In fact, football had a difficult start in the U.S. for this very reason. The difficulty peaked in the 1905 college season, which left 18 players dead and 159 with serious injuries. Reformers called for the game's banishment, but it was saved thanks to intervention by Theodore Roosevelt and the Military Academy at West Point, who suggested that the sport merely modify its rules. Once that was done, college football became an enormous success. But again, colleges played their games on Saturday: the Sunday question would be left to the professionals.

Some claim that the first professional football game occurred in 1895, in Latrobe, Pennsylvania. Whatever the case, a professional league certainly emerged in 1902: it faded quickly because its games were played on Saturday and could not compete with more popular college football. A new professional league began in Canton, Ohio, in November 1915—this time, its games were on Sunday. The foremost reason for this was the continued and overwhelming popularity of Saturday's college football. A second reason was that professional football developed strongest in medium-sized steel and coal towns of Pennsylvania and Ohio, where Catholics and more liberal Protestants dominated the population, where fewer Blue Laws therefore existed against Sunday play, and where the players were millworkers, with their only full day off being Sunday. Sunday was the best day for not only the players but also for fellow workers who came to watch.

This pattern did not transfer well to the South, where Sunday had become, ironically—given the region's colonial reputation for laxity—somewhat stricter than elsewhere: among Baptists, Southern Methodists, and Christian Evangelicals, Sunday play did not sit well, and until the 1960s pro teams that emerged in the South were always on its edges,

such as Washington, D.C., Texas, Kansas, and Missouri. The northern
states of Massachusetts, Pennsylvania, and New York also had Blue
Laws, especially against Sunday commerce (and therefore admission
fees), into the 1920s. Hence, the Midwest was the heartland of Sunday
and professional football.

There it was already clear by 1915 that blue-collar workers were
willing to pay fifty cents to one dollar on Sunday to watch pro teams
play, especially when they featured such stars as Jim Thorpe. The
league's full emergence was delayed by World War I, but soon afterward it was vibrant again and the National Football League was officially born in 1921. In Massillon, Canton, Detroit, Dayton, and Toledo,
pro football on Sunday took strong root, as the game seemed more accessible than college football to the local populations: tickets were
cheaper and the players usually came from their own social class,
whereas college players tended to be middle class. Across the country,
however, professional Sunday football still ranked behind college football, professional baseball, and even high school football in popularity.

This was largely because pro football was seen to go against certain
ethics accepted and promoted in collegiate and YMCA-type sports:
namely, fair play and the gentleman's ethic. These were hardly universal in college sports, as Amos Alonzo Stagg demonstrated convincingly, but they were seen as the ideal. Pro football, in contrast, *looked*
dirtier, and the "pro" element made the goal to win offensively blatant
to some: there was still a prejudice against athletes "selling their loyal-
ties," winning at all costs, or engaging in excessive training and commercialism. Where was the pure joy of the sport and the devotion to a
worthy institution of higher learning? Pro sports were also believed to
be more susceptible to gambling, and in fact almost every newspaper
account of early pro games mentioned the heavy betting that went on.

That football pros played on Sunday was another objection, at least
for many outside the Midwest. By World War I a main reason college
players used fake names when moonlighting with the pros was not
merely to stay eligible for college games but because of opposition by
certain factory owners and the college players' parents to Sunday football. In many places, there was organized religious opposition to Sunday football, particularly where there were Calvinist or evangelical
churches in town. But unchurched people didn't mind Sunday games,

and neither did more and more churched players and fans, right along-side Father Lynch in Chicago. Indeed, professional teams sought out many Notre Dame players, and plenty of priests sponsored church and community teams that later became professional organizations. Such people did not think of themselves as less religious for organizing Sunday football; they simply had a different notion of Sunday and of the relationship between religion and sports. To them it was no more dangerous—probably even less so—than the relationship between religion and learning. More Sunday play wasn't merely philosophical of course: the continued growth of businesses that catered to leisure also mattered greatly. But re-envisioning the sport certainly played a role.

The first Sunday arguments over professional football occurred in 1919 in New York, when the New York Giants announced plans to organize a team at the Polo Grounds. Because a ban on Sunday baseball in New York had just been lifted, football organizers assumed that this would apply to their sport as well. They were wrong: The city refused permission for Sunday football. The reasons were not clear, but the fact that professional baseball was held in higher esteem than professional football likely figured in. Only in 1925 did the New York football Giants receive permission to play on Sunday in the new NFL.

Even by then, and for many decades to come, the professional game clearly lagged behind the college game. In the early 1920s, average attendance at a Sunday NFL game was 3,000, one-tenth to one-twentieth that of a major college game. This changed in 1925 with the appearance in the NFL of Red Grange, already famous from his college days. Around 70,000 came one Sunday that year to the Polo Grounds to watch his Chicago Bears play the Giants.

But the first signs of consistent prosperity in the league emerged only in the 1940s, when attendance averaged more than 25,000—still far behind college football but encouraging. The Sunday league was also helped by the entry of so many college graduates after 1935, most of whom still worked at other careers in the off-season to make ends meet. On the 1941 Bears, there were future surgeons, dentists, and lawyers. Still, it was said that if a person played professionally, it hurt his chances of coaching in college, or even high school. Such remained the second-rate status of the game.

During the 1950s this all changed, as the professional game improved its image further and expanded its coverage. The NFL was not only getting closer to challenging its Saturday rival, college football, but was getting ready to take its place as a prominent Sunday afternoon ritual among large numbers of Americans.

The year 1950 itself was a crucial turning point. Rival professional leagues that had popped up were now subjected, rules were changed to make the pro game more interesting, and most important, regular television coverage began, as one team after the other began broadcasting games to regional audiences on Sunday.

Baseball and boxing had been televised regularly for several years already. In fact the first year of NFL television was not as impressive as for these sports. But within years, major and minor league baseball saw their attendance decline, and some blamed it on too much television: Branch Rickey felt that radio had inspired people to get to the ballpark, but now television kept them away. Others blamed reduced attendance on the growth of suburbs, further removed from downtown stadiums, and increased opportunities for other forms of recreation. But pro football got a big boost from television, as average attendance grew to 40,000 by 1960.

Televised professional football also changed general Sunday daytime programming. Ordinarily, Sunday mornings and afternoons were filled with the networks' required quotas of public-service broadcasts, and critics spoke of the Sunday afternoon "ghetto"—apparently *Wide, Wide World* wasn't terribly popular. Networks figured they had nothing to lose by trying football, and they were more right than they could ever have dreamed. By 1954 more than 90 percent of American homes had a television, and some 37 percent of them were tuned to Sunday afternoon football. In 1956 the first nationally televised games began, thanks to a unified contract with CBS for all twelve teams, raising the game's profile even higher. Two to three cameras were used for each game, and telecasting was in black and white.

It was enough to create even more fans for the game, including women and novices who now understood it better, and to establish Sunday afternoon football as a ritual in many homes. The single game usually credited with boosting interest most, and helping to launch professional football's ascent as American's favorite sport, was the 1958 championship game at Yankee Stadium between the New York Giants and the Baltimore Colts. It was the first sudden-death finish in league history: ordinarily, tie games were simply left that way, and when time expired with the score even, many viewers that Sunday turned off their sets, thinking the game was over. But most of the record 10.8 million viewers saw the Colts finally win, and along with the 64,000 at the game they were "limp" with exhaustion afterward, according to the *New York Times*. They were also hooked: for the rest of the decade and beyond, pro football dominated Sunday afternoon programming, at least during the twelve Sundays of the NFL season.

Again, this occurred in a context that did not necessarily ignore traditional religion, either for players or for fans. Ray Nitschke, regarded as one of the toughest players in the NFL, said that "some people couldn't understand how a group of rough football players could pray together before a game. But we did, and I think this really brought the team closer together." Johnny Unitas, the Colts' quarterback in the famous overtime game, went to early Mass on game days, then went home for orange juice, eggs, sausage, coffee cake, and the Sunday paper, and babysat the younger kids while his wife and older children went to the next Mass. When they returned, he went to the stadium.

Vince Lombardi was an even better example of mixing Sunday religion and Sunday football—a more enthusiastic layman's version of Father Lynch at St. Nick's, only a few hours away. Lombardi grew up with the "trinity" of family, religion, and sports. Football in particular was so intertwined with his religious and patriotic sensibilities that there was no need for a second thought about Sunday play: the game represented his highest values, and what better day to express those? If religion was part of his daily life and even manifested in his sport, then why shouldn't that sport be part of his Sunday life?

Lombardi was Catholic, and Catholics generally were more comfortable with Sunday play, as already suggested, but this did not mean that the sentiment was universal. Growing up in New York, Lombardi was part of a Sunday afternoon sandlot team, yet at his high school, Cathedral, sports were looked down upon, especially football, as crass on any day. According to the *Cathedral Annual* of 1931, football brought many undesirable physical, moral, and intellectual results. Indeed football "indubitably leads to the adoption of questionable ethical practices and unsportsmanlike conduct. It sanctions the evasion of rules, trickery, undesirable recruiting practices bordering on professionalism, and a lack of courtesy." Despite this context, Lombardi would find his niche in football anyway, beginning as a player at Fordham University, a Catholic school, where he was part of the "seven blocks of granite" who made up the line.

The Jesuits ran Fordham, and they had no small influence on Lombardi's philosophy toward sport. Part of this was their famous emphasis on pragmatism and their favoring of means above ends. If football, for instance, could be a means of teaching lasting truths, then the day on which it was played might hardly matter. Moreover, Jesuits believed in striving for perfection, and that perfection was attainable by anyone who had enough desire and zeal. Finally the Jesuits believed in hierarchical order, so that although free to pursue a chosen path, one also owed submission to superiors. Lombardi took all these lessons to football—indeed, he came to see it as the ideal arena for demonstrating them. Football was therefore a religious act to Lombardi, not a diversion.

When he finished playing at Fordham and began coaching at northern New Jersey's St. Cecilia High School, or "Saints" as everyone called it, his team always played on Sunday—mostly because Saints had no stadium, and Sunday was the only day the stadium of the public high school was free. But clearly this was unimportant to Lombardi, and the benefits of playing on Sunday were obviously superior to any benefits of not playing. Unlike at his own high school, football and religion "were conjoined in every manner possible" at Saints. And although religion required one to play fairly, Lombardi's vision of football and religion also required one to win. He equated loss with weakness and sin. This was how he could justify saying in later years, without apology, that "nothing stoked the fire to win like hatred of the opponent." It was quite a transformation of the Sermon on the Mount: certainly, hating was not desirable, but if it helped one to attain an even more desirable goal, then so be it. Lombardi was so keen on this point already that he would not talk to a rival high school coach if he saw him at Sunday Mass on game day.

At Saints, the game and the preparations for it even resembled holy rites. After players put on their pads and uniforms, Lombardi led them from the basement locker room and up the marble steps of the school's church, "their cleats clickity-clacking" all the way, where they attended Mass and received communion. They knelt in a semicircle around the altar to pray. Upon emerging from the church, the team was greeted by nuns, who gave them "sacramentals," such as little bleeding hearts of red felt, to stuff inside their pants and helmets; Lombardi always put his under the sock of his left shoe. Then the team climbed on the back of an oil truck and rode to the stadium. On the way they sang their fight song, "On Cecilia," the tune lifted from "On Wisconsin." Then a final ritual before the kickoff: Lombardi gathered the players for the Lord's Prayer. Thousands were in the stands, as football was a main source of Sunday entertainment for the people of northern New Jersey during the 1940s.

After coaching at Saints, Lombardi worked for a time at Fordham, but moved to the NFL in 1954 with the New York Giants, where his attitudes toward football and religion (and Sunday sport) were made more apparent than ever. He coached offense while another famously Christian coach, the Southern Protestant Tom Landry, handled the defense. In New York too, Lombardi insisted, if less explicitly than at Saints, that football and religion were interchangeable in their promotion of sacrifice, discipline, obedience, and more. He said so even more forcefully when he became a head coach at Green Bay in 1959, in the heart of NFL country. He was especially close to members of the Catholic Norbertine monks in town, who ran schools, a parish church, and a college, and like Lombardi promoted an active view of religion. As enthusiastic as he was about them, they in turn were fanatical about Packer football. Priests of all stripes were his special guests at games and practices, and he let them in even when reporters had been kicked out of a "secret" practice. Lombardi was also good about getting tickets for nuns, who used up a large part of his fifty-seat allotment. Before games, Lombardi attended Sunday Mass close to his home, at St. Matthew's. He sat only six rows back, but the priest tried not to look Lombardi's way because the coach's visage was so intense. After games, he socialized with priests and other friends in his own basement recreation room, with lots of talk (especially if the Packers had won), whiskey, beer, scotch, chips, and hot crabmeat dip. Later on Sunday evening, Lombardi liked to eat at a restaurant, usually seated next to a priest, and grew quieter by the minute, for he was already thinking about next Sunday's game. In fact, he said, Sunday night was his worst time of the week.

The people of midwestern Green Bay merged football and religion as easily and naturally as Lombardi or the Norbertine monks. It was one of the most densely Catholic regions of the U.S., its ten Catholic elementary schools and two high schools were full, and there were ten different Catholic churches in the small city, with ninety-four Masses on Sunday, whether the Packers were playing or not. In other words, their love for Sunday football did not preclude their religious devotion in the least.

Likewise, fewer and fewer athletes expressed discomfort about playing on Sunday, including those from the South. Most religiously minded athletes and coaches with aspirations to the professional game—whether Catholic like Lombardi or Protestant like Landry or Fran Tarkenton later on—followed the Lombardi model, either by simply accepting the necessity of the Sunday schedule, or more positively in believing that the possible virtues to be gained from playing outweighed the virtues of not playing. A man presenting himself as a sort of freelance chaplain to the New York Giants in the 1960s told their coach, Allie Sherman, that the players were "worthy American heroes" and that "each man needs to know the good Lord's guidance, each man should be blessed by it on Sunday morning." The team already had a Catholic chaplain, and Catholic players went to Mass on Sunday morning before games anyway, but this man wished to lead a nondenominational service for other players. He showed Sherman a file of newspaper clippings and photos of himself with members of the Baltimore Colts. "These boys are undefeated," he reminded Coach Sherman, "in a tone not quite so bold as to suggest he was responsible for that, yet not so humble as to exclude the possibility." Sherman consulted his quarterback, Fran Tarkenton: "Maybe it's a good thing. All those Southern boys—don't you think they might get something out of it?" Tarkenton wasn't necessarily against, but he worried that nobody knew the man: preachers down South "could get a man rolling his eyes and climbing the walls if they wanted to," and

they didn't need that before a game. And so in the end the team po-
litely told the man no.

Certainly the most basic thing about the pro game was the "pro":
these players were paid. But that didn't stop some of them, or observers, from treating it in reverential terms. One of the Giants' players, Aaron Thomas, sat with his head in his hands before a game, as if
praying. He also told one writer, "I love the way the pro game is laid
out, the beauty of the passing techniques. I tell you, I leave a huddle
when my pass play has been called and I'm so full of that great feeling
of anticipation that I can barely keep it all to myself." Before a game,
there was very little noise or movement in the locker room, causing the
same writer to be choked up by "the purity of the drama." When the
Giants won a game, their permanent chaplain, Father Benedict Dudley,
led them in a "victory prayer," with everyone down on one knee. And
then they all said the Lord's Prayer together. It was only a game, everyone said, but "to these guys and their fans it was the essence of their
lives." It was the cosmic struggle, it was the ancient Greeks appeasing
and worshiping their gods precisely by engaging in sport on their holi-
est days, it was more than diversion, it was more than the everyday,
and thus it was perfectly worthy of Sunday.

THE AMERICAN GAME ON SUNDAY

Although professional baseball early on played most of its games on
days other than Sunday, Sunday was soon the most popular day. Naturally it didn't take long for the Sunday question to arise here as well.

From their beginning in the early 1870s, pro baseball teams played
on Sunday for the usual reason that it was the one free day for most
fans. But the new National League, founded in 1877, banned Sunday
play, as part of a campaign to make baseball respectable among the
middle classes, who tended to be more Sabbatarian than working
classes. Midwestern Cincinnati, a heavily German town used to a fun-
loving Sunday, was expelled from the league in 1880 for scheduling
games on Sunday, but this only contributed to the foundation of a new
league, the American Association, in 1882, which allowed Sunday
play. Some minor league professional teams played on Sunday, some
did not, depending on the severity and enforcement of local Blue Laws.

Even more amateurs played baseball on Sunday, because most Blue Laws focused on commerce, not play. The only issue with regard to amateurs, then, was whether baseball per se was suited to Sunday. "Social gospelers," famous for their broad views of religion and their social outreach, had no problem with it, arguing that strict Sabbatarianism was driving many working-class men away from church. And besides, if the rich and well-to-do could enjoy themselves every day of the week, when most people were working, then why shouldn't those "most people" enjoy playing or even watching a game on their one day free from work? Better to incorporate sport into Sunday than to drive people from church by excluding sport, better for them to get rest and recreation through sport than through drinking or gambling.

A. G. Spalding responded to those who wished to restrict even amateur Sunday baseball, "I think baseball is the best exercise in the world for a youth," and Sunday was their only day to try. Moreover, he believed that of all the games they could play, it built best the assorted virtues that made up American individuality, which he named as courage, confidence, combativeness, dash, discipline, determination, energy, eagerness, enthusiasm, pluck, persistency, performance, spirit, sagacity, success, vim, vigor, and virility. The character Sherm mentioned earlier put it more mystically—"It's just that it's such a joy to play the great game of baseball. It's the most glad be-all and the end-all of all things on earth that a man can do. . . . You can throw your whole soul into it and it still isn't enough. There's always more yet to do to make it perfect. It's like kittens playing to learn how to mouse better. Oh, it's great."

Many Americans felt the same way and thus found no objection to its being played on Sunday, even professionally. By the mid-1880s the professional game was wildly popular, most of all on Sunday, when crowds might number five to ten thousand, at least in areas where Sunday play was allowed. Chicago's minor league teams tended to set their attendance records on Sundays. When the American Association and National League merged in 1891, the popularity of Sunday games was such that the new league decided to let each team decide its own Sunday policy, according to local Blue Laws and taste. Some teams were afraid to lose the middle-class crowd, but cities with large populations of recent immigrants went ahead anyway with Sunday play, including nearly every midwestern team. Sabbatarians argued against Sunday play on the grounds of protecting against noise, defending public morals, and safeguarding religious beliefs. Norman Bingham countered Spalding's praise of Sunday baseball by discounting the sport altogether, on any day: it was overemphasized, it promoted trickery and dishonesty, and it was to blame for a decline in morality among youth. Others emphasized the greed of the professional game, and the low reputations, modest social origins, drinking habits, and generally meager wages of the players (all sure signs of immorality). R. J. Floody wrote in 1906 that Sunday baseball "neither instructs, edifies nor ennobles. It interferes with the rest and quiet of religious people," not to mention pulling children away from Sunday school. And the popular evangelist Sam Jones of Georgia fumed, "There is not a more corrupting thing this side of Hell than baseball."

One of the early figures who helped to make the game of baseball socially acceptable, although not Sunday play (for he never played then), was the fortuitously named Billy Sunday. Raised in an orphanage, Billy's athletic prowess was clear early on. One of the fastest men in America, he took that speed to baseball and made the professional ranks. There he saw firsthand why the sport had a bad image, for many players were indeed rowdy, hardened drinkers and womanizers, and the game itself not yet the gentrified pastime envisioned by Ted Morgan. Instead it featured frequent fights and relentless verbal abuse of opponents by players and fans. Billy was not as hardened as some, but in 1886 he underwent a religious conversion—ironically, while out drinking with fellow players in Chicago.

Soon he joined YMCA Bible Study and attended evening and morning services on Sundays: he had time enough because his team, the Chicago White Sox, didn't yet play on Sunday. Sportswriters loved him because he was different: an exciting player who was involved at church and did volunteer work. Gradually, religion became more important to him than baseball, and he began to preach—so much that people were sure he would give up the game and preach full time, especially when the Sunday question inevitably arose. In 1891 the Cincinnati Reds offered him $5,000 a year to play for them—but the Reds played on Sunday, and Billy was leaning toward quitting baseball anyway.

He did quit, and took a full-time job with the YMCA, at one-fifth his baseball salary, and went on to attain even greater fame as an evangelist preacher, paving the way for such figures as Billy Graham. He preached dramatically on all the favorite evangelical themes: the power of prayer, the inerrancy of the Bible, the eradication of vice, standing up for America, morality, home and family, motherhood, prayer, the evils of evolution and drink and the flesh and certain amusements and alien political philosophies, and the need to keep the Sabbath. But unlike some evangelists who preached against baseball, Billy punctuated his message with his sporting past. He boxed the devil, and like a baseball player taunted him, cursed him, spat at him, and called him names. In this physical approach to preaching, he would have pleased Sam Jones, who said that religions were "turning into crocheting societies for women." Not a sermon of Billy Sunday. He hoped to reach unchurched men by using baseball slang and gestures, winding up like a pitcher to throw a fastball at the devil, stepping up to the plate for Jesus, running across the stage and sliding headfirst along the floor, his hand groping for the base, imitating a sinner coming home to be saved. Once he yanked a slat from the pulpit, held it like a bat, and said he was going to get a hit off the devil. "Oh Lord, there are a lot of people who step up to the collection plate at church and fan . . . Oh Lord, give us some coaches out at this Tabernacle so that people can be brought home to you. Some of them are dying on second and third base, Lord, and we don't want that." At all times he exuded an aggressive, militant masculinity—muscular Christianity at the pulpit rather than in the sports arena. Teddy Roosevelt and the biblical David were Sunday's models, and his favorite hymn was "Onward Christian Soldiers." Like Luther Gulick, Sunday said Christ was tough and "not a sissified sort of galoot that let everybody make a doormat out of him."

Such praise of sport did not wholly sanctify baseball. The psychologist Mary Brownell concluded in a 1925 study that there was nothing inherently good or bad in baseball (or any other sport) that would cause one necessarily to reap moral success or failure. One who engaged in sport could just as well be made a cheat as a moral paragon. Baseball produced not only Christy Mathewson, a famed pitcher who graduated from college and would not play on Sunday, but also Grover Cleveland Alexander, who in addition to pitching was a hard-living, notorious drinker: in fact, each man won exactly the same number of games, suggesting that their moral choices had little to do with their skill at baseball. Jackie Robinson would later brutally say, "Baseball, like some other sports, poses as a sacred institution dedicated to the public good, but it is actually a big, selfish business with a ruthlessness that many big businesses would never think of displaying."

Still, the positive rhetoric and image of baseball promoted by Billy Sunday and Christy Mathewson had its effect. If these two themselves would not play on Sunday (Mathewson would later manage on that day), they helped to make the game respectable, and helped especially Protestant believers to consider Sunday baseball, even the professional version, as a possibly suitable activity. By 1906 most major league teams were playing on Sundays, usually less so in the East and South, and one third of the total attendance in a given major league city came on Sundays, estimated the *New York Times,* followed by Saturday. And plenty of preachers after 1900 were not opposed at all. An Episcopal priest in Chicago, identified by the *Chicago Tribune* in 1906 as a "shining light" of the church, had a son who was a baseball reporter, and the family's dinner conversations, even on Sunday, focused on local teams. This priest would not himself attend games on Sunday, but he adjusted the start of church services during the postseason so that his flock might arrive at the stadium in time for the first pitch. And within a minute of his last "Amen" on Sunday, he was on his new telephone asking his son the score. Rabbi Charles Fleischer spoke up for Sabbath baseball, played or watched, in 1911, arguing that it was irrational and short-sighted to expect people to give the whole of their free day to worship or mere abstinence from toil; employees were "grounded six days a week," and had few chances to witness a game "on which their hearts are set . . . Six days a week they toil over littered desks or over heartless machines, dreaming of the game, longing for an opportunity to witness one, and then when the day of freedom comes the game is closed through mere narrow prejudice." Liberal Protestants argued that baseball taught important lessons essential to Christian moral development—something like Sunday school—including virility and manliness.

During World War I and beyond, including after the crisis of the Black Sox scandal in 1919, baseball continued to work on its image, sponsoring Sunday concerts and especially tying baseball to patriotism: playing baseball on any day was now an expression of one's Americanism, and that could trump even traditional religious objections to Sunday play. "The Star-Spangled Banner" was first played at a baseball game in 1918, and rapidly caught on—a practice that surely contributed to its being declared the U.S. national anthem in 1931. Partly because of these sentiments, the last laws against Sunday play faded as well. The New York Giants and Cincinnati Reds (managed by Christy Mathewson) agreed to stage a Sunday game in New York in 1917, as a test of the city's Blue Laws against Sunday baseball. A lawsuit followed, but the teams were upheld in their decision, mainly because the game was meant to support the war effort. Even if patriotism would not work on Eric Liddel during the 1924 Olympics, it worked well on many Americans. A related reason given in favor of Sunday baseball was that baseball helped Americanize so many immigrants, more of whom could attend games on Sunday than otherwise. The last teams without Sunday baseball were the Boston Red Sox (until 1929), Philadelphia Athletics (until 1933), and Pittsburgh Pirates (until 1934).

By 1950 there was little thought among players or fans about Sunday baseball, which was at least as American, and perhaps still more so, than Sunday football. Sunday remained the day of highest attendance for baseball, and the day (along with American holidays) for double-headers.

This was certainly evident with one of the most popular teams of the 1950s, the Brooklyn Dodgers. Around 3 million people lived in Brooklyn by now, which would have made it the second largest metropolis in the United States if it were not already part of New York City. It had eight colleges, 6,000 acres of parks, 1,200 churches and synagogues, 8,000 factories, and a host of ethnic groups from earlier decades of immigration, including Jews, Irish, Italians, Scandinavians, and Germans, as well as more black Americans than ever. They didn't all get along perfectly. But they were united by a few things: almost all were part of an ethnic minority, almost all were poor, and they all had the Dodgers to make them feel they belonged every day of the week. Baseball in Brooklyn, as in many places, was more than sport, but part of people's very identity. When Walter O'Malley announced in 1956 that the team was moving to Los Angeles, one writer conducted a survey among Brooklynites of the three worst human beings in history: the winners were Hitler, Stalin, and O'Malley.

On any given day during the long season, including Sunday, the Dodgers' game could be heard all over the borough, so that even if one were not at Ebbets Field in person, one could follow things just by walking down the street. The most die-hard listeners were especially in the bars, where the Sunday crowd was large, listening to the game and talking about the team, or debating who was the best New York center fielder: Mantle of the Yankees, Mays of the Giants, or Snider of the Dodgers? Those who cheered the Yankees or Giants in Brooklyn bars were told to go back to where they belonged. One Yankees fan responded, "I got a right to cheer my team, this is a free country." The response: "This ain't no free country, chum, this is Brooklyn."

But the real action was at Ebbets Field itself, where two games were often played on home Sundays. At thirty-two thousand seats, it was smaller than the Giants' Polo Grounds or Yankee Stadium by at least half, and thus everything was easily visible and intimate. One of the team's sponsors was Old Gold cigarettes, and any Dodger who hit a home run was rewarded with a carton of Old Golds, which was slid down the screen behind the catcher from the press box while everyone around yelled "Wooooooo!" There was also the famous Abe Stark sign in right field: "Hit this sign, win a suit!" Gladys Gooding was the organist who played "Three Blind Mice" when the umpires made an unpopular call. The Dodgers Symphony played "The Worms Crawl In" when a strikeout victim from the visiting team walked back to the dugout, with a loud thump on the bass drum when the player sat down, and "Somebody Else Is Taking My Place" when a visiting pitcher was removed. Happy Felton, the fat man in a Dodgers uniform, hosted a popular radio show thirty minutes before the game called *The Knot-Hole Gang*, even though he knew very little about baseball. Tex Rickart, the public-address announcer, was famous for his playful style, with such sentences as "A little boy has been found lost," and "Will the fans along the outfield railing please remove their clothes."

Because of their small stadium, it was important for the Dodgers to draw the largest possible crowds, and thus for decades they had been innovators in trying to broaden the appeal and status of the game. This included attracting women to the stadium with Ladies' Days. Marianne Moore, who won the Pulitzer Prize for poetry, was a famous Brooklyn fan. And despite male domination in bars and at the stadium, Brooklyn's single most famous fan was Hilda Chester, who sold hot dogs and peanuts at Yankee Stadium on the Dodgers' off-days, and wore her unmissable hula skirt and rang her ten-cent cowbell while watching at Ebbets Field on her days off from work.

The young Doris Kearns was another female fan from Brooklyn. Many Sundays she spent at the home of her best friend Elaine, whose extended family always visited that day for a lively get-together. Sunday fun was lacking in Doris's home, where her mother was too sickly to have many people over. But next door on Sunday she could find dinner, music, dancing, canasta, and lively conversation, including about the Dodgers.

Sometimes Sunday might include a game at Ebbets Field itself. Doris was the only girl on her playground who could talk to the boys about baseball, for her early years revolved around the "dual calendars of the Dodgers and the Catholic Church," which more specifically meant Ebbets Field and St. Agnes Parish Church. Before her first live game, in the summer of 1949, she approached the stadium with great anticipation; to her it "looked like a train station in a dream, with dozens of gilded ticket windows." The floor tiles included baseball stitching, and in the center of the ceiling a large chandelier was made of baseball bats. Walking up the tunnel to the stands, her father told her she was "about to see the most beautiful sight in the world"—and in fact the reddish-brown infield, the "impossibly green grass," and the packed stands were just that. They were so close to the field they could hear the players talking to each other, and she seemed to know all the fans around her, including her first-communion teacher Sister Marian, cracking roasted peanuts nearby.

Such feelings of reverence and familiarity nullified any question of whether to attend a game on Sunday. Like Vince Lombardi, she blended easily her feelings for the Dodgers and her Catholic faith. Her spiritual life didn't merely include the Dodgers but featured them, as was the case for many Brooklynites. When first baseman Gil Hodges got off to a terrible start in 1953, the clergy of Brooklyn led prayers for him one Sunday. At Doris's first confession, in preparation for her first communion, she confessed not only how many times she had talked in church, disobeyed her mother, and so on, but also how often she had wished harm to certain talented rivals of the Dodgers. The priest, incredulous, asked for specifics. "I wished harm to Allie Reynolds," she began, the Yankee pitcher. She wanted him to break his arm. "And how often did you make this wish?" "Every night before going to bed, in my prayers." He asked whether there were others. "Oh, yes," and she went on to list more. But instead of urging Doris to stop harboring ill will, the priest provided a suitably Brooklyn answer: how would she feel if all these injuries occurred and then the Dodgers undeservedly won the Pennant and World Series? He assured her that "they will win the World Series someday fairly and squarely," and she would be all the happier for it. That moment finally came in 1955, with the Dodgers' victory over the hated Yankees, in seven games, when all the papers screamed out, "THIS IS NEXT YEAR!" (in reference to the Brooklyn mantra "Wait 'til next year"). A young Lew Alcindor (later Kareem Abdul-Jabbar) yelled happily out of his window, while a devoted fan named Ira Schneider danced on his fire escape with neighbors until one A.M., declaring in the first person plural that typifies "participating" fans, "We had beaten the Yankees and we were better men for it."

Obviously the Dodgers were about more than baseball. They were part of the American struggle, and at least unconsciously the greater cosmic struggle represented by sports—which helps to explain how fans became so upset, excited, angry, and deliriously happy over "just a game." For many, believers or not, these struggles were holy struggles, and that they occurred on Sunday was hardly a problem, certainly not in Catholic and Jewish Brooklyn. In fact, the fifth game of the 1955 series, held on Sunday, drew the largest World Series crowd ever at Ebbets Field, 36,796. Just as from the start, the Sunday crowds were still biggest in baseball.

AMUSEMENTS

Naturally there were other sports besides football and baseball on the vast Sunday marketplace, including golf at some five thousand courses by now, increasingly popular tennis, or the spectator sports of basketball and stock-car racing—especially popular in the Bible-believing South, with pitstop church services on Sunday morning for the crews, prerace invocations, and unapologetic ties to Christianity. Who could doubt the legitimacy of either drivers or spectators in that context? Racing was a chance to profess one's Christian values in specifically Southern form. And naturally there were far more activities than sport alone—in fact so many more that Neil Postman's 1986 book *Amusing Ourselves to Death* certainly applied to the 1950s, with Sunday a leading player.

A popular Sunday destination around cities were amusement parks and nature parks, just as in Europe. Coney Island, perhaps the earliest amusement park in the United States when founded before 1900, was still crowded in the 1950s. As ever, it attracted most of its 35 million annual visitors on Sundays. In the hot summer, more than a million bathers packed the beach that day alone—a scene the French observer H. J. Duteil unsympathetically described in 1953 as follows: "Hundreds of thousands of people, sometimes a million or more, stretch out side by side, in the sun, a spectacle of unforgettable ugliness." Lawrence Ferlinghetti explained that he was not impressed by the Woodstock rock festival in 1969, with its half-million naked people gathered in a small place to have a good time, because that happened every weekend on Coney Island.

Bathhouses lined the beach, and beyond them were the amusements, including roller coasters, Virginia reels, whips, waxworks, sideshows, corn on the cob, cotton candy, taffy, fries, hot dogs, and soft drinks. One could also ride a mechanical horse in old Steeplechase Park, opened in 1897, or on rainy days (as well as sunny) attend the Pavilion of Fun, two acres of nauseating amusement beneath weatherproof steel and glass. Coney Island's popularity, especially on Sunday, hardly pleased everyone, as reflected in the title of one of many memoirs of the place: *Sodom by the Sea*.

Rather tamer were America's nature parks, and once again New

York provided a leading model. Central Park, inspired by European examples, was the first landscaped public park in the U.S. and thus became known as the "People's Park." Although grounded in democratic rhetoric, in fact the park had its origins in the interests of the wealthy: opening between 1858 and 1860, it was meant to promote the "cosmopolitan nature of the city" but also to increase real estate values by compressing the little residential land available on Manhattan Island. The wealthy and middle classes who surrounded the park flocked easily to it on various days. Working-class people and more recent immigrants, often the same, lived farther away and tended to prefer Coney Island for their Sunday outings. But between 1870 and 1900, Central Park became more genuinely democratic, thanks largely to faster and cheaper transportation that brought working-class people to the heart of Manhattan.

The park had Saturday afternoon concerts and skating as well, but Sunday was the busiest day, as it was in London or Paris. The *New York Times* called Sunday in Central Park the "People's Pleasure Ground," the "People's Pleasure Day," the "Holiday of the Poor." One-fourth of all the park's visitors arrived on Sunday, so that the carriages that dominated the week stood out less that day. The new Sunday crowds were large enough that they soon united to protest the famous Sunday-only rule of "Keep Off the Grass" and other Sunday restrictions: the grass was the main draw for urban families, and Sunday their best day to use it. Working-class families brought their baskets of "cheap luxuries," some apples or peaches, homemade pie and sandwiches, and they wanted to sit on grass beneath the trees. Some also wanted to play baseball. The Presbyterians, Reformed, and Methodists of New York wanted Sunday to be a quiet day, with church at the center and the park subdued, but liberals, freethinkers, and immigrants wanted more—especially Germans, who argued for Sunday concerts and boat services in Central Park. The local Sabbath Committee dug in its heels for decades, insisting that although they might follow Europe in landscaping parks, they would not follow Europe's Sunday pastimes. But Sunday restrictions were changed during the 1870s, in response to popular demand, with the advent of boat rentals, pony rides, and concerts. The American Museum of Natural History opened in the late nineteenth century on the edge of the park, and three-quarters of its visitors came on Sunday. By the 1950s these were all old hat, as was Sunday baseball, but at least the baseball backstops were brand new. Other sorts of Sunday recreation, not to mention political demonstrations, followed in the years after.

Although this look at sport and amusement has focused on those of the large, public variety, it is only fair to end the chapter where many Americans ended Sunday as well—at home. A *Good Housekeeping* article in 1955, "What to Do When It Rains on Sunday," explored some of the domestic amusements possible on an American Sunday afternoon. The target audience was women, while the setting was presumably in the suburbs, for its list of suggested activities would for some Americans come perilously close to the numbing pursuits of an English Sunday at home. For others, however, it was quite satisfactory. The list went as follows:

> Go out in the rain and get wet, recapturing the happy childhood delight of sloshing in puddles, not minding if you get splashed.
>
> Plan a perfect crime story.
>
> Do pencil-and-paper things, such as making up a simple crossword puzzle based on family jokes or personal experiences, or a genealogy of your family, or a paper doll with complete wardrobe, or some extra-special Christmas cards by cutting up the cards you received last year and combining them for lavish new effects.
>
> Relax with your records, by settling down to a whole symphony or opera, or your collection of Bing Crosby, or sort your collection into some easy-to-find order.
>
> Check the Sunday paper to see whether any local church offered evensong.
>
> Write a letter to someone you don't know—your congressman, a favorite author, or your local newspaper, possibly calling attention to a billboard that obscures traffic or suggesting photographs of particularly lovely gardens in your neighborhood.

Make something new out of something old, by covering an old wastebasket with bright magazine covers, or cutting out flowers and fruits from pictures and gluing them on a battered tray, or making a "set" of your cream and lotion jars and bottles by painting the tops with nail polish.

Give yourself an all-out, salon-style beauty treatment, including a long, lazy bubble bath, a pedicure, an entirely different hairdo, curling your eyelashes, using eye lotion and mascara, and broadening your brows with an eyebrow pencil.

Wash your dog.

Send off for all the things you've been meaning to—the seed catalogue, the prints from the Metropolitan Museum, the reducing plan, the trial bottle of perfume, the mail-order gadget.

Take down an atlas and open it at random. You'll be amazed at the fun you can have looking at maps. Look up anything you like—the capital of Iceland, or how many airline miles New York is from Paris, or where Hoboken is in relation to Manhattan. See how many towns in Idaho you can name before turning to a map of that state. Guess (and look up) what are the second largest cities in European and Asian countries.

Rearrange your wardrobe, play a game you haven't played in a long time, read a book from your childhood or a classic, spend a nostalgic hour looking at old letters, make some food you've never tried before, or make something to freeze and get that "money in the bank" feeling about having it there whenever you want it, take inventory of your possessions (useful in the event of fire and theft, and gratifying to see how much you're really worth), memorize something for show-off purposes, and so on.

There is much more, but this conveys well enough how some imagined suburban women might like to confront the day.

The list hardly mentions another important suburban activity by now present in the United States as in England: reading the Sunday newspaper. This institution was established for good during the Civil War, when hunger for news was so high that any opposition to Sunday distribution was overwhelmed by sheer demand. When the war ended, Sabbatarians insisted that the papers should cease. Whitlaw Reid of the *New York Tribune* listened, and dropped the Sunday edition. But he noted that even as many people praised and congratulated him for doing so, they then walked off and read someone else's Sunday paper. And so he started the Sunday edition again. By 1890 there were 660 Sunday papers in the U.S., despite the old Puritan dictum against "worldly" reading. In fact, religionists joined in that reading, as Sunday papers learned that they could also serve as important vehicles for churches, and thus gain a greater acceptance.

The American version of the Sunday paper emerged in the 1890s, thanks to the famous wars between William Randolph Hearst and Joseph Pulitzer, who saw the Sunday paper as potentially both news and entertainment for the often homebound populace. Especially Pulitzer established the early Sunday formula: a few pages of the usual news and editorials, but especially spreads devoted to "exaggerated and sensationalized stories involving science or pseudo-science, plus a similar dose of some crime material, plus some pages of stage comments with emphasis on legs, plus a sob sister–type of advice to girls and lovers, the exploitation of some prominent literary or social figure (preferably European), sports, and society, and color supplements."

One early American clergyman called such a Sunday paper "the common sewer of our social life, the cesspool of all shames and scandals." But by the 1950s the Sunday paper was far more respectable, with an entire section usually devoted to religion, and the original formula merely updated in suburban form: comics, syndicated Sunday magazines heavy on celebrities, a local Sunday magazine, features, sections on gardening and women and high arts and sports, and more editorials, sports, and advertising than usual. Many Sunday papers of the 1950s reached over three hundred pages; the *New York Times* stood at six hundred and weighed more than four pounds. Surveys revealed that, despite the advent of television, people might spend one and a half hours with the Sunday paper. Such a vast amount of precious time would not have been spent this way in a purely Continental country on Sunday.

The *Good Housekeeping* article neglected altogether a brand-new and perhaps even more important at-home activity on Sunday: watching television. If the newspaper, then the gramophone, and then the radio were successively the latest attractions of stay-at-home Sundays in previous generations, then television was the rage of the 1950s. Different figures of set ownership exist, but one study cited an increase from 55 percent of households in 1951 to 94 percent by 1958. Moreover, never had any other medium taken up such a large proportion of the average person's leisure hours, including on Sunday. Besides afternoon football and baseball, Sunday evening television was a big favorite among Americans; some of the most popular shows of the week were aired that night. Television made not only the NFL and baseball widespread Sunday rituals, but many other shows besides.

Not everyone was thrilled at the growing popularity of TV. The president of Boston University, Daniel March, famously commented in 1951 that if the television craze continued "we are destined to have a nation of morons." In 1961, Newton Minow, chair of the Federal Communications Commission under President Kennedy, feared that the prophecy was already true. He complimented programmers for their worthwhile programs, but there were too few such shows: sit down and watch one day from beginning to end, he invited, and "I can assure you that you will observe a vast wasteland. You will see a procession of game shows, violence, audience participation shows, formula comedies about totally unbelievable families, blood and thunder, mayhem, violence, sadism, murder, Western badmen, Western goodmen, private eyes, gangsters, more violence and cartoons. And, endlessly, commercials—many screaming, cajoling, and offending. And most of all, boredom. True, you will see a few things you will enjoy. But they will be very, very few." In addition to such general complaints, others raised questions about the suitability of television for Sunday, especially given that evening's focus on light entertainment.

But as with other popular Sunday activities, television shows too were tinged with Americanism—despite, or because of, Senator Joe McCarthy's tainting of Hollywood. Television even helped to give patriotism a more uniform look. Until the mid-1950s, nationwide programming was not possible, because television beams did not bend: the curvature of the earth prevented broadcasts beyond a limited region. But the advent of cable television made national broadcasts a reality, and these transformed American cultural life, even beyond the broadcasting of sporting events, into more standardized ideals and language, whatever the particular sort of program.

Family dramas generally dominated between 1954 and 1964, such as *Father Knows Best, Ozzie and Harriet, Dennis the Menace,* and *Leave It to Beaver,* almost all of them showing parents, especially fathers, directing children toward correct moral choices—with morality based heavily on capitalism, consumerism, and quasi-religious (American) notions of right and wrong. Quiz shows were next in popularity. On Sunday afternoon, besides sports, one might also choose among highbrow conversations with such people as Sir Osbert Sitwell, an English poet and satirist, who showed off his ancestral estate on NBC one Sunday; the famous thinker Arnold Toynbee; or the former prime minister of Ireland, Eamon De Valera. And, of course, there was religious programming, led by Archbishop Sheen, Billy Graham, and Norman Vincent Peale.

But the favorite time for viewing on Sunday was in the evening, when lighter fare was indeed featured but was made respectable by its appeal to the whole family. This usually included variety shows, such as *The Ed Sullivan Show,* the premier variety-style show, airing between 1955 and 1971, and *The Wonderful World of Disney.* Less famous but highly popular at the time was *The Dinah Shore Chevy Show,* a one-hour musical variety hour scheduled at nine o'clock Eastern time on Sunday evenings—the prime slot in the entire viewing schedule of the week. Her show reflected not only many of the values of the 1950s but also its conflicts and tensions.

Although ethnically Jewish, Shore was portrayed as generically all-American. Although a working woman with nannies at home, she acted domestically—promoting cars and suburban living and her family and insisting that she placed more importance on being Mrs. George Montgomery than Dinah Shore. Although her hair and skin were lightened and her nose reduced and her teeth filed down and straightened, she was meant to look "natural," by American standards. Although feminine, she could not be too alluring, the sort wives would be jealous of. Although she preferred a "slinky sheath style to show off her svelte figure and 23-inch waistline," her fans insisted on "a bouffant-skirted, Southern-belle style that fit her husky Tennessee accent." Her hair was medium length and feminine, but never "vampy."

Thus constructed, she smiled while she sang, "energetically snapping her fingers or enthusiastically punching the air." She was "tan, fit, good-natured, the ideal image of the girl next door," rather than some sultry star, and especially female viewers liked that she bought her own wardrobe rather than wear "couturier-donated clothes." Clearly she was meant to appeal to the ever-growing suburban, car-hungry culture of the U.S., and the best time to get that message out, felt the sponsors, was Sunday night, for six long years.

On the American Sunday marketplace, one could therefore find just about anything found on Sunday in England *or* the European Continent—not only quiet and strict and churchgoing Sundays, but extensive professional and amateur sports, television, all sorts of parks, and arguably even more shopping. Not every enterprise was open for business, of course, some areas of the country were quieter than others, and only some tensions in American society were more explicit that day than otherwise. Still, taken as a whole, the American Sunday looked at least as busy as Sunday anywhere else did, if not more so.

This was what led Alexis McCrossen to call the American Sunday by now both a holy day and a holiday. After all, some Americans still followed the Puritan meaning of Sunday—a holy day. Others disregarded any religious constrictions at all and made it a day solely for recreation—what "holiday" now means. But still more Americans engaged in both holy day and holiday sorts of activities. Especially for this last group, it was not as if holy day and holiday merely coexisted on Sunday, in parallel but never intersecting worlds. Through their deeds if not their conscious thoughts, this group restored the two words, which have come to be seen as opposites, to the single meaning they had had when born in medieval English: merely different spellings of exactly the same thing.

A WORD AFTER

Asse, Belgium, the Annual Kiwanis Barbecue,
a Sunday in June, Recently

What strikes me most today is not the odd chain of circumstances that brought me here, nor the wonderful food and convivial atmosphere so common at festivities organized by otherwise reserved Belgians, nor the tranquil setting in this gently sloping park situated behind a former villa, nor even this culturally bombarded country's recent adaptation of an American form of outdoor dining. Rather it is that the obvious moment for such an occasion is understood by all to be Sunday. Only an outsider unaccustomed to this assumption would even notice.

My friend Louis, who invited me, is busy with ten other Kiwanis behind an enormous expanse of smoky grills, while his wife Charlotte walks past bearing plates heaped with food. Knowing no one else in the crowd of hundreds, I wave hello to these two and decide that by joining in to help I might not only meet new people but have a chance to gather more sentiments about Sunday, a topic much on my mind lately—for conversation, as usual in Belgium, is sure to become more spirited and wide-ranging as the evening wears on. Louis points me to the person in charge, who trusts me to clean off tables but not to hand anything out.

My hopes for conversation are somewhat dashed when I realize just how much food and drink people are consuming and therefore just how fast I must work in order to keep up. After all, this is no grab-a-paper-plate-and-clean-up-after-yourself affair: there is no paper plate or paper cup or plastic fork in sight, but instead a whole assortment of delicate glasses, serious cutlery, and heavy plates, and each course means a new set of all three. I have been to many Belgian dinners over the years and therefore am not terribly surprised that standards are just as high at a barbecue as in a dining room, in regard to the setting as well as the food. And what food, even if it is all cooked by amateurs: eight different sorts of meat, serving tables piled with perfectly prepared vegetable, potato, and rice dishes, and more, as if everyone was born with the same perfect sense of how such things should be cooked, dished up, and consumed. I have no doubt that the event will last long, with courses judiciously spaced over several hours: before-dinner drinks, hors d'oeuvres, main dish(es), dessert with coffee, then finally cheese and after-dinner drinks and cigars, plus beer and wine throughout, with each sort of beer in its own special glass. But at last people's appetites slacken, the pace of clearing slows, and conversation does indeed begin.

Of course, much of this does not involve me, beyond a hello or a thank you. But as people run out of topics with one another, they look my way and start chatting. There's nothing like a foreign accent to arouse curiosity (or fear), and upon hearing mine, interest picks up: What in the world am I doing here? With the especially curious and friendly, such as Hubert and Katleen, my very foreignness allows me to ask even less delicate questions of my own, such as how in the world such overwhelmingly trim people, who generally eat so carefully, can put away such unbelievable quantities of food and drink today. "Yes," nods Hubert soberly, as if to concede an unalterable fact of life, "we're

Burgundians." He means the short-lived medieval nation, centered in what is now Belgium, that was famous for its lavish tastes in dress, art, music, food, and wine. "But remember," he points in characteristic Belgian fashion to the sky with a warning finger, "it's not an everyday thing—only special occasions." Still, such occasions are pretty frequent, I reply, and Sunday seems to be an especially favorite day for them. "The perfect day," explains Hubert. Everyone is free, and family and friends can more easily get together. Now that I think about it, every table I had cleared was full of people obviously connected to many other people—grandparents, parents, young adults, teenagers, and young children. When it emerges that Hubert has taken up golf, I wonder aloud whether he ever plays on Sunday. "Of course not," he implies with his expression, then says, "That's a day for family," a sentiment not in the least diminished by the fact that his children are all grown. As for all the food—well, Sunday is a feast day, isn't it?

Here's where knowing a bit of etymology came in handy: if holy day and holiday have come to be seen as competitors in English, in Hubert's native Dutch, or his proficient French, there is no such confusion. Instead, there is only one crystal-clear label: "feast day," or *feestdag*. Sunday was the original feast day, and is still the greatest. The feast part always implied more than food—something like general celebration, and included church—but the feasting was unmistakable and never clandestine, unlike my own Super Bowl get-togethers. Clearly it still meant at least two things on Sunday in Belgium: church for those who pleased, but certainly lots of food and drink and family.

What about all the work involved? I ask Hubert, with a teasing nod toward the perspiring men at the barbecues and my weary legs. "I've cleared your place at least four times." "And many thanks," he replies, explaining that it takes a lot of effort to make a good feast day, just like at Christmas. He's been on the other end often enough himself, and in his mind it is clear that the benefits to the many justify the labor of the few, especially when it comes to the food: that's why all the bakeries, restaurants, and cafés are open on Sunday in Belgium—they choose another day to close. And those working can feel good that they've contributed to making the day nice for others, and that their turn to rest will come.

When I have finished helping in the kitchen, Hubert and Katleen ask me to join them for more talk and consumption. I notice, however, that it's ten-thirty by now, and that the invitation had specified from four until ten. "I guess that ending time means nothing?" I ask Louis, who is nearby, still cleaning. "Absolutely nothing," he confirms. Belgians could be fairly regimented about various things: this day is for that, that day for this, and at this very barbecue there is a wonderfully complicated system of drink coupons, purchased in one corner, redeemed in another, and stamped with the official words "entitles the bearer to one glass of . . ." But such regimentation apparently did not extend to the ending time of Burgundian-inspired feasts. Louis continues: "People put a closing time as a suggestion, a gesture to civilization and politeness, or perhaps to save face if the party is bad, but everyone knows it means nothing. To really be polite, people stay after the ending time, to show they've had fun. If this were Holland, people would go home right at ten. But they do things differently there," he says, shaking his head.

The people lingering at this late hour suggest by their actions that they are reluctant for this Sunday evening to end. But there is no real sense of pathos or melancholy, as in the French "Sunday in the Country," and certainly none of the gloom of the old English Sunday or Belgian wartime Sunday. Here at the barbecue, and in other places I'd been recently in Belgium, even the end of Sunday remains a happy moment, which I can explain only by people's focus not on Sunday's ending but on the certainty that another fun Sunday will come again soon. There is no sad prospect of Monday, no relief that a dull Sunday is finally over, but rather just as in the days of Ernest Claes—or for that matter the Burgundians—the happy assurance of Sunday's return next week. Each perspective is right in its way, but the adoption of one or the other certainly influences the prevailing mood.

Surely there are melancholy Sundays in Belgium too nowadays, especially among people less affluent and socially connected than these Kiwanis. I have seen some of this Sunday malaise myself, and read some of the poetry recounting it. But other poems and memoirs I have read here about Sunday are full of anticipation: on Sunday it never seemed to rain (impossible in wet Belgium), on Sunday there were delicate pastries, chicken, grandparents, chocolate at breakfast, sport, scouts, family, more family, culture, music, choir robes, cyclists, dirty children, special Dubec cigarettes, the best wine, and aromatic cigar smoke. And other Sunday experiences I have known here, in all sorts of social circles, only confirmed that the spirit of anticipation still dominated Belgian Sundays, just as it had in centuries past: it is as abundant among the members of the Distinguished Mustache Club, who sit next to me on the train one Sunday, sporting straw hats and matching T-shirts and gigantic fantastic mustaches while on their way to some sort of fair, as it is at this well-heeled barbecue.

The survival of old Sunday traditions in Belgium, if in new form, makes me wonder about the survival and transformation of other traditions featured in this book, and so I set out for a few final impressions.

In the Netherlands I see that Sunday is, as Louis suggested, generally more subdued than in Belgium. I find this ironic, given that the Dutch tend to be louder and that David Beck enjoyed so many Sunday banquets himself. Perhaps over time the Reformed preachers had a bigger impact than they thought. Or perhaps it is because the Dutch simply have some of the strictest laws against Sunday trading in all of Europe, and these contribute greatly to the quiet. Obviously, Sunday is still sacred in this sense, even if it may make the day more melancholy than in Belgium, at least when away from the coast or the largest cities. In some areas the Sunday quiet is explicitly religious, with a few of the devout even walking to church in old-style clothing. And if some urban churches have been converted to multipurpose cultural centers, some 35 percent of the population was still claiming in 1997 to attend Sunday services. I attend a few myself, starting with a Reformed service in the old university town of Leiden. The converted Gothic church looks much as it would have in the seventeenth century, although the moving sermon is delivered by a female preacher, the clothing is updated, and a loud organ now proudly accompanies hymns. I also attend a Reformed service around the corner that is more firmly rooted in the past: the old church is in the octagonal Reformed shape designed just for preaching, and an authentic fire-and-brimstone sermon lasting nearly an hour leaves the thin crowd, including me, rather cold. Finally, I visit one of Amsterdam's old hidden Catholic churches, where the sense of heroic devotion is still almost tangible.

In France, the Sunday afternoon crowds I encounter each week at the Jardin du Luxembourg, one of Paris's most popular parks, remind me of the Sunday bustle witnessed by Louis Morin a hundred years before. Nearly half of the French report that they still devote part of Sunday to a promenade, and this is certainly evident in the park, along with tennis, basketball, soccer, toy boats, a fantastic children's playground, and hardly an inch of space left to sit on the grass. The outlying parks of Paris are also still crowded on sunny Sundays, while museums are crowded every Sunday, especially on free-admission Sundays. And because fresh fruit, vegetables, and baked goods are as crucial as ever for Sunday dinner—at home or in a restaurant—these are for sale here and there in small shops: the French know the Burgundian influence too. Outside of these small vendors of food and drink, most people are not working: for although one French law guarantees businesses the right to trade when they please, another insists on compulsory rest for employees, preferably on Sunday, and in practice this means that the second cancels the first. Some of the nonworking are at church: plenty of the churches in Paris are rather empty, but St. Étienne du Mont is warm and Notre Dame is jam-packed for Masses.

Most at Notre Dame appear to be curious tourists, but how to explain crowded Sunday Masses in such small towns of Brittany as Noyal Muzillac? I squeeze in there among locals, some of whom will also visit a chapel in a field that afternoon, where the silence is otherworldly and the "intention" books full of emotional vows. Most head after Mass directly to one of the village's two cafés, located just across from the church doors: men in one, women in the other, and after an hour they switch. Later on Sunday in Brittany, the beach is busy too, just like the beaches of Louis Morin, so that when the tide is high it seems there will not be enough sand for everyone who would like to sit down. Sunday in France seems to me as full as ever, even without large trucks on the road, banned on Sundays since 1996. It is full enough that most establishments are closed on Monday morning. This is partly connected to the latest reduction of the workweek, to 35 hours, but perhaps it marks as well the return of St. Monday. That's how some churchmen see it, who complain like their distant predecessors that people need Monday to recover from Sunday.

In England, the stone church that was built in the village of Marden in the lifetime of Joanna le Schirreve still stands on the church green. A new parish vestry hall nearby is fittingly the home of, among other things, the popular Sunday Club, for children ages three to ten, who meet friends, play games, and learn—all much safer than wandering around ponds. If this setting looks rather medieval, other Sunday remains around England are more reminiscent of the 1930s, or of present-day France, the Netherlands, and Belgium. One can dine out easily enough on Sunday now, such as at the Albion Tavern in Faversham, Kent, which dutifully "guards the traditions of an English Sunday lunch," or a lovely establishment I try in Cambridge where the biggest draw is decidedly not the food but the unforgettable garden. In fact, England's laws regarding Sunday opening in general have been similar to those in Europe since at least 1994, when, said one observer, the old English Sunday passed into history, "largely unmourned by a society which now finds solace in shopping rather than singing hymns." Yet in my experience, plenty still find solace in hymns too. Overall figures for church attendance in England are middling, at just above 25 percent, and apparently much worse for the dominant Church of England. Still, I attend a C of E service in a small town south of London and find the modest church full and lively. The larger, barnlike building of an evangelical congregation is likewise full, the singing enthusiastic, and energy high. There is also more public Sunday sport now than in the 1930s, including extensive amateur Sunday football leagues, or cricket and football live or on television.

If many English seem content with this new Sunday, it is deeply lamented by the still-active if much-reduced Lord's Day Observance Society and its magazine *Day One*, which wishes to keep Sabbatarian ideals alive. I read a recent, typical issue, which included an article on the rarity of car theft on Sunday: a representative of Admiral Car Insurance explains that thieves too "want to spend Sunday with their families." Other articles oppose the expansion of shopping hours, and condemn Sunday sport. Michael Jones of New Zealand, whom some consider the greatest rugby player ever, is praised like Eric Liddel for having refused to compete on Sunday, even though this decision cost him fame and opportunity. An English player named Glyn Blaize is similarly praised. (It strikes me that such examples always seem to come from English-speaking Christian athletes.)

The LDOS does not praise, however, the triple-jumper Jonathan Edwards, who for years refused to compete on Sunday but then changed his mind. After failures at the 1988 and 1992 Olympics convinced him that missing important competitions was hindering the full development of his gift, Edwards adopted the stance of most Christian athletes before and since: his ability was granted by God and should therefore be put on display whenever possible, even on Sunday, for others to share. He believed that God himself had said as much, in a 1993 dream: he was not to be merely a "Christian ornament" or curiosity on the sideline but was to promote an even higher Christian purpose by participating and achieving. In 1995 Edwards went on to set a world record, then won the silver medal at the 1996 Olympics, before retiring and becoming a frequent presenter on the program *Songs of Praise.* Meanwhile, he criticized the movie *Chariots of Fire,* which recounted Liddel's heroics, for suggesting that a Christian should never compete on Sunday. To Edwards, the decision was personal, and even higher things were at stake.

And so goes the mix of old and new in other Western countries. Sunday churchgoing tends to be on the decline, but not everywhere. As late as 1997, Ireland boasted 89 percent for at least occasional attendance, while Poland, Portugal, Slovakia, Italy, and Belgium were not far behind at around 50 percent. France, Germany, and the Scandinavian countries brought up the rear at 5 to 10 percent, and half of Swedes declared themselves unbelievers. Yet as one scholar states, religion "is always declining and reviving." Moreover, neither high nor low figures are any more indicative now than they were a century ago, as 75 percent of all Europeans still consider themselves Christian, if in a broad and not-necessarily-churchgoing sense.

Surprisingly, long-strict Scotland is one of four countries with the loosest Sunday opening laws in Europe, although its Sabbatarian roots are still evident in such places as the Sunday-policed Isle of Lewis. Scotland's Canadian namesake, Nova Scotia, maintains the strict Sunday vigilantly. But Canada as a whole struck down its national Lord's Day Act in 1985, prompting some delighted religious leaders to say that it would force modern Christians "to confront the heresy" that religion is a Sunday matter only: as one put it, "The problem we face is not so much how to keep the Sabbath holy, but how to remind ourselves that the rest of the week is part of God's creation as well." If this sounded terribly radical and progressive, it was right out of the second century AD.

Finally, in the United States, the churchgoing and commercial and sportive traditions evident through the 1950s on Sunday are now more evident than ever. About 60 percent of Americans are still tied to a traditional church, not far from the peak of 69 percent in 1960, and some 45 percent of Americans claim to go to church on Sunday. Some traditional churches are fading in urban areas, but some are still vibrant, as at Bethel AME in Baltimore, now 220 years old, with its impressive chorus, sharply dressed ushers, and 3,500 worshipers each week. And new forms of churches are always emerging, in response to new commercial and recreational rhythms, going from a building-centered, classroom-centered, and Sunday-centered model to something more flexible. These include services at drive-in theaters, beaches, resort hotels, and campgrounds, and sometimes on weeknights—based on the premise suggested in the 1950s that a family weekend away might be more sacred than church time. Those who hold to traditional models resist such changes, believing that they are grounded in growing secularism, materialism, and even hedonism. But defenders can point out that ancient Christians met on Sunday around their working hours, and that forms of Sunday worship have regularly changed over the centuries, from gatherings in private homes in ancient Rome, to the medieval cathedral, to evangelicals who for centuries took the church into the wider culture, to the enlarged-suburban-living-room churches of the 1950s. Each was an idiom of a particular time.

The commercial Sunday thrives too. In fact Alexis McCrossen contends that the driving force of the busy American Sunday is not secularism but consumerism. Certainly consumerism could be included in one's definition of secularism, but the self-definition of those doing most of the consuming is Christian: 85 percent of all Americans still consider themselves so. Demand for services and products is so great that even those seeking a more Sabbatarian version of Sunday can hardly escape; for they too on Sunday want telephones, heat, air conditioning, electricity, dairy products, and many other everyday necessities once regarded as luxuries. And the general desire for goods on any day helps drive more public forms of consumerism on Sunday, including shopping. Most states still have Blue Laws, but these tend to restrict specific sorts of Sunday trade rather than trade generally, and so Sunday shopping is far more common in the U.S. than in church-avoiding Germany or Denmark. This is driven in part by those who view shopping as recreation, and in part by competition, but both are fueled by the supremely high value Americans place on consumer goods and a strong economy. As long as prosperity is a top priority, then it's hard to imagine that Sunday trading will be seen as wrong. The same with "hard work": as long as it is a virtue, then it is likely to be present on Sunday too. Americans work significantly more hours per year than Germans, Dutch, Norwegians, and even Brits. They also take shorter vacations and retire later—and generally have more commercial-oriented Sundays. A culture's most sacred values tend to show up on its sacred days as well.

Certainly this is true of the last element of the American Sunday: sport. If some Americans participate in or watch sports out of indifference toward religion, most have learned to fit them into their religious sensibilities, thanks to the continuing tendency to sacralize sport—either as American civil religion or in the terms of traditional religion. A few Christian athletes, as in England, cannot reconcile their religious beliefs with playing on Sunday, but most follow the thinking of the triple-jumper Jonathan Edwards. Pete Brock, a former lineman for the New England Patriots, put it best in 1978: "I now approach Sunday afternoon [football games] as a worship service. The Bible tells me, 'Present your bodies as a living and holy sacrifice, acceptable to God . . .' God has blessed me with a large body, great strength and the ability to play this difficult game. My responsibility is to play to one hundred percent of my ability as a way of thanking Him for what He's done for me." Jerry Falwell, the well-known founder of Liberty University, stated a wish that Liberty would someday "knock the bejabbers out of Notre Dame, in the name of the Lord." William Heyen, in his poem "If Jesus Played Football," expressed the view that surely Jesus would have been a wide receiver, "great at catching," feinting, precise cuts, "knocking off helmets with a stiff arm," and "spiking the ball in the end zone." He didn't say whether he would have played on Sunday. Interteam, interfaith prayer circles have long been forming after NFL games. By 1984 professional baseball's "baseball chapel" had four thousand players attending every Sunday in both minor and major leagues, and these continue.

Critics of sacralization have increased since the 1950s. The author James Michener noted in 1976 that football was a strange mix of patriotism, sex, violence, and religion, so that at halftime he could not tell whether he was in a striptease show, an armory, a cathedral, or a stadium. The former NFL player Dave Meggysey claimed that the league tolerated any sort of ordinarily unethical behavior in the pursuit of victory. The sociologist Harry Edwards concluded that U.S. sports did not develop Christian morals but rather ignored them—promoting "macho attitudes" that carried over into ordinary life, especially in relationships with women, who became viewed as just something else to be conquered. Frank Deford in 1976 satirized the worshipful attention to sport by calling it "Sportianity"—part of what William James called our national disease: "the bitch-goddess of success." Robert Higgs has more recently and similarly concluded that sport is more about business than religion, so why all the posturing? He did not mind athletes "witnessing" as long as they did not witness that they won because God helped them to. As Jack Sareela, a minister at the University of Florida, put it, Christianity was about a guy who died on the cross, who looked a lot like a loser, and who even appealed to and associated with losers. In this vein, Deford took the Fellowship of Christian Athletes to task, pointing out ex-members who complained that the organization wouldn't "let you go, once they get their teeth in. At least not when you're on top—have a bad season and suddenly they've got no interest in your soul." By marching out only the winning Christians, the emphasis was more on the winning than on the Christian.

Despite such criticisms, or the warning of Pope John Paul II that Sunday has been overwhelmed by sport, sport remains as popular on Sunday in America as on any other day—and in some cases even more so. The NFL Championship, renamed the Super Bowl in 1966 but still held on Sunday, is the supreme sporting event of the year. In fact it is larger than sport: the Super Bowl boasts 75 percent of the twenty-four most-watched television shows ever broadcast in the United States. The halftime show has evolved from featuring Up With People, or marching bands forming clever letters, to such icons as Aerosmith. The coin toss was once conducted by plain old referees but now involves a solemn ceremony with football legends and sacred rites. The national anthem is not only sung but performed at benedictory length by such celebrities as Barry Manilow, Whitney Houston, and Cher. Former players express their faith by saying "I believe in the Super Bowl." One scholar explains that it's not the violence or the commercial aspect or the outcome that attracts people to the Super Bowl but its value in American civic religion: as the Romans knew well, a multicultural nation needs transcendent sacred myths that unite everyone, and thus even non–sports fans watch the Super Bowl, where the national myths are most clearly on display.

Yet such reverential talk continues to go beyond civic religion. The 1977 film *Oh God!* has a preacher respond to questions about his spiritual credentials with the line, "Why, I gave the prayer at this year's Super Bowl!" as if there were no higher recommendation. This was satire, of course, but others were serious. Norman Vincent Peale, still going strong in the 1970s, said that "if Jesus Christ were alive today, he would be at the Super Bowl," with presumably little thought as to whether it was on Sunday. If he picked corn on Sunday, why would he not throw around a ball, or watch others do so? Various churches adjust their schedules on Super Bowl Sunday, putting giant televisions right in the church to create a fellowship experience, or developing a "holy huddle." One pastor holds a pregame service that includes a "kickoff at 10:45," pregame prayer, an anthem ("Amazing Grace"), a cheer, and finally a huddle with the "team owner," Jesus. The sermon contains every possible biblical reference to athletics and is otherwise riddled with sports clichés about fumbling and being thrown for losses but always getting up and trying again. And testimonials from Christian athletes are played at halftime rather than the entertainment offered by the network.

My own family can't quite sacralize the Super Bowl, but most of them do love sports and understand perfectly well the appeal of participating in a unifying cultural event. And so the get-togethers continue, now without my grandmother, who, Super Bowl or not, was usually a lot of fun and is missed. I would have liked to tell her what I'd learned so far about how Sunday got to be where it is—the Puritan traditions, the various Continental traditions, and still other influences present today, either separately or all mixed together, and how things changed over time. She might have been interested, but she might just as well have tuned me out and switched to one of her favorite TV shows. That was something else I would have liked to ask her: How in the world could she find so many modern entertainments and Sunday habits offensive, yet be such a big fan of *The Benny Hill Show,* even on Sunday? To me it was at best silly and at worst coarse; to her, resembling as it did the slapstick comedy on which she grew up, it was "real" entertainment. In this great mystery, I suspect, lies some insight into how cultural values in general, and Sunday values in particular, have regularly changed across generations.

It seems safe to say that this process will continue: Sunday will change as the world around it changes. It also seems safe to say that, whatever the changes, Sunday will retain its extraordinary character, however one might understand that. For it has been fed by centuries of aspirations, and in spite of countless disappointments, it continues to be reinforced by such sublime pleasures as an inspiring Sunday sermon in Leiden, the unsurpassed Sunday air of Paris, the serenity of Sunday in Cambridge, or the aromas and scenery and unrestrained sociability of a long Sunday dinner in Belgium.

BIBLIOGRAPHICAL NOTES

These notes are partly "Suggestions for Further Reading" and partly the usual scholarly acknowledgment of works that have been helpful to me. Mostly I merely list those works, in alphabetical order within each topic or subtopic, but when specific references seem especially called for, I have given them. The structure of each chapter note follows the structure of the chapter itself, although some longer lists, with works that apply to the entire chapter, are interspersed. Works are cited fully the first time they are mentioned in each chapter note, thereafter abbreviated. Readers who require other specific references may contact me through the publisher.

A WORD BEFORE

Sunday neurosis: Discussed in J. Shulevitz, "Bring Back the Sabbath," *New York Times Book Review* (March 2, 2003): 50–53.

A *Sunday in the Country* (France, 1984), directed by B. Tavenier. G. Michel, *The Sunday Walk* (London, 1968; translated from the French by Jean Benedetti). On cold Mondays, see E. Zerubavel, *The Seven Day Circle* (New York, 1985), 110.

Some general scholarly studies of Sunday: J. N. Andrews, L. R. Conradi, *History of the Sabbath and the First Day of the Week* (Washington, D.C., 1912); D. Baugard, "Pour une anthroposociologie du dimanche: Signification, représentation et pratique, temps de travail et temps hors-travail," *Loisir et société* 20/1 (1997): 161–88; D. Botte et al., *Le dimanche* (Paris, 1965); H. G. Cowan, *The Sabbath in Scripture and History* (Kansas City, 1948); *Dimanche: Le temps suspendu* (Paris, 1989); T. Eskenazi, D. Jarrington, W. Shea, eds., *The Sabbath in Jewish and Christian Traditions* (New York, 1991); J. A. Hesey, *Sunday: Its Origin, History, and Present Obligation* (London, 1889); V. J. Kelly, *Forbidden Sunday and Feast-Day Occupations: An Historical Synopsis and Theological Commentary* (Washington, D.C., 1945); H. Kingsbury, *The Sabbath: A Brief History of laws, petitions, remonstrances and reports, with facts, and arguments, relating to the Christian Sabbath* (New York, 1840); A. H. Lewis, *A Critical History of Sunday Legislation from 321 to 1888* (New York, 1888); W. Rybczynski, *Waiting for the Weekend* (New York, 1991); K. A. Strand, ed., *The Sabbath in Scripture and History* (Washington, D.C., 1982); C. Van de Wiel, "Les temps sacrés: Les jours de fête et de pénitence dans le droit canonique (canons 1244–1253)," *Questions liturgiques* 78/4 (1997): 243–67; L. Voye, "Du dimanche. . . . l'evolution des pratiques dominicales," *Lumen vitae* 47/2 (1992): 187–99.

Some popular depictions of Sunday: F. Hastings, *Sundays round the World* (London, 1897); P. Jounel, *Le dimanche* (Paris and Ottawa, 1990); B. Larbey, *A Month of Sundays* (Oxford, 1986); F. Morel, C. Patry, *Les habits du dimanche* (Paris, 1999); M. E. Connolly, "Sunday at Carriganee," *Irish Monthly* 24 (1896): 521–26; S. M. Fitzgibbon, "Our Sunday Gipsying," *Irish Monthly* 37 (1909): 581–82; A. Furlong, "Sunday in the Bar'nies," *Irish Monthly* 33 (1905): 601–08; K. Knox, "Garland Sunday," *Irish Monthly* 22 (1894): 488–89; E. O'Leary, "Sunday Outing," *Irish Monthly* 50 (1922): 323–28; C. J. Quirk, "Sunday Evening," *Irish Monthly* 56 (1928): 359; M. Rock, "A Last Sunday in Ireland," *Irish Monthly* 19 (1891): 101; M. Rock, "Sunday in the Country," *Irish Monthly* 19 (1891): 536–39; M. Rock, "A Sunday Outing," *Irish Monthly* 26 (1898): 495–99; M. Russell, "Irish Farmer's Sunday Morning," *Irish Monthly* 7 (1879): 96–102, and "Rustic Sunday," *Irish Monthly* 27 (1899): 169–79; P. A. Sheehan, "Sunday in Dartmoor," *Irish Monthly* 22 (1894): 80–88; L. W. Tentler, "One Historian's Sundays," in *Religious Advocacy and American History*, B. Kuklick and D. G. Hart, eds. (Grand Rapids, Mich.): 209–20.

Some other incidental titles: M. Ferguson, *Zondag en maandag* (Amsterdam, 1960); C. Swinkels, *De Dames van de Zondag* (Brugge, Belgium, 1973); T. Klopfer, *The Anthracite Idiom, or Sundays we are closed, go around the back* (Scranton, Pa., 1995); C. Applewhite, *Sundays: One Day a Week She Was Good* (New York, 1979).

Some inspirational, pastoral, and critical titles: G. N. Davies, "The Christian Sabbath," *Reformed Theological Review Melbourne* 42/2 (1983): 33–41; T. Edwards, *Sabbath Time: Understanding and Practice for Contemporary Christians* (New York, 1982); E. Farley, "A Missing Presence," *Christian Century* 115/9 (March 18, 1998): 276–78; J. Hilton, "From Sabbath to Lord's Day: Examining the Ethics of Sunday," *Faith and Mission* 17/3 (2000): 65–78; E. J. Kilmartin, "The Basis of the Sunday Mass Obligation," *Bread from Heaven* (1977): 151–61; A. Martin, "Notes sur le Sabbat," *Foi et Vie* 13–51; K. H. Miskotte, *In ruimte gezet, overdenkingen over den zin van den Zondag* (Amsterdam, 1941); W. Muller, *Sabbath: Restoring the Sacred Rhythm of Rest* (New York, 1999); C. E. Pocknee, "Sunday—The Eucharist and the Resurrection," *Church Quarterly Review* 165 (1964): 66–72; H. Rennings, "The Christian Sunday and Special Purpose Sundays," *Times of Celebration* (1981): 78–82; W. Rordof, "Le dimanche: Source et plénitude du temps liturgique chrétien," *Cristianesimo nella storia* 5/1 (1984): 1–9; W. Rordof, "Sunday: The Fullness of Christian Liturgical Time," *Studia Liturgica* 14 (1982): 90–96; G. H. Williams, "Sabbath and the Lord's Day," *Andover Newton Quarterly* 19/2 (1978): 121–28.

1 PROLOGUE: SUNDAY ASCENDANT

The metaphor of the river: E. Laverdiere, "The Origins of Sunday in the New Testament," *Sunday Morning: A Time for Worship* (Collegeville, Minn., 1982): 11–27.

The Day of the Sun

Especially helpful for this and the next section was E. Zerubavel, *The Seven Day Circle* (New York, 1985), 6–59; see also A. Aveni, *Empires of Time: Calendars, Clocks, and Cultures* (Boulder, Colo., 2002), 88–89; P. K. Seidelmann, ed., *Explanatory Supplement to the Astronomical Almanac* (Sausalito, Calif., 1992); S. Waterhouse, "The Planetary Week in the Roman West," in K. Strand, ed., *The Sabbath in Scripture and History* (Washington, D.C., 1982), 308–22. A host of internet sites offer information of varying reliability, such as www.calendar-zone.com.

Sun Day Becomes the First Day
General works on the Sabbath (see also Zerubavel and the next section below):
N.-E. Andreasen, *The Old Testament Sabbath: A Tradition-Historical Investi-
gation* (Missoula, Mont., 1972), and *Rest and Redemption: A Study of the Bib-
lical Sabbath* (Berrien Springs, Mich., 1978); J. N. Andrews, L. R. Conradi,
History of the Sabbath and First Day of the Week (Washington, D.C., 1912); E.
Fromm, *You Shall Be as Gods: A Radical Interpretation of the Old Testament
and Its Tradition* (New York, 1966); J. B. Jordan, *Sabbath Breaking and the
Death Penalty: A Theological Investigation* (Tyler, Tex., 1986); H. Webster,
Rest Days: A Study in Early Law and Morality (New York, 1916).

Sacred time and space: E. Muir, *Ritual in Early Modern Europe* (Cambridge,
1997), 73, referring to Émile Durkheim's *Elementary Forms of the Religious
Life* (New York, 1954).

Seven-day biorhythms: Aveni, 88–89.

*The Day of the Lord, Pagan and Jewish Influences,
The Lord's Day Around AD 150*
General works: See "Some General Scholarly Studies of Sunday" in the notes to
"A Word Before," above. A wonderful survey I saw late was H. J. de Jonge,
"Zondag en sabbat: over het ontstaan van de christelijke zondag," unpublished
talk, University of Leiden, February 2006. Also various works by S. Bacchiocchi,
Anti-Judaism and the Origin of Sunday (Rome, 1975), *Divine Rest for Human
Restlessness: A Theological Study of the Good News of the Sabbath for Today*
(Rome, 1980), *From Sabbath to Sunday: A Historical Investigation of the Rise of
Sunday Observance in Early Christianity* (Rome, 1977), and "Remembering the
Sabbath: The Creation-Sabbath in Jewish and Christian History," in *The Sab-
bath in Jewish and Christian Traditions*, in T. C. Eskenazi, D. J. Harrington, and
W. H. Shea, eds. (New York, 1991): 69–97; then R. J. Bauckham, "Sabbath and
Sunday in the Post-Apostolic Church," in D. A. Carson, ed., *From Sabbath to
Lord's Day* (Grand Rapids, Mich., 1982): 251–98; S. O. Bäck, *Jesus of Nazareth
and the Sabbath Commandment* (Åbo, Sweden, 1995); R. Beckwith, W. Stott,
*This Is the Day: The Biblical Doctrine of the Christian Sunday in Its Jewish and
Early Church Setting* (London, 1978); R. Cabie, "Le dimanche et le temps pascal
au temps d'Origene" *Recherches et tradition: Mélanges patristiques offerts à
Henri Crouzel, S. J.* (Paris, 1992): 47–60; F. H. Colson, *The Week* (Cambridge,
1926); J. P. Cotton, *From Sabbath to Sunday: A Study in Early Christianity*
(Bethlehem, Pa., 1983); R. Dufay, *Le dimanche hier et aujourd'hui* (Paris, 1979);
E. Ferguson, "Sabbath: Saturday or Sunday. A Review Article," *Restoration
Quarterly* (1980): 172–81; R. C. D. Jasper, review of Bacchiocchi, and Beckwith
and Stott, *Journal of Ecclesiastical History* 30 (1979): 475–76; L. L. MacReavy,

The Sunday Repose From Labour: An Historico-Theological Examination of the Notion of Servile Work (Leuven, Belgium, 1935); R. M. Nardone, "The Church of Jerusalem and the Christian Calendar," in *Standing Before God: Studies on Prayer in Scriptures and in Tradition with Essays* (New York, 1981); R. Odom, *Sabbath and Sunday in Early Christianity* (Washington, D.C., 1977); W. Rordorf, *Sunday: The History of the Day of Rest in the Earliest Centuries of the Christian Church* (London, 1968); K. A. Strand, *The Early Christian Sabbath: Selected Essays and a Source Collection* (Worthington, Ohio, 1979); K. Strand, "From Sabbath to Sunday in the Early Christian Church: A Review of Some Recent Literature, Part I: Willy Rordorf's Reconstruction," *Andrews University Seminary Studies* 17 (1979): 333–43; "Part II: Samuele Bacchiocchi's Reconstruction," *Andrews University Seminary Studies* 16 (1979): 85–104; W. Swartley, *Slavery, Sabbath, War, and Women: Case Issues in Biblical Interpretation* (Scottsdale, Pa., 1983); J. M. Vermaak, "Sabbats—en Sondagsviering in die eerste vier eeue N.C.," *Acta patristica et byzantia* 20 (1991): 85–95.

The new Lord's Day: The leading advocate is probably Rordorf, *Sunday*. The transferred Sabbath: This view was especially developed by Puritans and other elements of English Christianity, discussed further in Chapter 3. One day in seven: The leading proponent of this is surely Bacchiocchi, in many works, who is an Adventist but whose work is praised by Catholics. A Calvinist view: See especially Beckwith and Stott. Carson's *From Sabbath to Lord's Day* is an interesting response to all of these interpretations.

Pagan and Jewish influences more specifically: S. Benko, *Pagan Rome and the Early Christians* (Bloomington, Ind., 1984); M. Bockmuehl, *Jewish Law in Gentile Churches* (Edinburgh, 2000); D. Flusser, "Tensions between Sabbath and Sunday," *The Jewish Roots of Christian Liturgy* (New York, 1990): 42–147; G. Halsberghe, *The Cult of Sol Invictus* (Leiden, Netherlands, 1972); A. Nocent, "Christian Sunday," *The Jewish Roots of Christian Liturgy* (New York, 1990): 130–41; F. A. Regan, *Dies Dominica and Dies Solis: The Beginnings of the Lord's Day in Christian Antiquity* (Washington, D.C., 1961).

Early worship: Many of the works above, such as Rordorf, 177–270, contain important information; more specifically see J. V. Bartlet, "Sunday Worship of the Primitive Christmas," *Biblical World* 26 (1905): 341–54; P. Bradshaw, *Early Christian Worship* (Collegeville, Minn., 1996); G. W. Butterworth, *Clement of Alexandria* (Cambridge, 1919); O. Cullmann, *Early Christian Worship* (Philadelphia, 1953); S. R. Llewelyn, "The Use of Sunday for Meetings of Believers in the New Testament," *Novum Testamentum* 43/3 (2001): 205–23; S. McKinion, *Life and Practice in the Early Church: A Documentary Reader* (New York, 2001). Paul's observations on worship in I Corinthians 14:26, Ephesians 5:18–20. One summary of Justin Martyr in Bradshaw. Benko devotes an entire chapter to the kiss, plus its later development, in M. Penn, *Kissing Christians: Ritual and Community in the Late Ancient Church* (Philadelphia, 2005). Clement's Sermon in Butterworth, *Clement*, 261–93, and Origen's approach in A. Monaci Castagno, "Origen the Scholar and Pastor," in M. Cunningham, P. Allen, eds., *Preacher and Audience: Studies in Early Christian and Byzantine Homiletics* (Leiden, Netherlands, 1998).

Other Sunday rituals: On sex, especially P. Brown, *The Body and Society* (Oxford, 1988), 256, 323; study groups starting on 104.

From Lord's Day to Christian Sunday
General works: Especially helpful was G. Bowersock, P. Brown, O. Grabar, eds., *Late Antiquity: A Guide to the Postclassical World* (Cambridge, Mass., 1999), which contains a number of insightful articles on especially worship and the religious context. Also P. Brown, *Authority and the Sacred: Aspects of the Christianisation of the Roman World* (Cambridge, 1995), *The Body and Society*, *The Rise of Western Christendom: Triumph and Diversity AD 200–1000* (Oxford, 1996); B. Ehrman, *The Apostolic Fathers I* (Cambridge, 2003); K. M. George, "Sunday, Pentecost and the Jubilee Tradition: A Patristic Perspective," in H. Ucko, ed., *The Jubilee Challenge* (Geneva, 1997): 99–103; J. Hillgarth, ed., *Christianity and Paganism, 350–750: The Conversion of Western Europe* (Philadelphia, 1969); Penn, *Kissing Christians;* C. Pietri, "Le temps de la semaine à Rome et dans l'Italie Chrétienne (IV–VIe S.)," in *Le temps chrétien de la fin de l'Antiquité au Moyen Age: IIIe–XIII siècles: Paris, 9–12 mars 1981* (Paris, 1984): 63–81. See further M. Salzman, *On Roman Time: The Codex-Calendar of 354 and the Rhythms of Urban Life in Late Antiquity* (Berkeley, 1990); R. Stark, *The Rise of Christianity* (Princeton, 1996); W. Thomas, *Der Sonntag im frühen Mittelalter* (Göttingen, 1929); M. Wallraff, *Christus Verus Sol: Sonnenverehrung und Christentum in der Spätantike* (Münster, 2001); F. A. Wright, *Select Letters of St. Jerome* (Cambridge, 1933). Eusebius's statement: Carson, *From Sabbath*: 282.

Church councils, Caesarius, and others on a Sabbath-like Sunday: Especially MacReavy, 302, 309–15; also 304 on Augustine and the Ten Commandments; Brown, *Authority*, 20–21, on Augustine too; also Carson, 300–02, on Augustine and the Ten Commandments. V. J. Kelly, *Forbidden Sunday and Feast-Day Occupations: An Historical Synopsis and Theological Commentary* (Washington, D.C., 1945), 34–38, and McKinion, 57–64.

Later worship: see above under "General works," but especially Bowersock, 23–49, 200–08, 249–53, 337, 509, 590, with McKinion, 57–64. On Jerome and Sunday, Regan, *Dies Solis*, 65–69.

2 SUNDAY MIDDLE-AGED

H. S. Bennett, *Life on the English Manor: A Study of Peasant Conditions, 1150–1400* (Cambridge, 1971; reprint of the 1937 edition) is important not only for the opening "Prologue" but its more analytical chapters on various topics. Also in the opener, information on housing from Bolton, 12, and Hanawalt, *Crime and Conflict*, 26; fields, meadow, and hay are from Bolton 14–18, 32; Latham, 36; Richardson, 100 (who also discusses priests as farmers); Bennett, 82, 106–17; Hanawalt, *Ties that Bound*, 113; Rodgers, 33–94 (full citations under "Work," below).

Work

Generally on material life and economy (much of this as well in "Medieval Society" below): J. L. Bolton, *The Medieval English Economy* (London, 1980); C. Dyer, *Making a Living in the Middle Ages: The People of Britain 850–1520* (New Haven, Conn., 2002); B. Hanawalt, *Women and Work in Preindustrial Europe* (Bloomington, Ind., 1986); W. O. Hassall, *How They Lived: An Anthology of Original Accounts Written Before 1485* (Oxford, 1962); M. Wood, *The English Mediaeval House* (London, 1965).

Generally on medieval society, family, and gender: J. Bennett, *A Medieval Life: Cecilia Penifader of Brigstock, c. 1295–1344* (New York, 1999); J. Bennett, A. Froide, eds., *Singlewomen in the European Past: 1250–1800* (Philadelphia, 1999); E. Britton, *The Community of the Vill: A Study in the History of the Family and Village Life in Fourteenth-Century England* (Toronto, 1977); D. Chadwick, *Social Life in the Days of Piers Plowman* (Cambridge, England, 1922); M. Clare Coleman, *Downham-in-the-Isle: A Study of an Ecclesiastical Manor in the Thirteenth and Fourteenth Centuries* (Suffolk, England, 1984); G. Egan, *The Medieval Household: Daily Living c. 1150–1450* (London, 1998); K. L. French, "To Free Them from Binding: Women in the Late Medieval English Parish," *Journal of Interdisciplinary History* 27/3 (1997): 387–412; A. Froide, *Never Married: Singlewomen in Early Modern England* (Oxford, 2005); F. and J. Gies, *Life in a Medieval Village* (New York, 1990); B. Hanawalt, *Crime and Conflict in English Communities, 1300–1348* (Cambridge, Mass., 1979); B. Hanawalt, *The Ties that Bound: Peasant Families in Medieval England* (Oxford, 1985); G. Homans, *English Villagers of the Thirteenth Century* (New York, 1960); T. J. Hunt, *The Medieval Customs of the Manors of Taunton and Bradford on Tone* (Frome, 1962); L. C. Latham, "The Manor and the Village," in G. Barraclough, ed., *Social Life in Early England* (New York, 1960); E. Miller, *The Abbey & Bishopric of Ely: The Social History of an Ecclesiastical Estate from the Tenth Century to the Early Fourteenth Century*

(Cambridge, 1951); F. W. Maitland, "The History of a Cambridgeshire Manor," in H. Cam, ed., *Selected Historical Essays of F. W. Maitland* (Cambridge, 1957), 16–40; S. Olson, *A Chronicle of All That Happens: Voices from the Village Court in Medieval England* (Toronto, 1996); N. Orme, *Medieval Children* (New Haven, Conn., 2001); E. Power, *Medieval People* (London, 1924); P. Schofield, *Peasant and Community in Medieval England, 1200–1500* (New York, 2003); D. M. Stenton, *English Society in the Early Middle Ages, 1066–1307* (Middlesex, England, 1951); J. Z. Titow, *English Rural Society, 1200–1350* (London, 1969).

Sunday legislation and emphasis: V. J. Kelly, *Forbidden Sunday and Feast-Day Occupations: An Historical Synopsis and Theological Commentary* (Washington, D.C., 1945); A. H. Lewis, *A Critical History of Sunday Legislation from 321 to 1888* (New York, 1888). Quote from Piers Plowman in Bennett, *English Manor,* 115. Hales and more in Strand, "Sabbath and Lord's Day"; Peckham in Lewis, 81; Aquinas and the *Decretals* in D. A. Carson, *From Sabbath to Lord's Day* (Grand Rapids, Mich., 1982), 302–04. Money, sex, and spilt blood from G. Duby, *The Legend of Bouvines: War, Religion, and Culture in the Middle Ages* (Berkeley, 1990), 1. Gregory of Tours in R. Dufay, *Le dimanche hier et aujourd'hui* (Paris, 1979), 39–41, and Priebsch, 26–28. Eustace of Flay in Jones, 166–68. Mirk's (Myrc) *Instructions for Parish Priests* has been edited by E. Peacock (London, 1868; revised and reprinted, 1981), 9–10 on holy days. Number and sorts of holy days, Meade, 97–98, Spencer, 24, Harvey, among others (below under "Mass").

The agricultural year: Bennett, *English Manor,* 82. Dialogue on hard labor from *Internet Medieval Sourcebook,* http://www.fordham.edu/halsall/sbook.html, "The Dialogue Between Master and Disciple: On Laborers, c. 1000." Bishop of Winchester from A. Brown (below), 81–83. Working alone in fields, Harvey, and Reiss, 47–52 (also below).

Mass

Generally on late medieval religion: R. and C. Brooke, *Popular Religion in the Middle Ages* (New York, 1984); A. Brown, *Popular Piety in Late Medieval England: The Diocese of Salisbury, 1250–1550* (Oxford, 1995); G. H. Cook, *The English Mediaeval Parish Church* (London, 1954); G. G. Coulton, *Medieval Village, Manor, and Monastery* (New York, 1960), and *Ten Medieval Studies* (Boston, 1906); E. Cutts, *Parish Priests and Their People in the Middle Ages in England* (London, 1898); E. Duffy, *The Stripping of the Altars: Traditional Religion in England 1400–1580* (New Haven, Conn., 1992); J. Fenton, "The Last English Style," *New York Review of Books* (December 18, 2003): 81–83; K. French, *The People of the Parish: Community Life in a Late Medieval English*

Diocese (Philadelphia, 2001); K. French, G. Gibbs, B. Kumin, *The Parish in English Life, 1400–1600* (Manchester, England, 1997); A. Gasquet, *Parish Life in Mediaeval England* (London, 1906); P. J. P. Goldberg, *Women in England, c. 1275–1525* (Manchester, England, 1995); R. Hutton, *The Pagan Religions of the Ancient British Isles: Their Nature and Legacy* (Cambridge, Mass., 1991); K. Kamerick, *Popular Piety and Art in the Late Middle Ages: Image Worship and Idolatry in England, 1350–1500* (New York, 2002); D. Meade, *The Medieval Church in England* (Folkestone, England, 1988); J. R. H. Moorman, *Church Life in England in the Thirteenth Century* (Cambridge, 1955); D. M. Owen, *Church and Society in Medieval Lincolnshire* (Lincoln, England, 1981); W. A. Pantin, *The English Church in the Fourteenth Century* (Notre Dame, Ind., 1962); N. J. G. Pounds, *A History of the English Parish* (Cambridge, 2000); H. G. Richardson, "The Parish Clergy of the Thirteenth and Fourteenth Century," *Transactions of the Royal Historical Society,* 3rd ser., 6 (1912): 89–128; J. Shinners, ed., *Medieval Popular Religion: 1000–1500* (Peterborough, England, 1997); C. Straw, *Gregory the Great: Perfection in Imperfection* (Berkeley, 1988); R. N. Swanson, *Religion and Devotion in Europe, c. 1215–1515* (Cambridge, 1995); R. N. Swanson, *Catholic England: Faith, Religion and Observance Before the Reformation* (Manchester, England, 1993), *Church and Society in Later Medieval England* (Oxford, 1989), and R. N. Swanson, "Le clergé rural Anglaise au bas moyen âge (vers 1300–vers 1530)," in P. Bonnassie, ed., *Le Clergé rural dans l'Europe médiévale et moderne* (Toulouse, France, 1995): 61–100.

Clothing: Orme, 73; Gies, 98–99; Owen, 118.

Church bells: G. R. Owst, *Preaching in Medieval England (c. 1350–1450)* (Cambridge, 1926), 156; also W. Moll, *Kerkgeschiedenis van Nederland vóór de Hervorming* (Utrecht, 1864), 277, who mentions the three bells—this may have been a peculiarly Dutch custom.

Churchyard as cemetery and playground: Homans, 384; Cook, 32; Cutts, 206; G. Owst, "The People's Sunday Amusements in the Preaching of Medieval England," *Holborn Review* (January 1926): 32–45; Owen, 105; and many more.

Church building: Meade; Fenton, 81; Owen, 113; and especially Cook, 17–20, 25, 28, 35, 40, 81–83, 87, 149–232.

Vestments and rituals: Cutts, 191–95; Gasquet, 155–61, 222.

Deacons, subdeacons, and holy water clerks: Bennett, *English Manor*, 322–36; J. Hillgarth, ed., *Christianity and Paganism, 350–750: The Conversion of Western Europe* (Philadelphia, 1969), 183–85; Cook; Cutts, 191–95, 299–302.

Rituals during church: Duffy, 110–29; Owst, *Preaching in Medieval England,* (below) 165–94; Orme, 200–02; Homans, 394–97; Mirk, 9; Cutts, 243; Coulton, *Ten Medieval Studies,* 117, and *Medieval Village,* 239. The version of the Lord's Prayer given here in Swanson, *Catholic England,* 89–90.

Church interior and the role of the laity: In addition to above, especially Cook and Duffy, see French, "To Free Them," 394; Kamerick, 4–8; A. Brown, 46, on parish spirituality, and chaps. 4–5; Cutts, 184–87; Fenton, 81. On the Sunday Christ murals, especially Reiss, below.

Social distinctions: See the subheading, "Medieval Society," above. Orme, 223, on the number of parishes and clergy. The vicar's glebe in Homans, 385, Pounds, 159, Richardson, 100; Pounds, 158, on the increasing distinction of the clergy from laypeople; also Bennett, *English Manor,* 322–36. On women in the crowd, Froide, *Never Married,* and Bennett and Froide, *Singlewomen,* 1–3. Other distinctions, Schofield, 13–22, Bolton, 14–22, 104; Britton, 20–37, 166–78.

Excommunication: One ritual in Mirk, 24.

Preaching: C. Muessig, ed., *Preacher, Sermon, and Audience in the Middle Ages* (Leiden, 2002); G. R. Owst, *Literature and Pulpit in Medieval England* (New York, 1961), 67, 114–18, 152, 287, and *Preaching,* 63, 169–94, with 326 on Jacob's Well; Cutts, 215, among others. Augustine and Chrysostom in S. McKinion, *Life and Practice in the Early Church: A Documentary Reader* (New York, 2001), 74–95. H. L. Spencer, *English Preaching in the Late Middle Ages* (Oxford, 1993), 78, and H. Pfander, *The Popular Sermon of the Medieval Friar in England* (New York, 1937), 8–9, on Arthur. Mirk, 15, for the Trinity metaphor. Many of these sources contain materials on women, see also K. Phillips, *Medieval Maidens: Young Women and Gender in England, 1270–1540* (Manchester, England, 2003), 143–45. Hassall, 318–19, for tithe story. Horror stories of Sunday-violators in Thurston, 41, Rodgers, 22.

The Sunday letter and Sunday Christ: D. Augsburger, "The Sabbath and Lord's Day during the Middle Ages," *The Sabbath and Scripture in History,* 190–215; W. R. Jones, "The Heavenly Letter in Medieval England," *Medieval Hagiography and Romance* (Cambridge, 1975): 163–78; C. A. Lees, "The 'Sunday Letter' and the 'Sunday Lists'," *Anglo-Saxon England* 14 (1985): 129–52; T. O'Loughlin, "The Significance of Sunday: Three Ninth-Century Catecheses," *Worship* 64/6 (1990): 533–44; V. O'Mara, *A Study and Edition of Selected Middle English Sermons: . . . A Sermon on Sunday Observance . . .* (Leeds, England, 1994); R. Priebsch, *Letter from Heaven on the Observance of the Lord's Day* (Oxford, 1936); A. Reiss, *The Sunday Christ: Sabbatarianism in English*

Medieval Wall Painting (Oxford, 2000); K. A. Strand, "Sabbath and Lord's Day During the Middle Ages," in Strand, ed., *The Sabbath in Scripture and History* (Washington, D.C., 1982); P. Brown, *The Rise of Western Christendom* (Oxford, 1996), 285. Trollope quoted in Spencer, 1.

Eucharist: Promoting fellowship, especially J. Bossy, *Christianity in the West, 1400–1700* (Oxford, 1985). Also Duffy, 98, 123–29, Cook, 149–206. Hassall, 132, on the oven dispute. Prayers in Mirk, 9; and perils of Mass in Mirk, 58, and Moll, 300–01; Bennett, *English Manor,* 266–70, on the devil's chapel.

Meat

Noise, markets, peddlers: Gies, 33; Owst, "People's Sunday Amusements," 32–33, 37; Hanawalt, *Crime and Conflict,* 85; Owen, 110; Homans, 384; Rodgers, 64–66, 73; Cook, 28, 32; Reiss, 47; Thurston, 46; Hassall, 165–66; Cutts, 206, among others. Women arguing in Goldberg, 230.

Material life, including housing and food: See this section above, especially Hanawalt, *Ties That Bound,* 133–62, and J. Bennett, "The Village Ale-Wife: Women and Brewing in Fourteenth-Century England," in Hanawalt, *Women and Work,* 20–36. Also Hassall, 133–48, Bennett, 232–34, Britton, 157–63, Gies, 94–96.

Names: Hanawalt, *Ties That Bound,* 174.

Makeup of households: See above too, also Britton, 65–66; Orme, 53–55; Hanawalt, *Ties That Bound,* 95–152; and Froide and Hanawalt above on single women.

Fun

The story of Joanna le Schirreve is discussed in R. Finucane, *The Rescue of the Innocents: Endangered Children in Medieval Miracles* (New York, 2000), 117–19, 137; 172–204 also includes his translations of the entire set of relevant documents.

Children's rhymes: Orme, 137, and games 182–84; plus Hanawalt, *Ties That Bound,* 183–91, 217.

Holy days, time, and recreation: C. Cheney, "Rules for the Observance of Feast-Days in Medieval England," *Bulletin of the Institute of Historical Research* 34 (1961): 117–47; E. Eisentraut, *Die Feier der Sonn- und Festtage seit dem letzten Jahrhundert des Mittelalters* (Amorach, Germany, 1914); B. Harvey, "Work and Festa Ferianda in Medieval England," *Journal of Ecclesiastical History* 23/4 (1972); B. Henisch, *The Medieval Calendar Year* (University Park, Pa., 1999); D. L. Higdon, "The Wife of Bath and Refreshment Sunday," *Papers on Lan-*

guage and Literature 8/2 (1972): 199–201; R. Hutton, *The Rise and Fall of Merry England: The Ritual Year, 1400–1700* (Oxford, 1994); R. Hutton, *The Stations of the Sun: A History of the Ritual Year in Britain* (Oxford, 1996); J. Le Goff, *Time, Work, and Culture in the Middle Ages* (Chicago, 1980); Owst, "People's Sunday Amusement"; A. W. Pollard, *English Miracle Plays: Moralities and Interludes* (Oxford, 1890); C. Reeves, *Pleasures and Pastimes in Medieval England* (Oxford, 1998); E. Rodgers, *Discussion of Holidays in the Later Middle Ages* (New York, 1940); H. Thurston, "The Medieval Sunday," *Nineteenth Century* 46 (July 1899): 36–50.

Churchmen and recreation: Pounds, 241–58, on the importance of play, plus Rodgers, 45–48; the tavern against the tabernacle is from Marc Therry, a Belgian scholar; Thurston, 46, 48; Higdon on refreshment Sunday; the king of heavy cheer in Swanson, *Catholic England*, 60–61; Hanawalt, *Crime and Conflict*, 99–100, on Sunday as the biggest day for murder; Bennett, *English Manor*, 106–17; Mirk, 30; the unfortunate Worcestershire priest, in Power, *Medieval People*, 31; Gies, 156–69, on Jude and Judas Iscariot; Spencer, 70, on hermaphrodites; Cook, 38; Owst, *Literature and Pulpit*, 438, on the devil's school, 393–95, 435; Owst, "People's Amusements," 34–36, 39, 41; Sunday sex in P. Brown, *The Body and Society* (New York, 1988), 256, and Reiss, 47–52; Reiss, 32, on greater concern about play than work. Plus section above on "Sunday, the Sunday Letter, Time, and Recreation." Aquinas on sport in Coulton, *Medieval Village*, 254–56, plus 272 on clerical condemnations in general. Owst, *Preaching in Medieval England*, 100, on the pardoner-friar rivalry, with the amusing play itself in Pollard, 114–25. Orme, 62–67, on children's accidents; also Finucane; and Hanawalt, *Ties That Bound*, 152, on candles not extinguished.

3 SUNDAY REFORMED

David Beck's journal has been edited by S. Veldhuijzen, as *Spiegel van mijn leven: een Haags dagboek uit 1624* (Hilversum, 1993). (Unless obviously elsewhere, all place names in this chapter are from the Netherlands.) Its value can be gauged by a look at R. Lindeman, Y. Scherf, R. Dekker, eds., *Egodocumenten van Noord-Nederlanders uit de zestiende tot begin negentiende eeuw: Een chronologische lijst* (Rotterdam, 1993), which lists 150 sixteenth- and seventeenth-century "ego-documents" (diaries, autobiographies) found in Dutch archives by a team of scholars in three years of searching. Most of these documents remain unpublished, most are autobiographies rather than diaries, and most focus on major events or impersonal information rather than everyday life and emotions. Beck wrote down what he did virtually every day in 1624, and perhaps in other years too, but this is the only surviving volume by him. A few other titles in the Lindeman work are described similarly to Beck's, but they are few indeed and from later years. See also R. M. Dekker et al., "Verstopte bronnen: Egodocumenten van Noord-Nederlanders uit de 16de tot 18de eeuw," *Nederlandse Archievenblad* 86 (1982).

Beck's dream of going blind on p. 15 of the journal, the dream of the Turk on 13 October. Other details from his life come from the journal itself, and Veldhuijzen's introduction, pp. 7–20, but I will not cite all of them here.

The Hague: Details taken from Beck's journal but also H. Rowen, *John de Witt: Grand Pensionary of Holland, 1625–72* (Princeton, 1978), two chapters entitled "Life in The Hague."

Sunday in the Netherlands: Countless works touch upon the subject, but two older works address it specifically: P. van den Berg, *De viering van den zondag en de feestdagen in Nederland vóór de Hervorming* (Amersfoort, 1914), on the centuries before the Reformation, and S. D. Veen, *Zondagsrust en Zondagsheiliging in de zeventiende eeuw* (Nijkerk, [1889]), which focuses on the seventeenth century.

The Word
Generally on the religious situation of the Dutch Republic, especially the Reformed religion, with English-language works listed first (various general works, listed under "Dutch Society," below, also treat religion): Begin with P. Benedict, *Christ's Churches Purely Reformed: A Social History of Calvinism* (New Haven, Conn., 2002), which includes a section on the Dutch; A. Duke, *Reformation and Revolt* (London, 1990); J. Elliott, "Protestantization in the Northern Netherlands, A Case Study: The Classis of Dordrecht 1572–1640" (dissertation, Columbia University, 1990); W. Frijhoff, *Embodied Belief: Ten Essays on Religious Culture in Dutch History* (Hilversum, 2002); D. E. Holwerda, ed., *Exploring the Heritage of John Calvin* (Grand Rapids, Mich., 1976); W. Janse, "The Protestant Reformation in the Low Countries: Developments in Twentieth-Century Historiography," *Reformation & Renaissance Review: Journal of the Society for Reformation Studies* 6/2 (2004): 179–202; B. Kaplan, *Calvinists and Libertines: Confession and Community in Utrecht 1578–1620* (Oxford, 1995); C. Kooi, *Liberty and Religion: Church and State in Leiden's Reformation, 1572–1620* (Leiden, 2000); J. Pollmann, *Religious Choice in the Dutch Republic: The Reformation of Arnoldus Buchelius (1565–1641)* (Manchester, England, 1999); B. Scribner, R. Porter, M. Teich, *The Reformation in National Context* (Cambridge, 1994).

Religious situation, in Dutch: Basic primary sources are in J. N. Bakhuizen van den Brink, et al., eds., *Documenta Reformatoria,* 2 vols. (Kampen, 1960), and the old synodal collections, W. Knuttel, *Acta der Particuliere Synoden van Zuid-Holland, 1621–1700,* 6 vols. (The Hague, 1908–16), and J. Reitsma, S. D. van Veen, eds., *Classicale Acta 1573–1620: Particuliere Synode Zuid-Holland,* 6 vols. (The Hague, 1892–99). These are now regularly supplemented with records from other synods. For secondary sources, several works by A. Th. van Deursen, including *Bavianen en Slijkgeuzen* (Assen, 1974), *Een dorp in de polder: Graft in de zeventiende eeuw* (Amsterdam, 1994), *Geleefd geloven: Geschiedenis van de protestantse vroomheid in Nederland* (Assen, 1996), *Plain Lives in a Golden Age: Popular Culture, Religion, and Society in Seventeenth-Century Holland* (Cambridge, 1991). Also R. Evenhuis, *Ook dat was Amsterdam,* 5 vols. (Amsterdam, 1965–78); W. Frijhoff, *Wegen van Evert Willemsz: Een Hollands weeskind op zoek naar zichzelf, 1607–1647* (Nijmegen, 1995); H. A. Enno van Gelder, *Getemperde Vrijheid* (Groningen, 1972); W. Janse, "De vestiging van de gereformeerde kerk 1572–1600," in C. Augustijn et al., *Reformatorica. Teksten uit de geschiedenis van het Nederlandse protestantisme* (Zoetermeer, 1996), 89–103; F. van Lieburg, "Geloven op vele manieren," in W. Frijhoff, ed., *Geschiedenis van Dordrecht II: 1572 tot 1813* (Hilversum, 1998), 271–304; J. van der Loos, *Vaderlandsche Kerkgeschiedenis* (Amsterdam, 1947); H. Roodenburg, *Onder censuur: De kerkelijke tucht in de gereformeerde gemeente van Amsterdam, 1578–1700* (Hilversum, 1990); G. D. J. Schotel, *De Openbare Eeredienst der Nederlandse Hervormde Kerk in de zestiende, zeventiende en achttiende eeuw* (Haarlem, 1870); C. van der Sluijs, *Puritanisme en Nadere Reformatie* (Kampen, 1989); J. Spaans, *Haarlem na de Reformatie* (The Hague, 1989); W. Verboom, *De catechese van de Reformatie en de Nadere Reformatie* (Amsterdam, 1986); A. Wouters, P. Abels, *Nieuw en Ongezien: Kerk en Samenleving in de classis Delft en Delfland 1572–1621,* 2 vols. (Delft, 1994); A. Wouters, P. Abels, *De Grote Kerkelijke Vergadering van 's-Hertogenbosch (1648)* (Den Bosch, 1986).

Generally on Dutch society, English-language works: K. H. D. Haley, *The Dutch in the Seventeenth Century* (London, 1972); J. L. Price, *Dutch Society: 1588–1713* (London, 2000); S. Schama, *The Embarrassment of Riches: An Interpretation of Dutch Culture in the Golden Age* (Berkeley, 1988); D. Barnes, *Street Scenes: Leonard Bramer's Drawings of 17th-century Dutch Daily Life* (Hempstead, England, 1991); P. van der Coelen, et al., eds., *Everyday Life in Holland's Golden Age: The Complete Etchings of Adriaen van Ostade* (Amsterdam, 1998); D. Haks, M. C. van der Sman, eds., *Dutch Society in the Age of Vermeer* (Zwolle, 1996); P. Zumthor, *Daily Life in Rembrandt's Holland* (New York, 1963). Some English travel accounts also offer interesting insights, including K. van Strien, *Touring the Low Countries: Accounts of British Travellers, 1660–1720* (Amsterdam, 1998), and *British Travellers in Holland During the Stuart Period* (Leiden, 1993); W. Temple, *Observations upon the United Provinces of the Netherlands* (Oxford, 1972).

On Dutch society, Dutch-language works: M. Prak, *Gouden Eeuw: Het raadsel van de Republiek* (Nijmegen, 2002); G. D. J. Schotel, *Het maatschappelijk leven onser Vaderen in de zeventiende eeuw* (Leiden, n.d.); H. Beliën, et al., eds., *Gestalten van de Gouden Eeuw: Een Hollands groepsportret* (Amsterdam, 1995); P. te Boekhorst, *Cultuur en maatschappij in Nederland, 1500–1850: Een historisch-antropologisch perspectief* (Boom, 1992); F. Boersma, *Dagboek van Nederland: Geschiedenis gezien door ooggetuigen* (Amsterdam, 1984); G. Dorren, *Eenheid en verscheidenheid: De burgers van Haarlem in de Gouden Eeuw* (Amsterdam, 2001); H. Hendrix, M. Meijer Drees, eds., *Beschaafde Burgers: Burgerlijkheid in de vroegmoderne tijd* (Amsterdam, 2001); J. de Jongste et al., *Vermaak van de elite in de vroegmoderne tijd* (Hilversum, 1999); E. Kloek, *Wie hij zijn, man of wijf: Vrouwengeschiedenis en de vroegmoderne tijd* (Hilversum, 1990); A. Schuurman, et al., eds., *Aards Geluk: De Nederlanders en hun spullen van 1550 tot 1850* (Amsterdam, 1997); H. Thomas, *Het dagelijks leven in de 17de eeuw* (Amsterdam, 1981); A. de Vrankrijker, *Het maatschappelijk leven in Nederland in de Gouden Eeuw* (Amsterdam, 1937); A. de Vrankrijker, *Mensen, leven, en werken in de Gouden Eeuw* (The Hague, 1981).

Church interiors: C. van Swigchem, T. Brouwer, W. van Os, *Een huis voor het Woord: Het protestantse kerkinterieur in Nederland tot 1900* (The Hague, 1984); Roodenburg.

Church services, including singing, preaching, communion, weddings: L. Vischer, ed., *Christian Worship in Reformed Churches Past and Present* (Grand Rapids, Mich., 2003), 19, 21; J. de Bruijn, ed., *Psalmzingen in de Nederlanden: Vanaf de zestiende eeuw tot heden* (Kampen, 1991), 187; also Roodenburg, 80, 90–102; Van Deursen, *Plain Lives,* 265, 270, and *Bavianen,* 56, 173; Elliott, 463–66, 470; Evenhuis, II; S. van Ruyven-Zeman, X. van Eck, H. van Dolder-De Wit, *Het geheim van Gouda. De cartons van de Goudse Glazen* (Zutphen, 2002); L. Taylor, *Preachers and People in the Reformations and Early Modern Period* (Leiden, 2003), includes J. Ford, "Preaching in the Reformed Tradition," T. Worcester, "Catholic Sermons," and J. Bosma, "Preaching in the Low Countries"; Beliën, 139; Dorren, 136; Van Veen, 22–28. Complaints about behavior in G. Stronks, "Het kerkvolk op de zondagen. De gereformeerde kerk en de sabbatsontheiliging, ca. 1580–1800," in J. van Laarhoven et al., eds., *Munire Ecclesiam: Opstellen over "gewone gelovigen"* (Maastricht, 1990), 139–52; Van Strien, *Touring,* 132, 204, 205; W. Teellinck, *Huys-boeck, ofte Eenvoudighe verclaringheende toe-eygheninghe, van de voornaemste Vraegh-stucken des Nederlandtschen Christelijcken Catechismi* (Middelburgh, 1639).

Dutch Treats

Attitudes toward family and children: B. Roberts, *Through the Keyhole: Dutch Child-rearing Practices in the 17th and 18th Century* (Hilversum, 1998); D. Haks, *Huwelijk en gezin in Holland in de 17de en 18de eeuw* (Utrecht, 1985).

Drinking and taverns: Schotel, *Maatschappelijk Leven*, 15, passim; Wouters and Abels, 83; Van Deursen, *Plain Lives*, 100; L. Jansen et al., *Herbergen in Nieuwkoop* (Nieuwkoop, 1990); P. Janssens, *Herbergen in Heemskerk* (Heemskerk, 1996); F. Assenberg, *Herbergen in Vlaardingen en Vlaardinger-Ambacht* (Vlaardingen, 1990); B. Hermesdorf, *De herberg in de Nederlanden: Een blik in de beschavingsgeschiedenis* (Arnhem, 1977).

Courting, weddings, feasting, dancing, games: Thomas, 35, 39–43, 70; Van Deursen, *Plain Lives*, 85–87, 107; G. Udinck, *Tot tijdverdrijf in ballingschap (1663–1665)* (Groningen, 1988), ed. H. Niebaum, F. Veldman, entries on niece Marie, such as January 31, February 7, March 29; Van Veen, 73; J. Jobse-van Putten, *Eenvoudig maar voedzaam: Cultuurgeschiedenis van de dagelijkse maaltijd in Nederland* (Nijmegen, 1995); A. Duker, *Gisbertus Voetius*, 4 vols. (Leiden, 1897–1914), on dancing; J. Faber, *Het aantekeningenboek van Dirck Jansz. (1604–1636)* (Hilversum, 1993); Van Strien. The mock battle in *Relatie van het wonderlijck gevecht ende belegeringe vande tafel, seer importante plaetze: by assault gewonnen, by de lief-hebbers vande goede chiere, ende haer-lieder geallieerde* (The Hague, 1655). The collection of songs, in *Den Nieuwen Verbeterden Lust-hof, Gheplant vol uytgelesene, eerlijcke, Amoreuse ende vrolijcke ghesanghen, als Mey, Bruylofts, Tafel, ende Nieu jaers-liedekens . . .* 3rd ed. (n.p., n.d.).

Willem Frederik's Sundays: J. Visser, *Gloria Parendi: Dagboeken van Willem Frederik, stadbouder van Friesland, Groningen en Drenthe, 1643–1649, 1651–1654* (The Hague, 1995); more on him in L. Kooijmans, *Liefde in opdracht: Het hofleven van Willem Frederik van Nassau* (Amsterdam, 2000).

Sunday work: Bosma, in Taylor; Van Strien, *Touring*, September 1718; Spaans, 134.

Sabbath Ideals and Obstacles

Preachers' complaints about Sunday behavior: The catechism excerpt in Van Veen, 103, also 45–51, 115–18, 135, 158; the 34 activities in 56–63; Van den Berg notes that the seventeenth-century arguments over Sunday were anticipated, even explicitly waged, during the Middle Ages as well—the specifics were different, but the basic issue was always the literal or figurative status of the fourth commandment. More complaints in the 164th session of the Synod of Dordt; Elliott, 463–66; Stronks, 147; H. Visser, *De geschiedenis van den Sabbatsstrijd onder de Gereformeerden in de zeventiende eeuw* (Utrecht, 1939), 60; Knuttel, 181; J. van den Berg, "Het stroomlandschap van de Gereformeerde Kerk in Nederland tussen 1650 en 1750," in F. Broeyer, E. van der Wall, et al., eds., *Een richtingenstrijd in de Gereformeerde Kerk: Voetianen en Coccejanen 1650–1750* (Zoetermeer, 1994); Brienen; Van Deursen, *Plain Lives,* 239–40; Evenhuis, II; T. Philadelphus, *Rust-daghs Vermaeck: of Ondersoeck hoe verre een Christen Mensch op des Heeren dagh sijn Playsieren, ende Genuchten mach op-volghen* (n.p., 1664); dancing above under "Courting," see also Duker, Voetius, II, 1643–44 work.

Obstacle of the Regents: Van Deursen, *Bavianen,* 27; Van Veen, 158; Knuttel, I, 45, IV, 51; Eliott, 477 passim; Wouters and Abels, 167–69; Dorren; Van Veen, 81; see any synodal minutes, which contain a multitude of complaints about magistrates not enforcing the Sabbath.

Obstacle of multiple religions: Bergsma, in Scribner et al., 74; Spaans; Wouters and Abels, I, 531; Bosma, in Taylor, 348; Van Deursen, *Plain Lives,* 233, 262, and *Graft,* 82–86; Pollmann; J. D. Bangs, *Pilgrim Life in Leiden* (Leiden, 1997); Van Strien, 131, 203; Dorren, 134; Frijhoff, *Embodied Belief,* 40; Duke, 246; B. Kaplan, "Fictions of Privacy: House Chapels and the Spatial Accommodation of Religious Dissent in Early Modern Europe," *American Historical Review* 107/4 (October 2002): 1031–64.

Obstacle of theological differences: V. Demeulenaere, "De zondag in het Ancien Regime: dag van God en dag van de mens" (licentiate thesis, Katholieke Universiteit Leuven, 1994), shows that Catholic desires for the observance of Sunday, in this case in the Spanish Netherlands, just south of the Dutch Republic, were much the same as Protestant. Luther, in S. Bacchiocci, "Remembering the Sabbath: The Creation-Sabbath in Jewish and Christian History," in *The Sabbath in Jewish and Christian Traditions,* T. C. Eskenazi, D. J. Harrington, and W. H. Shea, eds. (New York, 1991): 69–97, especially 81. Also K. Strand, "Sabbath and Sunday in the Reformation Era," in K. Strand, ed., *The Sabbath in Scripture and History* (Washington, D.C., 1982), 215–28; R. B. Gaffin, *Calvin and the Sabbath* (Geneva, 1998); J. Kaiser, *Ruhe der Seele und Siegel der Hoffnung: die Deutungen des Sabbats in der Reformation* (Göttingen, Germany, 1996); D. Augsburger, "Sunday in the pre-Reformation Disputations in French Switzerland," *Andrews University Seminary Studies* 14 (1976): 265–77; J. Peters, "Sonntagsverbrecher in Schwedisch-Pommern: Zur bäuerlichen Belastbarkeit durch Arbeitsrente," *Jahrbuch für Wirtschaftsgeschichte* 1982 (4): 89–113; J. H. Primus, "Calvin and the Puritan Sabbath: A Comparative Study," in D. Holwerda, ed., *Exploring the Heritage of John Calvin* (Grand Rapids, Mich., 1976); D. F. Schulz, "Gottes Werktage: die Heiligung der Zeit in den Kirchen der Reformation bis zur Mitte des 20 Jahrhunderts," *Kerygma und Dogma* 28 (1982): 91–112; L. Schümmer, "Le sabbat, le dimanche: Un jour pour Dieu, un jour pour l'homme," *Revue réformée* 45 (1994): 39–51; D. Smith, "Die Calvinistiese Sondagbeskouing met spesiale verwysing na Sondagsport en die uitsending daarvan," *Hervormde Teologiese Studies* 46/4 (November 1990): 596–612.

The Shadow of the English Sabbath

The early modern English Sabbath: Bownd's work is *The doctrine of the sabbath: plainely layde forth, and soundly proued by testimonies both of holy scripture, and also of olde and new ecclesiasticall writers* (London, 1595). Helpful secondary sources were B. Ball, *The Seventh-Day Men: Sabbatarians and Sabbatarianism in England and Wales, 1600–1800* (Oxford, 1994); D. Como, *Blown By the Spirit* (Stanford, 2004); J. T. Dennison, *The Market Day of the Soul: The Puritan Doctrine of the Sabbath in England, 1532–1700* (New York, 1983); L. A. Govett, *The King's Book of Sports. A history of the declarations of King James I, and King Charles I, as to the use of lawful sports on Sundays* (London, 1890); R. L. Greaves, "The Origins of English Sabbatarian Thought," *Sixteenth Century Journal* 12/3 (1981): 19–34; D. S. Katz, *Sabbath and Sectarianism in Seventeenth-Century England* (Leiden, 1988); D. S. Katz, "Jewish Sabbath and Christian Sunday in Early Modern England," in *Jewish Christians and Christian Jews*, R. Popkin and G. Weiner, eds. (The Hague, 1994): 119–30; K. L. Parker, *The English Sabbath: A Study of Doctrine and Discipline from the Reformation to the Civil War* (Cambridge, 1988); K. L. Parker, "Never on a Sunday: Why Sunday Afternoon Sports Transformed Seventeenth-Century England," *South Atlantic Quarterly* 95/2 (1996): 339–64; K. L. Parker, "Thomas Rogers and the English Sabbath," *Church History* 53/3 (1984): 332–47; J. H. Primus, *Holy Time: Moderate Puritanism and the Sabbath* (Macon, Ga., 1989); J. H. Primus, "The Dedham Sabbath Debate: More Light on English Sabbatarianism," *Sixteenth Century Journal* 17/1 (1986): 87–102; J. H. Primus, "Sunday: The Lord's Day as a Sabbath—Protestant Perspectives on the Sabbath," in *The Sabbath in Jewish and Christian Traditions*, T. C. Eskenazi, D. J. Harrington, W. H. Shea, eds. (New York, 1991): 98–136; L. Racaut, "The Book of Sports and Sabbatarian Legislation in Lancashire, 1579–1616," *Northern History (Great Britain)* 33 (1997): 73–87; J. K. Ruhl, "Religion and Amusements in Sixteenth and Seventeenth-Century England: 'Time might be better bestowed and besides wee see sin acted'," *British Journal of Sports History* 1/2 (1984): 125–65; W. B. Whitaker, *Sunday in Tudor and Stuart Times* (London,

1933); H. Sul, "The King's Book of Sports: The Nature of Leisure in Early Modern England," *International Journal of the History of Sport* 17/4 (2000): 167–79.

Comparisons to Scotland: R. Brackenridge, "Enforcement of Sunday Observance in Post-Revolution Scotland," *Scottish Church History Society Records* 17/1 (1969): 33–45; L. Leneman, "Prophaning the Lord's Day: Sabbath Breach in Early Modern Scotland," *History (Great Britain)* 74/241 (1989): 217–31; J. McGavin, "Kirk, the Burgh, and Fun," *Early Theatre: A Journal Associated with the Records of Early Drama* 1 (1998): 13–26; M. Todd, "Profane Pastimes and the Reformed Community: The Persistence of Popular Festivities in Early Modern Scotland," *Journal of British Studies* 39/2 (2000): 123–56.

Dutch efforts to implement the English Sabbath: Willem Teellinck, *De Rusttijdt: Ofte Tractaet van d'onderhoudinge des Christenlijken Rust Dachs* (Rotterdam, 1622), plus his *Huys-boeck,* 2–4. More on him and the early struggle in Van Veen, 113; Frijhoff, *Evert Willemsz,* 303; Van den Berg, "Stroomlandschap," 14; Stronks, 142–43; Visser, *Sabbats-strijd,* 57–82; Willem Ames, *The Marrow of Theology,* 287–300; Jacobus Burs, *Threnos, or Lamentation Showing the Causes of the Pitiful Condition of the Country and the Desecration of the Sabbath* (Tholen, 1627).

Coccejus and later debates: Van Veen, 121–53, among others. More specific studies include W. van Asselt, *Johannes Coccejus: Portret van een zeventiende-eeuws theoloog op oude en nieuwe wegen* (Herenveen, 1997); Visser, *Sabbats-strijd;* and F. A. van Lieburg, *De Nadere Reformatie in Utrecht ten tijde van Voetius* (Rotterdam, 1989).

English in the Dutch Republic: J. Leynse, *Preceding the* Mayflower: *The Pilgrims in England and in the Netherlands* (New York, 1972), 91–100, 203; K. Sprunger, *Dutch Puritanism: A History of English and Scottish Churches of the Netherlands in the Sixteenth and Seventeenth Centuries* (Leiden, 1982); K. L. Sprunger, "English and Dutch Sabbatarianism and the Development of Puritan Social Theology (1600–1660)," *Church History* 51/1 (1982): 24–38; Van Veen, 21; Van Strien, 201; Bangs, 16.

Baboons and Papists on Sunday
Mennonites: W. J. Kühler, *Geschiedenis van de Doopsgezinden in Nederland,* 2 vols. (Haarlem, 1940).

Remonstrants: L. van Aken, *De Remonstrantsche Broederschap in Verleden en Heden* (Arnhem, 1947).

Catholics: Kaplan, "Fictions"; P. W. F. M. Hamans, *Geschiedenis van de Katholieke kerk in Nederland* (Brugge, 1992); F. Hoppenbrouwers, *Oefening in volmaaktheid: De zeventiende-eeuwse rooms-katholieke spiritualiteit in de Republiek* (The Hague, 1996); B. Te Lintelo, *Ketters en Papen in Twente* (Hengelo, 1988); L. J. Rogier, *Geschiedenis van het Katholicisme in Noord-Nederland in de 16de en 17de eeuw,* 5 vols. (Amsterdam, 1964); G. Rooijakkers, *Rituele repertoires: Volkscultuur in oostelijk Noord-Brabant, 1559–1853* (Nijmegen, 1994); W. Tepe, *XXIV Paepsche Vergaderplaetsen* (Amsterdam, 1984); M. Wingens, *Over de grens: De bedevaart van katholieke Nederlanders in de zeventiende en achttiende eeuw* (Nijmegen, 1994). Also C. Dessing, "De toestand der Katholieken te Zevenbergen tijdens de republiek," *Bossche Bijdragen* 18 (1941–45); G. Hilhorst, "Het Kerspel Schalkwijk," *Archief van het Aartsbisdom Utrecht* (1884): 56; J. H. Hofman, "Het Kerspel Olst," *Archief van het Aartsbisdom Utrecht* (1892): 90; C. Kooi, "Converts and Apostates: The Competition for Souls in Early Modern Holland," *Archive for Reformation History* 92 (2001): 195–214; J. van der Loos, "De pastoors der Statie Soeterwoude na de Hervorming," *Bijdragen tot de geschiedenis van het bisdom Haarlem* 26 (1901): 147–48; M. Olthof, "Leusden en Hamersveld," *Archief van het Aartsbisdom Utrecht* (1909); H. N. Ouwerling, "Uit de Kerkgeschiedenis van Deurne," *Bossche Bijdragen* (1922–23); L. Scholte, "Limmen," *Bijdragen tot de geschiedenis van het bisdom Haarlem* 13 (1886); M. Spiertz, "De godsdienstig leven van de katholieken in de 17de eeuw," *Algemene Geschiedenis der Nederlanden,* vol. 8, (Haarlem, 1979), 344–57.

4 SUNDAY À LA MODE

Louis Morin and his book: L. Morin, *Les dimanches parisiens, notes d'un décadent* (Paris, 1898). On Morin, see H. Boucher, "Louis Morin," *International Studio* 10 (1900–06): 242–54; R. Hesse, *Les artistes du livre: Louis Morin* (Paris, 1930); review of L. Morin, *French Illustrators,* in *Nation* 57 (1893): 454–55; M. H. Spielmann, "Louis Morin," *Magazine of Art* (1901): 151–58; E. Bayard, *La caricature et les caricaturistes* (Paris, 1900).

Sunday and the people: R. Marx, "Dimanches de Paris," in *Les types de Paris* (Paris, 1889).

Industrialization, urbanization, class in Europe and France: Broadly, R. Merriman, *A History of Modern Europe* (New Haven, Conn., 1996), R. Magraw, *France 1815–1914: The Bourgeois Century* (London, 1983), J. Popkin, *A History of Modern France,* 3rd ed. (Upper Saddle River, N.J., 2006), A. Horne, *Seven Ages of Paris* (London, 2002), and T. Zeldin, *France, 1848–1945,* 2 vols. (Oxford, 1973). Also J. Aubert, *Paris autrefois* (Lyon, 1995); J. P. Chaline, *Les bourgeois de Rouen: Une élite urbaine au XIXe siècle* (Paris, 1982); G. Crossick, H.–G. Haupt, *The Petite Bourgeoisie in Europe, 1780–1914* (London, 1995); H.–G. Haupt, "The Petty Bourgeoisie in Germany and France in the Late Nineteenth Century," in J. Kocha, A. Mitchell, eds., *Bourgeois Society in Nineteenth-Century Europe* (Oxford, 1993), 302–22; H. Kaelble, "French Bourgeoisie and German Bürgertum, 1870–1914," in Kocka and Mitchell, 273–301; P. Parkhurst Ferguson, *Paris as Revolution: Writing the Nineteenth-Century City* (Berkeley, 1994); A. Gérard, Y. Katan, P. Saly, H. Trocmé, *Villes et sociétés urbaines au XIXe siècle: France, Grande-Bretagne, États-Unis, Allemagne, Autriche* (Paris, 1992); B. Smith, *Ladies of the Leisure Class* (Princeton, 1981); E. Weber, *Peasants into Frenchmen: The Modernization of Rural France, 1870–1914* (Stanford, 1976).

Leisure, entertainments, and recreation generally: L. Abrams, *Workers' Culture in Imperial Germany. Leisure and Recreation in the Rhineland and Westphalia* (New York, 1992); Y. Berce, *Fête et révolte* (Paris, 1976); A. Corbin, ed., *L'avenèment des loisirs, 1850–1960* (Paris, 1995); G. Cross, *A Quest for Time. The Reduction of Work in Britain and France, 1840–1940* (Berkeley, 1998), and G. Cross, *Time and Money: The Making of Consumer Culture* (London, 1993); G. Cross, ed., *Worktime and Industrialization: An International History* (Philadelphia, 1988); H. Cunningham, *Leisure in the Industrial Revolution, c.1780–c.1880* (New York, 1980); A. Daumard, *Oisiveté et loisirs dan les sociétés occidentales au xix siècle* (Abbéville, France, 1983); C. Rearick, *Pleasures of the Belle Époque: Entertainment and Festivity in Turn-of-the-Century France* (New Haven, Conn., 1986); V. Schwartz, *Spectacular Realities: Early Mass Culture in Fin-de-Siècle Paris* (Berkeley, 1998); B. Stern Shapiro, ed., *Pleasures of Paris: Daumier to Picasso* (Boston, 1991).

Some guidebooks and descriptions and images of France around 1900, especially Paris: L. Beaumont-Maillet, *Atget Paris* (Paris, 1892), G. Le Gall, *Atget: Life in Paris* (Paris, 1998), and W. Wiegand, ed., *Eugène Atget: Paris* (New York, 1998), on the well-known photographer's turn-of-the-century images; also L. Besse, A. Bernard, *Huit jours à Paris: Guide des étrangers et des promeneurs . . .* (Paris, 1864); M. Carriere, G. Coistaz, *Le livre de Paris 1900* (n.p., 1994); J. Claretie, *La vie à Paris*, 20 vols. (1880–1901); E. Frébault, *La vie de Paris: Guide pittoresque et pratique du visiteur* (Paris, 1878); G. Grison, *Paris horrible et Paris original* (Paris, 2001, after 1882 edition); L. Ulbach, *Guide sentimental de l'étranger dans Paris, par un Parisien* (Paris, 1878).

Some specific studies of the French Sunday, past or recent (religiously oriented works are below, under "Holy Sunday," and some others are mentioned separately): The outstanding recent survey is R. Beck, *Histoire du dimanche: De*

1700 à nos jours (Paris, 1997), plus his "C'est dimanche qu'il nous faut: Les mouvements sociaux en faveur du repos dominical et hebdomadaire en France avant 1906," *Le mouvement social* 184 (1998): 23–51. See also G. E. Coubard d'Aulnay, *Le dimanche d'un garçon* (n.p., 1841); J.-F. Barrielle, *Quand dimanche était jour de fête* (Paris, 1982); E. Bersier, *Le dimanche* (Paris, 1864); J. Bouttier, *Le dimanche, dialogue* (Lille, 1849); Y. Brisset de Morcour, *La police séculaire des dimanches et fêtes dan l'ancienne France* (Paris, 1936); "Le dimanche à Paris: Extrait de la press (du samedi 7 Juillet 18 . .)," Bibliothèque National, 32511; J. C. David, "L'observation des dimanches et fêtes a Paris en juin 1814, D'après un memoire inédit de l'abbé Morellet," *Revue d'histoire moderne et contemporaine* 33 (October–December 1986): 645–60; R. Dufay, *Le dimanche: Hier et aujourd'hui* (n.p., 1979); G. Coquiot, *Dimanches d'eté* (Paris, n.d.); R. Marx, "Sunday Closed," *L'histoire* 41 (1982): 89–91; A. Mossé, "Notes historiques sur le repos hebdomadaire," *Jour. d. économistes* 6/15 (1907): 335–50; H. Sebastiani, *La question du repos hebdomadarie dans l'industrie* (Paris, 1904); R. Watin-Augouard, *L'application & la réforme de la loi du 13 juillet 1906 sur le repos hebdomadaire* (Paris, 1909); and such "mood" titles as J.-L. Petitrenaud, *52 omelettes du dimanche soir: Par les plus grands chefs de France* (Geneva, 2000), M. Le Drian, *Le dimanche on va au restaurant* (Paris, 1994); or the children's book S.-V. Rosabianca, *Un dimanche avec . . . Renoir* (Geneva, 1990).

Some examples of Sunday issues in other European countries at the time: R. Lanzavecchia, "Per la storia del movimento sociale cattolico: La lega del riposo festivo di torino," *Bollettino del 'archivio* 20:2 (1985): 330–37; S. Laube, "Religiosität, Arbeit und Erholung: Bayerische Heiligentage im 19. Jahrhundert," *Zeitschrift für bayerische Landesgeschichte* 61:2 (1998): 347–82; P. Niemeyer, "Die Sonntagsruhe vom hygienischen Standpunkte," *Sammlung und Vorträgen fur das deutsche Volk* 4 (1880): 377–400; C. Wischermann, "Streit um Sonntagsarbeit: Historische Perspektiven einer aktuellen Kontroverse," *Vierteljahrschrift fur Sozial und Sirtschaftsgeschichte* 78:1 (1991): 6–38.

The *décadents*: M. Calinescu, *Faces of Modernity: Avant-Garde, Decadence, Kitsch* (Bloomington, Ind., 1977); A. Carter, *The Idea of Decadence in French Literature, 1830–1900* (Toronto, 1958); J. Przybo, *Zoom sur les décadents* (Paris, 2002); J. Siegel, *Bohemian Paris* (New York, 1986); R. Thornton, *The Decadent Dilemma* (London, 1983). The website on www.dandyism.net.

On the Boulevard

In addition to guidebooks and entertainments listed above, see Chantal George, "Les premiers visiteurs du Louvre," *L'Histoire* 130 (February 1990): 32; Balzac, in Gérard et al., 133; also J. Csergo, "Extension et mutation du loisir citadin, Paris XIXe–début XXe siècle," in Corbin, 121–68.

Of Cafés and Dance Halls

In addition to Rearick, 83, Csergo, and others listed above under "Leisure entertainments," F. Gasnault, *Guinguettes et lorettes. Bals publics et danse sociale entre 1830 et 1870* (Paris, 1986); Shapiro, 123, on prostitutes.

Mass?

For more on religion, see the works listed under "Holy Sunday," below.

Au Restaurant

P. Andrieu, *Histoire du restaurant en France* (n.p., 1955); Chatillon-Plessis, *La vie à table à la fin du 19e siècle* (Paris, 1894); A. Huetz de Lemps, J. R. Pitte, *Les restaurants dans le monde et à travers les âges* (Grenoble, 1990); S. Mennell, *All Manners of Food: Eating and Taste in England and France from the Middle Ages to the Present* (Oxford, 1985); L. Moulin, *Les liturgies de la table: Une histoire culturelle du manger et du boire* (Antwerp, 1988); R. L. Spang, *The Invention of the Restaurant: Paris and Modern Gastronomic Culture* (Harvard, 2000); M. Twain, *Innocents Abroad* (New York, 2002), 76.

The Infield of Longchamps

In addition to Horne, 270, Rearick, and other works on entertainment above, see on sport R. Holt, *Sport and Society in Modern France* (London, 1981); E. Weber, "Gymnastics and Sports in Fin-de-Siècle France: Opium of the Classes?" *American Historical Review* 86 (Feb 1971): 70–98; P. Arnaud, J. Camy, eds., *La naissance du mouvement sportif associatif en France. Sociabilités et formes de pratiques sportives* (Lyon, 1986). On horses, N. de Blomac, *La gloire et le jeu: Des hommes et des chevaux (1766–1866)* (Paris, 1991). And on the draw of the suburbs and urban parks, B. Cabadoce, "Jardins ouvriers et banlieue: Le bonheur au jardin?" in A. Faure, ed., *Les premiers banlieusards. Aux origines des banlieues de Paris* (Paris, 1991), 202; M. Conan, I. Marghieri, "Figures on the Grass: The Public Gardens of Paris," *Landscape* 31:1 (1991): 29–35. On Proust and omnibuses in Paris, Shapiro, 52. Warnings against omnibuses in Ulbach, chapter "Paris en Voiture."

To the Country!, And Again!

G. E. Coubard d'Aulnay, *Le dimanche d'un garçon* (n.p., 1841). Jean Gabin in D. Baugard, "Pour une anthroposociologie du dimanche: Signification, représentation et pratique, temps de travail et temps hors-travail," *Loisir et société* 20/1 (1997): 172–79. Also Frébault, 287–325. Merriman, 355, on bicycles.

Pleasure Train
Corbin, 35, on the emergence of "the beach" in the eighteenth century; but Chaline, 203–17, on the lack of appeal of coastal towns until the First World War,
even in such close-lying places as Rouen.

Working Sunday
Smallpox in Kocka and Mitchell, 355–56. In this and other sections Beck, *Dimanche,* has very helpful things to say, as on 145 and 245 about the revolutionary calendar. Also Cross, *Quest for Time,* 82–83, and other works under
"Industrialization" above. J. Lefort, *Du repos hebdomadaire au point de vue de
la morale de la culture intellectuelle et du progrès de l'industrie . . . ouvrage
couronné par l'Académie des sciences morales et politiques* (Paris, 1874). Merriman, 832, on birthrates. Specific studies of St. Monday include J. Kaplow, "La
fin de la Saint-Lundi, étude sur le Paris ouvrier au XIX siècle," *Temps libre* 2
(1981): 108; H. Polge, "Le dimanche et le lundi," *Annales du Midi* 87:121
(1975): 15–36; J. Reulecke, "Vom blauen Montag zum Arbeiterurlaub.
Vorgeschichte und Entstehung des Erholungsurlaubs für Arbeiter vor dem ersten
Weltkrieg," *Archiv für Sozialgeschichte* 16 (1976): 205–48. Zola depicts an im-
peccable Sunday among workers, noted in D. Hollier, *Against Architecture: The
Writings of Georges Bataille* (Cambridge, Mass., 1989), in an 1868 editorial in
La tribune. The commercial animation in Beck, "C'est dimanche."

Jean and Marie in F. Le Play, *Les ouviers des deux mondes,* 5 vols. (Paris,
1857–85), second series (1895–90); revised and abridged (n.p., 1983). Also the
water-carrier, Sophie-Victoire, the 59-year-old laborer and his 43-year-old wife,
the cabinetmaker and his wife, the surveyor in Guise, the tailor in Meusnes. Useful were H. Leyret, *En plein faubourg: Notations d'un mastroquet sur les moeurs
ouvrières* (Paris, 1895); P.-J. Proudhon, *De la célébration dimanche considérée
sous les rapports de l'hygiène publique, de la morale des relations de famille et
de cité . . .* (Paris, 1850).

The postmistress in J. Bouvier, *Mes memoires, une syndicaliste feministe,
1875–1935* (Poitiers, 1936), and her broader *Histoire des dames employées
dans les postes, télégraphes et téléphones de 1714 à 1929* (Paris, 1930), and
Beck, *Dimanche,* 191.

Strikes and problems: Beck, "C'est dimanche," 28, 39, and *Dimanche,* 301–02,
316–18, passim; Cross, *Quest for Time,* 82–83.

Sunday Horrible
Works mentioned include G. de Maupassant, *"A Parisian Bourgeois' Sundays,"
and Other Stories* (London, 1997); Charles Foley, *Le dimanche d'un bureau-*

crate (Paris, 1883); plus interpretations of Seurat in Y. Contempré, *Un dimanche après midi à l'île de la Grande Jatte* (Paris, 1978); C. McKay, "Presence and Absence: Seurat and the 'Bathers,' National Gallery, London," *History Workshop Journal* 45 (1998): 240–45; R. McMullen, "Sunday Afternoon on the Island of La Grande Jatte," *Horizon:* 82–94, and countless others.

J. Vallès, *Le dimanche d'un jeune homme pauvre: Le septième jour d'un condamné* (Paris, 1860), plus Siegel, who discusses Vallès specifically from 195 on; also Shapiro, 20. Vallès's obituary in *Le monde illustré,* 21 February 1885. A Bohemian pedigree exists on the "dandyism" website mentioned above, where the quote from Baudelaire may be found as well.

Holy Sunday
Auguste's story in *Notre-Dame du dimanche à Saint-Bauzille de la Sylve* (Hérault) (n.p., 1897). On the same shrine, B. Billet, *Notre-Dame du dimanche. Les apparitions à Saint-Bauzille-de-la-Sylve. L'événement—Le message* (Paris, 1973).

Apparitions of Mary in the nineteenth century, besides those in Lourdes: See D. Blackbourn, *Marpingen* (New York, 1995), for a German example, and V. Turner, E. Turner, *Image and Pilgrimage in Christian Culture* (New York, 1978), ch. 6, "Apparitions, Messages, and Miracles: Postindustrial Marian Pilgrimage." Also R. Gibson, *A Social History of French Catholicism, 1789–1914* (London, 1989), 145–51, and Beck, *Dimanche,* 251–53, passim. More accounts and discussion in A. Badts de Cugnac, *Relation complète de la guérison de Mme la comtesse Hedwige de Chatillon obtenue à Lourdes le dimanche 31 mai 1885* (Amiens, 1885); Abbé Janvier, *Vie de la Soeur Saint-Pierre, carmelite de Tour* (Tours, 1881); P. Boutry, "Marie, la grande consolatrice de la France au XIX siècle," *L'Histoire* 50 (1982): 31. On nineteenth-century religion more broadly, Gibson, and Yves-Marie Hilaire, *Une chrétienté au xix siècle? La vie religieuse des populations du diocese d'Arras (1840–1914),* 2 vols. (Lille, 1977); M. Lagrée, *Religion et culture en Bretagne, 1850–1950* (Paris, 1992); M. Launay, *Le bon prêtre: Le clerge rural au XIX siècle* (n.p., 1986); P. Pierrard, *La vie quotidienne du prêtre Français au XIXe siècle, 1801–1905* (Paris, 1986).

Church attendance and Sunday complaints: Merriman, 850, Beck, *Dimanche,* 278, Weber, 364, and F. Gibon, *Le dimanche de l'homme des champs* (Paris, 1902), 16. Other religiously minded complaints of the current Sunday in W. W. Atterbury, *Le dimanche aux États-Unis* (New York, n.d.); *Le bulletin de la ligue populaire pour le repos du dimanche.* 1889–1910; P. Collot, *Instructions sur le dimanche et les fêtes en général . . .* (Marseille, 1831); *Le dimanche. Avis a tout le monde, surtout aux habitants des campagnes* (Paris, 1854); *Un dimanche au village* (n.p., n.d.); F. Gibon, *Les bienfaits du dimanche* (Paris, n.d.); A. Gicquel

des Touches, *Le dimanche chez les nations Protestantes* (n.p., 1889); R. Lavol-
lée, *Le dimanche et les chemins de fer* (Paris, 1889); Abbé Jacques-Isidore Mul-
lois, *Le dimanche aux classes elevées de la société, ou manuel de l'oeuvre du
dimanche* (Paris, 1854), and *Le dimanche au peuple* (Paris, 1854); W. de
Nordling, *Le repos du dimanche et le service des chemins de fer* (Paris, 1890);
M.-I. Tourte-Cherbuliez, *Un dimanche: Scènes familières* (Geneva, 1857). There
were various journals devoted to more religious Sundays as well, such as *Le dimanche catholique* (1874–1922); *L'observateur du dimanche* (1854–68), and
Le repos du dimanche (1890–1914).

Cissey: L. Bastien, *Vie de M. de Cissey, promoteur de l'oeuvre dominicale de
France* (Paris, 1893).

Sunday-keeping and birthrates: One broader study from an earlier period of rel-
evance, H. J. Voth, "Seasonality of Conceptions as a Source for Historical Time-
Budget Analysis: Tracing the Disappearance of Holy Days in Early Modern
England," *Historical Methods* 27:3 (1994): 127–32.

Rimbaud: Excerpts from the poem "les poètes de sept an."

Consternation and expansibility: see Marx.

5 SUNDAY OBSCURED

The last Sunday before war: K. van Isacker, *Mijn land in de kering 1830–1980*,
2 vols. (Antwerp, 1978–83), 1: 248; C. Verschaeve, *Oorlogsindrukken* (Ghent,
1996), 174. Birds' nests are a frequent object of desire among boys in the novels
of Ernest Claes; his quote is from *Daar is een mens verdronken* (Leuven, 1950),
29. (Unless obviously elsewhere, place names in this chapter are from Belgium.)

The best single source for all aspects of the First World War in Belgium is the
masterful S. Schaepdrijver, *De groote oorlog: Het koninkrijk België tijdens de
eerste wereldoorlog* (Amsterdam, 1997). More recently, see also L. De Vos, *De
eerste Wereldoorlog* (Leuven, 2003). In English, W. Groom, *A Storm in Flanders: The Ypres Salient, 1914–1918* (Washington, D.C., 2002); J. Horne, A.
Kramer, *German Atrocities: A History of Denial* (New Haven, Conn., 2001);
relevant parts of E. H. Kossmann, *The Low Countries 1780–1940* (Oxford,
1978); S. Marks, *Innocent Abroad: Belgium at the Paris Peace Conference of
1919* (Chapel Hill, N.C., 1981); and L. Zuckerman, *The Rape of Belgium* (New
York, 2004). Bibliography in P. Lefèvre, J. Lorette, *La Belgique et la première
guerre mondiale: Bibliographie—België en de Eerste Wereldoorlog: bibliografie*
(Brussels, 1987), and P.-A. Tallier, S. Soupart, *België en de eerste wereldoorlog:
Bibliografie, deel 2, 1985–2000* (Brussels, 2000).

Old Sunday

For some Irish examples of sentimentality for Sunday, see "Some Popular Depictions" under the note to "A Word Before."

Political, social, religious, economic context: Schaepdrijver, 11–40; Van Isacker, 1: 179–88; L. Van Molle, "Voorstellingen van de agrarische samenleving in België rond 1900," in L. Pil, *Boeren, burgers en Buitenlui: Voorstellingen van het landelijk leven in België vanaf 1850* (Leuven, 1990); and J. Polasky, "Transplanting and Rooting Workers in London and Brussels: A Comparative History," *Journal of Modern History* 73 (September 2001): 528–60.

Claes and Sunday: "De nieuwe parochie," in *Die schone tijd* (Antwerp, 1949); *Het leven en de dood van Victalis van Gille* (Leuven, 1951).

Saturday night haircut: Claes, "Janneke de Kleermaker en Fiel Ekster," in *Ernest Claes vertelt* (Antwerp, 1944).

Racing doves: Van Isacker, 1: 186; Y. Vandenbrande, *Vinkt tussen de twee wereldoorlogen, 1918–1940* (Deinze, 2001), 276–77. Sander's story in *Pastoor Campens Zaliger* (Antwerp, 1935). Also "Pastoor Munte," in *Sichemsche Novellen* (Leuven, 1921), and the fast-reading pastor in "De nieuwe parochie." Streuvels example from " 's Zondags," a part of "Lenteleven," in *Volledig Werk,* 4 vols. (Brugge and Utrecht, 1971–73), vol. 1.

Sunday Mass: J. van Haver, *Voor u, beminde gelovigen. Het rijke roomse leven in Vlaanderen (1920–1950)* (Tielt, 1995), 22–40; Vandenbrande, 130–59; Claes, "De nieuwe parochie," *Pastoor Campens, De Witte* (Amsterdam, 1920), *Studentenkosthuis 'Bij Fien Janssens'* (Leuven, 1950), *Voor de open poort* (Leuven, 1952), "Pastoor Munte," and *Daar is een mens.*

After Mass, and lunch and vespers: Van Isacker, 1: 230–31; Van Haver; Claes, *Voor de open poort,* and the others just cited; Vandenbrande, 32.

Catechism and Sunday clothing: Claes, *Whitey,* "Pastoor Munte," "Janneke de Kleermaker," *Studentenkosthuis.* Vandenbrande, 29–30.

Fanfare: Claes, *De fanfare "De Sint-jansvrienden"* (Brussels, 1924).

Excursions: Claes, *Studentenkosthuis.*

Cafés: Claes, *Onze smid* (Brussels, 1928), "De mambers van 't konsèl," in *Sichemsche Novellen* (Leuven, 1921); Van Isacker, 1: 194–96; Vandenbrande, 101, on women on Sunday.

Streuvels's tragic Sunday: "Zomerzondag," part of "Lenteleven," in *Volledige Werk.* Abraham Hans in his *Roeselare in den Oorlog* (Roeselare, 1919), 7.

Sunday in Trenches
Generally: Again much information comes from Schaepdrijver, *De groote oorlog.* Dix quote in S. Weintraub, *Silent Night: The Remarkable Christmas Truce
of 1914* (London, 2001), 6. On the ancient Israelites, V. Nikiprowetzky, "Le
Sabbat et les Armes dans l'histoire ancienne d'Israël," *Revue des études juives*
159/1-2 (2000): 1-17; the truce of God and Bouvines in G. Duby, *The Legend
of Bouvines: War, Religion, and Culture in the Middle Ages* (Berkeley, 1990), 1;
P. Catteeuw, *Jozef van Herck: Memorieboekje 1915* (Kontich, 2002), 5 September 1915. More broadly, M. Shevin-Coetzee, F. Coetzee, *World War I and European Society: A Sourcebook* (Lexington, Mass., 1995); C. F. Horne, ed.,
Source Records of World War I (Lewiston, N.Y., 1998), vol. 2.

More memoirs and sources of soldier life: L. Barthas, *De oorlogsdagboeken van
Louis Barthas, tonnenmaker* (Amsterdam, 1999); P. Chielens, et al., *Karel
Lauwers: Kunstenaar & soldaat, Antwerpen 1892–Lendelede 1918* (Ieper,
2000); E. Claes, *Uit mijn soldatentijd* (Le Havre, France, 1917); E. Claes, *Uit
den oorlog: Namen 1914* (Antwerp, 1919); J. De Cuyper, E. H. André, *Journal
de campagne, 1914–1917: Oorlogsboek van een hulpdokter bij het Belgische
leger* (Brugge, 1968); J. Dewaele, *De oorlog van Valentin* (Koksijde, 1999); *Het
evangelie van de Zondag,* in Algemene Rijksarchief, Brussels; M. Gerstmans, *De
oorlogsdagen in Augustus 1914 te Sint-Truiden: De belevenissen van een bran-
cardier* (St. Truiden, 1964); A. Gysel, *Decker's dagboek, 1914–1919: Notities
van een oorlogsvrijwilliger* (Ghent, 1999); A. Gysel, *De grote oorlog van onder-
lieutenant Arthur L. Pasquier* (Ghent, n.d.); A. Gysel, *In der Modderbrij: Oorlogsdagboek van R. Snoeck* (Ghent, 1998); A. Gysel, *Oorlogsdagboek Ieper
1914–1915: Zuster Margriet-Marie* (Ghent, 2002); J. Laffin, *On the Western
Front: Soldiers' Stories from France and Flanders, 1914–1918* (Surrey, England,
1998); G. De Landtsheer, *Eugeen Van Mieghem: Kunstenaar in oorlogstijd,
1914–1918* (Ieper, 2002); F. Pijnaert, G. Schaeck, *Dagboek: Belevenissen als
oorlogsvrijwilliger met vertrek en terugkeer uit de oorlog 1914–1918* (Lan-
degem, 1974); P. Sagenstem, *Mijn oorlogsdagboek* (Antwerp, 1938); I. Samson,
Brieven, indrukken en beschouwingen (Amsterdam, 1917); A. Sevens, *Uit het
oog, uit het hart! Rozen uit het kampleven* (Antwerp, 1919); Verschaeve, *Oorlogsindrukken;* J. Vols, "Zo was mijn oorlog: Uit het dagboek van een
brankardier," Brussels, Legermuseum, At-14 VI 152.

Studies of soldier and front life: see especially T. Ashworth, *Trench Warfare,
1914–1918: The Live and Let Live System* (London, 1980), but also Schaepdrijver, chap. 6, and P. Chapman, T. Smith, *In the Shadow of Hell: Behind the
Lines in Poperinghe* (London, 2001). Also K. Adriaenssens, "1914–1918: Ma-
teriële, culturele en morele aspecten" (licentiate thesis, Katholieke Universiteit
Leuven, 1984); R. Christens, K. De Clercq, *Frontleven 14–18. Het dagelijks*

leven van de Belgische soldaten aan de Ijzer (Tielt, 1987); F. Deflo, *De literaire oorlog: De Vlaamse prozaliteratuur over de eerste wereldoorlog* (Aartrijke, 1991); C. Depoorter, *1914–1918: De oorlog achter het front* (Poperinge, 1999); J. R. Leconte, *Aumôniers militaires Belges de la guerre 1914–1918* (Brussels, 1969); M. Meul, "De oorlogsmeters van de Belgische soldaten tijdens de eerste wereldoorlog (1914–1918)" (dissertation, Katholieke Universiteit Leuven, 2002); J. Meyer, *La vie quotidienne des soldats . . .* (Paris, 1966); *Mis en gebedenboek van den Vlaamschen soldaat* (Bussum, 1917).

Free Sunday

Many of the works in the last section overlap into this section, because Belgian soldiers were fighting in the free territory; but see more specifically S. Debaeke, *Ik was 20 in '14* (Koksijde, 1999); A. Gysel, *Jane de Launoy, 1914–1918: Oorlogsverpleegsters in bevolen dienst* (Ghent, 2000); J. Simons, *Oorlogsvlaanderen* (n.p., 1921); A. Van Walleghem, *De oorlog te Dikkenbussche en Omstreken* (Brugge, 1967). Claes on the French in *Bei uns in Deutschland* (Brussels, 1919), 88–89.

Occupied Sunday

The chief memoirs for this section are S. Streuvels, *In oorlogstijd: Het volledige dagboek van de eerste wereldoorlog* (Brugge, 1979); V. Loveling, L. Stynen, S. Van Peteghem, B. Van Raemdonck, *In oorlogsnood, Virginie Lovelings dagboek 1914–1918* (Ghent, 1999), with V. Van Conkelberge, S. Van Peteghem, *Index bij Virginie Lovelings dagboek, 1914–1918, In oorlogsnood* (Ghent, 2001); A. Deprez, ed., *Verzameld Journalistiek Werk van Karel van de Woestijne* (Ghent, 1986–95), vols. 7–9; and L. Gille et al., *Cinquante mois d'occupation* (Brussels, 1919). Helpful in reading these memoirs was S. de Schaepdrijver, "Drie Vlaamse schrijvers en de *Groote Oorlog*: De oorlogsaantekeningen van Virginie Loveling, Stijn Streuvels en Cyriel Verschaeve," *Handelingen van de Maatschappij voor geschiedenis en oudheidkunde te Gent,* Nieuwe Reeks 56 (2002): 283–98.

Other useful memoirs: J. Demarée, F. Vanhove, *Oorlog in de Belgique: Het oorlogsdagboek van schoenmaker Felicien Vanhove uit Zarren, 1914–1917* (Veurne, 2000); E. Denys, *'t Is Oorlog, Pastoor!* (Koksijde, 2001); E. Denys, *Uitgedreven: Oorlogsdagboek over Clercken* (Antwerp, 1922); K. Dumoulin, *Getuigen van de grote oorlog: Getuigenissen uit de frontstreek* (Koksijde, 2001); Elf Novembergroep, *Van den grooten oorlog* (n.p., n.d.); J. Geldhof, *Oorlogsdagboeken over Ieper,* 2 vols. (Ieper, 1974–77); *Heures de Détresse* (Brussels, 1915); L. Devliegher, *Oorlogsdagboeken uit de streek tussen Ijzer en Leie* (Brugge, 1972); J. Gits, *Izegem 14–18,* 2 vols. (Izegem, 2001); J. N.-E. Fonteyne, *Kinderjaren* (Antwerp, 1939); L. Slosse, *Oorlogsdagboek van Rumbeke in 1914–1918* (Brugge, 1962); E. I. Strubbe, "Een halve eeuw uitgaven van West-vlaamse oorlogsdagboeken uit de eerste wereldoorlog," in Van Walleghem, *De oorlog te Dikkenbusche,* 5–27; L. Ureel, *De Kleine mens in de grote oorlog: Getuigenissen van twee generaties dorpsonderwijzers uit de frontstreek* (Tielt, 1984); H. Vanden Abeele, *Oorlogsdagboek van eenen gemeente secretaris* (n.p., 1924); A. Vierset, *Mes souvenirs sur l'óccupation allemande* (Paris, 1932).

Useful general and local studies of occupied Belgium: A point of comparison in English is H. McPhail, *The Long Silence: Civilian Life Under the German Occupation of Northern France, 1914–1918* (London, 2001). W. Baekelmans, *Ons volk tegen den Duitsch* (Antwerp, 1924); L. de Bondt, *De grote oorlog in de regio Londerzeel* (Londerzeel, 1999); A. Capiteyn, ed., *Gent en de eerste wereldoorlog: Het stadsleven* (Ghent, 1991); R. Casteels, G. Vandegoor, *1914 in de regio Haacht: Kleine dorpen in de grote oorlog* (Haacht, 1993); D. Clybouw et al., *Grimbergen 1914: Vier dorpen in de grote oorlog* (Grimbergen, 1994); S. Debaeke, J. Lermytte, *Merkem in de kijker: Het dorp anno 1900, tijdens de grote oorlog en de heropbouw* (Veurne, 1995); D. Decuypere, *Het malheur van de Keizer: Geluwe 1914–1918* (Geluwe, 1998); V. Degrande, *Assebroek, 1914–1918* (Brugge, 1989); L. Van der Essen, *Inval en oorlog in België: Van Luik tot den Yser: Benevens schets der diplomatische onderhandelingen die aan het konflikt zijn voorafgegaan* (Leiden, n.d.); *Hasselt Bezet: De eerste wereldoorlog* (Hasselt, 1998); E. van Hoonacker, *Kortrijk 14–18* (Kortrijk, 1994); R. Houthaeve, *Moorslede, 1914–1918* (Moorslede, 1997); F. Keersmakers, *Een dorp in de oorlog. Oorlogsgebeurtenissen te Duffel, 1914–1918* (Duffel, n.d.); R. Lampaert, *Reninge onder vuur* (Koksijde, 2002); J. Muls, *De val van Antwerpen* (Ghent, 1918); P. Van Nuffel, *De Duitschers in Aalst* (Aalst, 1921); J. Paquay, *Tongeren gedurende de Duitsche bezetting* (Tongeren, 1920); L. Schepens, *Brugge bezet: 1914–1918, 1940–1944: Het leven in een stad tijdens twee wereldoorlogen* (Tielt, 1985); A. A. H. Struycken, *De oorlog in België: Verspreide opstellen* (Arnhem, 1916); R. De Swert, "Mechelen in het eerste jaar van de Grote Oorlog, 1914–1915" (dissertation, Katholieke Universiteit Leuven, 1990); M. Vanderschaeghe, *La vie quotidienne à Stavelot pendant la guerre* (Stavelot, 1982); M. Vansuyt, M. van den Bogaert, *De militaire begraafplaatsen van W.O.I in Vlaanderen,* 5 vols. (Erpe, 2000–01); K. Verhelst, M. M. V. Raf van Laere, *De eerste wereldoorlog in Limburg,* 2 vols. (Hasselt, 1997); F. Verschoren, *De eerste jaren van den oorlog in het land van St. Gummarus* (Lier, 1919); C. Vlaminck, *Het etappengebied in België tijdens den oorlog 1914–1918* (Brussels, 1922).

Novels and literary studies: H. Klein, *The First World War in Fiction* (London, 1978); S. de Schaepdrijver, "Death Is Elsewhere: The Shifting Locus of Tragedy in Belgian Great War Literature," *Yale French Studies* 102 (2002): 94–114. In Dutch, A. G. Christiaens, *De grote oorlog: Novellen over 14–18* (Leuven, 1994);

E. Claes, *Oorlogsnovellen* (Leuven, n.d.); J. Crets, *België vrij! Verzen van den oorlog 1914–1917* (Rotterdam, 1917); S. Debaeke, *Humor in de oorlog: Bizarre en grappige verhalen, anekdoten, foto's uit de grote oorlog 1914–18* (Koksijde, 1994); F. Timmermans, *Pallieter* (Lier, 1916), was only one of many, with Claes and Streuvels, to write war stories and novels. Claes's story of the mother and three soldiers is *De moeder en de drie soldaten* (Amsterdam, 1939).

Various aspects of the occupation: J. Delbecke, *Kinderen in de eerste wereldoorlog* (Tielt, 2000); D. Huybrechts, *Les musiciens dans la tourmente* (Anseroeul, 1999); G. Pelkmans, "De Belgische oorlogsindustrie in de eerste wereldoorlog" (dissertation, Katholieke Universiteit Leuven, 1986); T. Termote, *Verdwenen in de Noordzee: De geschiedenis van de Duitse U-boten aan de Belgische kust in de eerste wereldoorlog en, opheldering over het lot van vijftien verdwenen onderzeeërs* (Erpe, 1999); G. Watkins, *Proof Through the Night: Music and the Great War* (Berkeley, 2003).

Visual images: K. Devolder, B. Symoens, *Bezet België 1914–1918: Tekeningen, prenten en foto's uit de oorlogsarchieven van het Algemeen Rijksarchief* (Brussels, 1998); *La Belgique occupée*; G. Durnez, *Een bloem in het geweer: Beelden uit de eerste wereldoorlog in Vlaanderen* (Hasselt, 1969); G. Durnez, G. De Maeyer, *Zeg mij waar de bloemen zijn: Beelden uit de eerste wereldoorlog in Vlaanderen* (Leuven, 1988).

Religion in the occupation: J. Art, *Herders en parochianen. Kerkelijkheidsgegevens betreffende het bisdom Gent, 1830–1914* (Ghent, 1979); R. Aubert, *Les deux premiers grands conflits du cardinal Mercier avec les autorités allemandes d'occupation* (Leuven, 1998); C. Borchgraeve, *God of genot? Vlaanderen 1918–1940* (Leuven, 1998); R. Burggraeve et al., *Van rechtvaardige oorlog naar rechtvaardige vrede. Katholieken tussen militarisme en pacifisme in historisch-theologisch perspectief* (Leuven, 1993); M. Cloet, ed., *Het bisdom Brugge* (Brugge, 1984); M. Cloet, ed., *Het bisdom Gent 1559–1991* (Ghent, 1991).

Prisoners and other exiles from Belgium: K. Cool, *Het leven van de Vlaamse krijgsgevangenen in Duitsland in de eerste wereld oorlog* (Brussels, 2002); R. Van Eenoo et al., *Vluchten voor de groote oorlog: Belgen in Nederland 1914–1918* (Amsterdam, 1988); *Het godsdienstig leven der Belgen in Nederland tijdens de oorlogsjaren 1914–1918* (The Hague, 1919); E. de Roodt, *Oorlogsgasten: vluchtelingen en krijgsgevangenen in Nederland tijdens de eerste wereldoorlog* (Zaltbommel, 2000).

Sunday Restored?
Materials especially from *Cinquante mois*, Streuvels, *In oorlogstijd*, and De Roodt, *Oorlogsgasten*. See another end-of-the-war celebration, on a Sunday, in

Plechtige intrede der soldaten van Tongerloo in hun dorp na den Europeeschen oorlog 1914–1918: Op zondag 18 mei 1919 (Tongerloo, 1919).

6 SUNDAY STILL

The BBC radio program was entitled *Hancock's Half Hour;* this episode, "Sunday Afternoon at Home," aired on 22 April 1958. Hancock was born in 1924 and thus had had many years to absorb the patterns of a suburban English Sunday.

England between wars: early quotes from Lord Snell of Plumstead, *The Case for Sunday Games* (London, 1933), 5–6. More broadly, R. Blythe, *The Age of Illusion: England in the Twenties and Thirties 1919–1940* (London, 1963); K. Caffrey, *'37–'39: The Last Look Round* (London, 1978); P. Dewey, *War and Progress, Britain 1914–1945* (London, 1997); R. Graves, A. Hodge, *The Long Week-end: A Social History of Great Britain 1918–1939* (New York, 1963); C. Grayling, *A Land Fit for Heroes: British Life After the Great War* (London, 1987); O. M. Hueffer, *Some of the English: A Study Towards a Study* (New York, 1930); J. McMillan, *The Way It Was 1914–1934* (London, 1979); M. Muggeridge, *The Sun Never Sets: The Story of England in the Nineteen Thirties* (New York, 1940); J. Stevenson, *British Society 1914–45* (London, 1984).

Images: H. Chapman et al., *Those Were the Days: A Photographic Album of Daily Life in Britain, 1919–1939* (London, 1983); J. L. Howgego, *London in the 20s and 30s from Old Photographs* (London, 1978).

Useful guidebooks and travel books of the time: J. Bone, *The London Perambulator* (New York, 1925); R. Bransten, R. McKenney, *Here's England: A Highly Informal Guide* (New York, 1955); C. S. Brooks, *English Spring* (New York, 1932); T. Burke, *City of Encounters: A London Divertissement* (Boston, 1932), *The English Townsman: As He Was and as He Is* (London, 1946), *Living in Bloomsbury* (London, 1939), *The London Spy: The Book of Town Travels* (New York, 1922); R. P. T. Coffin, *Book of Crowns and Cottages* (New Haven, Conn., 1925); J. Flanner, *London Was Yesterday, 1934–1939* (New York, 1975); C. Hamilton, *Modern England as Seen by an Englishwoman* (New York, 1938); Homeland Association, *Dear Old London* (London, 1928); B. James, *London on Sunday: A Sort of Guide Book* (London, 1964); E. V. Lucas, *Introducing London* (London, 1925) and *London Afresh* (London, 1937); H. V. Morton, *In Search of England* (London, 1932), *The Call of England* (London, 1951), *When You Go to London* (London, 1927), *The Spell of London* (London, 1931), and *I Saw Two Englands: The record of the journey before the war and after the outbreak of war in the year 1939* (New York, 1943); F. Muirhead, ed., *London and Its Environs* (London, 1918); F. Muirhead, ed., *Sights of Lon-*

don (London, 1953); C. Stratton Parker, *English Summer* (New York, 1931); W. S. Scott, *Bygone Pleasures of London* (London, 1948); C. C. Van Loren, *A London Omnibus* (London, 1927); K. D. Wiggin, *Penelope's English Experiences* (Champaign, Ill., 2002).

"Part of our religion": in D. Brailsford, *Sport, Time, and Society: The British at Play* (London, 1991), 105, who also comments there on the Early Closing Association. More on the ECA in W. Rybczynski, *Waiting for the Weekend* (New York, 1991), 117, who also treats the emergence of the weekend. On the insufficient reduction of work hours in the week, G. Cross, *Time and Money: The Making of Consumer Culture* (London, 1993); also D. Brailsford, *A Taste for Diversions: Sport in Georgian England* (Cambridge, 1999), 74.

The Old, Old Reputation

Some helpful studies of the English Sunday: Chronologically, one may proceed with K. Parker, *The English Sabbath: A Study of Doctrine and Discipline from the Reformation to the Civil War* (Cambridge, 1988); W. B. Whitaker, *Sunday in Tudor and Stuart Times* (London, 1933); W. B. Whitaker, *The Eighteenth-Century English Sunday: A Study of Sunday Observance from 1677–1837* (London, 1940); J. Wigley, *The Rise and Fall of the Victorian Sunday* (Manchester, 1980); D. Eshet, "Life, Liberty and Leisure: Sunday Observance in England and the Cultural Ideology of Modern Leisure" (dissertation, UCLA, 1999). Also I. Bradley, "The English Sunday," *History Today* 22/5 (1972): 355–63; P. Carus, "Christian Sunday," *Open Court* 20 (1906): 360–66; W. Hodgkins, *Sunday: Christian and Social Significance* (London, 1960); M. Levy, *Der Sabbath in England: Wesen und Entwicklung des englischen Sonntags, von Dr. Max Levy* (New York, 1966); and more specialized studies in P. Goetsch, "The Sunday in Victorian Literature," in U. Broich, T. Stemmler, G. Stratmann, eds., *Functions of Literature: Essays Presented to Erwin Wolff on His Sixtieth Birthday* (Tübingen, Germany, 1984): 227–49; R. L. Greaves, "The Origins of English Sabbatarian Thought," *Sixteenth Century Journal* 12/3 (1981): 19–34; B. Harrison, "The Sunday Trading Riots of 1855," *Historical Journal* 8/2 (1965): 219–45; W. S. F. Pickering, "The Secularized Sabbath: Formerly Sunday; Now the Weekend," *Sociological Yearbook of Religion in Britain* (1972): 33–47; P. F. Skottowe, *The Law Relating to Sunday* (London, 1936); J. Sutherland, "Thackeray, the Oxford Election, and the Sunday Question," *Bodleian Library Record* 9/5 (1977): 274–79; D. Brooke, "The Opposition to Sunday Rail Services in North-Eastern England, 1834–1914," *Journal of Transport History* 6/2 (1963): 95–109; D. R. Williams, "Never on Sunday: The Early Operation of the Cinematography Act of 1909 in regard to Sunday Opening," *Film History* 14/2 (2002): 186–194. Others are listed under specific topics below.

Various quotes: F. Engels, "Parsonocracy in Prussia," *Northern Star* 341 (May 25, 1844). Also Louis-Auguste Martin, *Le Dimanche à Londres* (n.p., 1863). Gigault de la Bedolliere in A. Gérard, Y. Katan, P. Saly, H. Trocmé, *Villes et sociétés urbaines au XIXe siècle: France, Grande-Bretagne, États-Unis, Allemagne, Autriche* (Paris, 1992), 321. "All to pieces" in R. Bransten, R. McKenney, *Here's England: A Highly Informal Guide* (New York, 1955). W. Irving, "A Sunday in London," *The Sketchbook of Geoffrey Crayon* (1819–20). A "lost day" in C. Laughlin, *So You're Going to England!* 2nd ed. (Boston, 1948), 395. Increasing choices in M. Harris, *Sunday London* (London, 1937), 7. See also "The Gloom of English Sunday," in *Every Saturday* 16 (1874): 148–51.

The Old, Old Struggle

Many of the studies of Sunday listed above, as well as more general studies, include long-standing debates over the day. In addition to those secondary sources, I list here contemporary documents that I consulted, divided into works before World War I and those after, mostly to give a sense of how furiously these debates raged—this is only a portion of the possibilities.

Prewar: E. A. Bernard, *The English Sunday: Its Origins and Claims* (London, 1903); J. Bridges, *The Sunday Railways Practically Discussed* (Edinburgh, 1847); R. Bolton, *A Letter to a Lady, on Card-Playing on the Lord's Day* (London, 1748); "The Catholic Sunday and Puritan Sabbath," *Catholic World* 23/133–38 (April–September 1876): 550–65; "Central Association for Stopping the Sale of Intoxicating Liquors on Sunday," *London Quarterly Review* 34/68 (1870): 389–413; J. F. Clarke, "Rational Sunday Observance" *American Periodical Series, 1800–1850*, 131 (1880): 497–506; J. W. Dawson, *The Day of Rest in Relation to the World That Now Is and That Which Is to Come* (London, 1887); P. Dearmer, *The Parson's Handbook* (Milwaukee, 1902); C. Dickens, *Sunday under three heads: As it is; As Sabbath Bills would make it; As it might be made* (London, 1836); F. W. Farrar, "The Sunday Question," *Forum* 28 (1899–1900): 140–145; J. Grant, *The Sabbath Delight: A Tract* (Kentish Town, 1838); T. Guthrie, *Sundays Abroad* (London, 1872); G. E. Harris, *A Treatise on Sunday Laws: the Sabbath—the Lord's Day: its history and observance, civil and criminal* (Rochester, 1892); E. Higginson, *The Sunday Questions, or, How Sunday came: how to use it best and how to legislate (and not legislate) about it* (London, 1856); C. Hill, *Continental Sunday labour; a warning to the English nation* (London, 1877); C. Hill, *Sunday: its influence on health and national prosperity* (London, 1876); J. Hughes, *Essay on the Christian Sabbath; including remarks on Sunday-drilling* (London, 1804); L. Joynes, *The Sabbath: a discourse to children* (London, 1826); "Memorials to Congress on the Subject of Sunday Malls," *Christian Examiner* 6 (1829): 226–41; Metropolitan Sunday Rest Association, *Report of the Proceedings of the Committee of the Metropolitan Sunday Rest Association during 1858 & 1859* (London, 1859); F. Meyrick, *Sunday Observance: an argument and plea for the Old English Sunday* (London, 1902); B. W. Noel, *Music and Pleasure on the Sabbath* (London, 1856); J. P. B. Phillips, "Our English Sunday," *King and Country: A Review and Magazine* (1902): 92–96; *The Removal of the Crystal Palace* (London, 1852); "Sunday and the Sabbath" and "Christian Sunday not the Jewish Sabbath," *London Quarterly Review* 8/16 (1857): 395–430; *The Sunday-opening of the lyceums and public gardens defended* (Manchester, 1840); J. Tilling, printer, *The Sunday Water-party: with some account of the Club at the Oak, of the trip to Richmond, and the melancholy disaster which befel them on their return home, whereby the whole party were drowned* (Chelsea, 1820); C. J. Vaughan, *A Few Words on the crystal palace question* (London, 1852); J. Ward, *A clear exposition of the Lord's day . . .* (Birmingham, 182-); J. Weir, *The New Crystal Palace and the Christian Sabbath* (London, 1852).

After 1918: Archdeacon of Worcester, "Sunday Observance," *Church Quarterly Review* 113 (1931–32): 185–194; "The English Sunday," *New Statesman* 36 (1930–31): 324–25; "The English Sunday," *Theology* 14/79 (1927): 1–7; C. Falkland, "English Sunday," *Listener* 9/208 (1933): 23; F. J. Harvey, *Sunday Observance: in church, state and home: a re-examination of Old Testament laws, of New Testament principles and of the question of liberty in modern life* (London, 1924); C. Penney Hunt, *In Defense of the Christian Sunday* (London, 1931); L. Hunter, *On Keeping Sunday* (London, 1928); A. Macrae, "In Praise of the English Sunday," *National Review* 79 (1922): 240–49; C. C. Martindale, "Sanctifying Sunday," *Month* 170 (Aug 1937): 118–25; W. Whitaker, "An Aspect of the Social Value of Sunday," *London Quarterly & Holborn Review* Series 6/5 (1936): 516–28. An example of more recent debate, F. Dillistone, "The Holy Hush of Sunday Morning," *Theology Today* 33/1 (April 1976): 15–23. The Anglican vicar in L. Hunter, *On Keeping Sunday* (London, 1928), 21.

More specifically on Scotland and Wales: An Englishwoman, "The English Sunday and the Scotch Sabbath," *Tait's Edinburgh Magazine* 25 (1858): 661–66; A. Kennedy, *Memories of Scottish scenes and Sabbaths more than eighty years ago* (Edinburgh, 1902); *The Christian Sabbath, considered in its various aspects by ministers of different denominations; with preface by Baptist W. Noel* (Edinburgh, 1850); G. MacDonald, *David Elginbrood*, pt. 1, chap. 8, pt. 2, chap. 12, pt. 3, chaps. 6–7; D. Maclean, *The law of the Lord's Day in the Celtic Church* (Edinburgh, 1926); W. Nixon, *Sixty-one pleas for Sabbath-breaking answered: and an appeal to various classes, regarding the sanctification of the Lord's-Day*

(Edinburgh, 1847); A. Smith, *Lock Up the Swings on Sundays* (Durham, 1998); J. G. Stewart, *The anti-Sabbatarian defenceless* (Glasgow, 1854). W. R. Lambert, "Welsh Sunday Closing Act, 1881," *Welsh History Review* 6 (1972/73): 161–89.

Mass Observation research in *Meet Yourself on Sunday: A Study for Mass-Observation* (London, 1949), which also includes "That Sunday Morning Feeling." S. Aumonier, "One Sunday Morning," *Overheard: Fifteen Tales* (Freeport, N.Y., 1972). Taking "pleasures sadly" in C. S. Brooks, *English Spring* (New York, 1932), 98. See also S. Jones, *Workers at Play: A Social and Economic History of Leisure, 1918–39* (London, 1986).

Class on Sunday, Lying Down and Eating Up, Staying In, Afternoons Out, Evenings Out

On leisure and Sunday generally: M. Billinge, "Recreation, Re-Creation and the Victorians," *Journal of Historical Geography* 22/4 (1996): 443–59; A. Howkins, J. Lowerson, *Trends in Leisure, 1919–1939* (London, 1979); G. R. Lavers, B. S. Rowntree, *English Life and Leisure: A Social Study* (London, 1951); R. Lennard, ed., *Englishmen at Rest and Play: Some Phases of English Leisure, 1558–1714* (Oxford, 1931); J. K. Walton, J. Walvin, eds., *Leisure in Britain, 1780–1939* (Manchester, England, 1983); J. Walvin, *Leisure and Society, 1830–1950* (London, 1978).

On leisure, Sunday, and class more specifically: P. Bailey, *Leisure and Class in Victorian England: Rational Recreation and the Contest for Control, 1830–85* (Buffalo, N.Y., 1978); R. Homan, "Sunday Observance and Social Class," *Sociological Yearbook of Religion in Britain* (1970): 78–92; R. Weight, "The Politics of Pleasure: The Left, Class Culture, and Leisure in England," *Journal of Urban History* 20/2 (1994): 252–70.

On women, leisure, class, and Sunday: N. Beauman, *A Very Great Profession: The Woman's Novel, 1914–39* (London, 1983); D. Beddoe, *Back to Home and Duty: Women Between the Wars, 1918–1939* (London, 1989); *Sunday Lunch with Mrs. Beeton* (Ward Lock, 1990); N. Humble, *The Feminine Middlebrow Novel: 1920's–1950's: Class, Domesticity, and Bohemianism* (Oxford, 2001); C. Langhamer, *Women's Leisure in England, 1920–60* (New York, 2000); C. M. Parratt, *"More than Mere Amusement": Working-Class Women's Leisure in England, 1750–1914* (Boston, 2001); C. M. Parratt, "Little Means or Time: Working-Class Women and Leisure in Late Victorian and Edwardian England," *International Journal of the History of Sport* 15/2 (1998): 22–53.

Polemics on the working class, leisure, and Sunday: Examples of earlier polemics besides Dickens's or Bernard's, in J. Kingsmill, *The Sabbath the working man's true charter: thoughts for thinking men of the industrial classes, on the Sabbath question* (London, 1856); R. Maguire, *A word to Sunday sellers: No. I of four special lectures to the working classes on the better observance of the Lord's Day* (London, 1857); R. Maguire, *A word to Sunday sellers: No. II of four special lectures to the working classes on the better observance of the Lord's Day* (London, 1857); J. B. Quinton, *Prize essays on the temporal advantages of the Sabbath, considered in relation to the working classes* (Philadelphia, 1849); J. A. Quinton, *Heaven's antidote to the curse of labor: or the temporal advantages of the Sabbath, considered in relation to the working classes* (New York, 1850); J. A. Quinton, *The workman's testimony to the Sabbath, or, The Temporal Advantages of that day of rest considered in relation to the working classes: being the first three of one thousand and forty-five competing essays on the Sabbath by working men* (Edinburgh, 1852); *Sunday Work: Seven Pamphlets, 1794–1856* (New York, 1972).

Later studies of working-class leisure and Sunday: W. Brierly, *Means-Test Man* (Nottingham, England, 1983); A. Davies, *Leisure, Gender and Poverty: Working-Class Culture in Salford and Manchester, 1900–1939* (Philadelphia, 1992); S. Jones, *Workers at Play: A Social and Economic History of Leisure, 1918–39* (London, 1986); S. G. Jones, *Sport, Politics, and the Working Class: Organized Labour and Sport in Inter-War Britain* (Manchester, England, 1988); D. Reid, "Iron Roads and the Happiness of the Working Classes," *Journal of Transport History* 17/1 (1996): 57–73; D. Reid, "Weddings, Weekdays, Work and Leisure in Urban England, 1791–1911: The Decline of Saint Monday Revisited," *Past & Present* 153 (1996): 135–63.

Contemporary surveys and studies of working-class leisure, especially by Mass Observation: A. Calder, D. Sheridan, eds., *Speak for Yourself: A Mass-Observation Anthology, 1937–49* (Oxford, 1985); G. Cross, ed., *Worktowners at Blackpool: Mass-observation and popular leisure in the 1930s* (London, 1990); P. Gurney, ed., *Bolton Working-Class Life in the 1930s: A Mass-Observation Anthology* (Brighton, 1998); C. Madge, T. Harrison, *Britain* (Middlesex, 1939); C. Madge, T. Harrison, eds., *First Year's Work, 1937–39* (London, 1938); *Meet Yourself on Sunday: A Study for Mass-Observation* (London, 1949); *The New Survey of London Life and Labour,* vol. 9, *Life and Leisure* (London, 1935); *The Pub and the People: A Worktown Study for Mass-Observation* (London, 1943); *Puzzled People: A Study in Popular Attitudes to Religion, Ethics, Progress and Politics in a London Borough for Mass-Observation* (London, 1947); B. Seebohm Rowntree, G. R. Lavers, *English Life and Leisure: A Social Study* (London, 1951); H. Spender, *Worktown: Photographs of Bolton and Blackpool Taken for Mass-Observation* (Bristol, 1982). And a couple of Orwell novels, *Down and Out in Paris and London* (New York, 1933) and *The Road to Wigan Pier* (London, 1937).

Memoirs: Phyllis Walden's Sunday is in "Speak for Yourself." Phyllis Willmott, in *Growing Up in a London Village: Family Life Between the Wars* (Atlantic Highlands, N.J., 1979). Other working-class memoirs with a bearing on Sunday include K. Armstrong, H. Beynon, eds., *Hello, Are You Working? Memories of the Thirties in the North East of England* (South Wellfield, England, 1977); W. Goldman, *East End My Cradle: Portrait of an Environment* (London, 1988). More middle-class memoirs: B. Blake, *Ankle-Strap Shoes on Sundays* (Bognor Regis, England, 1982); A. Clarke, *Growing Up in the 1920s* (London, 1986); E. Elias, *On Sundays We Wore White* (London, 1978); C. G. Harper, *A Londoner's Own London* (London, 1927); P. Oakes, *From Middle England: A Memory of the 1930s* (New York, 1980); G. Raverat, *Period Piece* (New York, 1952).

Miscellaneous memoirs and literature related to leisure and Sunday: *Fifty Years, Memories and Contrasts: A Composite Picture of the Period 1882–1932* (London, 1932); L. Halward, *To Tea on Sunday* (London, 1936); R. Kipling, *Un beau dimanche anglais* (Paris, 1925), and *My Sunday at Home* (London, 1895); M. Muggeridge, *Chronicles of Wasted Time: Chronicle I, The Green Stick* (New York, 1973); G. Orwell, *A Clergyman's Daughter* (London, 1986); A. Rosener, *Sunday Collection: Thirty Twentieth-Century Poems about Sunday* (1995); B. Shaw, "A Sunday on the Surrey Hills," in his *Tales* (New York, 1932).

Related studies on daily and home life: B. Brandt, *The English at Home* (London, 1936); V. Chernichewski, *Anthropological Report on a London Suburb* (London, 1935); M. V. Hughes, *London at Home* (New York, 1931); E. McMurray, *At Home in the Thirties: the Ekco Collection of Trade Catalogues* (London, 1995).

Upper-class leisure: Goetsch; A. G. MacDonell, *England Their England* (New York, 1934), chap. 6; V. Nicholson, *Among the Bohemians: Experiments in Living, 1900–1939* (New York, 2002); N. Courtney, *In Society: The Brideshead Years* (London, 1986); L. Lewis, *The Private Life of a Country House* (Gloucestershire, 1997); A. Tinniswood, *A History of Country House Visiting: Five Centuries of Tourism and Taste* (Oxford, 1989); not to mention various novels of Evelyn Waugh (such as *Brideshead Revisited)* and the Mitford sisters.

Churchgoing and Not
Religion: C. G. Brown, *The Death of Christian Britain: Understanding Secularism 1800–2000* (London and New York, 2001); R. C. Churchill, *The English Sunday* (London, 1954); H. Davies, *Worship and Theology in England: The Ecumenical Century, 1900–1965* (Princeton, N.J., 1965); R. Gill, *The Myth of the Empty Church* (London, 1993); A. Hastings, *A History of English Christianity*

1920–2000 (London, 2001); E. Routley, *Twentieth Century Church Music* (New York, 1964); S. C. Williams, *Religious Beliefs and Popular Culture in Southwark c. 1880–1939* (Oxford, 1999).

On preaching more specifically, including guidebooks for tourists: H. Davies, *Varieties of English Preaching 1900–1960* (London, 1963); A. Gammie, *Preachers I Have Heard* (London, 1945); M. Harris, *Pulpits and Preachers* (London, 1935); J. Marchant, *Wit and Wisdom of Dean Inge* (London, 1927); D. Simpson, *Chats with Chums: Twenty-four Sunday Morning Addresses to Boys and Girls* (London, 1928); L. H. Waring, *Sundays in London with Farrar, Parker, Spurgeon and Others* (New York, 1906).

The dream is in *A Sunday Morning's Dream on Public Worship* (London, 1930). The various quotes regarding attendance and belief and Sunday are from works in the "Mass Observation" note above, especially Rowntree and Lavers, and *Meet Yourself on Sunday,* as well as Brown, *Death.*

Another approach to secularization is in P. Richter, "Seven days' trading make one weak? The Sunday trading issue as an index of secularization," *British Journal of Sociology* 94/45/3 (London): 333–48. See for a recent synthesis of studies that reject the theory, R. Stark, R. Finke, "Secularization, R.I.P." in their *Acts of Faith: Explaining the Human Side of Religion* (Berkeley, 2000).

The Good Book(s)

In addition to the large list under "Class on Sunday," see for Sunday schools specifically: P. B. Cliff, *The Rise and Development of the Sunday School Movement in England, 1780–1980* (Redhill, England, 1986); T. W. Laqueur, *Religion and Respectability: Sunday Schools and Working Class Culture, 1780–1850* (New Haven, 1976), and various reviews of Laquer, such as by A. Briggs, in *Journal of Ecclesiastical History* 31 (1980): 125–26, C. G. Brown, in *Economic History Review* 2/31/2 (1978): 302–03, and D. Pals, in *Church History* 47 (1978): 338–39. Also K. D. M. Snell, "The Sunday-School Movement in England and Wales: Child Labour, Denominational Control and Working-Class Culture," *Past & Present* 164 (1999): 122–68; M. Dick, "The Myth of the Working-Class Sunday School," *History of Education* 9/1 (1980): 27–41; F. Reid, "Socialist Sunday Schools in Britain, 1892–1939," *International Review of Social History* 11/1 (1966): 18–47; and R. Findlay, "The World Marches Forth on the Feet of Little Comrades . . . Or Does It? The Socialist Sunday School Movement in Late Nineteenth Century Scotland," *Cahiers Victoriens et Edouardiens: Revue du Centre d'Études et de Recherches Victoriennes et Edouardiennes de l'Université Paul Valéry, Montpellier* 54 (Oct 2001): 147–48.

Reading: Graves, *Long Weekend,* has much material, as do J. McAleer, *Popular Reading and Publishing in Britain, 1914–1950* (Oxford, 1992); R. Scott, "The Sunday Periodical: Sunday at Home," *Victorian Periodicals Review* 25/4 (1992): 158–62. And see the section on Women and Leisure above, under "Class."

Afternoons Out (More)
Hyde Park: Wiggins, 8–9; A. Milton, *London in Seven Days: A Guide for People in a Hurry* (New York, 1923); Morton, *When You Go to London;* Henry James, *English Hours* (New York, 1960), 11.

Driving and cycling: A. Christie, *The Golden Ball and Other Stories* (Boston, 1991), 131–47; J. Brown, S. Ward, *Village Life in England, 1860–1940* (London, 1985), 10–11.

Rambling: T. Burke, *The Outer Circle: Rambles in Remote London* (New York, 1921); C. Cameron, *Green Fields of England* (New York, 1930); H. H. Symonds, *Walking in the Lake District* (London, 1935). And recent studies, A. Holt, "Hikers and Ramblers; Surviving a Thirties Fashion" *International Journal of the History of Sport* 4 (1987): 56–67; H. Walker, "The Popularization of the Outdoor Movement, 1900–1940," *British Journal of Sports History* 2/2 (1985): 140–53.

Expanding Sunday Sport
Lord Snell of Plumstead, *The Case for Sunday Games* (London, 1933). More on Liddel appears in J. Benge, *Eric Liddell: Something Greater than Gold* (Seattle, Wash., 1998); S. Magnusson, *The Flying Scotsman* (New York, 1981); D. Mc-Casland, *Eric Liddell, Pure Gold* (Grand Rapids, Mich., 2001); D. P. Thomson, *Eric H. Liddell: Athlete and Missionary* (Perthshire, Scotland, 1971).

English sport in general: D. Birley, *Playing the Game: Sport and British Society, 1910–45* (Manchester, 1995), and *Sport and the Making of Britain* (Manchester, 1993); D. Brailsford, *British Sport: A Social History* (Cambridge, 1992), *Sport and Society: Elizabeth to Anne* (London, 1969), *A Taste for Diversions: Sport in Georgian England* (Cambridge, 1999), "The Lord's Day Observance Society and Sunday Sport, 1834–1914," *Sports Historian,* on www.umist.ac.uk/sport/brailsfd.html, and "Sporting Days in Eighteenth Century England," *Journal of Sport History* 9/3 (1982): 41–54; H. Cantelon, R. Hollands, eds., *Leisure, Sport and Working-Class Cultures: Theory and History* (Toronto, 1988); N. Garnham, "Both Praying and Playing: 'Muscular Christianity' and the YMCA in North-east County Durham," *Journal of Social History* 35/2 (Winter 2001): 397–407; R. W. Henderson, "The King's Book of Sports in England and

America" *Bulletin of the New York Public Library* 52/11 (1948): 539–53; R. Holt, *Sport and the British: A Modern History* (Oxford, 1989); R. Holt, ed., *Sport and the Working Class in Modern Britain* (Manchester, 1990); S. G. Jones, "State Intervention in Sport and Leisure in Britain between the Wars," *Journal of Contemporary History* 22/1 (1987): 163–82; J. Lowerson, "Sport and the Victorian Sunday: The Beginnings of Middle-Class Apostasy," *British Journal of Sports History* 1/2 (1984): 202–220; S. Magee, *Ascot: The History* (London, 2002); T. Mason, ed., *Sport in Britain: A Social History* (Cambridge, 1989); C. Tennyson, "They Taught the World to Play," *Victorian Studies* 2/3 (1958–59): 211–22. Also T. Livesey, *Babes, Booze, Orgies and Aliens. The Inside Story of Sport Newspapers.*

Golf: B. Darwin, *British Golf* (London, 1946); D. R. Benson, ed., *Fore! The Best of Wodehouse on Golf* (New York, 1983); on caddying, Lowerson, 214, and H. Longhurst, *Only on Sundays* (London, 1964), 58–61.

Cricket, boxing, and greyhound racing: Many of the studies above discuss both, but also J. Williams, *Cricket and England: A Cultural and Social History of the Inter-war Years* (London, 2003).

Football (soccer): A. J. Arnold, *A Game That Would Pay: A Business History of Professional Football in Bradford* (London, 1988); N. Fishwick, *English Football and Society 1910–1950* (Manchester, 1989); D. Russell, *Football and the English: A Social History of Association Football in England, 1863–1995* (Preston, 1997); J. Walvin, *The Only Game: Football in Our Times* (Harlow, 2001). On Sunday football, T. Smith, *When Sunday Comes. A History of the Langburgh Sunday Football League, 1974–99*; P. Moulds, *Manchester Amateur Sunday Football League: 40th Anniversary Brochure (1947–87).*

Pools: M. Clapson, *A Bit of a Flutter: Popular Gambling and English Society, c. 1823–1961* (Manchester, 1992); *How to Win a Fortune in Football Pools* (London, 1938); J. Hilton, *Why I Go In For the Pools* (London, 1936); E. Johnstone, *Profit From Football Pools* (London, 1937); Mass Observation, *First Year's Work*, 32–41; *London Life and Labour*, 275–76; Rowntree, Seebohm, and Lavers, 124–76; Brailsford, *Sport, Time, and Society*, 24–25; Holt, *Sport and the British*, 182–86; Walvin, *Leisure and Society*, 140.

Evenings Out (More)

Much material is drawn from the leisure and sporting sections above, plus specifically on music, J. Nott, *Music for the People: Popular Music and Dance in Interwar Britain* (Oxford, 2002); on radio, A. Briggs, *The Golden Age of Wireless* (London, 1965); and on pubs the already mentioned and indispensable Mass Observation, *The Pub and the People: A Worktown Study.*

A copy of Chamberlain's speech is on www.yale.edu/lawweb/avalon/wwii/gb3.htm. Churchill's reinstatement of bell-ringing is mentioned in R. Jenkins, *Churchill: A Biography* (New York, 2001), 2.

7 SUNDAY ALL MIXED UP

Copies of four *Wide, Wide World* programs may be consulted at the Library of Congress, with the following titles and call numbers: "A Sunday in Autumn" (16 October 1955, VBG 7801–7802), "A Sunday Afternoon With Youth" (13 November 1955, FDA 0111–0112), "Sunday Driver" (29 April 1956, FDA 0144–0146), and "American Sunday: A Visit With the Three Faiths" (25 November 1956, FCB 2337–2339). The program was announced in the *New York Times,* "Oct. 16 TV bow set for 'Wide World,' NBC to 'Transport Viewer in Air, on Land and Under Water, in New Show," September 9, 1955; twenty episodes of the program were to air that year, approximately every other Sunday from 4:00 to 5:30 P.M.

The "spiritual marketplace" is discussed in R. Ellwood, *The Fifties Spiritual Marketplace: American Religion in a Decade of Conflict* (New Brunswick, N.J., 1997).

Foundations

A most helpful general study of the American Sunday is Alexis McCrossen's *Holy Day, Holy Day: The American Sunday* (Ithaca, N.Y., 2000). Also A. McCrossen, "Neither Holy Day Nor Holiday," *Southwest Review* 82 (Summer 1997): 366–81. Both are especially strong on the nineteenth and early twentieth centuries.

Studies of the American Sunday to 1800: A. M. Earle, *The Sabbath in Puritan New England* (New York, 1891); W. U. Solberg, *Redeem the Time: The Puritan Sabbath in Early America* (Cambridge, Mass., 1977).

Studies of the nineteenth-century Sunday to World War I: R. Z. Chamlee, *The Sabbath Crusade, 1810–1920* (Washington, D.C., 1968); J. F. Gilkeson, "The Rise and Decline of the 'Puritan Sunday' in Providence, Rhode Island," *New England Quarterly* 59/1 (March 1986): 75–91; K. Knortz, *Der amerikanische Sonntag* (Zurich, 1891); H. E. Cox, "Daily Except Sunday: Blue Laws and the Operation of Philadelphia Horsecars," *Business History Review* 39/2 (1965): 228–42; A. M. McCrossen, "Sabbatarianism: The Intersection of Church and State in the Orchestration of Everyday Life in Nineteenth-century America," *Religious and Secular Reform in America* (1999): 133–58.

Some useful examples of the debate over the nineteenth-century Sunday (to World War I): S. Andrews, *The Sabbath at Home* (Philadelphia, 1837); W. W.

Atterbury, *Le Dimanche aux Etats-Unis* (New York, n.d.); H. W. Bellows, *Our American Sunday: A Paper . . . read at the National Conference of Unitarian and Other Christian Churches, October 25, 1872* (Boston, 1872); J. Q. Bittinger, "The Sabbath in Relation to Civilization," *Andover Review* 12/69 (1889): 275–90; H. A. Boardman, *A Plea for Sabbath Afternoon* (Philadelphia, 1870); H. M. Brooks, *New England Sunday* (Boston, 1886); J. W. Chadwick, "Why the Fair Must be Open on Sunday," *Forum* 14 (1892–93): 541–50; F. W. Evans, *Sabbaths vs. the People: Shaker Address to the American People, Male and Female* (Pittsfield, Mass., 1892); J. S. Fairly, *Sunday Observance and Sunday Desecration* (n.p., 1893); W. L. Fisher, *History of the institution of the Sabbath Day, being a plea for liberty of conscience in opposition to Sabbath conventions* (Philadelphia, 1846); R. J. Floody, *Scientific Basis of Sabbath and Sunday: a new investigation after the manner and methods of modern science* (Boston, 1906); E. Gibson, *The sinfulness of neglecting and profaning the Lord's Day* (Philadelphia, 1815); E. G. G., "The Uses and Capabilities of Sunday," *Christian Examiner and Religious Miscellany* 4/15 (1851): 55–79; O. P. Giftford, "Why the World's Fair Should be Opened on Sunday," *Arena* 7 (1893): 193–96; G. E. Harris, *A treatise on Sunday laws: the Sabbath—the Lord's day: its history and observance, civil and criminal* (Rochester, 1892); F. M. Holland, "Should the World's Fair Be Open on Sunday?" *Open Court* 5 (1892): 2722; International Congress on Sunday Rest, *Sunday, the world's rest day: an illustrated story of the Fourteenth International Lord's Day Congress held in Oakland, California, July 27th to August 1st, 1915, during the Panama-Pacific International Exposition* (Garden City, N.Y., 1916); R. M. Johnson, *Report in relation to the Sunday mail* (Washington, D.C., 1830); W. Kincaid, *Sunday: a holiday or a holy-day?* (Oswego, N.Y., 1885); J. Lee, *Sunday Play* (New York, 1910); A. H. Lewis, *The Catholicization of Protestantism on the Sabbath question* (Plainfield, N.J., 1897); A. H. Lewis, *The Sabbath question from the Roman Catholic standpoint* (Chicago, 1894); *Swift decadence of Sunday: what next?* (Plainfield, N.J., 1899), and *The Evolution and future of Sunday Legislation* (Plainfield, N.J., 1905); A. Mackay-Smith, *The Sunday Newspaper: an address delivered before the Church Club of Philadelphia on the Evening of February 26, 1906* (n.p., 1906); "Moral Sunday Sports," *Open Court* 9 (1895): 4354; New York Sabbath Committee, *The Soldier's and Sailor's Sabbath* (New York, 1862); D. Oliver, *The foreign visitant: containing interesting observations and remarks made by an inhabitant of Terra Incognita on the character and manners of the inhabitants of this earth, particularly in relation to the Lord's Day* (Boston, 1814); H. C. Potter, "Sunday and the Columbian Exposition," *Forum* 14 (1892–93): 194–200; *Rome's challenge: why do Protestants keep Sunday?* (Battle Creek, Mich., 1893); *The Sabbath in Europe: the holy day of freedom, the holiday of despotism* (New York, 1858); P. Schaff, *The Anglo-*

American Sabbath: an essay read before the National Sabbath Convention, Saratoga, August 11, 1863 (New York, 1863); W. A. Scott, *The Bible, God's crystal palace for all nations* (New Orleans, 1854); J. G. Shea, "The Observance of Sunday and Civil Laws for its Enforcement," *American Catholic Quarterly Review* 8 (1883): 139–52; N. Smith, "Shall Sunday be preserved?" *Forum* 2 (1886–87): 182–89; J. L. Spaulding, "Why the World's Fair should be Opened on Sunday," *Arena* 7 (1893): 45–47; E. C. Stanton, "Our Boys on Sunday," *Forum* 1 (1886): 191–98; B. Sunderland, *Sunday not the Sabbath, all days alike holy: a controversy between the Rev. Dr. Sunderland, Wm. Henry Burr, and others* (Washington, D.C., 1872); D. Swing, "What the American Sunday Should Be," *Forum* 12 (1892): 120–27; Theologos, *Shaving: a breach of the Sabbath and a hindrance to the spread of the Gospel,* 2nd ed. (London, 1860); M. M. Trumbull, "Ministers on Sunday Closing a Sunday Fourth of July," *Open Court* 7 (1893): 3684–86; M. R. Vincent, *Pleasure-Sunday a Labor Sunday: A Sermon* (New York, n.d.); L. Wells, *A mother's plea for the Sabbath: in a series of letters to an absent son* (Portland, Maine, 1847); G. M. Whicher, "Sunday in Germany," *Andover Review* 19 (1893): 565–69.

Studies and debates of Sunday in the twentieth century: H. Armerding, "Lord's Day is Not Passé," *Christianity Today* 12 (August 16, 1968): 1076–78; parts of S. Bacchiocchi, *Divine Rest for Human Restlessness: A Theological Study of the Good News of the Sabbath for Today* (Rome, 1980), and S. Bacchiocchi, *The Sabbath Under Crossfire: A Biblical Analysis of Recent Sabbath/Sunday Developments* (n.p., 1998); C. Bridenbaugh, "The Boston Sabbath," *New England Quarterly* 7/2 (1934): 325–26; R. Cohen, *Sunday in the Sixties* (New York, 1962); J. D. Douglas, "Toward a Brighter Sunday," *Christianity Today* 8 (1964): 894; T. B. Douglass, "Christian Use of Sunday," *Social Action* (U.S.) 26 (1959): 21–27; J. Gurrieri, "Catholic Sunday in America: Its Shape and Early History," *Sunday Morning: A Time for Worship* (Collegeville, Minn., 1982); B. Johnson, "On Dropping the Subject: Presbyterians and Sabbath Observance in the Twentieth Century," in *The Presbyterian Predicament: Six Perspectives,* M. J. Coalter, J. M. Mulder, L. B. Weeks, eds. (Louisville, Ky., 1990), 90–108; R. O. Johnson, "The Sunday Question, Henry E. Jacobs, and Confessional Reappraisal in Eastern Lutheranism," *Lutheran Quarterly* 13/3 (1999): 285–303; D. J. McMillan, ed., *Influence of the Weekly Rest-Day on Human Welfare: A Scientific Research* (New York, 1927); L. Schmidt, *Consumer Rites: The Buying & Selling of American Holidays* (Princeton, N.J., 1995); L. B. Weeks, "The Scriptures and Sabbath Observance in the South," *Journal of Presbyterian History* 59/2 (Summer 1981): 267–84; D. Schneider, "The Controversy over Sunday Movies in Hastings, 1913–1929," *Nebraska History* 69 (1988): 60–72.

Examples of recent works intended especially as pastoral or inspirational or critical or just practical "things to do" for Sunday or Sabbath or both: W. O. Carver, *Sabbath Observance: The Lord's Day in our Day* (Nashville, Tenn., 1940); M. J. Dawn, *Keeping the Sabbath Wholly: Ceasing, Resting, Embracing, Feasting* (Grand Rapids, Mich., 1989); T. Edwards, *Sabbath Time: Understanding and Practice for Contemporary Christians* (New York, 1982); K. G. Greet, *Enjoying Sunday* (London, 1956); N. M. Guy, *Why I Observe the Lord's Day* (Hamilton, Bermuda, 1964); E. Farley, "A Missing Presence," *Christian Century* 115/9 (March 18, 1998): 276–78; C. Kiesling, *The Future of the Christian Sunday* (New York, 1970); K. B. Mains, *Making Sunday Special* (Waco, Tex., 1987); W. H. Marsh, *The Presbyterian View Toward Sunday Theatricals in America* (1958); M. Mason, "Making the Most of Sunday," *International Journal of Religious Education* 10/5 (1934): 23; R. Odom, *The Lord's Day on a Round World* (Nashville, Tenn., 1970); D. Pate, *52 Sabbath Activities for Teen Groups* (n.p., 1995); B. Patterson, "Rest? Never on Sunday," *Christianity Today* 30/13 (1986); G. Robinson, *Fifty-Two Things to Do on Sabbath* (Washington, D.C., 1983); R. E. Ring, "Please don't call Sunday the Sabbath," *Dialog* 25 (1986): 139–140; G. L. Rose, *Our Day of Rest: A Graphic History of the Sabbath and the Lord's Day, with That of the Calendar and the Law* (Glendale, Calif., 1946); D. Schaper, *Sabbath Sense: A Spiritual Antidote for the Overworked* (Philadelphia, 1997); J. Stafford, *Children Are Bored on Sunday* (New York, 1945); L. M. Weidlich, "The Sunday Friends: The Group and Their Quilts," *Uncoverings* 18 (1997): 67–93.

Economic aspects of Sunday: D. Laband, D. Heinbuch, *Blue Laws: The History, Economics, and Politics of Sunday Closing Laws* (Lexington, Mass., 1987); A. Raucher, "Sunday Business and the Decline of Sunday Closing Laws: A Historical Overview," *Journal of Church and State* 36 (1994): 13–33; J. A. Siguaw, P. M. Simpson, "Effects of Religiousness on Sunday Shopping and Outshopping Behaviours: A Study of Shopper Attitudes and Behaviours in the American South," *International Review of Retail, Distribution and Consumer Research* 7/1 (January 1997): 23–40.

Sacralization accommodation, and Sunday change: See especially H. S. Jacoby, *Remember the Sabbath Day? The Nature and Causes of Changes in Sunday Observance since 1800* (Philadelphia, 1945); also F. W. Dunford, P. Kunz, "Neutralization of Religious Dissonance," *Review of Religious Research* 15 (1973): 2–9; J. B. Jordan, *Sabbath Breaking and the Death Penalty: A Theological Investigation* (Laguna Hills, Calif., 1986); W. McLoughlin, R. Bellah, eds., *Religion in America* (Boston, 1968); R. Stark, R. Finke, "Secularization, R.I.P." in their *Acts of Faith: Explaining the Human Side of Religion* (Berkeley, 2000); W. Swartley, *Slavery, Sabbath, War, and Women: Case Issues in Biblical Interpre-*

tation (Scottsdale, Pa., 1983); H. H. Ward, *Space-age Sunday* (New York, 1960); W. Rybczynski, *Waiting for the Weekend* (New York, 1991). McCrossen, in both her book and her articles, has many sensible things to say about this process as well.

Literature and memoirs with Sunday elements: C. Bukowski, "A Minor Impulse to Complain; Sundays Kill More Men than Bombs; Monday Beach, Cold Day," *Midwest* 3 (1961–62): 20–23; F. Scott Fitzgerald, "Crazy Sunday," in *Babylon Revisited and Other Stories* (New York, 1996); C. Jackson, *Earthly Creatures: Ten Stories* (Freeport, R.I., 1971), including "Sunday Drive"; J. Kerouac, *On the Road* (New York, 1955); N. Krasna, *Sunday in New York: A Comedy* (New York, 1962); W. Macken, *God Made Sunday: and other Stories* (New York, 1962); N. Marden, *Sunday Dinner: Essays and Anecdotes* (New York, 1972); P. O'Donovan, *Birthday Blues, or, It Feels Like Sunday but There's No Football On* (Inverness, Calif., 1980); M. Sandoz, *Sandhill Sundays and Other Recollections* (Lincoln, Neb., 1970); J. Steinbeck, *Travels With Charley* (New York, 1961); R. Taylor, *Chicken Every Sunday: My Life with Mother's Boarders* (New York, 1943).

American Religion on Sunday in the 1950s
America generally: A. Cooke, *America Observed: From the 1940s to the 1980s* (New York, 1988); P. Daniel, *Lost Revolutions: The South in the 1950s* (Washington, D.C., 2000); H.-J. Duteil, *The Great American Parade* (New York, 1953); S. Douglas Franzosa, *Ordinary Lessons: Girlhoods of the 1950s* (New York, 1999); J. Oakley, *God's Country: America in the Fifties* (New York, 1986); R. Schwartz, *An Eyewitness History: The 1950s* (New York, 2003). Also E. Lindop, *America in the 1950s* (Brookfield, Conn., 2002), and N. Finkelstein, *The Way Things Never Were* (New York, 1999), have some useful information.

American society, including suburban life: R. Fishman, *Bourgeois Utopias* (New York, 1987); N. Harris, "The Changing Landscape: Spaced Out at the Shopping Center," in *Cultural Excursions: Marketing Appetites and Cultural Tastes in Modern America* (Chicago, 1990), 278–88; J. Hudnut-Beumler, *Looking for God in the Suburbs: The Religion of the American Dream and Its Critics, 1945–1965* (New Brunswick, N.J., 1994); E. Kaledin, *Daily Life in the United States, 1940–1959: Shifting Worlds* (Westport, Conn., 2000); C. La Rocco, "If You Build It, They Will Shop: The Evolution of Malls in America," *Financial History* 78 (Spring 2003): 16–19; D. Macrae, *The Americans at Home* (New York, 1952; reprint of a nineteenth-century work); T. Mennel, "Victor Gruen and the Construction of Cold War Utopias," *Journal of Planning History* 3/2 (2004): 116–50; J. Merritt, *Day by Day: The Fifties* (New York, 1979).

American religion generally: S. Curtis, *A Consuming Faith: The Social Gospel and Modern American Culture* (Baltimore, 1991); M. H. Ducey, *Sunday Morning: Aspects of Urban Ritual* (New York, 1977); Ellwood, *Fifties Spiritual Marketplace;* J. Fisher, *The Catholic Counterculture in America, 1933–1962* (Chapel Hill, N.C., 1989); M. Frady, *Billy Graham: A Parable of American Righteousness* (Boston, 1979); T. Hangen, *Redeeming the Dial: Radio, Religion, and Popular Culture in America* (Chapel Hill, N.C., 2002); P. Heidebrecht, *Faith and Economic Practice: Protestant Businessmen in Chicago, 1900–1920* (New York, 1989); W. Herberg, *Protestant, Catholic, and Jew: An Essay in American Religious Sociology* (Chicago, 1955); W. B. Lawrence, *Sundays in New York* (Lanham, Md., 1996), 179–213 especially; W. McLoughlin, R. Bellah, eds., *Religion in America* (Boston, 1968); W. Newman, P. Halvorson, *Patterns in Pluralism: A Portrait of American Religion, 1952–1971* (Washington, D.C., 1972); R. Stark, C. Glock, *American Piety: The Nature of Religious Commitment* (Berkeley, 1968); F. Szasz, *Religion in the Modern American West* (Tucson, Ariz., 2000); L. Weeks, "God's Judgement, Christ's Command: Use of the Bible in Nineteenth-Century American Political Life," *Bible in American Law Politics and Political Rhetoric* (1985): 61–77; J. Wind, J. Lewis, eds., *American Congregations,* vol. 1: *Portraits of Twelve Religious Communities* (Chicago, 1994).

Sermons and preachers' memoirs: H. Fosdick, *Riverside Sermons* (New York, 1958); J. O. Chatham, *Sundays Down South: A Pastor's Stories* (Oxford, Miss., 1999); B. Graham, *Just As I Am* (New York, 1977); M. Warner, ed., *American Sermons: The Pilgrims to Martin Luther King, Jr.* (New York, 1999).

Catholic Sunday in America

A. Ehrenhalt, *The Lost City: Discovering the Forgotten Virtues of Community in the Chicago of the 1950s* (New York, 1995); L. Cunningham, ed., *A Search for Solitude: Pursuing the Monk's True Life. The Journals of Thomas Merton, 1952–1960,* vol. 3 (New York, 1996); Fisher, *Catholic Counterculture;* D. A. Lord, *That Wonderful Sunday Mass* (St. Louis, 1955); J. F. Powers, *Wheat That Springeth Green* (New York, 1988); F. Sullivan, "I Remember a Church," *Good Housekeeping* 49 (November 1954): 226–29; various pieces from the *American Ecclesiastical Review:* F. Connell, "Sunday Mass," 134 (1956): 276–77, and "Sunday Work," 134 (1956): 275; R. McCormick, "Reflections on Sunday Observance," 161 (1969): 55–61; W. Schmitz, "Servile Work on Sunday," 132 (1955): 118–19, and "Length of Sunday Sermon," 134 (1956): 418; "Sunday Observance," 127 (1952): 71–72; "The Sunday Sermon," 130 (1954): 124; "Work on Sunday," 120 (1949): 343.

Protestant Strains on Sunday
J. C. Harper, *Sunday: A Minister's Story* (Boston, 1974). Methodist examples are from Ward. The main story is in L. Cryderman, *No Swimming on Sunday: Stories of a Lifetime in Church* (Grand Rapids, Mich., 2001). Lucy Forsyth Townsend's story is in Franzosa. The Mormon information is from *Church Ideal of a Sacred Sabbath* (n.p., n.d.); Deseret Sunday School Union, *Recreation and play: containing extracts from magazine articles, addresses, text books, government bulletins, etc., bearing upon the subject of the recreation, play and amusements of children and young people* (Salt Lake City, 1914); B. H. Roberts, *The Lord's Day: reasons for the observance by the Latter-day Saints of the first day of the week as the Christian Sabbath or the "Lord's Day"* (Independence, Mo., 1926); J. N. Watkins, *Savoring the Sabbath: A Young Mother Shows How Families Can Find Joy Through Keeping the Lord's Day Holy* (Bountiful, Utah, 1980); J. W. Kennedy, "Sunday Among the Suburban Salt Lake Saints," *Christianity Today* (1998): 27; W. A. Wilson, "Mormon Narratives: The Lore of Faith," *Western Folklore* 54 (1995): 303–26. Also an unpublished paper by B. Cannon, T. Merrill, "Ox in the Mire? The Battle Over Sunday Closing Laws in Utah, 1943–1971."

Ethnic and Racial Strains
Judaism and Blue Laws: A. R. Block, *Love Is a Four Letter Word* (Freeport, 1970); N. Cohen, *Jews in Christian America: The Pursuit of Religious Equality* (New York, 1992); E. Evans, *The Lonely Days Were Sundays: Reflections of a Jewish Southerner* (Jackson, Miss., 1993); R. Cohen, "Blue Sunday," *Christian Century* 78 (1961): 9–12; M. Kramer, "Is America a Christian Country? Sunday Closing Laws vs. Sabbath Observing Jews," *Tradition* 4 (1961): 5–20; K. M. Olitzky, "The Sunday-Sabbath Movement in American Reform Judaism: Strategy or Evolution?" *American Jewish Archives* 34 (1982): 75–88; also Laband and Heinbuch, and Raucher. "Sunday Law Hits Midtown Stores: Police Drive on West Side Yields 58 Summonses, Some on Illegal Work Charges," *New York Times*, January 24, 1955. Also "Sunday Selling: A New Service Raises a Hot Dispute," *Time*, October 22, 1956.

Latino Sundays: J. Dolan, A. Figueroa Deck, eds., *Hispanic Catholic Culture in the U.S.: Issues and Concerns* (Notre Dame, Ind., 1994); J. Dolan, G. Hinojosa, eds., *Mexican Americans and the Catholic Church, 1900–1965* (Notre Dame, Ind., 1994); J. Dolan, J. Vidal, eds., *Puerto Rican and Cuban Catholics in the U.S., 1900–1965* (Notre Dame, Ind., 1994); E. Rivera, *Family Installments: Memories of Growing Up Hispanic* (New York, 1982); Piri Thomas, *Savior, Savior, Hold My Hand* (Garden City, N.Y., 1972).

Black Sundays: See especially T. Branch, *Parting the Waters: America in the King Years, 1954–63* (New York, 1988); R. Lischer, *The Preacher King: Martin Luther King, Jr., and the Word That Moved America* (Oxford, 1995); and W. M. McClain, *Come Sunday: The Liturgy of Zion* (Nashville, Tenn., 1990). Ehrenhalt, 174–84; M. Frederick, *Between Sundays: Black Women and Everyday Struggles of Faith* (Berkeley, 2003); H. Hampton, S. Fayer, S. Flynn, *Voices of Freedom: An Oral History of the Civil Rights Movement From the 1950s Through the 1980s* (New York, 1990); Macrae, *Americans at Home,* 354; J. Titon, *Give Me This Mountain: Reverend C. L. Franklin, Life History and Selected Sermons* (Urbana, Ill., 1989).

Sacralizing Sunday Sport

Sacralizing sport: See McCrossen's works, but also W. Baker, *If Christ Came to the Olympics* (Sydney, 2000); A. Banks, "Jocks for Jesus: Fellowship of Christian Athletes Marks 50 Years," *Salt Lake Tribune,* February 28, 2004, C3; J. Dunn, *Sharing the Victory: The Twenty-Five Years of the Fellowship of Christian Athletes* (New York, 1980); J. Hefley, *Running with God: The New Christian Athletes* (New York, 1975); R. Higgs, *God in the Stadium* (Lexington, Ky., 1995); S. Hoffman, *Sport and Religion* (Champaign, Ill., 1992); R. Kimball, *Sports in Zion: Mormon Recreation, 1890–1940* (Urbana, Ill., 2003); F. Manfred, *No Fun on Sunday: A Novel* (Norman, Okla., 1990); B. Milton, "Sport as a Functional Equivalent of Religion" (dissertation, University of Wisconsin, 1972); J. Price, *From Season to Season: Sports as American Religion* (Macon, Ga., 2001); C. Putney, *Muscular Christianity: Manhood and Sports in Protestant America, 1880–1920* (Cambridge, Mass., 2001); D. Wiggins, "Work, Leisure, and Sport in America: The British Traveler's Image," *Canadian Journal of History of Sport* 13/1 (1982): 28–60; J. D. Willis and R. Welton, "Religion and Sport in America: The Case for the Sports Bay in the Cathedral Church of Saint John the Divine," *Journal of Sports History* 4 (1977): 189–207; and more below. On Vernon Law, see Moffi, below, under "The American Game on Sunday," and S. Frey, *Winning Spirit III: An Inside Look at LDS Sports Heroes* (Provo, Utah, 2000). Prebish's article is mentioned by V. Scott, "Sport Is a Religion in America," *Chronicle of Higher Education* (May 16, 1984): 25–27.

Some economic aspects: T. Jable, "Sports, Amusements, and Pennsylvania Blue Laws, 1682–1973" (dissertation, Pennsylvania State University, 1974); and R. J. Allen, "Sunday Racing Finishes Out of the Money," *Christian Century* 97 (1980): 1077–78, which shows that not every effort to push for Sunday sport won out, even with good economic arguments.

On churches' attitudes to Sunday play: See "Studies and Debates of Sunday in the Twentieth Century," above, and *American Religion on Sunday in the Fifties.*

The Sunday Game
The "insult to the country" is in E. Lindop, *America in the 1950s* (Brookfield, Conn., 2002), and N. Finkelstein, *The Way Things Never Were* (New York, 1999). The visiting Frenchman was Duteil, above. T. Morgan, *Wilderness at Dawn: The Settling of the North American Continent* (New York, 1993).

Miscellaneous titles: E. Asinof, *Seven Days to Sunday* (New York, 1968); V. Bagli, *Sundays at 2:00 with the Baltimore Colts* (Centreville, Md., 1995); V. Biever, ed., *Super Sunday: The Inside Slant on the Ultimate Game* (New York, 1998); B. Chandler, *Violent Sundays* (New York, 1984); I. Fryar, *Sunday Is My Day* (Sister, Ore., 1997); M. Fulks, ed., *Super Bowl Sunday: The Day America Stops* (Kansas City, Mo., 2000); M. Holovak, *Violence Every Sunday* (New York, 1967); R. Nathan, *Super Sunday: Yesterday, Today, & Tomorrow* (n.p., 1994); K. Rappoport, *Super Sundays* (New York, 1980).

Sources and studies: W. Brewer, *"The game of football," a sermon preached by the head master of St. Matthew's School, San Mateo, Cal.* (San Francisco, 1897); M. Cope, *The Game That Was: An Illustrated Account of the Tumultuous Early days of Pro Football* (New York, 1971); E. Fitzgerald, *Johnny Unitas* (New York, 1961); M. Herskiwitz, *The Golden Age of Pro Football: A Remembrance of Pro Football in the 1950s* (New York, 1974); M. S. Maltby, *The Origins and Development of Professional Football* (New York, 1997); D. Maraniss, *When Pride Still Mattered: A Life of Vince Lombardi* (New York, 1999); K. McClellan, *The Sunday Game: At the Dawn of Professional Football* (Akron, 1998); R. Peterson, *Pigskin: The Early Years of Pro Football* (New York, 1997); H. Roberts, *The Story of Pro Football* (New York, 1953); C. K. Ross, *Outside the Lines: African Americans and the Integration of the National Football League* (New York, 1999); R. Wells, *Mean on Sunday: The Autobiography of Ray Nitschke* (New York, 1973); R. Whittingham, F. Roe, *Sunday Mayhem: A Celebration of Pro Football in America* (Lanham, Md., 1987).

The American Game on Sunday
Miscellaneous: V. Bove, *And on the Eighth Day God Created the Yankees* (Plainfield, N.J., 1981); G. Early, "Birdland: Two Observations on the Cultural Significance of Baseball," *American Poetry Review* (July/August 1996); C. Evans, W. Herzog, eds., *The Faith of 50 Million: Baseball, Religion, and American Culture* (Louisville, Ky., 2002); W. Knickerbocker, *Sunday at the Ballpark* (Lanham, Md., 2000); L. Moffi, *This Side of Cooperstown: An Oral History of Major League Baseball in the 1950s* (Iowa City, Iowa, 1996); A. O'Toole, *Branch Rickey in Pittsburgh* (Jefferson, N.C., 2000); S. A. Riess, *Touching Base: Professional Baseball and American Culture in the Progressive Era* (Urbana, Ill.,

1999); B. Kelley, *The Negro Leagues Revisited: Conversation with 66 More Baseball Heroes* (Jefferson, N.C., 2000); B. Kelley, *Voices From the Negro Leagues: Conversations with 52 Baseball Standouts* (Jefferson, N.C., 1998); R. Ruck, *Sandlot Seasons: Sport in Black Pittsburgh* (Urbana, Ill., 1987).

Billy Sunday: R. A. Bruns, *Preacher: Billy Sunday and Big-time American Evangelism* (New York, 1992); L. W. Dorsett, *Billy Sunday and the Redemption of Urban America* (Grand Rapids, Mich., 1991); J. Hall, "Sunday in St. Louis: The Anatomy and Anomaly of a Large-scale Billy Sunday Revival," *Presbytaerian* 10 (1984): 99–110; R. F. Martin, "Billy Sunday and Christian Manliness," *The Historian* 58 (1996): 811–23.

Brooklyn Dodgers: H. Frommer, *New York City Baseball: The Last Golden Age, 1947–1957* (New York, 1985); D. Kearns Godwin, *Wait Till Next Year* (New York, 1997); P. Golenbock, *Bums: An Oral History of the Brooklyn Dodgers* (New York, 1984); C. Prince, *Brooklyn's Dodgers: The Bums, the Borough, and the Best of Baseball, 1947–1957* (Oxford, 1996).

Amusements

N. Postman, *Amusing Ourselves to Death: Public Discourse in the Age of Show Business* (New York, 1985).

Stock-car racing: M. Howell, *From Moonshine to Madison Avenue: A Cultural History of the NASCAR Winston Cup Series* (Bowling Green, 1997); J. Menzer, *The Wildest Ride: A History of NASCAR* (New York, 2001); P. Newberry, "Drivers Keeping the Faith," *Salt Lake Tribune*, February 10, 2004, B3.

Golf and country clubs: J. Mayo, *The American Country Club: Its Origins and Development* (New Brunswick, N.J., 1998); R. Moss, *Golf and the American Country Club* (Urbana, Ill., 2001).

Parks: C. Denson, *Coney Island: Lost and Found* (Berkeley, 2002); O. Pilat, *Sodom by the Sea: An Affectionate History of Coney Island* (Garden City, N.Y., 1943); *A Look at the U.S.A., 1955*; R. Rosenzweig, E. Blackmar, *The Park and the People: A History of Central Park* (Ithaca, N.Y., 1992).

What to do: J. and K. Lawrence, "What to Do When It Rains on Sunday," *Good Housekeeping* (January 1955): 60, 177.

Sunday newspaper: W. A. Hachten, "The Metropolitan Sunday Newspaper in the United States: A Study of Trends in Content and Practices" (dissertation, University of Minnesota, 1961); J. A. Haney, "A History of the Nationally Syndicated Sunday Magazine Supplements" (dissertation, University of Missouri, 1953); I. Lewis, "Envisioning Consumer Culture: Comic Strips, Comic Books, and Advertising in America, 1890–1945" (dissertation, University of Rochester, 1993); C. M. Schulz, *Sunday's Fun Day, Charlie Brown: A New Peanuts Book* (New York, 1962).

Television: W. Boddy, *Fifties Television: The Industry and Its Critics* (Urbana, Ill., 1990); N. Leibman, *Living Room Lectures: The Fifties Family in Film and Television* (Austin, Tex., 1995); F. J. MacDonald, *Don't Touch That Dial!* (Chicago, 1991); A. McNeil, *Total Television* (New York, 1980); S. Mickelson, *The Decade That Shaped Television News: CBS in the 1950s* (Westport, Conn., 1998); M. Shapiro, *Television Network Daytime and Late-Night Programming, 1959–1989* (Jefferson, N.C., 1991); J. Thumin, *Small Screens, Big Ideas: Television in the 1950s* (London, 2002); V. Adams, "News of TV and Radio," *New York Times,* January 2, 1955 (Sunday).

Radio: M. Hilmes, *Radio Voices* (Minneapolis, 1997); J. D. Swartz and R. C. Reiner, *Handbook of Old Time Radio* (Metuchen, N.J., 1993).

Also J. Klobuchar, *Sunday at the Met* (Minneapolis, 1971).

A WORD AFTER

Information on recent church attendance comes from specific studies below, but more general information also is from the Institute for Social Research at the University of Michigan, a study entitled "Study of Worldwide Rates of Religiosity, Church Attendance," on www.umich.edu/~newsinfo/Releases/1997. See also N. Knox, "Religion Takes a Back Seat in Western Europe," *USA Today,* August 10, 2005, and "Faith Fades Where it Once Burned Strong," *New York Times,* October 13, 2003. See also a study explaining the imprecision (usually excessively high) of self-reported attendance figures, in "A Quick Question: Did You Attend Church Last Week?" from the Hartford Institute for Social Research, hirr.hartsem.edu/research/quick_question40.html.

Information on European trade is in T. Askham, T. Burke, D. Ramsden, *Current EC Legal Developments: EC Sunday Trading Rules* (London, 1990).

Belgium: P. van Ostaijen, *Belgiese Zondag* (n.p., 1994), a poem. Also H. De Dijn, et al., *De zondag in de postmoderne cultuur* (Leuven, 1994); C. Swinkels, *De Dames van de Zondag* (Brugge, 1973).

The Netherlands: G. Dekker, J. de Hart, J. Peters, *God in Nederland: 1966–1996* (Amsterdam, 1997); Maarten 't Hart, *Mammoet op Zondag* (Amsterdam, 1977); M. Ferguson, *Zondag en maandag* (Amsterdam, 1960), especially 52–68; *Mensen op Zondag* (The Hague, 1957).

France: R. Beck, *Histoire du dimanche: De 1700 à nos jours* (Paris, 1997), final chapters; D. Botte et al., *Le dimanche* (Paris: Éditions du Cerf, 1965);

England: Sunday football league directory on www.sunday-football.co.uk/. *Day One*, May–August 2002, includes "Sunday Off for Car Thieves," "Tackling Glyn Blaize," "News Around the Nation," "Liddel Centenary." Jonathan Edwards online at *Soon*, www.soon.org.uk/page41.htm. M. Jones on stats.allblacks.com/Profile.asp?ABID=443. M. Sansom, "Sunday Trading," *Anvil* 9 (1992): 4–7; M. Schluter, D. Lee, *Keeping Sunday Special: The Fight Against the Shops Bill* (London, 1998); R. Higbed, *British Sunday Observance Law* (London, 1958); D. Nicholson-Lord, "Few Mourn as the Great English Sunday Dies," on ask.elibrary.com. The Albion tavern on www.albiontavern.com/index2.htm.

Other countries: Ireland, M. Maher, "Sunday in the Irish Church," *Irish Theological Quarterly* 60/3 (1994): 161–84, and V. Ryan, *The Shaping of Sunday: Sunday and Eucharist in the Irish Tradition* (Dublin, 1997); Scotland, P. Mewett, "Sabbath Observance and the Social Construction of Religious Belief in a Scottish Calvinist Community," in *Missionaries and Anthropologists* (Williamsburg, Va., 1983) 2:183–98; Canada, T. Sinclair-Faulkner, in *Christian Century*, 102 (1985): 549–50; A. M. C. Waterman, "Lord's Day in a Secular Society: A Historical Comment on the Canadian Lord's Day Act of 1906," *Canadian Journal of Theology* 11 (1965): 108–123; "Hamm Bends, Allows Sunday Shopping," *Halifax Soundoffs*, May 8, 2003.

United States, old and new religions: "Hip New Churches Pray to a Different Drummer," *New York Times*, February 18, 2004; J. Wind, J. Lewis, eds., *American Congregations*, vol. 1, *Portraits of Twelve Religious Communities* (Chicago, 1994); S. Prothero, *American Jesus* (New York, 2003), 4, 11. Debates over Sunday still live, as in "Sabbath Debate Will Never Rest," *Salt Lake Tribune*, July 24, 2004; Y. Yang, *Jesus and the Sabbath in Matthew's Gospel* (Sheffield, 1997), and its criticism in B. Viviano, *The Catholic Biblical Quarterly* 61/1 (January 1999): 175–78; and R. Reymond, "Lord's Day Observance: Man's Proper Response to the Fourth Commandment," *Presbytaerion* 13 (1987): 7–23. But ecumenical efforts live too: *The Lord's Day and the Sabbath: Catholic-Jewish reflections* (Los Angeles, 1994).

Commerce: D. Laband, D. Heinbuch, *Blue Laws: The History, Economics, and Politics of Sunday Closing Laws* (Lexington, Mass., 1987); N. Ferguson, "Why America Outpaces Europe (Clue: The God Factor)," *New York Times*, June 8, 2003; T. Early, "Revolution of the Absent," *Spectrum* 46 (1970): 4–6, 27; W. Rybczynski, *Waiting for the Weekend* (New York, 1991), 74, 215, 222, 231; "Bergen Residents Against Sunday Shopping," on www.keepthebluelaws.com.

Recreation in general: J. Spring, "Seven Days of Play," *American Demographics* 15/3 (1993): 50–53. K. Cure, *Fodor's Sunday in New York: 2,184 Relaxing, Uplifting, Caloric, Historic, Romantic Weekend Things to Do Without Your Kids* (New York, 1995); D. Mangain, *Sunday in San Francisco* (New York, 1996); C. Seligman, *Fodor's Sunday in San Francisco: 1,638 Relaxing, Uplifting, Caloric, Historic, Hip and Romantic Weekend Things to Do* (New York, 1994); M. Wooster, *Somewhere to Go on Sunday: A Guide to Natural Treasures in Western New York* (Buffalo, N.Y., 1991).

Sports: Brock in S. Hoffmann, *Sport and Religion* (Champaign, Ill., 1992), 111, with Michener on 129; W. Heyen, "If Jesus Played Football," *America* 157 (24 October 1987): 265; Falwell in J. Price, *From Season to Season: Sports as American Religion* (Macon, Ga., 2001), 23. Critics: "Are Sports Good for the Soul?" *Newsweek* 11 (January 11, 1971): 51–52; and F. Deford, "Endorsing Jesus," *Sports Illustrated*, April 26, 1976; R. Higgs, *God in the Stadium* (Lexington, Ky., 1995).

More on Sunday sports: D. W. Chen, "Cardinal O'Connor Now Criticizes Sunday Little League and Soccer Games," *New York Times* 147 (1998); N. M. Christian, "Parents Object to Cardinal's Comments over Playing Little League Games on Sundays," *New York Times*, May 18, 1998; "Sports vs. the Sabbath," *Deseret Morning News*, May 1, 2004; "Sunday Sports an Issue for LDS Community," *BYU NewsNet*, October 14, 2003; "Golf: A Year Later, Miller Has Some Regret," *Salt Lake Tribune*, July 5, 2005.

On the Super Bowl more specifically: "Super Bowl Sunday Stokes Creative Fires of Clergy Nationwide," *Johnson City Press*, January 25, 1995; "Holy Huddle: Churches Are Changing Their Schedules to Help Football Fans Keep the Faith," *Associated Press*, January 1, 2005; D. I. Kertzer, "The Super Bowl's Strange Tribe: Why We're Bonded by TV's Biggest Sunday," *TV Guide*, January 25, 1992.

ACKNOWLEDGMENTS

Thanks first to the David M. Kennedy Center for International Studies, and the College of Family, Home, and Social Sciences, both at Brigham Young University, for research support. While working on another project, under a Franklin Research Grant from the American Philosophical Society, I happened to come upon some important materials for this book as well, and thus must indirectly thank that institution.

Thanks to the staff at a variety of libraries and archives who willingly and capably answered questions and went out of their way to provide information and advice. I mention especially, in France, the Bibliothèque National; in the Netherlands, the Koninklijke Bibliotheek in The Hague, and the library of the Rijksuniversiteit Leiden; in Belgium, the Koninklijke Bibliotheek in Brussels, the library of the Katholieke Universiteit Leuven, and Jan Vande Weyer at the Koninklijke Museum van het Leger en de Krijgsgeschiedenis (or War Museum); in England, the library of the University of Cambridge; and in the U.S., the Library of Congress, the library of Brigham Young University, and the many libraries that cooperated with the latter in providing an abundance of interlibrary loan materials.

Thanks to the countless people who provided ideas, suggested sources, and told personal anecdotes. I especially recall a host of stimulating conversations among the residents of the Quint, in Leuven, Belgium, namely Jan Roegiers, Rob Brustens, Hedwig Schwall, Toon Barten, and Herman and Monique van der Wee, who were remarkably tolerant and even enthusiastic as the topic of Sunday arose again and again at dinner. To name just a few elsewhere, I thank Steven Buick, Annette Bishop, Simon Ditchfield, Richard Rex, Martin Dotterweich, Geoffrey Parker, and Elizabeth Emery. Patrick Allitt offered several ideas, while John Craig introduced me, for better or worse, to the Sunday of Tony Hancock. I'm sure I spoke about Sunday with just about every colleague in my own department at BYU, and in the French department, and I benefited even from casual comments; those I can still remember include Corry Cropper, Darryl Lee, Susan Rugh, Ignacio Garcio, Jeff Shumway, Kendall Brown, Don Harreld, Tom Alexander, Brian Cannon, and Neil York; my apologies to the many I certainly neglected. I also benefited from a string of efficient and intelligent research assistants, who ran down many leads, suggested materials, and put together an impossible number of notes: Kathryn Fleming, Rebekah Sanders, Anna Sanford, and Diana Wise.

I owe special thanks to those brave colleagues who read parts, albeit sometimes impossibly long parts, of earlier phases of the manuscript and offered helpful criticism. These included nearby Scott Sprenger, Glenn Cooper, Rich Kimball, and Malcolm Thorp, and farther away Clair Schen, Wim Janse, Leen van Molle, Sophie de Schaepdrijver, Elizabeth Sage, and Jim Fisher. Eddy Put and Diarmaid MacCulloch did the unthinkable and read the whole, a favor that I can hardly repay, much less their usual wise advice. Various nonhistorians likewise read parts of the manuscript and provided invaluable suggestions, including Kevin Kenner and a local book club consisting of Susan Abbott, Sherry Baker, Margie Brown, Kris Frederickson (who *is* a fellow historian), and Jane Lawson. My wife Paula belongs to this group and read not only her portion there but nearly the entire manuscript; for her helpful comments, and the inconveniences of various research trips, my many thanks.

Perhaps my most fundamental debt is to my agent John Ware, for his unfailingly intelligent comments and service, but here specifically for putting me in touch with Walt Bode, the person who first approached him with the idea of a book about Sunday. I generally prefer (probably foolishly) to invent my own topics for books, but when Walt told me about this one, I knew that I would like to try it, as I'd thought about the subject in a general way for decades. Thanks as well to Clare Alexander, for a most enlightening lunch in Cambridge on how one might approach this amorphous subject; to Trace Murphy at Doubleday for believing so strongly in the book; and to Darya Porat for working so efficiently on the details of its production.

My last and broadest debt is to those many people who more through deed than word helped me to see the various sides of Sunday. These include my large and mostly fun-loving family, with whom I have passed most of my Sundays through the years, beginning with Andrew, Jonathan, and Kate, continuing with my siblings Lloyd, Karen, Vicki, David, Kathryn, Steven, and Donald and their own families, on to my admirably long-suffering and good-humored parents, Lloyd and Kay, and ending with a swarm of laughing grandmothers happily named Lorine and Lorraine and Lorinda and Hallie who, fortunately for me, always seemed to be buzzing around my childhood home. Also inspiring were many friends in Belgium, France, the Netherlands, and Sweden, who in some cases for more than twenty years have gladly shown the expanded possibilities of Sunday, including Yvonne and Raymond Aerts, Donat and Gerlinde Aerts, Louis and Charlotte De Ridder (also Els, Koen, Kristien, Walter, Stefaan, and Karel), Hubert and Katleen Peynsaert (also Patrick, Barbara, Karien, and Dominique), Patricia Rijmenants, Frank Boidin, Simone Dunon, Eddy Put, and Maria Leon (also Liesbeth, Pieter Jan, and Katelijne), Bengt Svensson and Annika Hedermo, Michel and Christiaan Cloet (also Peter en Stef), and Marc and Marie Chevalier (also Nicolas, Antony, and Pierre). My heartfelt thanks to all for their hospitality and good humor.

INDEX